Buried Treasure

Buried Treasure

The Collected
Church Times *Sunday Readings*

Cally Hammond

CANTERBURY
PRESS

© Cally Hammond 2025

Published in 2025 by Canterbury Press
Editorial office
3rd Floor, Invicta House,
110 Golden Lane,
London EC1Y 0TG, UK
www.canterburypress.co.uk

Canterbury Press is an imprint of Hymns Ancient & Modern Ltd
(a registered charity)

Hymns Ancient & Modern® is a registered trademark of
Hymns Ancient & Modern Ltd
13A Hellesdon Park Road, Norwich,
Norfolk NR6 5DR, UK

All rights reserved. No part of this publication may be reproduced,
stored in a retrieval system, or transmitted,
in any form or by any means, electronic, mechanical,
photocopying or otherwise, without the prior permission of
the publisher, Canterbury Press.

Cally Hammond asserted her right under the Copyright, Designs and
Patents Act 1988 to be identified as the Author of this Work

Scripture quotations are from New Revised Standard Version Bible:
Anglicized Edition, copyright © 1989, 1995 National Council of the
Churches of Christ in the United States of America. Used by permission.
All rights reserved worldwide.

British Library Cataloguing in Publication data

A catalogue record for this book is available
from the British Library

ISBN: 978 1 78622 567 2

EU GPSR Authorised Representative
LOGOS EUROPE, 9 rue Nicolas Poussin, 17000, LA ROCHELLE, France
E-mail: Contact@logoseurope.eu

No part of this book may be used or reproduced in any manner for the
purpose of training artificial intelligence technologies or systems.

Typeset by Regent Typesetting

Contents

Preface   xxvii
Abbreviations   xxix

Introduction   xxxi

Year A

The First Sunday of Advent
Isaiah 2.1–5; Psalm 122; Romans 13.11–end; Matthew 24.36–44   2

The Second Sunday of Advent
Isaiah 11.1–10; Psalm 72.1–7, 18, 19 [*or* 72.1–7]; Romans 15.4–13;
Matthew 3.1–12   4

The Third Sunday of Advent
Isaiah 35.1–10; Psalm 146.1–10 or *Canticle:* Magnificat;
James 5.7–10; Matthew 11.2–11   6

The Fourth Sunday of Advent
Isaiah 7.10–16; Psalm 80.1–8, 18–20 [*or* 80.1–8];
Romans 1.1–7; Matthew 1.18–end   8

Christmas Day (Set II readings)
Isaiah 62.6–end; Psalm 97; Titus 3.4–7; Luke 2.[1–7] 8–20   10

The First Sunday of Christmas
Isaiah 63.7–9; Psalm 148 [*or* 148.7–end]; Hebrews 2.10–end;
Matthew 2.13–end   12

The Second Sunday of Christmas
Jeremiah 31.7–14; Psalm 147.13–21; Ephesians 1.3–14;
John 1.[1–9] 10–18   14

The Epiphany
Isaiah 60.1–6; Psalm 72.[1–9] 10–15; Ephesians 3.1–12;
Matthew 2.1–12   16

The Baptism of Christ (The First Sunday of Epiphany)
Isaiah 42.1–9; Psalm 29; Acts 10.34–43; Matthew 3.13–end   18

The Second Sunday of Epiphany
Isaiah 49.1–7; Psalm 40.1–12; 1 Corinthians 1.1–9; John 1.29–42   20

The Third Sunday of Epiphany
Isaiah 9.1–4; Psalm 27.1, 4–12 [or 27.1–11]; 1 Corinthians 1.10–18; Matthew 4.12–23   22

The Fourth Sunday of Epiphany
1 Kings 17.8–16; Psalm 36.5–10; 1 Corinthians 1.18–end; John 2.1–11   24

The Presentation of Christ in the Temple (Candlemas)
Malachi 3.1–5; Psalm 24.[1–6] 7–end; Hebrews 2.14–end; Luke 2.22–40   26

Sunday before Lent, Proper 1 (4–10 February)
Isaiah 58.1–9a [b–12]; Psalm 112.1–9 [end]; 1 Corinthians 2.1–12 [13–end]; Matthew 5.13–20   28

Sunday before Lent, Proper 2 (11–17 February)
Deuteronomy 30.15–end or Ecclesiasticus 15.15–end; Psalm 119.1–8; 1 Corinthians 3.1–9; Matthew 5.21–37   30

Sunday before Lent, Proper 3 (18–24 February or 24–28 May)
Leviticus 19.1–2, 9–18; Psalm 119.33–40; 1 Corinthians 3.10–11, 16–end; Matthew 5.38–end   32

The Second Sunday before Lent
Genesis 1.1—2.3; Psalm 136 [or 136.1–9, 23–26]; Romans 8.18–25; Matthew 6.25–34   34

The Sunday next before Lent
Exodus 24.12–end; Psalm 2 or Psalm 99; 2 Peter 1.16–end; Matthew 17.1–9   36

The First Sunday of Lent
Genesis 2.15–17; 3.1–7; Psalm 32; Romans 5.12–19; Matthew 4.1–11   38

The Second Sunday of Lent
Genesis 12.1–4a; Psalm 121; Romans 4.1–5, 13–17; John 3.1–17   40

The Third Sunday of Lent
Exodus 17.1–7; Psalm 95; Romans 5.1–11; John 4.5–42   42

The Fourth Sunday of Lent ('Refreshment' Sunday)
1 Samuel 16.1–13; Psalm 23; Ephesians 5.8–14; John 9.1–41   44

Mothering Sunday
Exodus 2.1–10 *or* 1 Samuel 1.20–end; Psalm 34.11–20 *or* 127.1–4;
2 Corinthians 1.3–7 *or* Colossians 3.12–17; Luke 2.33–35
or John 19.25–27   46

The Fifth Sunday of Lent (Passion Sunday)
Ezekiel 37.1–14; Psalm 130; Romans 8.6–1; John 11.1–45   48

Palm Sunday
Liturgy of the Palms: Matthew 21.1–11; Psalm 118.1–2, 19–end
[*or* 118.19–24]
Liturgy of the Passion: Isaiah 50.4–9a; Psalm 31.9–16 [*or* 31.9–18];
Philippians 2.5–11; Matthew 26.14—end of 27
or Matthew 27.11–54   50

Good Friday
Isaiah 52.13—end of 53; Psalm 22 [*or* 22.1–11 *or* 22.1–21];
Hebrews 10.16–25 *or* Hebrews 4.14–16; 5.7–9;
John 18.1—end of 19   52

Easter Day
Acts 10.34–43† *or* Jeremiah 31.1–6; Psalm 118.1–2, 14–24
[*or* 118.14–24]; Colossians 3.1–4 *or* Acts 10.34–43†;
John 20.1–18 *or* Matthew 28.1–10   54

The Second Sunday of Easter
[Exodus 14.10–end; 15.20, 21]; Acts 2.14a, 22–32†; Psalm 16;
1 Peter 1.3–9; John 20.19–end   56

The Third Sunday of Easter
[Zephaniah 3.14–end]; Acts 2.14a, 36–41†; Psalm 116.1–3, 10–17
[*or* 116.1–7]; 1 Peter 1.17–23; Luke 24.13–35   58

The Fourth Sunday of Easter
[Genesis 7]; Acts 2.42–end†; Psalm 23; 1 Peter 2.19–end;
John 10.1–10   60

The Fifth Sunday of Easter
[Genesis 8.1–19]; Acts 7.55–end†; Psalm 31.1–5, 15–16 [*or* 31.1–5];
1 Peter 2.2–10; John 14.1–14   62

The Sixth Sunday of Easter
[Genesis 8.20—9.17]; Acts 17.22–31†; Psalm 66.7–18;
1 Peter 3.13–end; John 14.15–21   64

The Seventh Sunday of Easter (Sunday after Ascension Day)
[Ezekiel 36.24–28]; Acts 1.6–14†; Psalm 68.1–10, 32–35
[or 68.1–10]; 1 Peter 4.12–14; 5.6–11; John 17.1–11 — 66

Pentecost (Whit Sunday)
Acts 2.1–21† or Numbers 11.24–30; Psalm 104.26–36, 37b
[or 104.26–end]; 1 Corinthians 12.3b–13 or Acts 2.1–21†;
John 20.19–23 or John 7.37–39 — 68

Trinity Sunday
Isaiah 40.12–17, 27–end; Psalm 8; 2 Corinthians 13.11–end;
Matthew 28.16–20 — 70

Sunday after Trinity, Proper 4 (29 May–4 June)
Continuous: Genesis 6.9–22; 7.24; 8.14–19; Psalm 46;
Romans 1.16, 17; 3.22b–28 [29–31]; Matthew 7.21–end
*Related: Deuteronomy 11.18–21, 26–28; Psalm 31.1–5, 19–24
[or 31.19–24]; Romans 1.16, 17; 3.22b–28 [29–31];
Matthew 7.21–end — 72

Sunday after Trinity, Proper 5 (5–11 June)
Continuous: Genesis 12.1–9; Psalm 33.1–12; Romans 4.13–end;
Matthew 9.9–13, 18–26
Related: Hosea 5.15—6.6; Psalm 50.7–15; Romans 4.13–end;
Matthew 9.9–13, 18–26 — 74

Sunday after Trinity, Proper 6 (12–18 June)
Continuous: Genesis 18.1–15 [21.1–7]; Psalm 116.1, 10–17
[or 116.9–17]; Romans 5.1–8; Matthew 9.35—10.8 [9–23]
Related: Exodus 19.2–8a; Psalm 100; Romans 5.1–8;
Matthew 9.35—10.8 [9–23] — 76

Sunday after Trinity, Proper 7 (19–25 June)
Continuous: Genesis 21.8–21; Psalm 86.1–10, 16–end [or 86.1–10];
Romans 6.1b–11; Matthew 10.24–39
Related: Jeremiah 20.7–13; Psalm 69.8–11 [12–17] 18–20
[or 69.14–20]; Romans 6.1b–11; Matthew 10.24–39 — 78

Sunday after Trinity, Proper 8 (26 June–2 July)
Continuous: Genesis 22.1–14; Psalm 13; Romans 6.12–end;
Matthew 10.40–end
Related: Jeremiah 28.5–9; Psalm 89.1–4, 15–18 [or 89.8–18];
Romans 6.12–end; Matthew 10.40–end — 80

Sunday after Trinity, Proper 9 (3–9 July)
Continuous: Genesis 24.34–38, 42–49, 58–67; Psalm 45.10–17
or Canticle: Song of Solomon 2.8–13; Romans 7.15–25a;
Matthew 11.16–19, 25–end
Related: Zechariah 9.9–12; Psalm 145.8–15; Romans 7.15–25a;
Matthew 11.16–19, 25–end   82

Sunday after Trinity, Proper 10 (10–16 July)
Continuous: Genesis 25.19–end; Psalm 119.105–112;
Romans 8.1–11; Matthew 13.1–9, 18–23
Related: Isaiah 55.10–13; Psalm 65.[1–7] 8–13; Romans 8.1–11;
Matthew 13.1–9, 18–23   84

Sunday after Trinity, Proper 11 (17–23 July)
Continuous: Genesis 28.10–19a; Psalm 139.1–11, 23, 24
[*or* 139.1–11]; Romans 8.12–25; Matthew 13.24–30, 36–43
Related: Wisdom of Solomon 12.13, 16–19 *or* Isaiah 44.6–8;
Psalm 86.11–17; Romans 8.12–25; Matthew 13.24–30, 36–43   86

Sunday after Trinity, Proper 12 (24–30 July)
Continuous: Genesis 29.15–28; Psalm 105.1–11, 45b [*or* 105.1–11]
or Psalm 128; Romans 8.26–end; Matthew 13.31–33, 44–52
Related: 1 Kings 3.5–12; Psalm 119.129–136; Romans 8.26–end;
Matthew 13.31–33, 44–52   88

Sunday after Trinity, Proper 13 (31 July–6 Aug)
Continuous: Genesis 32.22–31; Psalm 17.1–7, 16 [*or* 17.1–7];
Romans 9.1–5; Matthew 14.13–21
Related: Isaiah 55.1–5; Psalm 145.[8–9] 15–22; Romans 9.1–5;
Matthew 14.13–21   90

Sunday after Trinity, Proper 14 (7–13 Aug)
Related: Genesis 37.1–4, 12–28; Psalm 105.1–6, 16–22, 45b
[*or* 105.1–10]; Romans 10.5–15; Matthew 14.22–33
Related: 1 Kings 19.9–18; Psalm 85.8–13; Romans 10.5–15;
Matthew 14.22–33   92

Sunday after Trinity, Proper 15 (14–20 Aug)
Continuous: Genesis 45.1–15; Psalm 133; Romans 11.1–2a, 29–32;
Matthew 15.[10–20] 21–28
Related: Isaiah 56.1, 6–8; Psalm 67; Romans 11.1–2a, 29–32;
Matthew 15.[10–20] 21–28   94

Sunday after Trinity, Proper 16 (21–27 Aug)
Continuous: Exodus 1.8—2.10; Psalm 124; Romans 12.1–8;
Matthew 16.13–20
Related: Isaiah 51.1–6; Psalm 138; Romans 12.1–8;
Matthew 16.13–20   96

Sunday after Trinity, Proper 17 (28 Aug–3 Sept)
Continuous: Exodus 3.1–15; Psalm 105.1–6, 23–26, 45b *or*
Psalm 115; Romans 12.9–end; Matthew 16.21–end
Related: Jeremiah 15.15–21; Psalm 26.1–8; Romans 12.9–end;
Matthew 16.21–end   98

Sunday after Trinity, Proper 18 (4–10 Sept)
Continuous: Exodus 12.1–14; Psalm 149; Romans 13.8–end;
Matthew 18.15–20
Related: Ezekiel 33.7–11; Psalm 119.33–40; Romans 13.8–end;
Matthew 18.15–20   100

Sunday after Trinity, Proper 19 (11–17 Sept)
Continuous: Exodus 14.19–end; Psalm 114 *or*
Canticle: Exodus 15.1b–11, 20, 21; Romans 14.1–12;
Matthew 18.21–35
Related: Genesis 50.15–21; Psalm 103.[1–7] 8–13;
Romans 14.1–12; Matthew 18.21–35   102

Sunday after Trinity, Proper 20 (18–24 Sept)
Continuous: Exodus 16.2–15; Psalm 105.1–6, 37–end
[*or* 105.37–end]; Philippians 1.21–end; Matthew 20.1–16
Related: Jonah 3.10—end of 4; Psalm 145.1–8;
Philippians 1.21–end; Matthew 20.1–16   104

Sunday after Trinity, Proper 21 (25 Sept–1 Oct)
Continuous: Exodus 17.1–7; Psalm 78.1–4, 12–16 [*or* 78.1–7];
Philippians 2.1–13; Matthew 21.23–32
Related: Ezekiel 18.1–4, 25–end; Psalm 25.1–8;
Philippians 2.1–13; Matthew 21.23–32   106

Sunday after Trinity, Proper 22 (2–8 Oct)
Continuous: Exodus 20.1–4, 7–9, 12–20; Psalm 19 [*or* 19.7–end];
Philippians 3.4b–14; Matthew 21.33–end
Related: Isaiah 5.1–7; Psalm 80.9–16; Philippians 3.4b–14;
Matthew 21.33–end   108

Sunday after Trinity, Proper 23 (9–15 Oct)
Continuous: Exodus 32.1–14; Psalm 106.1–6, 19–23 [or 106.1–6];
Philippians 4.1–9; Matthew 22.1–14
Related: Isaiah 25.1–9; Psalm 23; Philippians 4.1–9;
Matthew 22.1–14 — 110

Sunday after Trinity, Proper 24 (16–22 Oct)
Continuous: Exodus 33.12–23; Psalm 99; 1 Thessalonians 1.1–10;
Matthew 22.15–22
Related: Isaiah 45.1–7; Psalm 96.1–9 [10–13];
1 Thessalonians 1.1–10; Matthew 22.15–22 — 112

Last Sunday after Trinity, Proper 25 (23–29 Oct)
Continuous: Deuteronomy 34.1–12; Psalm 90.1–6, 13–17
[or 90.1–6]; 1 Thessalonians 2.1–8; Matthew 22.34–end
Related: Leviticus 19.1–2, 15–18; Psalm 1; 1 Thessalonians 2.1–8;
Matthew 22.34–end — 114

Bible Sunday (Last Sunday after Trinity)
Nehemiah 8.1–4a [5–6] 8–12; Psalm 119.9–16;
Colossians 3.12–17; Matthew 24.30–35 — 116

All Saints' Day (1 November)
Revelation 7.9–end; Psalm 34.1–10; 1 John 3.1–3;
Matthew 5.1–12 — 118

The Fourth Sunday before Advent
Micah 3.5–end; Psalm 43 [or 107.1–8]; 1 Thessalonians 2.9–13;
Matthew 24.1–14 — 120

The Third Sunday before Advent
Amos 5.18–24; Psalm 70; 1 Thessalonians 4.13–end;
Matthew 25.1–13 — 122

The Second Sunday before Advent
Zephaniah 1.7, 12–end; Psalm 90.1–8 [9–11], 12 [or 90.1–8];
1 Thessalonians 5.1–11; Matthew 25.14–30 — 124

Christ the King: The Sunday next before Advent
Ezekiel 34.11–16, 20–24; Psalm 95.1–7; Ephesians 1.15–end;
Matthew 25.31–end — 126

Year B

The First Sunday of Advent
Isaiah 64.1–9; Psalm 80.1–8, 18–20 *or* [80.1–8];
1 Corinthians 1.3–9; Mark 13.24–end　　　　　　　　　　130

The Second Sunday of Advent
Isaiah 40.1–11; Psalm 85.1–2, 8–end [*or* 85.8–end];
2 Peter 3.8–15a; Mark 1.1–8　　　　　　　　　　　　　132

The Third Sunday of Advent
Isaiah 61.1–4, 8–end ; Psalm 126 *or Canticle:* Magnificat;
1 Thessalonians 5.16–24; John 1.6–8, 19–28　　　　　　134

The Fourth Sunday of Advent
2 Samuel 7.1–11, 16; *Canticle:* Magnificat *or* Psalm 89.1–4, 19–26
[*or* 89.1–8]; Romans 16.25–end; Luke 1.26–38　　　　136

Christmas Day (Set III readings)
Isaiah 52.7–10; Psalm 98; Hebrews 1.1–4 [5–12]; John 1.1–14　　138

The First Sunday of Christmas
Isaiah 61.10—62.3; Psalm 148 [148.7–end]; Galatians 4.4–7;
Luke 2.15–21　　　　　　　　　　　　　　　　　　140

The Second Sunday of Christmas
Jeremiah 31.7–14; Psalm 147.13–end; Ephesians 1.3–14;
John 1.[1–9] 10–18　　　　　　　　　　　　　　　　142

The Epiphany
Isaiah 60.1–6; Psalm 72.[1–9] 10–15; Ephesians 3.1–12;
Matthew 2.1–12　　　　　　　　　　　　　　　　　144

The Baptism of Christ (The First Sunday of Epiphany)
Genesis 1.1–5; Psalm 29; Acts 19.1–7; Mark 1.4–11　　　146

The Second Sunday of Epiphany
1 Samuel 3.1–10 [11–20]; Psalm 139.1–5, 12–18 [*or* 1–9];
Revelation 5.1–10; John 1.43–end　　　　　　　　　　148

The Third Sunday of Epiphany
Genesis 14.17–20; Psalm 128; Revelation 19.6–10; John 2.1–11　　150

The Fourth Sunday of Epiphany
Deuteronomy 18.15–20; Psalm 111; Revelation 12.1–5a;
Mark 1.21–28　　　　　　　　　　　　　　　　　　152

The Presentation of Christ in the Temple (Candlemas)
Malachi 3.1–5; Psalm 24.[1–6] 7–end; Hebrews 2.14–end;
Luke 2.22–40   154

Sunday before Lent, Proper 1 (4–10 February)
Isaiah 40.21–end; Psalm 147.1–12, 21 [147.1–12];
1 Corinthians 9.16–23; Mark 1.29–39   156

Sunday before Lent, Proper 2 (11–17 February)
2 Kings 5.1–14; Psalm 30; 1 Corinthians 9.24–end;
Mark 1.40–end   158

Sunday before Lent, Proper 3 (18–24 February or 24–28 May)
Isaiah 43.18–25; Psalm 41; 2 Corinthians 1.18–22; Mark 2.1–12   160

The Second Sunday before Lent
Proverbs 8.1, 22–31; Psalm 104.26–end; Colossians 1.15–20;
John 1.1–14   162

The Sunday next before Lent
2 Kings 12.1–12; Psalm 50.1–6; 2 Corinthians 4.3–6; Mark 9.2–9   164

The First Sunday of Lent
Genesis 9.8–17; Psalm 25.1–9; 1 Peter 3.18–end; Mark 1.9–15   166

The Second Sunday of Lent
Genesis 17.1–7, 15–16; Psalm 22.23–end; Romans 4.13–end;
Mark 8.31–end   168

The Third Sunday of Lent
Exodus 20.1–17; Psalm 19 [*or* 19.7–end]; 1 Corinthians 1.18–25;
John 2.13–22   170

The Fourth Sunday of Lent ('Refreshment' Sunday)
Numbers 21.4–9; Psalm 107.1–3, 17–22 [*or* 107.1–9];
Ephesians 2.1–10; John 3.14–21   172

Mothering Sunday
Exodus 2.1–10 *or* 1 Samuel 1.20–end; Psalm 34.11–20 *or* 127.1–4;
2 Corinthians 1.3–7 *or* Colossians 3.12–17; Luke 2.33–35 *or*
John 19.25–27   174

The Fifth Sunday of Lent (Passion Sunday)
Jeremiah 31.31–34; Psalm 51.1–13 *or* Psalm 119.9–16;
Hebrews 5.5–10; John 12.20–33   176

Palm Sunday
Liturgy of the Palms: Mark 11.1–11 *or* John 12.12–16;
Psalm 118.1–2, 19–end [*or* 118.19–end]
Liturgy of the Passion: Isaiah 50.4–9a; Psalm 31.9–16 [*or* 31.9–18];
Philippians 2.5–11; Mark 14.1–end of 15 *or* Mark 15.1–39
[40–end]   178

Good Friday
Isaiah 52.13—end of 53; Psalm 22 [*or* 22.1–11 *or*
22.1–21]; Hebrews 10.16–25 *or* Hebrews 4.14–16; 5.7–9;
John 18.1—end of 19   180

Easter Day
Acts 10.34–43† *or* Isaiah 25.6–9; Psalm 118.1–2, 14–24
[*or* 118.14–24];
1 Corinthians 15.1–11 *or* Acts 10.34–43†; John 20.1–18
or Mark 16.1–8   182

The Second Sunday of Easter
[Exodus 14.10–end; 15.20, 21]; Acts 4.32–35†; Psalm 133;
1 John 1.1—2.2; John 20.19–end   184

The Third Sunday of Easter
[Zephaniah 3.14–end]; Acts 3.12–19†; Psalm 4; 1 John 3.1–7;
Luke 24.36b–48   186

The Fourth Sunday of Easter
[Genesis 7.1–5, 11–18; 8.6–18; 9.8–13]; Acts 4.5–12†; Psalm 23;
1 John 3.16–end; John 10.11–18   188

The Fifth Sunday of Easter
[Baruch 3.9–15, 32—4.4 *or* Genesis 22.1–18]; Acts 8.26–end†;
Psalm 22.25–end; 1 John 4.7–end; John 15.1–8   190

The Sixth Sunday of Easter
[Isaiah 55.1–11]; Acts 10.44–end†; Psalm 98; 1 John 5.1–6;
John 15.9–17   192

The Seventh Sunday of Easter (Sunday after Ascension Day)
[Ezekiel 36.24–28]; Acts 1.15–17, 21–end†; Psalm 1;
1 John 5.9–13; John 17.6–19   194

Pentecost (Whit Sunday)
Acts 2.1–21 *or* Ezekiel 37.1–14; Psalm 104.26–36, 37b
[*or* 104.26–end]; Romans 8.22–27 *or* Acts 2.1–21;
John 15.26–7; 16.4b–15   196

Trinity Sunday
Isaiah 6.1–8; Psalm 29; Romans 8.12–17; John 3.1–17   198

Sunday after Trinity, Proper 4 (29 May–4 June)
Continuous: 1 Samuel 3.1–10 [11–20]; Psalm 139.1–5, 12–18;
2 Corinthians 4.5–12; Mark 2.23—3.6
Related: Deuteronomy 5.12–15; Psalm 81.1–10;
2 Corinthians 4.5–12; Mark 2.23—3.6   200

Sunday after Trinity, Proper 5 (5–11 June)
Continuous: 1 Samuel 8.4–11 [12–15] 16–20 [11.14–end];
Psalm 138; 2 Corinthians 4.13—5.1; Mark 3.20–end
Related: Genesis 3.8–15; Psalm 130; 2 Corinthians 4.13—5.1;
Mark 3.20–end   202

Sunday after Trinity, Proper 6 (12–18 June)
Continuous: 1 Samuel 15.34—16.13; Psalm 20;
2 Corinthians 5.6–10 [11–13] 14–17; Mark 4.26–34
Related: Ezekiel 17.22–end; Psalm 92.1–4, 12–end [or 92.1–8];
2 Corinthians 5.6–10 [11–13] 14–17; Mark 4.26–34   204

Sunday after Trinity, Proper 7 (19–25 June)
Continuous: 1 Samuel 17.[1a, 4–11, 19–23] 32–49; Psalm 9.9–end;
or 1 Samuel 17.57—18.5, 10–16; Psalm 133; 2 Corinthians 6.1–13;
Mark 4.35–end
Related: Job 38.1–11; Psalm 107.1–3, 23–32 [or 107.23–32];
2 Corinthians 6.1–13; Mark 4.35–end   206

Sunday after Trinity, Proper 8 (26 June–2 July)
Continuous: 2 Samuel 1.1, 17–end; Psalm 130;
2 Corinthians 8.7–end; Mark 5.21–end
Related: Wisdom 1.13–15; 2.23–24; *Canticle:* Lamentations 3.23–33†
or Psalm 30; 2 Corinthians 8.7–end; Mark 5.21–end   208

Sunday after Trinity, Proper 9 (3–9 July)
Continuous: 2 Samuel 5.1–5, 9–10; Psalm 48;
2 Corinthians 12.2–10; Mark 6.1–13
Related: Ezekiel 2.1–5; Psalm 123; 2 Corinthians 12.2–10;
Mark 6.1–13   210

Sunday after Trinity, Proper 10 (10–16 July)
Continuous: 2 Samuel 6.1–5, 12b–19; Psalm 24; Ephesians 1.3–14;
Mark 6.14–29
Related: Amos 7.7–15; Psalm 85.8–end; Ephesians 1.3–14;
Mark 6.14–29   212

Sunday after Trinity, Proper 11 (17–23 July)
Continuous: 2 Samuel 7.1–14a; Psalm 89.20–37;
Ephesians 2.11–end; Mark 6.30–34, 53–end
Related: Jeremiah 23.1–6; Psalm 23; Ephesians 2.11–end;
Mark 6.30–34, 53–end   214

Sunday after Trinity, Proper 12 (24–30 July)
Continuous: 2 Samuel 11.1–15; Psalm 14; Ephesians 3.14–end;
John 6.1–21
Related: 2 Kings 4.42–end; Psalm 145.10–19; Ephesians 3.14–end;
John 6.1–21   216

Sunday after Trinity, Proper 13 (31 July–6 Aug)
Continuous: 2 Samuel 11.26—12.13a; Psalm 51.1–13;
Ephesians 4.1–16; John 6.24–35
Related: Exodus 16.2–4, 9–15; Psalm 78.23–29; Ephesians 4.1–16;
John 6.24–35   218

Sunday after Trinity, Proper 14 (7–13 Aug)
Continuous: 2 Samuel 18.5–9, 15, 31–33; Psalm 130;
Ephesians 4.25—5.2; John 6.35, 41–51
Related: 1 Kings 19.4–8; Psalm 34.1–8; Ephesians 4.25—5.2;
John 6.35, 41–51   220

Sunday after Trinity, Proper 15 (14–20 Aug)
Continuous: 1 Kings 2.10–12; 3.3–14; Psalm 111;
Ephesians 5.15–20; John 6.51–58
Related: Proverbs 9.1–6; Psalm 34.9–14; Ephesians 5.15–20;
John 6.51–58   222

Sunday after Trinity, Proper 16 (21–27 Aug)
Continuous: 1 Kings 8.[1, 6, 10–11] 22–30, 41–43; Psalm 84;
Ephesians 6.10–20; John 6.56–69
Related: Joshua 24.1–2a, 14–18; Psalm 34.15–end;
Ephesians 6.10–20; John 6.56–69   224

Sunday after Trinity, Proper 17 (28 Aug–3 Sept)
Continuous: Song of Solomon 2.8–13; Psalm 45.1–2, 6–9
[or 45.1–7]; James 1.17–end; Mark 7.1–8, 14, 15, 21–23
Related: Deuteronomy 4.1–2, 6–9; Psalm 15; James 1.17–end;
Mark 7.1–8, 14, 15, 21–23   226

Sunday after Trinity, Proper 18 (4–10 Sept)
Continuous: Proverbs 22.1–2, 8–9, 22–23; Psalm 125;
James 2.1–10 [11–13] 14–17; Mark 7.24–end
Related: Isaiah 35.4–7a; Psalm 146; James 2.1–10 [11–13] 14–17;
Mark 7.24–end 228

Sunday after Trinity, Proper 19 (11–17 Sept)
Continuous: Proverbs 1.20–33; Psalm 19 [or 19.1–6] or
Canticle: Wisdom of Solomon 7.26—8.1; James 3.1–12;
Mark 8.27–end
Related: Isaiah 50.4–9a; Psalm 116.1–8; James 3.1–12;
Mark 8.27–end 230

Sunday after Trinity, Proper 20 (18–24 Sept)
Continuous: Proverbs 31.10–end; Psalm 1; James 3.13—4.3, 7–8a;
Mark 9.30–37
Related: Wisdom of Solomon 1.16—2.1, 12–22 or
Jeremiah 11.18–20; Psalm 54; James 3.13—4.3, 7–8a;
Mark 9.30–37 232

Sunday after Trinity, Proper 21 (25 Sept–1 Oct)
Continuous: Esther 7.1–6, 9, 10; 9.20–22; Psalm 124;
James 5.13–end; Mark 9.38–end
Related: Numbers 11.4–6, 10–16, 24–29; Psalm 19.7–end;
James 5.13–end; Mark 9.38–end 234

Sunday after Trinity, Proper 22 (2–8 Oct)
Continuous: Job 1.1; 2.1–10; Psalm 26; Hebrews 1.1–4; 2.5–12;
Mark 10.2–16
Related: Genesis 2.18–24; Psalm 8; Hebrews 1.1–4; 2.5–12;
Mark 10.2–16 236

Sunday after Trinity, Proper 23 (9–15 Oct)
Continuous: Job 23.1–9, 16–end; Psalm 22.1–15;
Hebrews 4.12–end; Mark 10.17–31
Related: Amos 5.6–7, 10–15; Psalm 90.12–end;
Hebrews 4.12–end; Mark 10.17–31 238

Sunday after Trinity, Proper 24 (16–22 Oct)
Continuous: Job 38.1–7 [34–end]; Psalm 104.1–10, 26, 35c
[or 104.1–10]; Hebrews 5.1–10; Mark 10.35–45
Related: Isaiah 53.4–end; Psalm 91.9–end; Hebrews 5.1–10;
Mark 10.35–45 240

Last Sunday after Trinity, Proper 25 (23–29 Oct)
Continuous: Job 42.1–6, 10–end; Psalm 34.1–8, 19–end [*or* 34.1–8];
Hebrews 7.23–end; Mark 10.46–end
Related: Jeremiah 31.7–9; Psalm 126; Hebrews 7.23–end;
Mark 10.46–end   242

Bible Sunday (Last Sunday after Trinity)
Isaiah 55.1–11; Psalm 19.7–end; 2 Timothy 3.14–4.5;
John 5.36b–end   244

All Saints' Day (1 November)
Isaiah 25.6–9; Psalm 24.1–6; Revelation 21.1–6a; John 11.32–44   246

The Fourth Sunday before Advent
Deuteronomy 6.1–9; Psalm 119.1–8; Hebrews 9.11–14;
Mark 12.28–34   248

The Third Sunday before Advent
Jonah 3.1–5, 10; Psalm 62.5–end; Hebrews 9.24–end;
Mark 1.14–20   250

The Second Sunday before Advent
Daniel 12.1–3; Psalm 16; Hebrews 10.11–14 [15–18]19–25;
Mark 13.1–8   252

Christ the King: The Sunday next before Advent
Daniel 7.9–10, 13, 14; Psalm 93; Revelation 1.4b–8;
John 18.33–37   254

Year C

The First Sunday of Advent
Jeremiah 33.14–16; Psalm 25.1–9; 1 Thessalonians 3.9–end;
Luke 21.25–36   258

The Second Sunday of Advent
Baruch 5 *or* Malachi 3.1–4; *Canticle:* Benedictus;
Philippians 1.3–11; Luke 3.1–6   260

The Third Sunday of Advent
Zephaniah 3.14–end; Canticle: Isaiah 12.2–end
[*or* Psalm 146.4–end]; Philippians 4.4–7; Luke 3.7–18   262

The Fourth Sunday of Advent
Micah 5.2–5a; Canticle: Magnificat *or* Psalm 80.1–8;
Hebrews 10.5–10; Luke 1.39–45 [46–55]   264

Christmas Day (Set I readings)
Isaiah 9.2–7; Psalm 96; Titus 2.11–14; Luke 2.1–14 [15–20] 266

The First Sunday of Christmas
1 Samuel 2.18–20, 26; Psalm 148 [*or* 148.7–end];
Colossians 3.12–17; Luke 2.41–end 268

The Second Sunday of Christmas
Jeremiah 31.7–14; Psalm 147.13–end; Ephesians 1.3–14;
John 1.[1–9] 10–18 270

The Epiphany
Isaiah 60.1–6; Psalm 72.[1–9] 10–15; Ephesians 3.1–12;
Matthew 2.1–12 272

The Baptism of Christ (The First Sunday of Epiphany)
Isaiah 43.1–7; Psalm 29; Acts 8.14–17; Luke 3.15–17, 21, 22 274

The Second Sunday of Epiphany
Isaiah 62.1–5; Psalm 36.5–10; 1 Corinthians 12.1–11; John 2.1–11 276

The Third Sunday of Epiphany
Nehemiah 8.1–3, 5–6, 8–10; Psalm 19 [*or* 19.1–6];
1 Corinthians 12.12–31a; Luke 4.14–21 278

The Fourth Sunday of Epiphany
Ezekiel 43.27—44.4; Psalm 48; 1 Corinthians 13; Luke 2.22–40 280

The Presentation of Christ in the Temple (Candlemas)
Malachi 3.1–5; Psalm 24.[1–6] 7–end; Hebrews 2.14–end;
Luke 2.22–40 282

Sunday before Lent, Proper 1 (4–10 February)
Isaiah 6.1–8 [9–end]; Psalm 138; 1 Corinthians 15.1–11;
Luke 5.1–11 284

Sunday before Lent, Proper 2 (11–17 February)
Jeremiah 17.5–10; Psalm 1; 1 Corinthians 15.12–20;
Luke 6.17–26 286

Sunday before Lent, Proper 3 (18–24 February or 24–28 May)
Genesis 45.3–11, 15; Psalm 37.1–11, 40–end [*or* 37.1–7];
1 Corinthians 15.35–38, 42–50; Luke 6.27–38 288

The Second Sunday before Lent
Genesis 2.4b–9, 15–end; Psalm 65; Revelation 4; Luke 8.22–25 290

The Sunday next before Lent
Exodus 34.29–end; Psalm 99; 2 Corinthians 3.12—4.2;
Luke 9.28–36 [37–43a]   292

The First Sunday of Lent
Deuteronomy 26.1–11; Psalm 91.1–2, 9–end [or 91.1–11];
Romans 10.8b–13; Luke 4.1–13   294

The Second Sunday of Lent
Genesis 15.1–12, 17–18; Psalm 27; Philippians 3.17—4.1;
Luke 13.31–end   296

The Third Sunday of Lent
Isaiah 55.1–9; Psalm 63.1–9; 1 Corinthians 10.1–13; Luke 13.1–9   298

The Fourth Sunday of Lent ('Refreshment' Sunday)
Joshua 5.9–12; Psalm 32; 2 Corinthians 5.16–end;
Luke 15.1–3, 11b–end   300

Mothering Sunday
Exodus 2.1–10 or 1 Samuel 1.20–end; Psalm 34.11–20 or 127.1–4;
2 Corinthians 1.3–7 or Colossians 3.12–17; Luke 2.33–35
or John 19.25–27   302

The Fifth Sunday of Lent (Passion Sunday)
Isaiah 43.16–21; Psalm 126; Philippians 3.4b–14; John 12.1–8   304

Palm Sunday
Liturgy of the Palms: Luke 19.28–40; Psalm 118.1–2, 19–end
[or 118.19–24]
Liturgy of the Passion: Isaiah 50.4–9a; Psalm 31.9–16 [or 31.9–18];
Philippians 2.5–11; Luke 22.14—end of 23 or Luke 23.1–49   306

Good Friday
Isaiah 52.13—end of 53; Psalm 22 [or 22.1–11 or 22.1–21];
Hebrews 10.16–25 or Hebrews 4.14–16; 5.7–9;
John 18.1—end of 19   308

Easter Day
Acts 10.34–43† or Isaiah 65.17–end; Psalm 118.1–2, 14–24
[or 118.14–24]; 1 Corinthians 15.19–26 or Acts 10.34–43†;
John 20.1–18 or Luke 24.1–12   310

The Second Sunday of Easter
[Exodus 14.10–end; 15.20, 21]; Acts 5.27–32; Psalm 118.14–end
or Psalm 150; Revelation 1.4–8; John 20.19–end   312

The Third Sunday of Easter
[Zephaniah 3.14–end]; Acts 9.1–6 [7–20]†; Psalm 30;
Revelation 5.11–end; John 21.1–19   314

The Fourth Sunday of Easter
[Genesis 7.1–5, 11–18; 8.6–18; 9.8–13]; Acts 9.36–end;
Psalm 23; Revelation 7.9–end; John 10.22–30   316

The Fifth Sunday of Easter
[Baruch 3.9–15, 32—4.4 *or* Genesis 22.1–18]; Acts 11.1–18;
Psalm 148 [*or* 148.1–6]; Revelation 21.1–6; John 13.31–35   318

The Sixth Sunday of Easter
[Ezekiel 37.1–14]; Acts 16.9–15†; Psalm 67;
Revelation 21.10, 22—22.5; John 14.23–29 *or* John 5.1–9   320

The Seventh Sunday of Easter (Sunday after Ascension Day)
[Ezekiel 36.24–28]; Acts 16.16–34†; Psalm 97;
Revelation 22.12–14, 16, 17, 20–end; John 17.20–end   322

Pentecost (Whit Sunday)
Acts 2.1–21† *or* Genesis 11.1–9; Psalm 104.26–36, 37b
[*or* 104.26–end];1 Romans 8.14–17 *or* Acts 2.1–21†;
John 14.8–17 [25–27]   324

Trinity Sunday
Proverbs 8.1–4, 22–31; Psalm 8; Romans 5.1–5; John 16.12–15   326

Sunday after Trinity, Proper 4 (29 May–4 June)
Continuous: 1 Kings 18.20, 21 [22–29] 30–39; Psalm 96;
Galatians 1.1–12; Luke 7.1–10
Related: 1 Kings 8.22–23, 41–43; Psalm 96.1–9;
Galatians 1.1–12; Luke 7.1–10   328

Sunday after Trinity, Proper 5 (5–11 June)
Continuous: 1 Kings 17.8–16 [17–end]; Psalm 146;
Galatians 1.11–24; Luke 7.11–17
Related: 1 Kings 17.17–end; Psalm 30; Galatians 1.11–end;
Luke 7.11–17   330

Sunday after Trinity, Proper 6 (12–18 June)
Continuous: 1 Kings 21.1–10 [11–14] 15–21a; Psalm 5.1–8;
Galatians 2.15–end; Luke 7.36—8.3
Related: 2 Samuel 11.26—12.10, 13–15; Psalm 32;
Galatians 2.15–end; Luke 7.36—8.3   332

Sunday after Trinity, Proper 7 (19–25 June)
Continuous: 1 Kings 19.1–4 [5–7] 8–15a; Psalms 42, 43
[*or* 42 *or* 43]; Galatians 3.23–end; Luke 8.26–39
Related: Isaiah 65.1–9; Psalm 22.19–28; Galatians 3.23–end;
Luke 8.26–39   334

Sunday after Trinity, Proper 8 (26 June–2 July)
Continuous: 2 Kings 2.1–2, 6–14; Psalm 77.1–2, 11–end
[*or* 77.11–end]; Galatians 5.1, 13–25; Luke 9.51–end
Related: 1 Kings 19.15–16, 19–end; Psalm 16;
Galatians 5.1, 13–25; Luke 9.51–end   336

Sunday after Trinity, Proper 9 (3–9 July)
Related: 2 Kings 5.1–14; Psalm 30; Galatians 6.[1–6] 7–16;
Luke 10.1–11, 16–20
Related: Isaiah 66.10–14; Psalm 66.1–8; Galatians 6.[1–6] 7–16;
Luke 10.1–11, 16–20   338

Sunday after Trinity, Proper 10 (10–16 July)
Continuous: Amos 7.7–end; Psalm 82; Colossians 1.1–14;
Luke 10.25–37
Related: Deuteronomy 30.9–14; Psalm 25.1–10;
Colossians 1.1–14; Luke 10.25–37   340

Sunday after Trinity, Proper 11 (17–23 July)
Continuous: Amos 8.1–12; Psalm 52; Colossians 1.15–28;
Luke 10.38–end
Related: Genesis 18.1–10a; Psalm 15; Colossians 1.15–28;
Luke 10.38–end   342

Sunday after Trinity, Proper 12 (24–30 July)
Related: Hosea 1.2–10; Psalm 85 [*or* 85.1–7];
Colossians 2.6–15 [16–19]; Luke 11.1–13
Related: Genesis 18.20–32; Psalm 138; Colossians 2.6–15 [16–19];
Luke 11.1–13   344

Sunday after Trinity, Proper 13 (31 July–6 Aug)
Continuous: Hosea 11.1–11; Psalm 107.1–9, 43 [*or* 107.1–9];
Colossians 3.1–11; Luke 12.13–21
Related: Ecclesiastes 1.2, 12–14; 2.18–23; Psalm 49.1–12;
Colossians 3.1–11; Luke 12.13–21   346

Sunday after Trinity, Proper 14 (7–13 Aug)
Continuous: Isaiah 1.1, 10–20; Psalm 50.1–8, 23–end [*or* 50.1–7];
Hebrews 11.1–3, 8–16; Luke 12.32–40
Related: Genesis 15.1–6; Psalm 33.12–end [*or* 33.12–21];
Hebrews 11.1–3, 8–16; Luke 12.32–40   348

Sunday after Trinity, Proper 15 (14–20 Aug)
Continuous: Isaiah 5.1–7; Psalm 80.1–2, 9–end [*or* 80.9–end];
Hebrews 11.29—12.2; Luke 12.49–56
Related: Jeremiah 23.23–29; Psalm 82; Hebrews 11.29—12.2;
Luke 12.49–56   350

Sunday after Trinity, Proper 16 (21–27 Aug)
Continuous: Jeremiah 1.4–10; Psalm 71.1–6; Hebrews 12.18–end;
Luke 13.10–17
Related: Isaiah 58.9b–end; Psalm 103.1–8; Hebrews 12.18–end;
Luke 13.10–17   352

Sunday after Trinity, Proper 17 (28 Aug–3 Sept)
Continuous: Jeremiah 2.4–13; Psalm 81.1, 10–end [*or* 81.1–11];
Hebrews 13.1–8, 15, 16; Luke 14.1, 7–14
Related: Ecclesiasticus 10.12–18 *or* Proverbs 25.6–7; Psalm 112;
Hebrews 13.1–8, 15, 16; Luke 14.1, 7–14   354

Sunday after Trinity, Proper 18 (4–10 Sept)
Continuous: Jeremiah 18.1–11; Psalm 139.1–5, 12–18 [*or* 139.1–7];
Philemon 1–21; Luke 14.25–33
Related: Deuteronomy 30.15–end; Psalm 1; Philemon 1–21;
Luke 14.25–33   356

Sunday after Trinity, Proper 19 (11–17 Sept)
Continuous: Jeremiah 4.11–12, 22–28; Psalm 14;
1 Timothy 1.12–17; Luke 15.1–10
Related: Exodus 32.7–14; Psalm 51.1–11; 1 Timothy 1.12–17;
Luke 15.1–10   358

Sunday after Trinity, Proper 20 (18–24 Sept)
Continuous: Jeremiah 8.18—9.1; Psalm 79.1–9; 1 Timothy 2.1–7;
Luke 16.1–13
Related: Amos 8.4–7; Psalm 113; 1 Timothy 2.1–7; Luke 16.1–13   360

Sunday after Trinity, Proper 21 (25 Sept–1 Oct)
Continuous: Jeremiah 32.1–3a, 6–15; Psalm 91.1–6, 14–end
[*or* 91.11–end]; 1 Timothy 6.6–19; Luke 16.19–end
Related: Amos 6.1a, 4–7; Psalm 146; 1 Timothy 6.6–19;
Luke 16.19–end   362

Sunday after Trinity, Proper 22 (2–8 Oct)
Continuous: Lamentations 1.1–6; *Canticle:* Lamentations 3.19–26
or Psalm 137 [or 137.1–6]; 2 Timothy 1.1–14; Luke 17.5–10
Related: Habakkuk 1.1–4; 2.1–4; Psalm 37.1–9; 2 Timothy 1.1–14;
Luke 17.5–10   364

Sunday after Trinity, Proper 23 (9–15 Oct)
Continuous: Jeremiah 29.1, 4–7; Psalm 66.1–11; 2 Timothy 2.8–15;
Luke 17.11–19
Related: 2 Kings 5.1–3, 7–15c; Psalm 111; 2 Timothy 2.8–15;
Luke 17.11–19   366

Sunday after Trinity, Proper 24 (16–22 Oct)
Continuous: Jeremiah 31.27–34; Psalm 119.97–104;
2 Timothy 3.14—4.5; Luke 18.1–8
Related: Genesis 32.22–31; Psalm 121; 2 Timothy 3.14—4.5;
Luke 18.1–8   368

Last Sunday after Trinity, Proper 25 (23–29 Oct)
Continuous: Joel 2.23–end; Psalm 65 [or 65.1–7];
2 Timothy 4.6–8, 16–18; Luke 18.9–14
Related: Ecclesiasticus 35.12–17 or Jeremiah 14.7–10, 19–end;
Psalm 84.1–7; 2 Timothy 4.6–8, 16–18; Luke 18.9–14   370

Bible Sunday (Last Sunday after Trinity)
Isaiah 45.22–end; Psalm 119.129–136; Romans 15.1–6;
Luke 4.16–24   372

All Saints' Day
Daniel 7.1–3, 15–18; Psalm 149; Ephesians 1.11–end;
Luke 6.20–31   374

The Fourth Sunday before Advent
Isaiah 1.10–18; Psalm 32.1–8; 2 Thessalonians 1; Luke 19.1–10   376

The Third Sunday before Advent
Job 19.23–27a; Psalm 17.1–9 [or 17.1–8]; 2 Thessalonians 2.1–5,
13–end; Luke 20.27–38   378

The Second Sunday before Advent
Malachi 4.1–2a; Psalm 98; 2 Thessalonians 3.6–13; Luke 21.5–19   380

Christ the King: The Sunday next before Advent
Jeremiah 23.1–6; Psalm 46; Colossians 1.11–20; Luke 23.33–43   382

For Barbara Virgo
Proverbs 31.10

Preface

The 'Principal Service' readings for Sundays and major festivals in the Church of England have been chosen with care, and for a purpose. They are based on the order set out in the Revised Common Lectionary (RCL), which is the result of decades of work and consultation among English-speaking Christian churches. 'Second Service' and 'Third Service' readings are an additional Church of England provision, not found in the RCL. They are not covered in this volume.

The RCL follows a three-year cycle: Year A is focused on Matthew's Gospel, Year B on Mark's, and Year C on Luke's. These three Gospels are collectively called 'synoptic', meaning that they have broadly the same outlook and approach. The fourth Gospel, John's, has a different style and character, and is used in all three years for specific times and seasons.

Each of the reflections in this book is a standalone exploration of the Church of England lections for a given Sunday. Some focus wholly on the Gospel; others look at the Old Testament/Hebrew Bible and the New Testament readings as well. It is easy to find the right reflection for each Sunday across the three years, A, B and C, in seasons like Lent and Easter, Advent and Christmas and Epiphany.

Outside of these seasons, in 'ordinary time', things are different. Ordinary time, or 'green time' (going by the traditional colour of vestments on these Sundays) may include Sundays before Lent and after Trinity. Because the date of Easter (calculated as the first Sunday after the first full moon after the spring equinox) varies between 22 March and 25 April, the number of Sundays after Trinity is not always the same. Ordinary-time Propers may be needed before Lent provision begins – with the second Sunday before Lent – in years when Easter is late. So each Sunday is assigned its own ('proper') set of readings *and* a date range.

In 2024, for example, Easter was quite early (31 March, so there were no ordinary-time Sundays between the Christmas season (which ends on 2 February) and the second Sunday before Lent. The eighth Sunday after Trinity in that year was on 21 July, so Proper 11 (for the Sunday between 17 and 23 July inclusive) was used. In 2025, though, when Easter was later, the eighth Sunday after Trinity was later, on 10 August: then Proper 14 (for the Sunday between 7 and 13 August) was required.

On the Sundays after Trinity, the Principal Service Lectionary provides alternative Old Testament readings and psalms. Those under the heading 'Continuous' allow the Old Testament/Hebrew Bible reading and its complementary psalm to stand independently of the other readings. Those under the heading 'Related' relate the Old Testament/Hebrew Bible reading and the psalm to the Gospel reading. As the Lectionary indicates, it is unhelpful to move from week to week from one sequence to another, so one sequence should be followed for the whole sequence of Sundays after Trinity.

So I had to make a choice: 'Continuous' or 'Related'? I based it on my own lectionary usage as a parish priest, and on the practice of other parishes. The 'Related' track may be preferred probably for two reasons. First, it encourages readers and worshippers to notice connections between different Bible writings. Second, it fits more easily into the pattern of seasons and festivals of the Church's year. Any reflection originally written in 2023–26 is focused only on the Gospel, which is the same for both tracks.

The easy way to know the readings for any date is to use a lectionary provided by the Church for each year, either in print form, or online, or via an app. A free resource is available at https://almanac.oremus.org and can be downloaded for diaries.

Abbreviations

AV	The Authorized ('King James', KJV) version, 1611
BCP	Book of Common Prayer 1552, 1662
NEB	New English Bible 1970
NIV	The New International Version 2011
NJB	The New Jerusalem Bible 1985
NRSV	The New Revised Standard Version 1989 (updated 2021)
RCL	The Revised Common Lectionary
REB	The Revised English Bible 1989 (update of NEB)
RSV	The Revised Standard Version 1952

Introduction

This book has had a long gestation. Over the past five years, from Advent 2020, I have been writing a weekly column for the *Church Times*, providing between 720 and 730 words on that Sunday's Principal Service readings. This 730 is a hard limit. I cannot ask for more words because the ideas are complex, or the reader deserves extra background information.

I have found this hard word-limit more helpful than frustrating. Time and again it obliges me to cut the soft words that give colour to what is written, but add little to build up the reader's understanding. Sometimes I aim to treasure and celebrate key words in the text. At other times, I must work those 730 words hard because I am conscious that the text can be misunderstood or even misused (the way John's Gospel presents 'the Jews' is a sensitive example). Occasionally, I use a deliberately oblique 'take' to try and surprise the reader with a fresh approach to stories they think they already know well.

I took on the job of writing the column with a worry about whether I would have enough to say. As it turned out, I have never *not* been inspired by the lections when I read them in preparation for writing. It has become the most enjoyable piece of writing I do each week, demanding that I investigate words and ideas to give readers access to facts and thoughts they might not otherwise come across without access to learned commentaries and other books. It has been important to me that what I say is in accordance with mainstream Christian orthodoxy. On rare occasions when it is not, I have flagged this up, so that the reader is free to take another path.

It is a great privilege to have access to the Bible, a privilege our forebears in the Church of England fought and died for. And it is a great act of daring to claim to be a reliable interpreter of God's holy word. As a priest in the Church of England, I take on this role whenever I preach, just as my fellow clergy do, Sunday by Sunday. But writing for the *Church Times*, I become, for a little part of each week, a Bible commentator of a very modest sort, and I relish the chance to go deep into the words and wisdom of the holy writings.

As I write this, I am in the middle of my fifth year of writing. Once I have completed a second Year A (2025–26), it will be time to hand on to another writer, with different skills and a fresh approach. But it will be hard to let go. Not least because of the many readers who, over the years, have been in touch to tell me how much they have enjoyed what I write, or to argue with me, or to send me thoughts and writings of their own, and, of course, to correct me with kindness ('speaking the truth in love', Ephesians 4.15).

But I am quite sure that the person who has benefited most from my weekly column has been 'me, myself, I'. I have tackled puzzles previously sidestepped and wrestled with thorny questions that might have driven me to preach on easier readings. Almost without noticing, the body of work has grown. If readers value reading it even half as much as I have enjoyed writing it, I will presume to count it a job well done.

YEAR A (MATTHEW)

H. Scriptures

Welcome dear book, souls joy and food! The feast
Of spirits, Heav'n extracted lyes in thee;
Thou art lifes charter, the Doves spotless neast
Where souls are hatched unto Eternitie.

In thee the hidden stone, the *Manna* lies,
Thou art the great *Elixir*, rare, and Choice;
The Key that opens to all Mysteries,
The *Word* in characters, God in the *Voice*.

O that I had deep Cut in my hard heart
Each line in thee! Then would I plead in groans
Of my Lord's penning, and by sweetest Art
Return upon himself the *Law*, and *Stones*.
Read here, my faults are thine. This Book, and I
Will tell thee so; *Sweet Saviour thou didst dye!*

Henry Vaughan (1621–95), from Silex Scintillans

The First Sunday of Advent

Isaiah 2.1–5; Psalm 122; Romans 13.11–end; Matthew 24.36–44

In AD 386, in a garden in Milan, this New Testament reading for Advent Sunday changed a man's life. He went on to change other lives, by his example (how he lived his life from then on) and by his teaching (the fruits of study and reflection, shared with others by writing and preaching).

His name was Augustine. He had travelled from north Africa to north Italy, searching for answers to the question of life, the universe, everything. He heard a voice telling him to pick up and read – but what? So he took up a book and read the first words his eyes fell on: 'put on the Lord Jesus Christ, and make no provision for the flesh, to gratify its desires' (Rom. 11.14).

Because he took the apostle Paul's words in Romans with the utmost seriousness, he let them change his life. For this is what our 'glorious liberty' (Rom. 8.21) consists in: the power to say 'yes' or 'no' to God.

Advent Sunday marks the beginning of the Church year. A new year is a good time for making resolutions. We often do so on 1 January, so why not make a Christian resolution on Advent Sunday? A resolution is not a solemn vow. It does not commit us to the same degree. It is more a statement of intent, a measuring stick we can keep coming back to as a check on how our good intentions are working out.

Sometimes in worship, Scripture readings fail to engage us, but not because the texts themselves are deficient. It may simply be that we are not yet ready to hear them properly. Sometimes we are determined not to take to heart their message, dreading the upheaval and self-denial that may ensue. The reader exhorts us at the beginning, '*Hear* the gospel of our Lord Jesus Christ …' We can hear, but do nothing. Or we can hear and act upon the voice that calls to us.

Taking the gospel seriously is not always the same as taking the Gospel literally. Those who read Matthew 24 in a literal way may find themselves convinced that an event called the Rapture could happen at any moment. The Rapture is a belief, in certain churches, that the coming of the Son of Man will be exactly as Matthew's Gospel states: sudden, unexpected and terrifying in its seeming arbitrariness. One will be taken, another left. The idea of a rapture also draws upon Paul's expectation that 'the Lord will come and not be slow': 1 Thessalonians 4.17 is the key text.

This separation of sheep from goats (Matt. 25.31–46) must be a matter of God's penetrating discernment. It cannot be mere caprice. Might it be that those selected for the Rapture (the term comes from the Latin word *rapio* for snatching something up) possess some quality of faith missing in those who are left behind?

Today's Gospel confirms that God's choice of whom to seize and whom to pass over is not arbitrary. Jesus insists that we have a choice, with an emphatic 'Know this!' The householder can choose to react to the warning by being ready. It sounds like hard work to keep up the constant vigilance required. Surely there must be lapses at times, when the householder (who stands for us) nods off while on guard.

Most of the time we can nod off (i.e. fall back into sin) without serious repercussions. Temptations are not street thugs awaiting their chance to begin an assault on someone. They are more stealth predators than overt assailants.

In the garden in Milan, everything came marvellously together to let Augustine embrace the faith he longed for. Conversely, it may take a hellish combination of many factors to draw us into sinning and falling short: being unobserved ('no one will know'); and having what passes in the world's eyes as an excuse ('she's been under such pressure!'); and the trivial nature of the individual steps into wrongdoing ('it was only one puff/sip/slice/fiver'). Together these factors fuse into a mighty force overcoming our resistance.

Augustine has much to teach us, but nothing is a better lesson than the life he lived in loving service of God and his people. All we really need, to make ourselves ready for that unexpected hour, is to love God, and our neighbour, and keep the faith.

The Second Sunday of Advent

Isaiah 11.1–10; Psalm 72.1–7, 18, 19 [or 72.1–7]; Romans 15.4–13; Matthew 3.1–12

Today's Gospel is the full-fat version of John the Baptist, not Baptist-lite. In common with Luke, Matthew uses a source that is not recorded in Mark or John, and it preserves for us an ominous conclusion (3.12) to the story of the Baptist's emergence from the desert and his role in proclaiming what Matthew calls 'the kingdom of the heavens'.

We do not usually learn about the good news in such a way. That warning about the cleaning out of the threshing floor does not even sound like good news. Matthew uses a distinctive word found nowhere else (what linguists call a *hapax*) for this image of judgement: *diakathariei*. The *-kathar-* bit means cleaning; the *dia-* bit tells us that the cleaning will be emphatic and thorough. Anyone who has ever done a clean-up job – on a mess, a wound, a muddy dog – that is subject to scrutiny and evaluation by someone else will know the anxiety that disrupts our equilibrium: 'Did I do a good enough job, or am I in trouble here?'

The imagery is not difficult to decode. This is the last act of a farmer whose working year is over. After this, there will be no more grain to winnow. The kernels of wheat contain the nutrition and the promise of life. Chaff, on the other hand, is empty. It keeps the shape of the whole grain of wheat, and superficially resembles it. But it is hollow, and worthless for anything except burning.

No one wants to be a speck of chaff at the last judgement. So why does the Gospel need this ominous tone to reinforce the warning? One simple answer is the gloomy predestinarian one, that we cannot help sinning and doing the evil we do not want (Rom. 7.19). Beyond that message there are other explanations – equally challenging, but less likely to freeze us in hopeless inactivity arising out of fear.

One explanation that jumps out from this Gospel is more than just a warning about judgement for Advent. On the contrary, it gives us a tool for applying to other texts as well, as we search the Scriptures, because we believe that in them we have eternal life (John 5.39). When the Pharisees and Sadducees came to be baptized by John, he completely failed on four out of the five marks of mission (tell, teach, tend, transform, treasure); and even his way of 'telling' was not easily recognizable as good news.

It takes a particular kind of vocation to dare to speak so brutally. John was either mad, bad or a prophet. To be uncompromising is characteristic of the prophetic calling, which is no doubt why prophets are so unpopular most of the time. I wonder if that uncompromising message was part of what drew the Pharisees in the first place, for they were prone to setting extreme standards of religious observance (Luke 11.42). That kind of holiness is something God can probably do without. If John and Jesus are right, it is mere gilding applied to the base metal of human arrogance.

The desire to be special is not wrong in itself, despite our misgivings about modern society's cult of celebrity. But the Baptist rips into these self-righteous people with a challenge that for me has become a yardstick, a standard I can apply in complicated questions of Church practice and Christian theology: 'Do not presume to say to yourselves, "We have Abraham as our ancestor"; for I tell you, God is able from these stones to raise up children to Abraham' (Matt. 3.9).

Whenever custom, legislation or ignorance mean that I find a Christian matter awkward, this is a test for me to apply. Does one Church doubt that another Church's communion is valid? God can raise up the body and blood of Christ from stones. Does one Christian believe that another's baptism is invalid? God can raise up a Christian baptized in the waters of their own true faith (just as martyrs are recognized as having been baptized in blood). This criterion works just as well on interpretations of the Trinity as it does on same-sex Christian marriage.

This does not mean that matters of order, faith and ethics are unimportant. But we need to be reminded (repeatedly, down the Christian centuries, it seems) that 'this extraordinary power belongs to God and does not come from us' (2 Cor. 4.7).

The Third Sunday of Advent

Isaiah 35.1–10; Psalm 146.1–10 *or Canticle:* Magnificat;
James 5.7–10; Matthew 11.2–11

I would like to begin with a word of appreciation to the prophet Isaiah for remembering people with weak hands and feeble knees (35.3). At some point in our lives, most of us will have to deal with one of these difficulties, or both. Not that the prophet can have imagined a future including surgery to replace joints and clever work-arounds for those like me whose grip strength is poor, such as rubber disks for getting lids off jars.

This passage of Isaiah delights us with its inclusiveness. It is a word of comfort for those whose ailments are not dramatic or disastrous but simply wearing and joy-reducing. The list of cures and healings mentioned by Isaiah is picked up centuries later in the Gospel, when Jesus sends John a message about the blind, the lame and the deaf. But he adds some new categories: lepers are cleansed, the dead are raised, and the poor get good news.

The logic of this sequence is hard to fathom. We might have expected the raising of the dead to be mentioned last, as a nature-defying climax to prove God's power. But no. It is followed by what feels to me, even though it probably should not, like an anti-climax. Having good news preached to you – which most of us have experienced one way or another – is hardly as remarkable as seeing the dead raised. I've had plenty of one, but never observed the other. Though I did once have to cross someone off the 'departed' section of the prayer list and put them back on the 'sick' section.

Both the raising of the dead and the hearing of good news have been traced by scholars to passages elsewhere in Isaiah (26.19; 61.1). But that still does not explain the logic of the sequence, and the concluding sentence, 'blessed is anyone who takes no offence at me', makes it even more puzzling.

Yet there is a logic to the shift from simple healings of physical ailments (blind, lame, deaf, lepers) to proofs of the kingdom (Resurrection, good news). Perhaps 'the poor' who get to hear the good news are meant to make us think of the 'poor in spirit' in the beatitudes of a few chapters before (5.3). That is my impression, given that the last part of Jesus' message to John the Baptist is adding a beatitude in here ('blessed is', 11.6).

When preparing to write, I had hoped that verse 6 would turn out to speak wisdom to a problem of our time: the giving and taking of offence. Could 'blessed is anyone who takes no offence at me' clarify for us the right balance between being sensitive and being over-sensitive? That would certainly be precious Bible wisdom.

But alas it does not. Not when you get into the meaning of the Greek word. It is a churchy kind of word, which has come down to us as the English word 'scandal'. It refers to a snare, or stumbling block, or something that causes offence, and is found almost nowhere in ancient literature apart from the Bible. The Old Testament has examples of the word 'scandal', and there it mostly means a snare. Whatever word we choose when we turn it into English, it must be something that makes us lose our footing.

With divine wisdom (unsurprisingly), Jesus anticipates the effect that preaching the good news is going to have on people. Like the first three beatitudes in Matthew 5, his solo beatitude here is countercultural. Prevailing wisdom says it is a bad thing to be poor or bereaved or meek. Here is a hint that encountering Jesus may upset our equilibrium and that finding him to be a stumbling block will be the common reaction to the man and his message.

Welcoming Jesus into our life is virtually impossible to do without causing some bumps in the level ground of daily life. It is a decision with consequences for every choice we make and even for our unspoken thoughts and feelings. From Paul's own experience within a single New Testament letter, Christ can be both our sure foundation (1 Cor. 3.10) and also a stumbling block (1.23, *skandalon*). It is hardly surprising if the Lord who has so discomposed our comfortable lives may indeed turn out to be a stumbling block for anyone who knows Jesus principally as a swear word.

The Fourth Sunday of Advent

Isaiah 7.10–16; Psalm 80.1–8, 18–20 [or 80.1–8];
Romans 1.1–7; Matthew 1.18–end

These readings touch on a unique selling point of Christian faith, enshrined in the Apostles' Creed and the Nicene Creed: that Jesus was 'born of the Virgin Mary' and 'incarnate by the Holy Ghost of the Virgin Mary'. If you tackle arguments by opponents of faith, you may find that the passages from Isaiah 7 and Matthew 2 both loom large. But I need to be more specific; I should say '*modern* opponents of faith'.

Most people, when they refer to the 'virgin birth' mean the virginal conception of Jesus, rather than the more apocryphal legends associated with Mary's purity before, during and after childbirth. And there was plenty of healthy scepticism in the early days of the Way from outsiders who could make no sense of a mingling of divine and human 'stuff' in the person of a single human being.

The criticism I am referring to gains much of its strength from nineteenth-century biblical inquiry, which saw the intensification of a new approach: historical criticism. In other words, treating the Bible like any other ancient document. Scrutinizing its date, authorship, place of origin, audience, intended purpose and genre. This was a revolution in thinking for Christians, imitating (and partly modelled on) the new science of evolution.

When the infancy narratives of Matthew and Luke began to attract this kind of scrutiny, opponents of Christianity, and some within the faith, sensed an opportunity. Where once miracles had been shining proofs of divine power (if one took it as a given that Scripture was sacred), they now became potential embarrassments to be minimized at all costs. The feeding of the 5,000? Obviously not a real tuck-in-and-scoff occasion but a symbolic sharing of tiny fragments. The healing miracles? Anything but the quasi-magical transformation of broken or dysfunctional bodies into whole ones.

A combination of the sceptical attitude and a historical-critical approach, applied to the virginal conception, created what looks like a clinching proof that that virginal conception was a fantasy, or a misunderstanding, or a clever piece of mis-selling. Who knew that biblical translation could be so controversial?

The argument goes like this. Isaiah 7.14 says, 'a young woman shall conceive and bear a son'. When translated into Greek (before Christ's birth) and Latin (afterwards), this became 'a virgin shall conceive'. Matthew used the Greek text of Isaiah as proof that God had foretold the virginal conception. Conclusion: this is therefore either a misunderstanding or a deliberate deceit to trick people into thinking that Jesus was more special than he really was.

When I first discovered that Christian faith could stretch my mind as well as my heart, it was thrilling. My faith no longer needed to sit in its own sealed compartment separate from the rest of my life as a student of ancient history and literature. And I had learned that the historical-critical method was the Truth, just as others learned the Bible as Truth. So I swallowed the argument I had been presented with and accepted that Isaiah had not prophesied a virginal conception, and Matthew had been at best mistaken, and at worst deceitful, in pretending otherwise.

Strangely, that did not make a difference to my belief in Jesus, whom I had not yet learned to divvy up into 'true God and true man'. Nor did I regard belief in the virginal conception as a corner-stone without which my faith would crumble. Back then I read *The Myth of God Incarnate*,[1] because it was new and controversial, not because I understood that calling God 'incarnate' might need explaining.

It is true that the Hebrew does not necessarily mean 'virgin', and that Matthew has read more significance into the text than perhaps he should. But the virginal conception does not stand or fall by that translation. His existing belief in it prompted Matthew to look for corroboration, which he found in Isaiah. What is more, we have not one but two accounts of it, which are different in their details and independent of each other, but similar in their shape. And it is normal for ancient life-stories to tell a birth narrative and then skip straight to adulthood, as Matthew does (and, with one adolescence-story, Luke also).

Scepticism and historical-critical scholarship are not the enemies of Christian faith. On the contrary, they are a big step forward into a faith that claims both head and heart for Jesus.

---

[1] John Hick, *The Myth of God Incarnate*, SCM Press, 1977.

Christmas Day (Set II readings)

Isaiah 62.6–end; Psalm 97; Titus 3.4–7; Luke 2.[1–7] 8–20

The message of the Christmas readings does not change, and here I am focusing on the shortest possible distillation of the three Sets specified for Christmas Day, Set II. First, from the Old Testament and epistle, us as we really are, and as Christ sees us, and as God would have us be: 'Sought out. Not forsaken (Isaiah). Saved (Titus)'.

There is no longer any need to travel in search of God, like Mary and Joseph, or the Magi. God has travelled to us and sought us out. We do not have to forsake all hope for ourselves and others, because God has not forsaken us. We may be sinking in a slough of despond or beaten down by countless troubles, but in God's eternal perspective, we are 'saved' – or to translate it slightly differently, we are 'safe'. No lasting harm can come to us.

Then we have six words (just one in Greek) from the Gospel: 'I am bringing you good news' (Luke 2.10).

This comes in a form we can easily grasp: the Christmas experience, Christian-style. John 1.1–14 is sublime, but with Luke and Matthew, and their stories of journeys and get-togethers, we can feel at home. Together, these Scripture fragments constitute a powerful Christmas message. The angel's words are good news for everyone. Racial identity and religious belief become irrelevant with the revelation that God's love for humankind is universal. If this is heresy, because God loves only Christians while the rest of the world can burn, well, call me a heretic.

Outside the Church, though, content creators and the media have Christmas schedules and pages to fill, and (to be fair) stereotypes to challenge. This can feel like a chipping away at our ideal imaginings until angelic glory loses its gleam, and peace and goodwill sound more like pie in the sky.

One example of this is the traditional Christmas story (caution: names and details may change from year to year) of the over-sharing parish priest, who tells the real story of Christmas while debunking 'mythical' Gospel stories of Jesus' birth. Preferably in front of the kiddies, straight after the school nativity play. And with plenty of parents within earshot, ready to be disgusted. Reader, I was nearly that parish priest once, when at one midnight Mass, assuming (wrongly) the church to be empty of under-10s, I declared from the pulpit, 'I don't believe in Father Christmas'. The guilt is with me still.

We need to keep the joy and the calling of Christmas woven together, as those Scripture fragments do, not least because it is always a tough time for some, not surprisingly when you think how much of our happiness is invested in it. And this year, more families than ever will be struggling.

One constructive exercise for when pressures and expectations are getting to us is to write a list of blessings. It may start slowly. Making the list in two columns, one 'positive' and the other 'negative', the negatives come quickly and plentifully to mind. To balance this, we need to take time, pause and think, so that gradually we recognize more of what is good in our lives. It helps if we can reflect on what makes the good things good. After all, it is human nature that the things that make us most comfortable and secure tend to become invisible, so that we take them for granted.

When we become Christians, we learn about the beatific vision, our ultimate perfecting in God's nearer presence. But we still have to go on in the human reality of hardships, doubts and difficulties in which we spend our earthly days. At Christmas, the divide between Christian truth and secular festivity seems stark. We can bridge the gulf by bringing that festivity into our worship. On the whole, we are good at this: at Christmas, occasional worshippers experience church at its most uplifting, and least naggy. We are not so good at bringing the solemn joy of the angelic 'good news' into secular winterval. Perhaps our faith-perspective comes across as judgemental.

Creating our list may help if we are under pressure in the festive season. But if there is a concrete stumbling block in the way of our happiness (domestic violence, addiction, abuse, debt, dying relationships), no list of blessings will magic it away. So, we should add a third column: things we are going to face up to once the food and gifts and decorations are cleared away.

The First Sunday of Christmas

Isaiah 63.7–9; Psalm 148 [*or* 148.7–end]; Hebrews 2.10–end; Matthew 2.13–end

Matthew 2 reads like an endorsement of oneiromancy (the interpretation of dreams). Indeed, it is a tale full of dreams – though not in a way that undermines the historical truth of events. Instead, this chapter, and the dreams that direct much of its action, help to form our understanding of the nativity (a historical fact) and the Incarnation (a theological fact).

Listening to someone telling you their dreams can sometimes be boring or uncomfortable. Our own dreams too may make us uncomfortable, but they are rarely boring. They can even be instructive. Perhaps Joseph's first dream was like this (Matt. 1.19–24). He must have gone to bed fretting about his fiancée's infidelity: how to do the right thing without dishonouring himself or shaming her?

Joseph does not reproach her for the shame her pregnancy could bring upon his family. Instead, the Gospel affirms that he is a righteous man: a signal that righteousness means showing compassion not judgement. He falls asleep, despite his inner disquiet, and then his dream reveals a way forward.

So much human wrongdoing is a matter not of positive choice but of people's inability to see a palatable alternative. The angel gives Joseph a way forward, not by solving the shame problem, but rather by showing that Mary's pregnancy is God's will, because this renders the shame unimportant. Joseph does the right thing, for the right reasons, as well as from compassion for his soon-to-be-wife. He sets aside his own ego, and shoulders the responsibility for the wellbeing of his strange foster-son.

This first dream prepares the way for several more. There is the dream of the Magi, which keeps them safe from Herod (2.12). This is followed by three further dreams for Joseph. Like his first dream, the second and third get an extra layer of authority, by being delivered through the agency of a divine messenger, an angel. This sets them apart from God's warning to the Magi (though that has its own distinctive quality, being, apparently, a shared dream) and from Joseph's fourth and final dream, which is only fleetingly recorded ('being warned in a dream', 2.22).

We are not told the angel's name. Luke's is the only Gospel to name Gabriel, and states that he was sent to Mary rather than Joseph. Gabriel effected communication between a human being and the Lord. His appearing and his message to Mary read like independent corroboration of Matthew's dreams. It helps if dreams have verification, and the angel provides it. The point is that Joseph's dreams are not wishful thinking, something born from his own mind or heart. Having trusted the angel once, he does not hesitate to trust again: he takes his wife and son into Egypt.

In this journey, we find an echo of Moses' travels out of Egypt into Midian (Ex. 2.15). Matthew seems to have crafted the story of the Holy Family's flight carefully to bring out its character as an example of what scholars call 'typology'. This means events in the Old Testament/Hebrew Bible prefiguring things in the New Testament.

Perhaps, though, Joseph obeys the angel because he himself is mindful of the example of his ancestor Moses, as well as recognizing the truth of the threat to his foster-son if Herod gets wind of his identity. He would surely have spoken with the Magi and taken appropriate measures after hearing of their distrust of King Herod, whom they detoured to avoid on their way home.

Matthew's Joseph is there at the beginning of Jesus' earthly existence, but then disappears from the Gospel story, as if, like Simeon's, his role has ended and his purpose has been fulfilled (Luke 2.29). So, to two final thoughts about the name: first, Matthew's is not the only 'Joseph' in Scripture to 'dream dreams' or to find himself in danger because of them (Gen. 37.5—41.32). Second, a serendipitous fulfilment: all four Gospels witness to another Joseph, who appears in the story after the apparent end of Jesus' life. He will honour the Saviour's body by seeing it safely laid to rest (Matt. 27.57, 59). Both men have their part to play in cherishing the incarnate Lord, who delivers himself into the hands of sinners, yes; but who, when he is at his most helpless, is content to be consigned to the care of two Josephs, both of them acting out of love, not blood.

The Second Sunday of Christmas

Jeremiah 31.7–14; Psalm 147.13–21; Ephesians 1.3–14;
John 1.[1–9] 10–18

Fullness is one of the less attractive side-effects of Christmas. Most of us eat too much; some of us drink too much. When we have eaten or drunk to the utmost, we declare that we are full. But when the witnesses to Jesus talk about 'fullness', they have something very different in mind. This Gospel is the only example of John using an idea (1.16) that figures repeatedly in Paul: in Greek it is *pleroma*. Like many a theological term, it has its roots in what is simple and familiar: in another ancient Greek text, you can eat your *pleroma* of cheese, for example. But in the New Testament, it has the sense of a number brought to completion: not just 'filled', then, but 'full-filled'.

This idea of full-fill-ment is closely connected to another idea in Ephesians, one that Paul (if Paul is the author of that letter) states repeatedly. That is destiny. Now, destiny is a much more problematic concept. For us, it presses a big red button labelled 'free will versus predestination' (you can see why the button needs to be big). That raises questions about how God's guiding hand in human history can be compatible with the free exercise of human will by which we declare ourselves to be Christians.

I describe elsewhere (page 194) how important and seductive an idea it was in Bible days for the future to be predictable. Foreknowledge of the future is a characteristic of God, but in itself that is not problematic. The problems only begin when we start to think and act as if we are predestined by God to be inside or outside his kingdom. That seems to strip us of free will, to make us pawns on a chessboard, and to condemn those who are not among the 'elect' to a damnation they have done nothing to deserve.

This is not a problem with a solution, I think, though I realize that others will disagree with me about the matter. In the twenty-first century, we can see the logical difficulties that arise when we affirm this belief. Because it seems to be an exclusivist idea, we want to play it down. But the Christian belief in God's providence (which, literally, means his 'foresight') is fundamental. We understand that God *is*, and the visions of him that occur in Scripture, rare as they are, give us some idea of the gap between our reality and his reality. There is God as we see him in Isaiah 6 and 1 Timothy 6.16: 'high and lifted up', in 'unapproachable light'. Then there is God-with-us, Emmanuel, the God we deal with every day in our prayers and sacraments, in our worship and of course in our observance of the Christmas season. God-with-us is close beside us always. We see him in the faces of those we love and even in the faces of people whom we do not know at all.

When we want to explore how God works within human history and in human time, we can struggle to see the bigger picture. The Bible readings for today are a snapshot. But instead of imagining them in an old-fashioned photograph album, we should picture something more like a hard drive or cloud storage. Thousands and thousands of photos go everywhere with us, in our pockets and bags. A few are treasured; the majority (perhaps because they are very similar and repetitive) are usually scrolled past in the hunt for those special images that tug at our heartstrings and make us smile as we remember.

That store of images is like the whole story of the Incarnation as we encounter it in the Bible. It reaches most obviously from Isaiah 7 into Revelation 12. In reality, it stretches from Genesis 1.26 to Revelation 22.20. In other words, it takes us from our first beginnings into God's eternal future, that Judgement that we spent Advent trying to make sense of.

From divine fulfilment, we have all received grace upon grace. That suggests an ever-growing heap of blessings. But we could translate it as 'grace in place of grace', suggesting the old covenant giving way to the new. This is one of those cases where I want to say that the evangelist has been deliberately ambiguous, and to good effect. If the text can mean either, it can also mean both.

The Epiphany

Isaiah 60.1–6; Psalm 72.[1–9] 10–15; Ephesians 3.1–12; Matthew 2.1–12

It makes sense to focus on the Gospel when we celebrate the Epiphany, especially in Year A, for the story of the Magi and their journey is Matthew's gift to the Church. No other Gospel mentions it. This does not mean that only Matthew thinks the Epiphany message matters to Christians. We have the reading from Paul to remind us about the inclusion of the gentiles (he mentions it twice). Also, Isaiah records God proclaiming it centuries before Christ's nativity.

Despite that instruction from God through his prophet, no such inclusion of the gentiles had been instituted. Either some Jewish people did not want to mix with gentiles; or the gentiles had no use for an act of welcome that was meaningless to them (because they did not call themselves 'gentiles' or know what the term meant); or both. I suspect it was both.

We find it easier to proclaim inclusive principles than to live them out, particularly when it will cost us something to uphold those principles. Still, it matters that the prophecy, with its principle of inclusion, was preserved in Scripture for us to keep coming back to. No one who claims to be a Christian should be able to say that they did not know God wants this from us.

Luke, himself a gentile, had worked hard in his Gospel, and in Acts, to smooth away possible sources of misunderstanding, where Jesus' Jewishness might be difficult for his gentile readers to understand. Not so Matthew, for whom Jesus is a new Moses, complete with his own miraculous infancy rescue and departure from Egypt (Ex. 2). It is Matthew's Gospel, with its sensitivity to Jewish history (as well as some less helpful moments, 27.25) that understands how broad is the gulf that needs to be bridged.

Perhaps it is unfortunate, for Matthew's inclusive message, how the English language has developed in its use of the term 'epiphany'. I can understand why people find it an attractive word-choice, for it sounds exotic (it is Greek) and it has four syllables to help it resound impressively. Within the Bible, it is used of Christ's first appearing (2 Tim. 1.10) and of his final appearing (1 Tim. 6.14). In neither of these two examples is it used in the way Christians now use it, to refer to that specific act of appearing (on the part of the Christ-child) and the act of acknowledgement by the three gentile wise men (marked by their giving of kingly gifts). At the time when the New Testament took shape, it was just a way of referring to any divine being materializing before a mortal, whether Christian or 'pagan'.

This makes me wonder what non-Christians make of us celebrating the Epiphany. We could try using the BCP alternative label, the 'manifestation of Christ to the gentiles', but manifestation sounds equally exotic and theological, and has even more syllables, so that is unlikely to help.

When it is used in ordinary speech, 'epiphany' may be nothing more than a synonym for 'appearance'. Sometimes I hear someone using it to describe their coming to a sudden and unexpected realization. Neither of these does anything like justice to our 'Epiphany'. But if we take them together, they do preserve some aspects of the fuller version that are genuinely important.

First, the Epiphany is an act of witness, something that we have to *see*. We may not be able to rival the Magi with a journey from the ends of the known world in search of the King of the Jews. But we can still imitate them, by a little pilgrimage: to church, to worship, to prayer.

Second, the Epiphany changes us, from a state of ignorance to a state of knowledge. We should not depart for our own country, not by any road, without having learned something, or realized something, or without being re-energized for whatever lies before us. Certainly, the vision that greets us when we behold our infant King, and know him for who and what he is, must be treasured. We depart bearing a knowledge more precious than any of the gifts we came with. But above all, that Epiphany vision is for sharing. The Light must beget light: for, taken all together, the three readings for the Epiphany are shot through with light – dawn light, starlight and, above all, divine light.

The Baptism of Christ
(The First Sunday of Epiphany)

Isaiah 42.1–9; Psalm 29; Acts 10.34–43; Matthew 3.13–end

The baptism of Jesus is a historical event. All four Gospels give their own version of it. Some argue that Matthew's version (3.17) deliberately echoes Psalm 2.7: 'the LORD ... said to me, "You are my son; today I have begotten you".' From early times, Christians looked to psalms for foreshadowings of Christ (68.18; 110.4 etc.). Psalm 22.1, 'my God, my God, why have you forsaken me?', is spoken by the Lord himself.

So there is nothing inherently problematic about God using a psalm-verse to affirm his Son's identity. But is Matthew 3.17 really a quotation of Psalm 2.7 at all? We tend to read the Bible looking for points of agreement, not difference. Thus we may fail to notice two facts that point in another direction. First, Psalm 2 does not refer to the Lord's son as the 'beloved'. Second, and more significant, Matthew records the voice from heaven as speaking in the third, not the second person.

I doubt that Matthew has cast the divine speech in the third person ('this is') rather than the second ('you are') by accident, or at random. His account is based upon Mark's Gospel, which was the first to be written. Yet Mark, like Psalm 2, uses the second person: 'you are my son, the Beloved' (1.11); it is possible that Mark intended us to detect an allusion to the psalm.

It looks like Matthew has changed the text deliberately. He would not take an unwarranted liberty in a way that obscured the original meaning; after all, these were not just any words, they were God's words. But one effect of his alteration is that, instead of hearing an affirmation from the Father *to* his Son, what we get is a public statement from the Father *about* his Son.

One commentator draws another parallel, this time with Jeremiah 31.20. There the old pre-Christian Greek translation of the Hebrew Bible, which we know Matthew used, has the phrase, 'my beloved son'. We could also point to Jeremiah 31.15 (= Matthew 2.18), for Matthew has referred to the Jeremiah prophecy about Rachel weeping for her dead children only a few verses before. It starts to look as if this part of the prophet, for whatever reason, was fresh in Matthew's mind when he was writing about Jesus' baptism.

Not all sons are 'beloved' when it comes to family relationships in the Bible. We only have to think of David's sons Absalom and Adonijah, and their competitive hostility to their father. But the loving relationship between God and the human being whom he calls his 'Son' is literally a matter of life and death, not just for the Son, but for the whole human race.

This brings us back to Matthew's report of God's words. If Matthew is right, what matters is not so much that God tells Jesus this, as that he tells *us*. We need to be taught both that Jesus is God's son and that, as such, he is 'beloved', lest we think that their relationship may be one of rivalry. Even divine fathers can be at odds with their sons (I think of Zeus and his father Cronos).

But there is a more powerful reason than these why Matthew gives the version he does. He is encouraging us to make a connection, to unlock another part of the mystery of Christ's identity. It is a connection so important that it may even have influenced his version of the baptism. All three synoptic Gospels record this later event, with its divine voice and its moment of revelation; we know it as the transfiguration (John's Gospel does not record it).

When Jesus is transfigured before Peter, James and John, God speaks an affirmation in the third person. But who is he speaking to? Moses and Elijah are there, but they surely know this truth already. That means that it must be spoken to the three disciples. All three of them have their moments of folly or self-centredness. But still, fallible and foolish as they are, they have been chosen to hear the voice of God himself, on that mountain of transfiguration, speaking to them, challenging them, calling them (Matt. 17.5; Mark 9.7; Luke 9.35). At the baptism, God is 'pleased' with Jesus. At the transfiguration, he is still pleased, but adds a command to the affirmation: 'Listen to him!' And so we do.

The Second Sunday of Epiphany

Isaiah 49.1–7; Psalm 40.1–12; 1 Corinthians 1.1–9; John 1.29–42

We are still celebrating the Epiphany of the Christ-child. So this is a good time to ask a fundamental question: do we celebrate because he is different from us or because he is like us? We can ask it another way: do we take the Epiphany of Christ into ourselves, or does Christ gather us up into his Epiphany?

If Christ is completely 'other', he can make no sense to us. And if he is just like us, whatever help he offers is no different from what we already receive from one another. Saying that he is both answers the question on the level of human feeling, but it falls short in terms of logic. Still, Scripture is here to help.

Christ is divine, not human; pre-existent, not created; and virginally conceived. We are none of those things. Better, then, to focus on what makes him comprehensible to us. He was born as a helpless infant; born into a family; born into poverty; born into a time when violence and instability were endemic.

The Isaiah reading encourages us to explores this, but not in terms of humanity as a lump, a big 'dollop of sin' (*massa peccati*) as Augustine expressed it on one of his gloomier days. Instead, Isaiah shows what it means, but also feels like, to be an individual human person: to be called, and named; to be gifted, protected, directed and acknowledged. To matter. Not all of us are called to be prophets. But prophets are recognizably like us, with their reluctance and self-doubt, their undeserved suffering.

The two themes that most attract my attention from these readings are calling and seeing. The call of a human person is that opening invitation from God to us-ward. The invitation to see is rather like our being told to wake up and pay attention to what is right in front of us. God calls us (Isaiah, John) and we, in our turn, call on God (1 Corinthians).

This encourages me to trust that every child changes the world by the fact of being born, even though most of us are born, live and die unnoticed by any but the people closest to us, whether family, or friends, or colleagues. Our 'mattering' to God cannot be on the basis of our status, achievements, or fame.

There is a fashionable message from secular wisdom that you can achieve anything you want to if only you try hard enough. Whether this is a teacher drawing a moral from the career of Harry Kane or a *Strictly* celeb drawing it from their samba in week six, does not matter. In reality, wanting something really badly, and striving for it, is never going to work for most of us. Most of us are Salieri, not Mozart (to pinch a moral from *Amadeus*).

Scripture is reassuringly realistic. Paul's honesty later in 1 Corinthians (9.24) is absolute: 'Do you not know that in a race the runners all compete, but only one receives the prize? Run in such a way that you may win it.'

We need a 'more excellent way' to understand our finitude in the context of divine eternity (1 Cor. 13). This Sunday's Gospel is stuffed with complex content, but what it asks of us repeatedly is a simple act of seeing – we might express this as 'looking *properly*'. 'See!' the Greek says twice, the Lamb of God is before us. The Spirit abides with him. The Holy Spirit is his instrument of regeneration. Jesus invites us, 'Come and see!' He has called us, chosen us and equipped us, before we even knew that we existed. By bringing his Epiphany to us, through the Incarnation, he shows us the way to bring ourselves to his Epiphany.

The answer to our question, therefore, is time. Our lives unfold in time and accrue meaning over time. God, who created time, made the first move, bringing the Epiphany to us in human time, so that in time we can take ourselves towards that Epiphany.

The Magi gave their presents, worshipped and then departed. Finding that the King of the Jews was a baby in the Gospel equivalent of a garage had not deterred them. They really were 'wise men' because they were called, and they came. They were enlightened, and they saw. Exactly the same possibilities lie before us. Sometimes God makes it all wonderfully simple.

The Third Sunday of Epiphany

Isaiah 9.1–4; Psalm 27.1, 4–12 [or 27.1–11]; 1 Corinthians 1.10–18; Matthew 4.12–23

We encounter 'the people who walk in darkness' many times in our readings of Isaiah over the years. Every winter we meet them afresh in the run-up to Christmas, and are reminded that the answer to their hope and prayer lies in the past, for they '*have* seen'. The answer to ours, on the other hand, lies in the future, for the prophecy declares that his authority '*shall* grow' and there '*shall be* endless peace' for the throne and kingdom that he will establish and uphold.

By the time that they appear in Epiphany 3, Christmas lies behind. Epiphany is about to shade into Lent. Now those walkers-in-darkness have a fresh significance. Matthew finds in them a confirmation of Jesus' identity as Messiah, for he leaves his home to begin the next phase of his life in the places foretold by Isaiah (Zebulun and Naphtali).

The label 'Messiah', so often treated as a mere surname, is really a title. If personal names tell others who we are, job titles tell others what we do. In the case of this title of Jesus, it looks backward and forward. For those who have been anointed, the experience is first a passive one (it is done to them). But from that moment, the experience turns into action, for they must now begin to live out the calling bound up in their anointing.

Yet that title, 'Messiah', is not merely a stamp of authenticity like a label or warranty. It announces what the anointed person is henceforth to become, from the moment when they enter this new phase of life and take on their new identity. This is what kings experienced in Old Testament times. It is what King Charles experienced in his coronation.

Isaiah had proclaimed a message to his own time, which in later centuries was received as God's will. Over the years, the notion of God's anointed one took clearer shape and began to be associated with royal descent, rescue and salvation. So when Andrew meets Jesus in John's Gospel (1.41) and brings the good news to his brother Simon with the words, 'We have found the Messiah', that excited outburst carries a great weight of expectation with it.

The name (as it is often treated) 'Christ' is so familiar to us as to become virtually invisible. The title 'Messiah', though, demands both attention and assent, for it is fundamental to how the four Gospels tell Jesus' story. Matthew, Mark and John all mention it in their opening chapters (1.18;

1.1; 1.41 respectively). Luke maximizes its impact by saving it up until it can be angelically proclaimed (2.11).

We are used to encountering Jesus in different ways, and calling him by many titles ('Christ/Messiah', 'Lord', 'Son of God', 'Son of Man', 'Word', 'King'). All of them help us to understand aspects of God the Son, extending the meaning of his Incarnation into political, religious, intellectual, family and social spheres. That breadth points to the universality of *Iesous Christos*.

Like Isaiah, Jesus proclaims a message to his own generation. It is a call to people around him to repent because the kingdom of the heavens is at hand. That call is as new and fresh today as it was to those who heard it in first-century Judaea. Written here is humanity's first person-to-person encounter with God's anointed, where we first learn that the Bible is so much more than just stories and history.

Jesus' call, 'Repent!' still speaks to us personally. A mere handful of words after it there comes his invitation to the first disciples: a miracle of call and response in the lives of people whose names we know. That historical event in which Simon, Andrew, James and John were summoned is also, immediately, always, our summons too. I hear the words 'Follow me', and I know that I am being called.

Over and over, the Gospel story speaks directly to whoever hears it or reads it or is immersed in it through music, art or drama. When the call sounds, 'Follow me', the people who walked in darkness find Christ the light. Finally, they see their way.

In the last verse of this Gospel, Jesus travels, teaches, preaches, heals. So unfolds the blueprint for his final years of earthly life, as the 'Logos' of the cross is found to be the power of God.

The Fourth Sunday of Epiphany

1 Kings 17.8–16; Psalm 36.5–10; 1 Corinthians 1.18–end; John 2.1–11

The steward at the Gospel wedding-feast is a realist. There is no euphemism about the guests being 'merry'. From his knowledge of such occasions, he expects those guests to 'become drunk'.

Perhaps stewarding wedding feasts was his full-time job and had taught him to expect the worst. More likely, he was a slave who belonged to the family and knew their ways and weaknesses.

How we eat together is a sensitive matter for human society. I once made a fuss about being stuck on the end of a wedding-breakfast top table. My only excuse is youth. It was my brother's wedding, and I could speak the truth to him (albeit more in selfishness than love) about the person who would have been my only company over several hours. I got my way and have felt guilty about it ever since.

Even princes get cross when someone changes their seating plan, so perhaps I should not feel too bad about it. In any case, weddings are a time when alcohol can sometimes be a kindly anaesthesia for family tension. As well as the celebration of a 'new life together in the community … which all should honour', there are less positive moments to endure. Rejected other-halves seethe and fume (quietly or not so quietly) in the presence of an ex's new partner. The recently bereaved pin a lips-only smile on for the day and keep it there till their jaws ache as badly as their heart. Mortified parents spend their whole day apologizing for over-excited children, as high on sugar as the older guests are on booze.

I would love to know more about the wedding couple. But the lack of information makes it plain that for John they are not the point. He wants our attention fixed on Jesus and the first of his signs. And a little on Mary too, given the way that he encourages his listeners and readers to focus on the tenor of her relationship with Jesus.

In the wider context of John's take on the good news, this couple and their wedding are just scenery and props for the unfolding of the 'greatest story ever told'. How was it that Jesus and his disciples (surely just 'friends' in the eyes of other guests) came to be invited? John does not tell us this either. And why on earth does he start the story of the first sign Jesus did with that whopping *non sequitur*: 'There was a wedding … and the mother of Jesus was there'?

We could take a devotional approach, and speak of her mystical consonance with the will of her son, and her respect for his authority. That makes for a pious moral, but it is hardly realistic. If the mother of one of my wedding guests had started to interfere by giving the waiting staff orders, I would have told her to pipe down.

Except not really. What I would really have done is to *want* to tell her to pipe down. And then grumble about it afterwards when I was safely out of earshot. And perhaps I might hope that the bridegroom would shrug off his friendship with that talented but peculiar guest who had brought along his interfering mother.

Grumbling afterwards is a pleasure reserved (if we are wise) for the journey home, when we are letting off steam to those we trust the most to share our views or forgive the multiple judgementalisms that underlie them. Some would say that this is two-faced rather than polite and perhaps a peculiarly British trait. That may be fair criticism. But this way of managing disagreement at family and social occasions has one invaluable advantage: it keeps the unkind word where it belongs, behind the 'fence of the teeth' (as Homer calls it). Once utter it aloud, and you have set free a demon that will torment your target, but almost certainly torment you too. Written words keep saying the same thing for ever, as Socrates remarked.

I used to find the wedding at Cana a dull Gospel. But prayer changed that. I focused on it regularly when praying the luminous mysteries of the rosary. As I painted and peopled the scene in my mind's eye, it transformed. A silken veil was drawn back and revealed a more intense reality in which humanity – at its most inconsequential and foolish – keeps company with God.

The Presentation of Christ in the Temple (Candlemas)

Malachi 3.1–5; Psalm 24.[1–6] 7–end; Hebrews 2.14–end; Luke 2.22–40

Do gates have heads? According to Psalm 24 they do. The fact is reiterated in a refrain (24.7, 9). It is common enough for the term 'head' to apply to the chief or the topmost part of something. Less common is the personification of gates and doors. Those entrances into the city stand symbolically for all its inhabitants, eager to welcome the 'King of glory' (a description of the Lord found only here in Scripture, yet important enough to be repeated four times in two verses). The fact that the doors are ancient is significant: the city has awaited this arrival for a long time. 'Lifting up your head' is a Hebrew way of expressing hope and expectation (also found in Luke 21.28).

'Doors need walls', I once heard a sermon begin (it was preached by an engineer). A door cannot do what doors do unless it is first part of a structure that defines a space, thus creating an inside and an outside. The doors and gates of a walled city are its weakest point when it is attacked from without. They are also its strongest point when we think about its dynamics within: a meeting point, a mixing point, the concrete expression of a belonging that is not a prison (no way out) but a refuge (doors open to let us in).

Our 'going out and coming in' is a biblical expression, familiar from the last verse of Psalm 121. That psalm is popular at Christian funerals, when verse 8 becomes a prayer on the threshold between mortal life and eternal life. A threshold is exactly what Simeon faces on this day, when Mary comes to be 'purified'. Through the Holy Spirit he has learned that, as the Gospel phrases it, he will 'not see death before he had seen the Lord's Messiah' (Luke 2.26).

He is often pictured in art as elderly, perhaps to contrast with the very young child, or because of the parallel proclamation that comes from Anna. I could not find this in the text, though some of my commentaries on the Gospel did assume that Simeon was old. It took wikipedia to enlighten me about a splendid eastern legend that the revelation had come as Simeon was translating Isaiah 7.14 from Hebrew into Greek – implying that he was at least 200 years old!

Simeon had been waiting for 'the consolation of Israel'. Anna spread the good news among those who were 'looking for the redemption of

Jerusalem'. For the prophetess, the arrival of Jesus was a reason to look to the future. For Simeon the righteous, meeting his Messiah was an ending. The poignancy of his situation has never been expressed better than in T. S. Eliot's 'A Song for Simeon'. Anna and Simeon together encapsulate the lifelong experience of encountering Christ, which is common to all of us who follow him. Anna reveals the redemption, Simeon the consolation, which Christ makes available to us too.

It has sometimes been taught by Christians that death is neither something they should fear happening to themselves, nor something that should cause them grief when it happens to others. The writer of Hebrews has this in mind when he explains Christ as destroying the power of death and liberating us from the fear of death (2.14–15). This might be seen as placing a heavy yoke on the shoulders of the faithful (despite Matthew 11.30). Not many of us (even great saints like Augustine) have faith strong enough to insulate us from sorrow at the death of loved ones. It may help to remember the kindly wisdom of Jeremy Taylor: 'It is not a sin to be afraid'.

The song of Simeon, known by its Latin incipit, *nunc dimittis* ('Now you send away') belongs to all our eventides. We sing it at the ending of the day. We sing it at the end of human journeys. Its use in Christian funerals has always been for me the acme of that mysterious mingled expectation and consolation that is the consigning of a human person to the deep waters of death, and all that lies beyond. As I was writing this, news happened to come to me of someone's death. It was expected and peaceful. So it was as natural as breathing for me to put down the phone and pray, 'Lord, now lettest thou thy servant depart in peace'.

Proper 1
Sunday between 4 and 10 February inclusive
(if earlier than the Second Sunday before Lent)

Isaiah 58.1–9a [b–12]; Psalm 112.1–9 [end];
1 Corinthians 2.1–12 [13–end]; Matthew 5.13–20

1 Corinthians 2 is a lot to absorb in one Sunday. Verse 15 alone is enough of a challenge. It poses a question that is always important for Christians, but especially in the run-up to Lent, when thoughts turn to the personal dimension of our discipleship: 'Those who are spiritual discern all things, and they are themselves subject to no one else's scrutiny.'

This letter is an early New Testament witness to the faith. It reveals a tension that re-echoes down Christian centuries from north Africa to Asia Minor; in the nations of Europe at the Reformation; and in the nonconformist revivalism, Pentecostalism and charismatic movements, which, closer to our own time, have posed their different challenges to the established Church of England.

There are different ways of taking Paul's statement, of course. But even the most authoritarian hierocrat cannot completely argue away its key idea. In the apostle's mind, there are different kinds of authority to which we are subject as human beings and as Christians. Human rulers are a straightforward instance of authority. The living witness of the first apostles and their successors is another. Textual authority is beginning to emerge in the shape of documents from Judaism. Other writings, too, are being copied and circulated; their authorship will become the guarantee of their authority.

But there is another form of authority, one that has no shape or form, no visible embodiment, no human endorsement: the Holy Spirit. People who are touched by the Holy Spirit themselves become 'spiritual'. Where the Spirit of God bestows authority, it bestows power as well. This makes it potentially dangerous, especially to the leadership and influencers of the emerging communities of the faithful which were coming to be called 'churches'.

A century or so after Paul, the Church's first Latin theologian was an African lawyer called Tertullian. He joined a group of Christians known as Montanists. He did so because they regarded the authority of the Spirit as supreme over other forms of revealed truth. One potential consequence of this was a canon of Scripture that should never be closed, because that would deny the possibility that the work of the Spirit was ongoing.

Being free to decide everything for ourselves, with 'only' the Spirit to guide us, has a wonderfully romantic aura about it. What it does not have is any way of resolving disagreements where both sides claim that their version is Spirit-authenticated truth.

When a person comes forward to offer themselves for ministry, they have to submit themselves repeatedly to the judgement of their fellow Christians. This tells us not that the Spirit is being ignored, but that we trust it to work not only in individuals but also in groups, including committees and congregations. All authority is God's. So if we claim that our opinion is synonymous with the will of God, one of the key proofs is not to be alone in holding it. One person, one opinion, one voice, can never make a church.

When we turn to the Gospel, authentication and authority are clearly in Jesus' mind as he preaches his sermon from the mount. He starts from what people are in their uncorrupt state: 'the salt of the earth', the 'light of the world'. Neither image is encouraging us to think of ourselves in individualistic terms.

Salt without its saltiness cannot be salt. But light is different. Once it is covered, it turns the illumination of a room into a light cast for the benefit of one person alone (like a torch under bedcovers). Worse still, if that light is placed under a basket, it illuminates no one, nothing. It might as well not exist at all. God's gifts to us are a fact, and they are shared among us all. We have all been baptized with the Holy Spirit. So any individual who claims to speak with the gift of the Spirit's authority needs to be listened to, but tested too.

In the end, like any gift from God, the gifts of the Spirit lie dormant until we bring them to life in our life by responding to Jesus' voice, our Lord speaking to each one of us as well as to all of us together. Then, together, we will put our light and salt to work for our own and others' good: as a beacon signalling the truth of Christ and as heavenly tasting food.

Proper 2
Sunday between 11 and 17 February inclusive
(if earlier than the Second Sunday before Lent)

Deuteronomy 30.15–end *or* Ecclesiasticus 15.15–end;
Psalm 119.1–8; 1 Corinthians 3.1–9; Matthew 5.21–37

Sometimes our response to Scripture is theoretical, because we ourselves have never experienced the situation it addresses. This could include murder, adultery or divorce (Matt. 5.21, 27, 31). At other times, our response is practical, because we have experienced just such a situation as the passage describes.

Jesus collapses the gulf between high crimes and low misdemeanours. Take the first example, murder. He shifts our gaze away from the fact of the deed and focuses it upon intentions and attitudes; the ultimate crime, murder, is then only the extremest end of the universal emotion that we call 'anger'.

We might have thought that being angry is not a sin at all, for in itself it hurts no one – except perhaps ourselves. But we have two truths to learn. First, sin is a continuum. The phenomenon of anger is not distinct from the crime of murder, but part of the same appetite for self-protection. Second, sin is both an event and a habit. Every step towards wrongdoing and away from goodness, even a small one, makes later temptations easier to succumb to and harder to resist.

Some of my reflection on sin as a continuum comes from my experience of addiction. I am addicted to two substances, nicotine and sugar. I found it relatively easy to give up nicotine (helped by patches) because I could cut it out completely – I decided never to smoke again. But I knew from previous attempts that one sneaky ciggie and I would be straight back to 20 a day.

Sugar (as carbohydrate) remains impossible to give up, because I need it (as carbohydrate). Too much is bad, but so is too little. So sugar is a better model for understanding how temptation and sin work in us. We cannot give up eating altogether. Nor can we just stop ourselves from feeling angry or jealous. But we can resolve to resist those feelings when they possess us. We can use them to spur us into righteous action.

The wisdom of Jesus' approach to sin is to connect our inner appetites and impulses to their outward expression in our deeds and attitudes. Anger and murder are aspects of the same problem, but Christianity does not advocate life in prison for losing one's temper (5.22). Nor does it see equivalence between four-letter expletives and Satan worship (5.37). Proportion and perspective still matter in evaluating the harms we do to ourselves and others.

One teaching for me stands out from the Gospel text, because I have a direct recollection of applying it myself, and seeing it applied by someone else, to two concrete situations. It is the verse that we sometimes use liturgically as an introduction to corporate confession at the Eucharist: 'Jesus said, before you offer your gift, go and be reconciled' (based on Matt. 5.23–4).

One goes back decades to my time in parish ministry. Two parishioners had a disagreement, and this led to one deciding to withdraw from a duty he had hitherto taken pride in. After a short time, he spoke with me about it and explained that he had listened to these words in a service and decided that the Christian thing to do was to get past the disagreement and to return to what he had done before. I cherish that moment as an example of a fellow Christian trying to live by the Gospel's calling.

The other relates to a time when I myself fell out with someone. I went to them and asked for reconciliation, even (tactlessly, perhaps) quoting this Gospel text as the catalyst for my request. At the time, reconciliation did not happen. In time, the bruises healed, but the scarring is permanent. Sometimes hurts cannot be healed, as when one party wants to move on while the other feels that the presenting problem has not been addressed. At other times, the wounds heal, but the battle-scars remain.

If there is a lesson to be drawn from this Gospel's catalogue of wrongdoing, perhaps it is that we cannot make hurts and harms as if they had never been. But we can always behave as we profess to believe, by being on the watch for opportunities to reconcile. Then, after we have tried to live out Romans 12.18 ('so far as it depends on you, live peaceably with all'), we can, as Bishop Westcott once put it, 'leave the issue to God's wisdom'.

Proper 3
Sunday between 18 and 24 February inclusive
(if earlier than the Second Sunday before Lent)

or

Sunday between 24 and 28 May inclusive
(if after Trinity Sunday)

Leviticus 19.1–2, 9–18; Psalm 119.33–40; 1 Corinthians 3.10–11, 16–end; Matthew 5.38–end

Of all the counter-intuitive religious teachings, surely one of the strangest is Jesus' command, 'Do not resist an evildoer'. We think of religion as being all about resisting evil. 'Fight valiantly as a disciple of Christ against sin, the world, and the Devil' says the baptismal liturgy.

But it is not the only surprise in store. More such teachings follow. Coming from the Sermon on the Mount they are compelling, for it is a distillation of Christ's teaching, an ethical counterpart to the life he lived as 'the great exemplar'. So Jeremy Taylor called Jesus, because he perfectly embodied his own precepts (in 1649).

It is easy to be distracted by detail in the Sermon on the Mount. Many single verses contain material for long meditation. But we need some sense of the context of the Sermon, to ensure our interpretation does not take on a life of its own. When studying the Bible, context matters.

Most scholarship is a routine business, hunting down references or excluding irrelevant material. It is like a potter hand-building an object rather than throwing it on a wheel: slowly refining, adding a little here, removing a little there. But occasionally those processes lead to something that does not just refine knowledge, but fundamentally changes it.

Good examples of this in science would be Galileo on heliocentrism, Newton on gravity, and Darwin on evolution through natural selection. In Classics, Milman Parry's studies of oral poetry transformed Homeric scholarship. In Old Testament studies, there is Wellhausen's hypothesis that Genesis is a composite work. In all cases, the ground-breaking discovery has been prefigured by the work of others, and has been amended, finessed or reformulated by later experts. But one person's visionary clarity takes human understanding forward – another click of the wheel toward crystal-clear focus.

In New Testament study, more than a century ago a theory had just such an effect. It considered the three synoptic ('same-point-of-view') Gospels, Matthew, Mark and Luke, and explained the mechanics of how they relate to one another.

Matthew and Luke both use Mark, which must therefore be earlier than both of them. But there is also a lot of stuff in Matthew and Luke that is not found in Mark. This led to the 'Q-hypothesis' ('Q' because of the German word for a source, *Quelle*). The Sermon on the Mount is widely regarded as a big chunk of a now-lost source, Q.

Like other great steps forward, the Q-hypothesis had its forerunners, and biblical scholars are still refining or challenging it in different ways. For now, what matters is that Q is a 'sayings source', a collection of Jesus' teachings that were heard, remembered and eventually written down, but in which elements of their oral origin are detectable.

In this passage, Jesus takes his listeners by surprise. This is tactical, a way to confound their unthinking acceptance of what sort of behaviour is conventionally seen as 'good' and 'bad' in God's eyes. Sometimes this takes the form of a flat contradiction (5.38–39, 43–44). In other cases, the underlying principle of the 'good' behaviour is pushed to a limit beyond what his audience would have anticipated (5.39–42).

The last section of the passage makes for difficult reading, and tentative preaching. What can we usefully say about Jesus putting this challenge before us (5.48)? It reads as if Jesus is setting us a spiritual goal that none of us would surely dare to set ourselves: that of modelling ourselves upon our heavenly Father. We are accustomed to the idea of modelling our self upon Jesus: Thomas à Kempis' *The Imitation of Christ* and Jeremy Taylor's *The Great Exemplar* are both classics of Christian devotion. But the imitation of *God*? To be 'perfect' like God our Father is beyond human imagining.

The problem of how to make ourselves perfect like God dissolves when we understand the Greek word *teleios*, which has been translated as 'perfect'. The underlying idea is wholeness, or completion, of what a thing ought to be. A *teleios* animal is full-grown. A *teleios* god is powerful and answers prayer. A *teleios* sacrifice is without blemish. Our goal, then is to be the most integrous version of ourselves, complete and fulfilled, that we possibly can. Being like God, it turns out, is not difficult after all, for we have been so from the beginning (Gen. 1.27).

The Second Sunday before Lent

Genesis 1.1—2.3; Psalm 136 [*or* 136.1–9, 23–26];
Romans 8.18–25; Matthew 6.25–34

If size matters, the most important of the lections for this Sunday is Genesis 1. If ratios matter, it is four times as important as the other two. What there is no denying is that it presents difficulties.

The belief that the world had a beginning sounds reasonable, even to modern science. But that it was created in six days does not. Nor does the idea that God, who 'ought' to be transcendent, rolls up his sacred sleeves and brings the world into being through hard graft.

Most of us who work for a living are tired by the end of the day, even when work has been enjoyable. If it took God all day to fashion each part of his creation, then it must indeed have been hard work, no mere wave of the hand or utterance of magic words.

Despite such complexities, finding nuggets of pure spiritual gold in Genesis 1 is not difficult. 'God created humankind in his image' (1.27); 'God saw everything that he had made, and indeed, it was very good' (1.31). What is difficult is making sense of these in the context of the rest.

I think of Genesis 1—2 as a game of two halves. The first chapter is priestly: it finds beautiful order, satisfying pattern, in the act of creating, so providing a blueprint for the human future from the beginning.

The second chapter, best read together with the first, is mythological, by which I mean that it tells stories about people that are more than just stories. Adam and Eve, shorn of their supposed names (which mean 'man' and 'woman'), are not only human individuals in historical time who exemplify that blueprint of striving and suffering; they are us. We hear their story and must apply it to ourselves.

This reminder that their story is our story is indispensable as we prepare for Lent to begin. In the 'Fall', Augustine detected a message that all are tainted by the sin of Adam with 'original sin'. This is sometimes treated – by those hostile to any teacher who counts as an elderly male (albeit one who cannot have been pale and who is never stale) – as a disastrous wrong turn for theology.

I disagree. Original sin is exactly what it says it is: the situation we are born into and in which our entire life is lived, which makes it impossible for us, by our own efforts, to reach God. It is by no means a wrong turn in the movement of Western theology, incompatible with the insight of

Eastern Christianity that we are called to become 'partakers of the divine nature' (2 Peter 1.4).

Knowing that in mature faith we take responsibility for how we live our lives and for our mistakes and sins, but yet have limited control over what harms we do to ourselves, others and the planet, is not a burden; it is a liberation. There is deep consolation in knowing, as every child should, that our parent will love us whatever we do, because sometimes we cannot help making mistakes.

The Gospel shows how the Genesis take on the human condition should work out in our lives. Jesus frames his teaching as a form of reasoning, using rhetorical questions to encourage us towards finding a better way of understanding ourselves and living for God. We applaud and quote his teachings on anxiety, but they do not magic our anxieties away. What they will do is to show us that anxiety is unavoidable because it is part of original sin. We must resist it constantly. Yet the answer is never more rigorism, tighter control.

Romans, on the other hand, takes a less down-to-earth approach, by personifying creation as an artefact with a purpose. It is subjected to futility; so are we. It is in bondage to decay; so are we. Most remarkably, it is a woman labouring to bring her child to birth. How Paul reached this exalted level of vision in his understanding of the Christ-event, I cannot imagine. But all of us must be glad that he did, for by his words he clothes our ineffable longings for God in garments of shining hope.

We can safely leave to a Pope the last word on the theme of these lections:

Good-Nature and Good-Sense must ever join;
To Err is Human[e]; to Forgive, Divine.
(Alexander Pope, *Essay on Criticism*, ll. 527–8)

The Sunday next before Lent

Exodus 24.12–end; Psalm 2 or Psalm 99; 2 Peter 1.16–end; Matthew 17.1–9

One word sums up this Sunday's readings; and the aim of the Lenten journey we are preparing; and even the aftermath of Lent and Passiontide when we undergo spiritual metamorphosis, from sluggish caterpillars into dazzling butterflies, freed from the cold constraints of earth.

Transfiguration. Mark and Luke tell the story as well as Matthew. Reflecting on why John does not record it, I concluded that he transfigured the transfiguration – into Jesus the light of the world. He does the same thing, after all, with Jesus the living bread, to expound the Eucharist. Perhaps he was reluctant to commit the most precious details of the gospel story to writing, where anyone could access them.

The transfiguration has been the traditional Gospel for the Sunday before Lent for centuries. It is a majestic word for a majestic reality, the moment when the veil of human mortality is drawn aside. Then we see not only Christ but also Moses and Elijah (who were once 'ordinary' human beings like the witnessing disciples) as they appear in heavenly glory.

This is how we believe and trust that we also shall one day be. Lent will encourage us to immerse ourselves more fully in the meaning of 'transfiguration', so there is work to be done. It requires a change of appearance, we know. But it will be a change of outer appearance that only happens because it is reflecting a new inner reality.

The first surviving use of the Latin word *transfiguratio* comes from a Roman polymath, Pliny the Elder. Such was his fascination with the natural world that he lost track of time and space while investigating the eruption of Vesuvius. That put an end, in AD 79, to his earthly existence, but not before he found time to say that 'there are problems concerning belief in an afterlife ... neither body nor mind possesses any sensation after death, any more than it did before birth – but vanity fabricates for itself a life lasting even into death, sometimes bestowing on the soul immortality, sometimes transfiguration'. He is scornful of the idea of transfiguration as 'making a god of one who has already ceased even to be human'.

Transfiguratio (the Greek equivalent is *metamorphosis*) is not always associated with loveliness or divinity. Pliny applied it to lycanthropy, and the Romans found werewolves quite as terrifying as we do. This confirms that it is not the label that adds exaltation to the event, but vice versa.

In Matthew's Greek, Jesus' clothing is 'white like light', giving a mystical feel, for sunlight is a powerful bleaching agent, whitening wherever its rays may reach. He has edited out Mark's more down-to-earth observation that the whiteness was 'such as no one on earth could bleach them' (Mark 9.3) – readers in earlier centuries would have known that fullers used urine as a principal bleaching agent. This is not the only occasion when we find Matthew drawn to the spiritual take on a down-to-earth gospel.

In October 2002, I had to absorb a new aspect of the transfiguration, when Pope John Paul II added a new set of prayers, the luminous mysteries (or 'mysteries of light'), to the traditional prayer known as the rosary. Working my way through the five meditations, from Christ's baptism, the wedding at Cana, and the ministry of healing and teaching to get to the transfiguration (the last of the five is the Eucharist), feels like a Lenten pilgrimage every time I undertake it: not in a spirit of miserable self-denial, but in purity and clarity, a simplicity that embodies Gospel truth. It is like an altar dressed in Lent array, a visible embodiment of what we preach.

Some ultra-sceptical exegetes deny that the transfiguration happened in Jesus' lifetime. They argue that it is a post-Resurrection appearance transplanted to a period before the Passion. If this were true (the evidence is not convincing), then what we have would be a free-floating chunk of Gospel, lacking a historical context to add depth to its message. The woman caught in adultery is a true example of this type (John 8.1–11).

Thankfully, we are not obliged to follow that ultra-sceptical line. The transfiguration has won our trust as a glimpse of eternity, a 'luminous mystery'. For it reveals in the adult Jesus (just as star and angels did for the infant), divine glory at home and at work in our world.

The First Sunday of Lent

Genesis 2.15–17; 3.1–7; Psalm 32; Romans 5.12–19; Matthew 4.1–11

Matthew, Mark and Luke, three Gospels with a similar point of view, all tell of Jesus' temptation. We know that this event matters because a version of it is set every year for Lent 1. Matthew and Luke are probably following the same source (no longer extant), which Mark either did not know or (more likely, Mark 1.13) chose not to retell it in full.

Of the three versions, I would choose Matthew's without hesitation. Losing Mark means losing the 'wild beasts' (Mark 1.13). Losing Luke means losing the information that the devil has been given authority over the world (Luke 4.6). Only Matthew tells the three temptations in full, in the correct order. The 'human' temptations come first, as the devil twice tries to get Jesus to prove his identity to himself; they lead to the third, Satan's true objective, to make Jesus worship a god who is not God (idolatry: Ex. 20.2).

Luke felt a need to explain how the devil can offer Jesus the kingdoms of the world. Matthew does not. He assumes that Satan is not telling the truth. John would surely agree (8.44). Luke also makes the end into a cliffhanger moment, with that disturbing image of the devil biding his time (4.13).

One detail that Matthew records, which is shared with Mark but lacking in Luke, is the angels who 'waited on' Jesus after his temptation. 'Waited on' makes me think of hovering restaurant staff. I wish the NRSV had stuck with the AV's translation, 'ministered to him'. Not just because of neophobia (which can be a positive survival strategy as well as a diehard preference for the archaic). The old translation is churchier. But it shows us Jesus in a way we need to keep in mind (see Matt. 26.7, for example): he receives ministry as well as offering it.

Following Christ means serving others, but also accepting the services that, out of love and faith, others offer to us. To be fully human, we should accept others' ministry to us, welcoming the part of recipient as well as giver.

The idea at the heart of this mutual offering and receiving of care is *diakonia*. The 'diaconate' may be a calling for the ordained, but *diakonia* is a mark of all Christians (1 Cor. 12.5; Eph. 4.14). Turned from Greek to Latin, *diakonia* becomes 'ministry' (*'minister'* is Latin for 'servant'). The Christian faith is, for everyone, a calling to ministry, to service of others. It applies to caring for people's bodies (their physical wellbeing), their minds (their capacity to approach God rationally) and their spirits (their need for growth in godliness).

Back to Matthew's ministering angels. The temptation story ends with their ministry, showing that those angels do more than just authenticate Jesus' divinity or defend him physically; the time for Michael and the angelic host to fight against the devil and his evil angels (Ps. 78.49; Rev. 12.7) is not yet.

I think the angels are there because the Son of God is also the Son of Man. In other words, he has angels to tend to him because that is the deal that God makes with all his children. We are not alone. We have angels to watch over us in this life (Matt. 18.10) and angels to help us from this life to the next (Luke 16.22). They do not tend Jesus (or us) because we are important (in a worldly sense), but because we are not.

Romans 5 encourages us with the thought that in Christ grace and righteousness will be ours. Whether or not angels are part of our spiritual thinking, Jesus our brother, who is the friend of sinners, has ensured that righteousness will be a 'free gift', not a struggle, an effort or – God forbid – a 'work'. Perhaps by now we have already failed in our chosen Lenten discipline. But Romans 5 keeps us hoping for that righteousness and grace.

And finally: unlike the synoptics, John does not record Jesus' wilderness temptation. But he does give us, in its place, a visual theology of the Son as the bridge spanning that otherwise eternal gulf between us and God, giving the angels a way to reach us, and giving us a way, in God's good time, of reaching God: 'Very truly, I tell you, you will see heaven opened and the angels of God ascending and descending upon the Son of Man' (1.51).

The Second Sunday of Lent

Genesis 12.1–4a; Psalm 121; Romans 4.1–5, 13–17; John 3.1–17

We might think that the whole purpose of faith is to prepare us for life eternal. 'Eternal life' features only a handful of times in Matthew, Mark and Luke. But it appears repeatedly after this first reference in John 3.15, and in John's letters, and in Romans (though not in today's passage).

The shortness of our attention spans, and our earthly lives, make us ill-equipped to understand eternal life. Scripture says we are like plants that are growing one day and burned the next (Ps. 90.5–6). Eternity, on the other hand, is a concept as unfathomable as infinity. We may accept infinity mathematically, yet be unable to grasp it imaginatively, because nothing in our lives is infinite, certainly not we ourselves.

This is a reminder of the limited usefulness of using comparisons when we try to talk about God. Theologians call such comparisons 'analogy'. God the Holy Trinity, we might say, is light or water, a single substance experienced in three forms (origin, process, effect; or vapour, liquid, solid). The inadequacy of such analogies has been recognized almost from the beginning (1 Tim. 6.15–16). It is not unreasonable to suppose that no analogies for God can ever be adequate. But that does leave us with a problem of how to talk about God at all.

So we feel obliged either to say nothing (which is impossible for a Spirit-filled, Jesus-shaped, God-directed heart) or to plough on regardless, using the outmoded, misleading language of parent, shepherd, bird, or anything else that seems at all to reflect the divine, to which we are helplessly yet hopefully attuned.

To say nothing, just because nothing is good enough, is a bad idea in our human relationships, so I can see no excuse for hiding behind apophaticism (the technical term for it) in our faith. Knowing that words are not enough to express my love for someone is not a reason for never telling them I love them. In practical terms, too, we rely on other people talking about God for us to learn about God. If previous generations of Christians had decided apophaticism was the way forward, Christianity would have died in its infancy.

Thus, we cannot, in good conscience, say nothing about God. Instead, we must shoulder our responsibility for saying something, somehow. One thing that may help us in this apparently impossible task is a fundamental distinction in how we know things (the technical term is epistemology). There are things (realities) and there are words (which describe those realities). In this instance, we are scrutinizing a two-word phrase; we need to relate the two words, 'eternal' and 'life', to something real so we can make sense of them. That real something is the actual eternal life that Jesus promises us. But we cannot learn the reality from the words, and we absolutely must not mistake the words for the reality.

Later in John's Gospel, Jesus tells us more about eternal life. It turns out not to be like a long holiday, or one of those endless childhood Sunday afternoons of the kind many of us remember from before the Sunday Trading Act of 1994. Jesus says: 'This is eternal life: that they may know you, the only true God, and Jesus Christ whom you have sent' (John 17.3).

That verse sounds odd on the lips of Jesus himself, speaking to his heavenly Father. Just like verses 13–17 of this Gospel for Lent 2, he speaks of himself in the third person. Predictably, some readers speculate whether a comment by the Gospel writer (or his source) has crept into the record of Jesus' actual words.

Human beings take pleasure from coming to know things, and from our faculty of imagination, which enables us to experience others' talents, traumas, emotions, as if they were our own. We call this empathy. It should come as no surprise that God, our Father, gives us this talent so that we can gain true knowledge even from things we do not understand, though our capacity for empathizing ('experiencing-with') with those who do.

Eternal life is knowing God. We can develop our knowledge of God by using our imagination and our instinct for making connections between things that (though not identical) share characteristics or properties. We must not abandon our duty to speak of the realities that lie beyond words.

The Third Sunday of Lent

Exodus 17.1–7; Psalm 95; Romans 5.1–11; John 4.5–42

The wilderness of Sin referred to in Exodus 17 makes a marvellous Lenten theme. Or at least it would do, if only it was 'sin' instead of 'Sin', a state of humanity, rather than a geographical location (close to mount Sinai).

The English word 'sin' is rooted in the idea of an offence or wrong, not necessarily something religious at all. Latin (*peccatum*) likewise. I like the Greek best, because it hints at an idea that is more generous to human intentions: at the heart of *hamartia* is 'going astray' or 'making a mistake'. In the three readings, we see a spectrum of sinning, from wrong actions like making a mistake (grumbling, lacking trust: Exodus); to a state of being (our inability to perfect ourselves: Romans); to a conversation that goes beyond the concept of sin by immersing us fully in the loving purposes of God (John).

'Sin' does not always mesh with our psychology-driven concept of ourselves. If nature has made us what we are, perhaps we are not responsible for either our own misdoings, or our happiness. But we can get past both nature and nurture, our genes and our upbringing, if we realize that Christ, who makes all things new, calls us to let the past go and take his guiding hand to walk into a future that we choose.

There is an aspect of our human nature that sometimes gets mixed up with our concept of sin, and it can lead to guilt, or a fear of looking within ourselves to find Christ, our inner teacher. That aspect is our appetites, or, we might say, our 'drives'. We are governed by appetites that exist to ensure our survival. They have to be powerful in the way that they influence, even direct our lives. We can no more excise them from our selves than we can decide we want our heart to stop beating. But there is a dark side to every appetite, which instead of protecting us can ruin us.

Among the chief physical appetites are hunger, thirst and sex. This Gospel has something to say about all three, and to do so it moves with breathtaking speed. We start from the simplest material we know, which falls freely upon us from above, and rises up from beneath our feet, and springs miraculously from the desert rock. Then, moments later, it transforms into a dizzying metaphysical vision of eternal life. A similar shift takes place from the need for simple sustenance, 'Rabbi, eat something' (John 4.31) to the truest source of life, 'my food is to do the will of him who sent me' (4.34).

The appetites of hunger and thirst are often sources of anxiety. As such, they are fixed in our minds as difficulties, as problems to be solved. Water would not come so easily to mind as an image of God's generosity if we had no taps in our houses; if we had to fetch, carry, or pump our own water every day like the Samaritan woman (see Gen. 24.15–20). Cain, the tiller of the ground, reaped the fruits of Adam and Eve's sowing (Gen. 3.17–19, 4.2; John 4.37): it took the 'sweat of his brow' to keep body and soul together.

Likewise, all kinds of excessive interest in what we eat, not just the gross excess of gluttony, can lead us into sin. C. S. Lewis makes the point beautifully with his finnicky eater in *The Screwtape Letters* (letter 17). Our modern fascination with what I mentally categorize as 'food porn' might have surprised him, but the misdirected appetite would not.

Sex is also an appetite that gets some attention in John 4, albeit in a more allusive way. Just as in the story of the woman caught in adultery, so here Jesus does not condemn the woman; but John shows how Jesus manages our going astray. He tries her with a question, which gives her options in replying: she can tell the truth; she can conceal the truth; or she can justify the truth (John 4.16–18).

She chooses right: to tell the truth. And then Jesus reveals that he knew the answer already. So why ask? Surely because he is giving her a chance (he is always giving us chances) to be honest about herself. No wonder she goes home saying that he told her everything she ever did.

The Fourth Sunday of Lent ('Refreshment' Sunday)

1 Samuel 16.1–13; Psalm 23; Ephesians 5.8–14; John 9.1–41

The Gospel for this Sunday is epic. But pity the Lectionary-compilers. How could it be reduced? It is still too short to begin where John begins, with Jesus' baptism. Or to take in the well in Samaria (Chapter 4). It cannot prefigure the Cross, as Jesus does when he teaches about living water pouring forth from the believer's belly (not heart, as John 7.38, NRSV, which obliterates the foreshadowing of the passion) during the feast of Tabernacles.

Water was a precious commodity in the holy city, and the pool of Siloam was famous for its living waters. 'Living' in this context means running water, rather than a standing pool. For the first Christians, it was important that baptism took place in 'living' water, a practice that continues among some churches to this day. My Welsh mother and sister were both baptized in a river near Horeb Chapel in Maenclochog. Mercifully, the pool for my baptism was warm, and clean, and filled by a tap.

John 9 is a combat, but not in the usual way of heroic contests. This is a contest for the truth, against received wisdom and determination to hold on to the past at the cost of the future. Jesus faces a series of characters: the disciples, the blind man, the Pharisees, the parents, 'the Jews'. At stake is nothing less than truth, compassion, piety, and the will of God.

All the intervening interactions take place within a frame: Jesus begins with the needs of an individual (he heals a blind man), whose belief and worship at the end make the proper response to the Son of Man. Meanwhile, some Pharisees declare their own righteousness, thereby convicting themselves of the sin of being determined not to see spiritually.

One approach to John 9, the way of the scholar, responds to our hunger for understanding. We try to make sense of the Gospel's component parts, assessing the theology embedded in physically and spiritually impaired humanity, drawing conclusions about the admittedly difficult balance of competing religious observance (to heal or to rest?). And we wrestle with the questions of theodicy that emerge from it all.

The other is the older way (I will not say 'better', because both are God-given, and for the fullness of faith we need both): to listen as we would with any other story. Then we can accept that the information we get is the information we need. There is no need to worry about whether there was ever such a thing as a kind and tolerant Pharisee, or a dependable and reliable disciple, or a self-doubting Jesus.

This approach, unlike the first, is something we have been trained in from early childhood. We learn life-principles from a conglomeration of such stories. People are not always what they seem (Beauty and the Beast; the Suffering Servant in Isaiah); poverty and inequality begin within families (Cinderella; the 12 sons of Jacob); the race is not always to the swift, nor the battle to the strong (the tortoise and the hare; Eccles. 9.11). All of these stories, and their morals, have direct parallels in the life of King David (who appears in today's Old Testament/Hebrew Bible lection), as well as in other Bible stories.

One reason why Chapter 9 reminds me of the passion is that it sets before the characters (and, by extension, us) a series of challenges. Repeatedly people's religious preconceptions, the rules they have been taught, clash with something that sounds wrong but feels right. A detail jumps out at me as the questioning unfolds. When the man's parents are questioned, they are afraid, because the answer they are being pressed for is not one that they can honestly give. They fear a backlash (being expelled from the synagogue) for speaking the truth. They are us in the face of a twitter-mob.

So the parents tell their questioners to ask the man himself. But when they find him, they do not ask him, they tell him. They must think they have nothing to learn. The man's response is worthy of Jesus himself, telling the truth while avoiding the tongue-trap:

I do not know whether he is a sinner. One thing I do know, that though I was blind, now I see.

Amazing grace was at work in that man, that day. And if that cannot lighten our load on this Refreshment Sunday, nothing can.

Mothering Sunday

Exodus 2.1–10 *or* 1 Samuel 1.20–end; Psalm 34.11–20 *or* 127.1–4;
2 Corinthians 1.3–7 *or* Colossians 3.12–17; Luke 2.33–35
or John 19.25–27

The 'baby in the bulrushes' is the earliest Bible story that I remember reading for myself, in a children's Bible. I liked the idea of Moses' name being based on the moment in his childhood when a passing Egyptian princess found him in his basket and 'drew him out of the water' (Ex. 2.10).

Decades later, I know about what scholars call 'aetiologies', those stories that explain how something or someone came to be named. Not to be confused, you medics, with aetiologies as doctors use the term, explaining the origin of a disease. Just recently, I learned that the aetiology conceals a potential embarrassment: Moses is the greatest prophet in Judaism – so why does he have an Egyptian name?

The aetiology in Exodus 2 is to reassure readers that Moses is a Hebrew, not an Egyptian. The Hebrew verb *mashah* ('draw') promotes a Hebrew origin. But the *m-s-s* consonants give it away: the same name is embedded in the famous pharaonic name Ra*meses*. It is Egyptian. It means 'son of'.

It is not surprising that no one in Judaism – or in Christianity for that matter – was keen to reject the unlikely etymology (it is in the Bible, after all!) in favour of the likelier one. But it would change our perspective on Moses completely if we dared to imagine that he might not have been a Hebrew after all, and that he grew up in Pharaoh's household because he really was part of Pharaoh's family.

Wanting to know where we come from is normal and natural. The popularity of genealogical research, and the attractions of genetic testing to find out more about our origins, bear witness to this truth of our humanity. There are risks involved that were unknown to our forebears – such as children discovering that their father is not their blood father – and these go some way to explain why some early societies policed female sexuality so rigorously. Blood matters. Paternity matters.

The baby in the bulrushes had no choice about growing up to become the leader of a people and the bringer of the law from heaven to earth. His life unfolded in a series of happenstances, which gradually acquired a direction: later on in Exodus 2 comes the story of how he killed an Egyptian, which strikes me as one of those crisis moments such as are found in many stories, in which a character takes a step, as if by chance, that will go on to govern their entire future.

Moses had made his choice. Whatever his origin, his loyalty came to attach itself to the oppressed Hebrews, whose God was now about to disclose himself out of the burning bush (Ex. 3.6). Rereading that passage now, I cannot help noticing an ambiguity about the words he hears: 'I am the God of your father, the God of Abraham, the God of Isaac, and the God of Jacob.'

Moses shows us one way in which the notion of family can be extended beyond mere confines of blood (as we used to say) and genes (as we say now): for he either comes from one racial group but is adopted by another (as Ex. 2.6–10 suggests), or he belongs to a birth family but makes a principled choice to stand with a different family, the children of Israel (Ex. 2.12–14, 19).

The Gospel of John shows us a different scene, but the same generous understanding of what is encompassed by 'family'. The settings are completely different, but there is an element of pressure in both. For Moses, it was the order from Pharaoh that Hebrew boys were to be thrown into the Nile (which adds a delicious irony to his having been drawn out of it by Pharaoh's own daughter). In the scene gathered about the Cross, the dying son looks to secure for his mother the best protection that he can, by entrusting her to one who was not a blood relative. Jesus was himself part of a blended family, for he had known Joseph's parenting as he grew. So naturally he saw beyond blood or genes.

In an era where we are discovering that who we are told we are does not have to be a prison we inhabit for the rest of our lives, it is good to realize that Scripture got there before us, long, long ago. When it comes to family, God really does seem to love wondrous variety.

The Fifth Sunday of Lent (Passion Sunday)

Ezekiel 37.1–14; Psalm 130; Romans 8.6–1; John 11.1–45

Here is a quiz question: 'What is the shortest sentence in the Bible?' It is hard for Bible-believing, church-going Christians to answer, for they will know that God did not write the Bible in English; and that even the Authorised Version is a translation, albeit one with an honoured and weighty history.

The standard answer to the question is John 11.35. To me, it feels like a proud moment for the English language: English rarely beats Latin for succinctness. The Greek uses three words; the Latin, four. But AV, RSV, and REB need only two: 'Jesus wept'. The NRSV spoils the power of that brevity, taking four words in its attempt to nail the precise meaning, but to no useful purpose (if it mattered that he *began* to weep, John would have told us when he stopped too).

At the centre of John's Gospel, the death and raising of Lazarus is a pivot, perfectly balancing its twin extremities, the flesh-ification, and the mort-ification, of the Son of God. Jesus embodies a uniquely human experience. Not even our closest genetic relatives, the apes, do this when distressed. They can certainly suffer, and make sounds expressive of distress. They even mourn. But they do not weep. The scientific term for producing tears is 'lachrymate'. (No need to be distracted here by crocodiles: apparently the eyes of some species water when they are eating, but it is not a distress response.)

It sometimes seems like John's Jesus is more superhuman than truly human. His signs of power, and his foreknowledge, not to mention his conversations with God the Father, are hardly proofs of what we have in common. Instead, they represent the great gulf between his humanity (perfect) and ours (flawed). At the centre, though, when it matters most to show it, when the terror and indignity of human dissolution is right in front of him (and us), he did what we do. Jesus wept.

'Jesus wept' is unimportant as a quiz answer. As a profanity, 'Jesus wept' appropriates the power of two short words, but empties them of their true meaning. What a waste that so many who use that profanity know nothing of its incarnational heart.

John 11.35 is not the only time in the Gospels, of course, that Jesus shows his emotions. On other occasions, we find him becoming angry, or exasperated, or moved with pity. There are times when we too feel like the young man in Wilhelm Müller's poem, when emotion robs us of words: *Ich kann nicht mehr singen, mein Herz ist zu voll* ('I can sing no longer, my heart is too full').

At times like that, Jesus more than once chooses to be alone, away from the gaze of others; as we do too. Soon we shall meet him in the garden of Gethsemane and look upon his desolation there. But even then, he keeps his friends close by: aware, perhaps, as they cannot be, that this will be the last time they spend together on earth in the old way, the way they have grown used to, the way that is too familiar to be properly valued.

The death of a friend is not a moment when we should feel obliged to display a stiff upper lip. Which is an odd phrase, now I come to think of it. When I am brought to tears, it is my lower lip that trembles and gives way. John Donne has said that the death of one person 'diminishes' us. That term encapsulates how death unravels the fabric of our common life, whether by the slowly pulled thread of a gradual deterioration, or by a gaping rent torn suddenly.

Collectively we go on living, fashioning fresh memories, weaving new relationships, patching that life-fabric so that it continues to hold together. It is not a silk-satin, smoothly perfect but slippery to sew, and hard to care for. It is a patchwork, marked and mended. And still beautiful.

There is a Japanese sewing technique called *sashiko*, a style of mending that, rather than trying to hide the damage to cloth, highlights it visibly with decorative stitching. It gloriously refuses to pretend imperfections away. That is a model for true courage in managing the distress of human dying. Weeping is not a weakness, any more than fear is a sin. We need not hide our grief. We too can weep.

Palm Sunday

Liturgy of the Palms: Matthew 21.1–11; Psalm 118.1–2, 19–end [*or* 118.19–24]
Liturgy of the Passion: Isaiah 50.4–9a; Psalm 31.9–16 [*or* 31.9–18]; Philippians 2.5–11; Matthew 26.14—end of 27
or Matthew 27.11–54

The behaviour of crowds has been part of psychology as an academic specialism since the days of Sigmund Freud, the father of modern psychology. Whatever we make of his theories, he undoubtedly probed many fundamental questions concerning what it is to be human.

Like Freud, we need to be thinking about crowd psychology if we are to understand the Passion Gospel fully. Any place where human beings gather together can become the setting for behaviours we would not exhibit alone or among friends. Most of us have experienced tensions between our individual conscience and our membership of a wider company.

We feel different when we are part of a crowd. In a football stadium, I am liberated to gloat ('You're not singing any more') or boast ('We're by far the greatest team the world has ever seen') in a way I would be ashamed to do in ordinary conversation.

Understanding crowd psychology can help us to negotiate our workplace; or to evaluate public debates in the House of Commons or the General Synod. In crowd situations, the safe place is usually with the majority. The place of danger is in the minority, standing out against a majority opinion when conscience forbids us to back down.

To be fickle is the archetypal characteristic of the mob. This is perfectly exemplified in these final days of Jesus' earthly life. When he enters Jerusalem, he is acclaimed as one of royal blood, as the Lord's chosen, and as a prophet, but he will be dead within the week. Fickleness is a quality that offends us, because our common life depends on being able to trust, and also to predict, people's behaviour. But even as we condemn it, we stand guilty of it, in our working lives and our personal lives, and even in our relationship with God. We find it so hard to exemplify the steadfastness that is at odds with fickle changeability.

For the Gospel of the Palms, the crowd was full of joy. How thrilling and inspiring it must have been to be there and participate, throwing our branches and crying aloud our hope and expectation. Perhaps it felt a little like taking part in the celebrations for King Charles' Coronation in 2023. Excitement kindled and passed from one person to the next in an atmosphere of festivity. This kind of crowd psychology can bring moments of sublime Christian joy when we participate in worship. I felt this at the funeral of a priest during one Lent. It was not a feeling that I could have experienced on my own at home, however strenuously I prayed for the repose of his soul.

But in the Gospel of the Passion, the crowd manifests its darker side, the shadow self of group psychology is revealed. And in case we want to say that we ourselves would not behave like them when part of such a crowd, a series of groups is revealed in quick succession, leaving us nowhere to hide. A group of religious leaders is spurred on by self-righteousness. A garrison of soldiers joins in tormenting a man when, one to one, they might have pitied and consoled him. A crowd bays for Barabbas, turning against the man they have been praising just days ago.

Strangely, the people who come closest to standing up against that group psychology are Mr and Mrs Pontius Pilate. She warns him not to get involved in action against 'that just man' (27.19). And he does try to heed her warning, or to honour his own conscience; perhaps both (27.24).

The word that psychologists use to describe the phenomenon at work in the Gospel crowds, and football crowds, and political crowds, is 'deindividuation'. Our responsibility gets diluted when we are part of a group; our shame and guilt responses are blunted; our anger, lust, greed and envy simply feel less wicked when other people are doing the same. 'Everyone was doing it' really does feel like an explanation rather than an excuse.

The overarching principle for Christians has to be that we must see the individual in every crowd, and behave to the crowd as we would to each constituent part of it. If Palm Sunday teaches us nothing else, it ought to teach us that our calling is not de-individuation but re-individuation.

Good Friday

Isaiah 52.13—end of 53; Psalm 22 [*or* 22.1–11 *or* 22.1–21];
Hebrews 10.16–25 *or* Hebrews 4.14–16; 5.7–9;
John 18.1—end of 19

Back in the days when I studied Latin poetry, Virgil held a special place as the gold medallist on the podium of poetic beauty and pathos. Everyone who reads his epic on the origins of Rome wrestles with what is called 'double motivation' or 'double perspective'. Virgil depicts a world of human beings striving and suffering, with a shadowy, partial awareness that the world they inhabit is thronged with another kind of being. The choices they make have their human motivation, but are also driven by the agendas of gods and goddesses.

This 'double perspective' is characteristic of epic literature. So perhaps we should not be surprised that it can help us to understand the epic Passion Gospel too, in which human beings make choices, while the writer shows us, the audience, the gap between what the characters in the story know and the epic providence that is working out in events.

We call this gap between the two perspectives at work in the story 'dramatic irony'. There is truth for us to absorb from the Passion as a one-off event in human history; but double motivation reveals another truth, for history is never only about the past. Elements of the Passion go on being played out in every human community from that day to this. The Passion is the purest distillation of the cup of human pathos and suffering that we drink from daily.

The centuries that have passed since the actual events of Good Friday have given us time to develop tools for interpreting this relationship between divine and human motivation. We do not only rely on the Gospel itself. There are writings from the past before the Passion (Isaiah, Psalm 22) and from the future after it (Hebrews), both of which help to close the gap and bring the two motivations together. They are tools for us to prise open meanings, securing for us the blessed assurance that the suffering we behold is not random or meaningless.

Double perspective helps us to sympathize with the problems faced by all the participants in the Passion epic. I cannot call it tragedy, because there is no fault or mistake in the protagonist (Jesus) dooming him to be the agent of his own downfall. But it is undoubtedly epic, because it deals with human beings in that grander scale of history. The characters in the Passion have only a partial understanding of their own actions and feelings, and an even vaguer sense of the possible consequences of their choices. But we see, and every year remind ourselves, that the redemption of the world is in their hands.

And this is literally crucial: by providing the divine perspective, the Gospel enables us to see as God sees. On Good Friday, we get a glimpse of what perfect and complete divine knowledge is like. There are good reasons why we come back year after year to witness the Passion of Christ. It is not rational argument that draws us. It is the comfort, the reassurance, the goodness, that we intuit when we see person after person make unkind, thoughtless, self-interested, cruel choices – and have them contribute to a divine epic of salvation in such a way that God's holy, heavenly purpose is achieved.

Tragic dramas usually end with some kind of resolution. But the Passion is epic, not tragedy, a kind of history in poetic form. It does not batter us into understanding with rational propositions, but makes concessions to our human nature. And in history, as in the habitations of God's eternity, there are no beginnings nor endings. Beyond the Passion Gospel's boundaries, human life flows on. Choices continue to be made; and made by people who only partially understand their own motivations (never mind God's), and scarcely think at all of the future those choices are helping to fashion.

Unlike the Gospel characters, we Christians today are privileged with insight into the meaning of those long-ago events. We can perceive, too, the hand of God at work. And unlike anything in Classical literature, we behold one character who bridges the divide between the two perspectives. In Jesus Christ, there are no gaps between one level of knowledge and another; no gulf between the human and divine. On this day long ago, a man hung dying on a cross. Then, and now, the story is only just beginning.

Easter Day

Acts 10.34–43† *or* Jeremiah 31.1–6; Psalm 118.1–2, 14–24
[*or* 118.14–24]; Colossians 3.1–4 *or* Acts 10.34–43†;
John 20.1–18 *or* Matthew 28.1–10

† The reading from Acts must be used as either the first or second reading.

'Who moved the stone?' asked Frank Morison in his 1930 book of that title.[1] Matthew had already given us the answer: an angel rolled the stone away (28.2). Morison's book looked into different accounts of what happened between Holy Saturday and Easter dawn. Reactions to the book showed that Christians and non-Christians alike wanted answers. I am convinced that Christians still want answers. They want to know what the Resurrection means.

Believers have doubts and difficulties with the Easter story, even as some non-believers struggle against its magnetic attraction. If the proof of the pudding is in the eating, we have some 'inward digesting' to do when it comes to the Paschal feast. We need to choose the correct exegetical cutlery. Our banquet of rich fare (Isa. 25.6) will require seasoning to suit individual palates. But first we need to gather the ingredients for the recipe.

Here my food metaphor breaks down. You cannot have a recipe with a hole in the middle where the signature ingredient should be. But a hole is exactly what our faith is rooted in: a space where a body should have been.

Only Matthew shows us the angel rolling back the stone. I think he was trying to reassure us that no one cheated by secretly removing the body. That seems to be why he records Pilate setting a company of soldiers to guard the tomb (27.65).

Our lives are full of things that we rely on but do not understand. From plumbing and electrics, to medical equipment and mobile phone technology, we accept that they are true and real because they work, and have measurable, predictable effects. For this reason, it should not be too difficult for us to give the Resurrection of Christ a hearing; and to sympathize with the women who were its first witnesses.

They were told something, and sent to share something, that they could not properly grasp, never mind 'make sense of' or 'believe in'. They

---

1 Frank Morison, *Who Moved the Stone,* Faber, 1930.

thought they knew what 'alive' and 'dead' meant. And they knew that Jesus was dead. Why else had they come to the tomb at dawn?

During his teaching ministry, Jesus spoke more than once about life and death. He was in no doubt which was preferable. I think that his most revealing comment is a woe pronounced upon the scribes and Pharisees: 'you are like whitewashed tombs, which on the outside look beautiful, but inside they are full of the bones of the dead and of all kinds of filth' (Matt. 23.27). I can think of no more astringent expression on his lips and no more painful judgement than to call someone (in the old words) a 'whited sepulchre'.

In Bible days, there was no grey area between life and death. This needs stating because we have made dying harder and more complicated, with the result that many of us will pass through a kind of half-life in which the mind decays but the body lingers. The Lord's command to 'Follow me, and let the dead bury their own dead' (Matt. 8.22) can seem harsh, but it is an honest preparation for Easter, when we learn to set aside the old understanding of death so as to lay hold of 'life that really is life' (1 Tim. 6.19).

In Luke's Gospel, two beings clothed in white knew, without being told, why the women had come to the tomb; they challenged them, 'Why do you look for the living among the dead? He is not here, but has risen' (Luke 24.5). But in Matthew, the angel speaks instead of Jesus' 'being crucified' and 'being raised'. This exchange between the two orders of created being, human and angelic, witnesses to a stage in the development of the Easter faith before Christians got entangled in philosophies of life and death. The bedrock of belief is not abstract meaning but concrete fact. Jesus was crucified. People saw it happen. They tended the man's dead body and laid it to rest in the grave. And Jesus was raised from the dead to a new way of being: 'He is not here' insists Matthew's angel (28.6).

We will see Jesus again, when we find our way home (28.10). This is the faith of the Church: those who believe in him, even though they die, will live, and everyone who lives and believes in him will never die (John 11.25–6).

The Second Sunday of Easter

[Exodus 14.10–end; 15.20, 21]; Acts 2.14a, 22–32[†]; Psalm 16; 1 Peter 1.3–9; John 20.19–end

[†] The reading from Acts must be used as either the first or second reading.

What's in a name? Perhaps nothing much. Names are sounds we apply to differentiate one thing, or one person, from another: so 'that which we call a rose by any other name would smell as sweet'.[1] But making mistakes about people's names matters. We can become annoyed when others do it to us. And when we stumble over someone else's name, misremembering or forgetting it, it can result in awkwardness, even shame.

This part of John's Gospel ends with a promise. We believe: and what he promises to us, as believers, is life 'in his name'. With no frivolous intention, I want to ask, would being saved in the Messiah's name have been so easy if he had been called Englebert? or (confining myself to biblical options) Maher-Shalal-Hash-Baz?

There is much to be said for the simplicity of a couple of syllables. We want to converse with our risen Saviour, to pray in and through his name, because that name in itself is powerful. It is even, all by itself, a prayer. It needs to be easy to say. It was decided before his Nativity. It is not an expression of his human personality, which was as yet unknown. But it was a distillation of his essence: 'God saves', or 'God, save!' Whether as a statement or a prayer, the name of Jesus opens up a path to God the moment that we utter it in faith.

When Adam named the animals in Genesis (2.19–20), his doing so was an act of power – not that the animals cared what name they were given, either as a species or as individuals. But humans do care. We care because (quite apart from the fact that our names represent the tastes and aspirations of our parents, not ourselves) people can make judgements on the basis of our names about the kind of person we are. Most of us are strongly influenced by others' judgements. No one who has watched *Red Dwarf* wants to be called Duane Dibley.

For early Christians, the name of Jesus was a key to unlock the mysteries of God. But even in the early days, within a hundred years of the Resurrection, the name they took from their Lord's calling as Messiah – 'Christians' – could provoke a different reaction, becoming a source of condemnation.

---

1 William Shakespeare, *Romeo and Juliet*, Act II, Scene 4.

When a Roman governor called Pliny wrote to the emperor Trajan for advice, he asked, 'Is it the mere name "Christian" which is punishable, even if innocent of crime, or rather the crimes associated with the name?' This shows how the label, the name, came with a weight of baggage. Trajan's response gives the lie to the Romans' reputation for persecution. He tells Pliny to punish any offences they commit, but not to hunt them down, and to accept their demonstrations of loyalty to the emperor.

Trajan was a humane ruler. He did not assume that a name bestowed by others must necessarily reflect the truth about those 'Christians'. He made a wise distinction between what label we apply to ourselves, or others, and who we actually are. That policy of judging by behaviour rather than labels is one that we today need to emulate, for in our own time too the name 'Christian' can have negative connotations, encouraging others to make hasty judgements based on a label, not on fact.

If the name of Jesus, and the label 'Christian', have an 'ick' factor attached to them in everyday life (not in Church circles of course), it cannot be because of the intrinsic unattractiveness of faith in the Son of God. Read 1 Peter 1 and you find a thrilling sense of exaltation, ecstasy even, at what God has done in Christ. Jesus has conquered death, and overcome the grimness of human disintegration. There is a snapshot of all that is most attractive and powerful in our Resurrection faith.

If that is not what other see when they look at us, it is our problem, and it needs fixing. Easter is the time to live out the divine splendour of the kingdom, the power and the glory of our risen Lord, Jesus Christ. I want to pray, with Jeremy Taylor, 'Lord, I glory in nothing so much as that I am a Christian, that thy name is called upon me. O my God, though I die, yet will I put my trust in thee' (*Holy Dying*, 1651).

The Third Sunday of Easter

[Zephaniah 3.14–end]; Acts 2.14a, 36–41†; Psalm 116.1–3, 10–17 [or 116.1–7]; 1 Peter 1.17–23; Luke 24.13–35

†The reading from Acts must be used as either the first or second reading.

You might think that there is nothing new to be said about the road to Emmaus. But somehow fresh insight comes every time I read it. That could be the effect of increasing age and a less retentive memory. A better explanation is that the Holy Spirit is at work in each encounter with the story. The Spirit reveals what we need to notice, when we need to notice it: whether that is a detail formerly undetected, or whether a fact already absorbed has suddenly presented itself in a new light.

This is how the Gospel works in us, revealing new insights in old materials (Matt. 13.51–53). It is possible because the 'us' we bring to every reading is a slightly different 'us'. We are always being changed by time, circumstance, experience. This time when I read the passage, two things surfaced, which I have, of course, encountered before, but this time they are sharply in focus.

The first thing is a point of circumstance. These two disciples are not – I repeat, not – apostles. They are just people. People who love the Lord. Yet not only do they see him after his Resurrection; they are also entrusted with the new way of being with him from that time on (the breaking of bread). One was called 'Cleopas', but the name of the other is not given.

That is encouraging from the historian's point of view. It suggests that Luke did not feel free to fill in facts and details when his source did not record them. He certainly fine-tuned his work to suit gentile audiences, but would not invent freely simply to tidy up the story.

The fact that only Cleopas is named suggests that Luke is indeed faithfully recounting a tradition from his special source (known as L). From the same source, now lost, Luke the writer must have drawn other characters like Zacchaeus, the prodigal son and the good Samaritan. One simple way to meditate on the Emmaus revelation is to give our name to that other disciple.

The other factor that had a new impact on me was the reaction of the two travellers to the man they met. Some readers will have spotted this ages ago, but it has only just come into focus for me.

Cleopas and the other disciple exclaimed, 'Were not our hearts burning within us while he was talking to us on the road, while he was opening the Scriptures to us?' (Luke 24.32). Think back a few verses, to when that actually happened (24.25–27). There was no trace there of that reaction, the surprise by joy, the burning heart within. Both of them had felt the moment with intense emotional force; neither of them had said a single word to the other about it.

Why not? We are not told. We need to use our imagination. Perhaps they had shared silent glances as they listened. Then they could genuinely say together, 'Did not our hearts burn within us?', for the face of each would have borne witness to what they felt.

There is another possibility, perhaps more realistic about how human beings respond to unexpected revelations. It may be that each of them felt a surge of emotion and spiritual excitement, but neither said anything because, well, because it sounded silly. Maybe it even felt disloyal, when, moments before, their faces and hearts had been so heavy; and when they had told the 'stranger' about the peculiar news the women had brought to them that morning, which led to their going to the tomb, but finding it empty, with no sign of the risen Lord.

The story of Emmaus is dramatic. In a stage-drama, the audience gains emotional pleasure from the moment called *anagnorisis* ('recognition'), in which one character suddenly realizes the true identity or nature of another. Sometimes it is chilling: at the end of *The Godfather*, the true Michael Corleone is revealed when the door shuts out his wife. Sometimes the pleasure springs from hope, like Eowyn before the Lord of the Nazgul in *The Lord of the Rings*, or Robin Hood at the archery contest. At that Emmaus meal, Cleopas and his companion experience an intense recognition when the 'stranger' breaks bread. We too share that pleasure, as we recognize them recognizing Jesus. That same pleasure of recognition is available to us at least every Sunday, for the rest of our earthly lives.

The Fourth Sunday of Easter

[Genesis 7]; Acts 2.42–end†; Psalm 23; 1 Peter 2.19–end; John 10.1–10

† The reading from Acts must be used as either the first or second reading.

In his Sermon on the Mount, Jesus asks, 'Is not life more than food, and the body more than clothing?' (Matt. 6.25). The question is rhetorical. Of course life is more than food and clothing. When I was still at school I read this in *King Lear*:

> O, reason not the need! Our basest beggars
> Are in the poorest thing superfluous.
> Allow not nature more than nature needs,
> Man's life is cheap as beast's.[1]

But I did not understand it then as I do now. Then, those were words of powerful pity, but their macrocosmic significance was as yet unfocused. Lear's revelation swept away the clutter of possessions and trappings of status, showing the person beneath the persona – king and beggar in common humanity.

What has triggered this reflection? The last verse of Sunday's Gospel. If Jesus has come to bring life – and more, *abundant* life – we need to know what such a life looks like, and how to live it. Rather than 'abundantly', I would translate, 'to the utmost' or 'in all its fullness'.

What drives many of us, much of the time, is a desire for possessing. Some people achieve this through status in their employment, which leads to wealth. Some find it in relationships, whether for good (in a like-minded company of friends or family) or bad (in the form of coercive control).

But possessing can make us anxious ('What if I lose it all?'). It can even become an end in itself. I was also at school when I first read George Eliot's *Silas Marner* and was saddened by the weaver's miserable half-life counting gold. But I remembered that his misery was rooted in a trust misplaced and idealism betrayed. Like an addict, Silas thought money made him feel safe, when really it created the anxiety it fed on. Gold was his prison, not his safe stronghold.

---

1 William Shakespear, *King Lear*, Act II, Scene 4.

The love of stuff can lead to addiction, debt, even murder. A stuff-filled life cannot be what Jesus means by 'life in all its fullness'. There is a sketch of that fullest form of life in Acts Chapter 4, in which people share what they have and distribute to those in need. But 2,000 years on, Luke's ideal has yet to be fully realized in the company of God's pilgrim people. And how many of us would truly welcome it if it were? As with the hearers of Jesus' sermon, I imagine a range of reactions: from 'It's all right for him to say that, he has no responsibilities' to 'That will be my life, starting today'.

Later, Lear said to a beggar, in words that I can still type from memory, 'Unaccommodated man is no more but such a poor, bare, forked [two-legged] animal as thou art'. He began to see how we cling to any fragment of stuff we can, to reassure ourselves that we exist and matter. It turned out that Lear could not shed the burdens of kingship while keeping the status. As long as property and status are our way of evaluating ourselves and seeking affirmation from others, we shall go on cutting ourselves off from 'life in all its fullness'.

Perhaps heroic sacrifice is required to secure our freedom from the lure of stuff. Now that is something Christians can be really good at: 'All the vain things that charm me most/I sacrifice them to his blood'.[2] 1 Peter shows that Christ's sacrifice is to be a model for us. But not by means of self-starvation, self-flagellation, self-hatred. We have been freed from sin for a simple purpose: to live a life of righteousness.

In John's Gospel, Jesus promises to be for us a Door (or Gate). As an image, it does not have the historical power of the Vine (the new Israel) or the emotional appeal of the Good Shepherd (the nurturing protector). But it is shows us a way between the world of stuff, and the kingdom of God. The Door opens to let us out of prison into light and freedom. The Door closes to keep us safe from harm, from that roaring lion who 'walketh about seeking whom he may devour' (1 Peter 5.8).

The message of all three readings is a message about who we are called to be. What we learn from them is that stuff cannot protect us. Neither can it liberate us. Christ, on the other hand, does both.

---

2 Isaac Watts, 'When I survey the wondrous cross', *Hymns and Spiritual Songs*, 1707.

The Fifth Sunday of Easter

[Genesis 8.1–19]; Acts 7.55–end†; Psalm 31.1–5, 15–16 [*or* 31.1–5]; 1 Peter 2.2–10; John 14.1–14

† The reading from Acts must be used as either the first or second reading.

I sympathize with Saul of Tarsus. While everyone else is getting stuck in to stoning the first Christian martyr, he stands apart, apparently applauding and approving what the crowd does. An isolated, peripheral figure in my imagination, he reminds me of myself, every time we took our children to an amusement park with rides. Motion sickness made this more of a torment than an entertainment for me. I too was always standing to one side, holding the coats.

Luke's apparently trivial comment is not merely a throwaway detail. It tells us something important about the crowd. They took off their coats to stone Stephen. They intended to get stuck in and put their best effort into his obliteration. It would be hard work. They would get too hot for coats. Here is a biblical equivalent for rolling up one's sleeves.

The same trivial remark tells us something about Saul too. Or rather it hints at something. When I stood apart from my group, holding the coats, I did so because I knew how awful it would feel to participate. I wanted to be part of the fun of the day, but not so much that I became sick. In the past when I have read this passage, I have always seen it simply as a first glimpse of the man who, following a time of persecuting the new faith, would become the apostle to the gentiles. But if Saul was such an eager persecutor, and (in this case) an apparently righteous one, responding to an egregious case of blasphemy, why was he looking after the coats? Why not join in with gusto, taking off his own coat, choosing a nice, jagged missile and hurling it at Stephen?

The lection misses out the end of the story, which is the first verse of Acts 8: 'And Saul approved of their killing him.' Perhaps that tells us all we need to know about how to judge Saul's actions. But I prefer the kinder possibility, that he was at least wondering if there was more to the new faith than blasphemy. Perhaps he rejoiced at Stephen's death because he hoped it would stop his own wondering, the allure of that new way of love and service.

It is in the nature of faith to have questions, to go in search of understanding. In this Gospel, John lays the groundwork for Thomas' scepticism at the Resurrection of Jesus by reporting his question, 'How can we know the way?' Once more, Gospel sublimity triggers in me memories of trivial and humdrum versions of the question at issue: how reluctant most of us are to stop while driving and ask for directions. How difficult it can be to listen to the answer and hold in our mind all the twists and turns of the journey ahead of us.

Finding 'the way' is not like following a satnav even when it sends us up a dirt track. Nor is it like trying desperately to remember whether it was 'right' or 'left' at the next crossroads. There is never a reason to become lost; because Jesus is always beside us, and he is the Way. He leads to the Father, and all who worship the Father come by the Way, whether they know it/him or not.

Philip's request (actually a command) to Jesus is a reprise of Thomas'. In both cases, Jesus gave an answer first, and then they asked for what he said was theirs already. They know the Way. They have seen the Father. Their requests show how little they have understood Jesus. It is surprising that they continued to follow him, however ineptly, when he seemed to be saying things, and making claims, that made him either 'mad, bad or God'. Their continuing companionship suggested that they trusted in him, even though they could make no sense of his divinity and misunderstood what he told them.

We can take courage from the fact that the disciples kept walking the way with Jesus. If they did not listen properly, because they thought they already knew what their extraordinary friend was going to say, well, they were hardly unique among humankind. Most of our close relationships are just the same. If this Gospel reminds us to be better at listening to those we love, at least one of its many purposes will have been accomplished.

The Sixth Sunday of Easter

[Genesis 8.20—9.17]; Acts 17.22–31†; Psalm 66.7–18;
1 Peter 3.13–end; John 14.15–21

†The reading from Acts must be used as either the first or second reading.

I once attended a memorial service in Oxford for my old Latin Tutor, Donald Russell. It followed the customary pattern for such events, interweaving elements of Christian liturgy with personal remembrances. As I looked around, recognizing people from another lifetime, there sprang into my mind Paul's words at the Areopagus (the 'rock of Ares', a place in Athens where justice was enacted): 'we too are his offspring' (Acts 17.28).

The congregation at the service was distinguished. But that was not the point. What mattered was that here was an assembly of one man's intellectual offspring, his family according to the mind. Not all of us were of equal distinction, but we were all changed by association with a teacher whose expertise in language was, frankly, epic.

Every teacher has the same daunting privilege of being remembered. Some stand out in the memory for their bullying or sarcasm; others for patience, or enthusiasm. For good or for ill, we do not forget them.

Christianity is something similar. A family, but not of blood, and not of learning either. A family we can join because we are like-minded, not because we have passed a test. We become members through a sacrament of new beginning, the death of the old life giving birth to the new one.

In the reading from Acts, Paul was facing a city full of strangers: strangers by blood, and strangers in terms of culture and society. He spoke into that alien audience, in a strange place, the truths that he believed they needed to know. Then he invited them to join a new family, the family of the Spirit. Outside the lection for Easter 6, that story concludes by saying that some scoffed and others procrastinated ('We will hear you again about this', Acts 17.32). But a few made their minds up then and there to join this new family of the Spirit.

Paul judged his audience well. Without compromising on Christian truth, he had looked around him with interested, noticing eyes, to see what he might have in common with the inhabitants of Athens. An image of an 'unknown god' and a line of verse from a foreign poet gave him a way to touch their hearts, so he could win those hearts for Christ.

Two centuries later, a more pugnacious preacher was doing things differently. He did not seek to win his audience through finding common ground. Confident in the superiority of the Christian cause, and hostile to everything that did not match his version of it, he asked belligerently, 'What does Athens have to do with Jerusalem? What does the Academy have to do with the Church? What do heretics have to do with Christians?'

His name was Tertullian. He may have been a lawyer; he certainly had the usual Roman education in how to argue a case, including denigrating his opponents. But abusing people who disagree with you is not a very good way to win them over. Not then, and not now.

How different was Paul's way of speaking at the Areopagus! The apostle had warmed the hearts of hearers with his courtesy and respect as he sought out what was good in what, to him, was 'other'. He took the trouble to observe and reflect. He talked to the crowd in terms that did not alienate them, but made them feel heard instead.

The Gospel suggests that Paul, not Tertullian, chose the way that was in tune with God's loving purposes. Jesus speaks of the Holy Spirit as an Advocate. In other words, a lawyer for the defence; one whose task it is to plead a case on behalf of guilty humanity, calling for judgement to be tempered with mercy, reminding our Father that we too are his children. Thundering denunciation could have been our fate. But, as one of their poets has said, 'to the divine it seemed otherwise' (*dis aliter visum*).[1]

Within the New Testament, we mostly see Christians as they were when they were not on the top of the pile socially, culturally, politically. Becoming history's top dog did not make Christians better or kinder. These readings encourage Christians today to recover the biblical model promoted by Peter and Paul: 'Interrogate your prejudices. Listen first. Do not resort to anger and hostility when others challenge you. Meet them instead with gentleness and reverence, and a clear conscience' (1 Peter 3.14–16).

---

1 Virgil, *Aeneid*, Book 2.148.

The Seventh Sunday of Easter
(Sunday after Ascension Day)

[Ezekiel 36.24–28]; Acts 1.6–14†; Psalm 68.1–10, 32–35 [*or* 68.1–10]; 1 Peter 4.12–14; 5.6–11; John 17.1–11

† The reading from Acts must be used as either the first or second reading.

This Gospel highlights a mystery. What on earth is 'glory'? The Bible tells us that glory is an attribute of God. Theologians suggest two kinds: intrinsic (how God is glorious in himself) and extrinsic (how God manifests his glory to us).

Glory is also a process. Father glorifies Son; Son glorifies Father. We glorify them both. Regular readers know that I love Latin; but by giving us the verb 'glorify', it makes it sound as if we make God glorious, when 'glorifying' means acknowledging God's glory, not creating it.

When we interpret words, we start with their original or literal meaning, which is concrete, physical. From this come derived meanings that are not. For example, we can talk of the 'root' of a problem because we know what the root of a plant is; or we can say that Christ will be 'a light to lighten the gentiles' because we know what the light of the sun is.

In the New Testament, 'glory' translates a Greek word, *doxa*. It is familiar from the label 'doxology', which we use for praise at the end of a psalm or hymn. *Doxa* starts by being a word for how things look, for their appearance. That led to the emergence of a further meaning: 'reputation, honour'. This is how, in Scripture, it developed into a term for divine splendour.

When the Old Testament/Hebrew Bible was translated into Greek, the translators used *doxa* to translate the Hebrew term *kavod*. That meant 'weighty, important'. It came to mean 'riches', as when Joseph tells his brothers about his 'glory' in Egypt (Gen. 45.13). The human mind moves easily between wealth and importance, then as now.

In moments when we feel close to God, our proximity enables us to see his glory. This is not the same as observing something that is beautiful. It is closer to ecstasy, that dissociation from the physical self, in which a vision comes. The vision need not be anything so grand as a one-to-one encounter with God. It is more about insight than physical sight, a feeling of clarity, reaching us like the voice of God himself, in a 'sound of sheer silence' (1 Kings 19.12).

The Greek word *doxa* has reminded us that one vital component of glory is that it is visible. We could call John's Gospel the Gospel of Glory, for the very moment of the Incarnation (John 1.14) is also the moment when the revelation of Christ's glory begins. John is in harmony with Luke. Both put glory at the centre of the Incarnation. That text in Luke we know as 'Nunc Dimittis' makes a statement of fact, that God expresses his glory in the salvation of his people (2.32).

John's Gospel is undoubtedly preparing us for the glory-fication of the Son of God. To understand how that works, we should read Chapter 17 as if we had never read it before, with no idea how the story would end. When we do that, we notice that the tone is triumphant. It sounds like 'glory' is a guarantee of winning, succeeding, earning the right to impose authority (17.2).

This way, Jesus' priestly prayer reads like many a prayer of ordinary people in Bible days, and still today. Shorn of that knowledge of what comes next, it sounds nakedly transactional ('I have done ABC for you; now you do XYZ for me', 17.4–5). That is not inappropriate, for prayer is supposed to be reciprocal. Both parties, beseecher and besought, get something out it. And it explains why the disciples were so devastated by Jesus' arrest and crucifixion. The prayer, at which we must remember that they were present (except for Judas), sets them up to expect a triumph, not some bitter and shameful humiliation. The Incarnation turns the meaning of glory inside out and upside down.

Above all else, God's glory is not an abstract quality, but something visible and close to us. The pillars of cloud and fire in the wilderness (Ex. 13.21) were not images of God's glory; they were epiphanies of it. God was right there, in the cloud and fire, among his pilgrim people.

We may still be unclear about what God's glory is. But one thing we know beyond reasonable doubt: that we have 'the light of the knowledge of the glory of God in the face of Jesus Christ' (2 Cor. 4.6).

Pentecost (Whit Sunday)

Acts 2.1–21† *or* Numbers 11.24–30; Psalm 104.26–36, 37b
[*or* 104.26–end];[1] 1 Corinthians 12.3b–13 *or* Acts 2.1–21†;
John 20.19–23 *or* John 7.37–39

†The reading from Acts must be used as either the first or second reading.

Here I go again, fussing about a Greek translation. At Pentecost, too – when we are celebrating the Holy Spirit breaking down language barriers. But translating is a tough job. No translation conveys its original perfectly. Language concepts rarely overlap completely across the obstacles of time and space. We go on needing the Holy Spirit to enable us to communicate.

Despite that first Pentecost, then, languages can still be barriers. The divisions of Babel are the fallout of the Fall. Without translators, we would have to learn Hebrew and Greek to read the Bible. Our holy writings are open to all, because the Spirit, who inspired the writers, inspires translators too. And the Spirit and the translators alike inspire us. Instead of the Bible being an obstacle, they make it an invitation. So spare a moment to say 'thanks be' for translators this Pentecost.

I still want to say something, though, about the NRSV translation of John 7.38. It is not wrong, but it does remind us of the barriers of word and thought that we need preachers, writers, fellow Christians – as well as newspapers like the *Church Times* – to help us break down, allowing Scripture to speak afresh to every generation. In that verse, we read that rivers of living water will flow out of the believer's 'heart'. But *koilia* does not really mean 'heart'. A closer translation is 'womb'. In John 3.4, for example, *koilia* is the word Nicodemus uses when he speaks to Jesus about being born anew from his mother's womb.

Whenever I feel that my love of language may be distracting from the Gospel message, through the tempting intrusions of linguistic questions, I try to keep in mind an observation of Augustine's, to bring me back to what matters. 'People whose nature is good', he says, 'love the truth in words, not the words themselves'.[2] He was a man who loved words. But he loved the Lord more.

---

1 Psalm 104.26–36, 37b in Common Worship equates to 104.24–34, 35b in BCP and NRSV.
2 Augustine, *Teaching Christianity*, 4.72.

What is the truth in these words, then? It is not as simple as choosing between one bit of anatomy and another. *Koilia* begins as a word for a cavity or hollow, particularly within the human body. The ancient medical writer Galen refers to the upper *koilia* (from neck to waist) and the lower *koilia* (from waist to groin). That shifts the focus from 'hollow' or 'cavity' to 'container'. Now I am reminded of George Orwell's depressing remark in *The Road to Wigan Pier* that a human being 'is primarily a bag for putting food into'.

In a natural shift of language over time, this 'bag' came to refer also to its contents. Thus *koilia* can refer to organs in the body, to intestines, lungs, heart, liver, and the like. 'Innards' has not the emotive power of the word 'heart'. It sounds unappealingly squelchy. This was probably why the translators felt that 'heart' was a better option. But Matthew 15.11 holds me back from agreeing with them. There, Jesus uses two terms in strong contrast to refer to internal organs, saying, 'whatever goes into the mouth enters the stomach (*koilia*), and goes out into the sewer; but what comes out of the mouth proceeds from the heart (*kardia*), and this is what defiles'.

I love words. But I love the truth in words more. So I need to discern what is the truth in Jesus' words. When he refers to 'the believer', he means us. When he speaks of 'rivers of living water', we have to ask what they are, and where they come from. The answer drops into my mind like a mechanism locking into place. Forget hearts, stomachs, chests and wombs. Turn to that deepest meaning of *koilia*. It is a hollow. A cavity. A space.

Without a *koilia*, we are full only of ourselves. There is no room in us for the love of God. This hollow is the place within us that stands open and ready to receive the Spirit of God. Only when we are filled with all the fullness of God (Eph. 3.19) can those living waters flow from us to water a thirsty, gasping world (Ps. 143.6).

I believe with all my heart, stomach, womb, innards and *koilia*, that without the Holy Spirit filling that hollow within me, I am an empty shell. Or just a bag, for putting food into. And rather an old bag at that.

Trinity Sunday

Isaiah 40.12–17, 27–end; Psalm 8; 2 Corinthians 13.11–end;
Matthew 28.16–20

> 'We pray together the grace: The grace of our Lord Jesus Christ, and the love of God, and the fellowship of the Holy Spirit be with us all evermore, Amen.'

The first prayer of all Christians in the Lord's Prayer. The second prayer of Roman Catholic Christians is the angelic salutation (Hail Mary). But the second prayer of this reformed Church of England is surely the Grace.

The Grace ends virtually every church meeting. If I am chairing a college meeting that is nothing to do with chapel, I feel the absence of this closing reminder that, as the politicians like to say, 'We're all in this together'. The Grace is an introductory or concluding formula in acts of worship too. It belongs, in short, to that privileged category of words that define us and what we believe. Like the creeds.

Our prayer books and our Bibles alike are stuffed with words that leave their mark on us. Some of the texts that speak to us most powerfully have their strong effect because (in part) they are spoken as personal: 'I was glad ...'; 'Lord, let me know mine end ...'; 'O that I had wings like a dove'; 'Thou art a place to hide me in.' Such words become part of our individual praying.

The Grace can be such a prayer, for an individual, of course. But it always points towards that greater whole in which we abide together. By its very nature (rather than by habit or common usage), it belongs to the category of the corporate. In other words, to us as the Body of Christ, as the Church.

This is partly a matter of phrasing. When we pray the Grace, we call the Lord Jesus *our* Lord. We also remind ourselves that we are not only individuals but elements in a whole, 'be with *us* all'. Unlike the Blessing that a priest or bishop declares *to* other people, the Grace is shared among us as equal Christian individuals. We ourselves ask for it. Only we ourselves can real-ize it.

This 'grace' is the gift of God the Son, a gift purchased despite the cost. The Father's gift is love, for love fulfils our yearning for relationship. Each person's life touches many others. If we hear of a life that does not, it fills us with pity and sadness. Even those few who withdraw from the world of other people (as hermits) do so in order to pray – for the world and other people.

The characteristic gift of the Holy Spirit makes Trinity Sunday – as much as Pentecost – the birthday of the Church. The Spirit is God our communicator, enabling us to convey feeling, and to be understood. The miraculous language that communicates perfectly, undoing Babel, may begin at Pentecost, but is it completed on Trinity Sunday, when we pray for the Holy Spirit to make us a 'fellowship'.

Centuries ago, older Latin translations of the Bible gave way to Jerome's Vulgate (Common) Bible, like King James and the RSV being superseded by the NRSV. One word that did not change was the word for the gift of the Holy Spirit here in 2 Corinthians 13.13. It remained as *communicatio*. A couple of writers tried out *societas* as an alternative, to emphasize community over communication. But it never caught on.

Communicatio feels right, and is right, because it creates a diagram for us, in the shape of a cross, or the points of a compass. On the horizontal axis, it joins person to person. On the vertical axis, it joins humanity to God. Our hearing of the word, and our receiving of God in sacramental signs, have both a horizontal and a vertical dimension. In both cases, what is created is fellowship through communication. Grace and love, in concert with the Spirit, no longer exist only to themselves. Through God's saving work in Christ, they reach and transform us, binding us to our God, who is Holy and Undivided Trinity.

For all that, both world and Church remain fallen. It is our earthly calling both to accept and to resist our fallenness. Individual churches fall out with one another, just like individuals in a congregation do. But we cannot in good conscience remain divided one from another, for that would be to resist the Spirit, and dishonour the threefold God who calls us to become partakers of the divine nature (2 Peter 1.4).

Proper 3
Sunday between 24 and 28 May inclusive
If this follows Trinity Sunday, Proper 3 is used (see page 32).

Proper 4
Sunday between 29 May and 4 June inclusive
(if after Trinity Sunday)

Continuous: Genesis 6.9–22; 7.24; 8.14–19; Psalm 46; Romans 1.16, 17; 3.22b–28 [29–31]; Matthew 7.21–end
*Related: Deuteronomy 11.18–21, 26–28; Psalm 31.1–5, 19–24 [*or* 31.19–24]; Romans 1.16, 17; 3.22b–28 [29–31]; Matthew 7.21–end

*The reflections that follow for the Sundays after Trinity (Proper 4 to Proper 25) focus on the Related sequence of readings – see page xiii [Preface] for an explanation.

My inspiration for this reflection was a sermon of Charles Spurgeon, the Baptist preacher, who came from Kelvedon, in my home county of Essex. It can be found online here: https://www.spurgeon.org/resource-library/sermons/the-two-builders-and-their-houses/#flipbook/

Jesus closes the Sermon on the Mount, his longest speech in any of the Gospels, with two warnings. The first is simple and direct, while the second is parabolic in form, so that the hearer must tease out its meaning. Both warnings contrast real religion with false, showing that equivalence of appearance is not always matched by an equivalence of nature. Both are free from oratorical flourishes, as if Matthew is showing us that Jesus needs no rhetorical tricks to persuade us that he speaks the truth.

The Baptist minister Charles Spurgeon has been called the 'Prince of Preachers'. Reading his passionate preaching on this Gospel helped me to overcome my aversion to the kind of parables that are too easily reduced to childish moral fables. The parable of the two builders is easy to read in that simplistic way. But Spurgeon, without calling it 'meditation', employs a meditative approach, using imagination to go deep into the message.

Both builders were skilled, he observes, for both were capable of constructing a dwelling. Both built houses, and the Gospel says nothing to suggest that one house was better than the other. The same could not be said, though, of the unseen foundations of the two houses. Spurgeon encourages us to look at the relationship between the builder (who stands for human individuals) and the house, which is what the Bible might call the 'operation', or 'works', of his hands. The first builder looked competent, and was. His house probably looked like the other from the outside. The difference lay within, unseen, where the rock-hewn foundations must have taken sweat (and perhaps blood and tears too) to complete.

The second builder attempted the same external work, a house. But out of view, its foundations were not competently built. We must conclude that the second builder wanted protection and security without having to invest his own blood, or sweat, or tears; and with minimal cost to himself in terms of blistered hands or sore muscles.

As we build, so we shall live. We have a choice whether to build our faith on strong foundations (the Rock who is Christ: 1 Cor. 10.4), or on shifting sands (1 Cor. 3.10–11). And we have just been told that people who cry 'Peace, peace!' are to be castigated for their delusion that they have done enough to keep 'in' with their Maker.

When both houses face the assaults of wind and flood, one fails the test. This directs Jesus' listeners to a vital question: what is this strong foundation upon which our faith must be built? Even within some other books of the New Testament, an answer to this question is beginning to be constructed. Ephesians 2.20 states that the apostles and prophets are the foundation of a building, and that the corner-stone (or keystone) of that same building is Christ. Hebrews 6.1–2 puts forward a list of hallmarks of faith: 'repentance from dead works and faith toward God, instruction about baptisms, laying on of hands, resurrection of the dead, and eternal judgement'.

But when Jesus ended his Sermon on the Mount, he was not yet prepared to explain that the Church would be built on the Rock that is Christ. Though the crowd is amazed because he taught with authority (Matt. 7.29), they have not yet fully understood God's salvific purpose, and plan, in Christ. Not until later in Matthew (21.42) does Jesus refer to the words of Psalm 118.22–3, and to himself as a fulfilment of them: 'The stone that the builders rejected has become the corner-stone; this was the Lord's doing, and it is amazing in our eyes'.

Now a keystone, or corner-stone, is not the same as a foundation stone. One fixes the building to the earth, the other lifts it skyward. But verse 44 reveals that Jesus is in fact both foundation stone and keystone: at least, that is my reading of his remark that 'anyone who falls on this stone will be broken to pieces; and it will crush anyone on whom it falls' (Matt. 21.44). Whether it crushes us by falling from above, or breaks us when we smash upon it, the Rock is Christ. And if we are not prepared to be broken, we cannot be re-formed in his likeness. As Spurgeon puts it: 'Pray earnestly for a broken heart. Remember it is the contrite spirit that God is pleased with.'

Proper 5
Sunday between 5 and 11 June inclusive
(if after Trinity Sunday)

Continuous: Genesis 12.1–9; Psalm 33.1–12; Romans 4.13–end; Matthew 9.9–13, 18–26
Related: Hosea 5.15—6.6; Psalm 50.7–15; Romans 4.13–end; Matthew 9.9–13, 18–26

This is a piecemeal Gospel, fragments of teachings tacked together. A middle section (Matt. 9.14–17), omitted from the lection, makes the patchwork even patchier. This is not the place for a single message.

A puzzle is lurking in the first verse of the passage. Sometimes we have to let such puzzles pass, in quest of a broader or deeper message in the Scripture. But in this case the puzzle is one we might prefer to tackle.

The puzzle is this: Matthew draws on Mark's Gospel, written earlier, for much of his narrative. And sure enough, Mark contains the story of the man, in Capernaum, whom Jesus called 'from the receipt of custom' (AV). But Mark says that the man's name was 'Levi'. Luke too calls him 'Levi' (5.27). That is strong evidence that the original story was about a man called Levi. Yet Matthew changes the name – to 'Matthew'.

One suggestion to explain the change is that 'Matthew' looks like the Greek word for a disciple, *mathetes*. True, that is a word repeated twice in the following verses; but such word play is usually flagged up in Scripture, not left to be discovered by over-imaginative commentators (Mark 3.16–17, for example, or Matt. 16.18).

A simpler explanation is that the writer of the Gospel we know as 'Matthew' changed the name because (a) he knew the name was in fact 'Matthew' and (b) he knew because he himself was that man. It need not be the case, though, that Jesus only ever called one tax-collector. He may have called many, just as he called many sinners of other kinds (9.10–11). Both versions may be true.

If it seems harsh to equate tax collection with sin, we must remember that wages were not the only method of payment for services back then. Those who set tax levels would not factor in payment for people doing the collecting, who were expected to add a percentage to make a living. So official tax levels would always be less than the sums that the collectors charged. No wonder tax-collectors were unpopular.

Matthew may have corrected Mark silently because he was confident that his version was more accurate. If we ask how he could be so sure, we end up in the same place where the early Church did, concluding that Matthew knew the tax-collector was called 'Matthew' because he was that tax-collector. A small puzzle leads to an important question: who is Matthew? Was he an evangelist, or disciple, or tax-collector? Perhaps he was all three.

We can do what Matthew did. We must apply our own experience to the good news and, at the same time, learn to recognize ourselves within it. If we are not the tax-collector, we may instead be the anxious parent or the marginalized woman; or a disciple, or onlooker, or simply a sinner sharing a meal with God's own Son.

That marginalized woman (9.20) has been ritually impure for more than a decade, presumably with a distressing condition called menorrhagia. One of my commentaries refers to her as 'the woman with an issue', which made me laugh. But it was written before the word 'issue' had become such a ubiquitous euphemism for 'problem', so I know I am being unfair.

Sometimes when I read Scripture, my mind detours into thoughts that the writer never intended me to think. That woman's touching of Jesus' clothes triggered thoughts about relics (objects that, some Christians believe, have healing power). Relics come in classes: first-class is a body part of the saint; second-class is an article or item of the saint's; and third-class is something that has been touched to a first or second-class relic.

I possess a third-class relic of Gwenffrewi (Winifred) bought from the shrine shop in Holywell. Do I think it can cure me? No. But do I think that touch matters? And that touching something a holy person has touched will be enough to effect healing? The answer, based on this Gospel, is, at least, 'possibly'. Jesus tells the woman that her faith, not her touching of his hem, has made her well. But she is human, and human beings are embodied creatures who need touch for understanding and belief. Her action (touching his clothes) and her healing (by his holiness, not magic powers or magic words) are the result of pure holiness having its natural effect on embodied humanity.

Proper 6
Sunday between 12 and 18 June inclusive
(if after Trinity Sunday)

Continuous: Genesis 18.1–15 [21.1–7]; Psalm 116.1, 10–17 [*or* 116.9–17]; Romans 5.1–8; Matthew 9.35—10.8 [9–23]
Related: Exodus 19.2–8a; Psalm 100; Romans 5.1–8; Matthew 9.35—10.8 [9–23]

The sending-out of the 12 disciples is like a *Race Across the World* challenge. Tough parameters are set. Instead of doing the 'sensible' thing and packing a change of clothing, some provisions, and all the insurance of stuff ('just in case'), they are not allowed to take any money or baggage. Nor are they permitted to plan ahead. For shelter and rest they must depend on the kindness of strangers ('Look where that got Blanche Dubois', they might have retorted[1]).

Their mission is to the 'lost sheep of the house of Israel'. They probably felt utterly unprepared. If so, anyone who is preparing for ordination this Petertide will sympathize wholeheartedly. Still, 'ready' is one thing; but 'willing' and 'able' matter much more. Following Jesus is a training in itself. It forms us.

Naturally, the disciples did as Jesus commanded them. Not even Judas Iscariot refused. Though they must have found it intimidating, they were impelled and inspired by the Lord's call, and by a force external to themselves, which we now recognize as the Holy Spirit.

The Gospel gives no hint that the disciples tried to negotiate with Jesus about the guidelines he had given them. They did not react like Moses when he tried to wheedle God into letting him off challenging Pharaoh, and leading the children of Israel through the wilderness. After a couple of feeble attempts to talk God out of his choice, Moses gave up on excuses, and instead spoke plainly the fearful reluctance of his heart: 'O my Lord, please send someone else' (Ex. 4.13).

Matthew does not tell us the outcome of that first mission. We have to rely on Jesus' wise judgement of people if we want to affirm here that they 'succeeded'. Despite being commissioned by their Lord, the disciples must have found it a nerve-wracking business. Without any education in public speaking, they had to proclaim good news. Without any medical

---
1 Tennessee Williams, *A Streetcar Named Desire*, 1947.

training, they had to cure the sick. If that were not hard enough, they had to raise the dead as well.

When it came to lepers, they were told to 'cleanse' rather than 'cure' them. This is an interesting distinction. Nowadays we would agree that both elements are necessary to recovery, that physical and mental healing are twin aspects of a single process.

Their last task was the most difficult of all: to do battle against the forces of evil. It is still a vital part of a Christian's duty, even though we do not express it using the language of 'demons'. It is good to reflect even for a moment on that aspect of our faith, for as Paul reminds us elsewhere (Eph. 6.11–12), there is more to life than the earthbound struggles of our physical existence.

The sending-out of the 12 disciples is like a dry run for the aftermath of Pentecost, when they knew, without having it explained in detail (Matt. 28.19–20), what they had to do for Jesus – because they had done it before. For this first apostolate ('sending-out'), the mission field would be restricted to the house of Israel (Matt. 10.5–6). Later, all the nations would become God's 'treasured possession', a 'priestly kingdom and a holy nation' (Ex. 19.6).

When Paul wrote to the Roman Christians, he too gave them clear guidelines (for organizing their church life), but not a comprehensive legal code that might encourage pharisaic scrupulosity. As Captain Barbossa says in *Pirates of the Caribbean*, 'The [pirate] code is more what you'd call *guidelines* than actual *rules*'. Flexibility matters amid the 'changes and chances of this fleeting world'.

Those guidelines suggest a method for responding to the challenges Christians would go on to face in the future. Paul explains in Romans 5.3–5 how each setback can feed in to future strength; and each increase in goodness can make the next setback something to learn from instead of being crushed by it.

This way of ordering common life is like a Bible equivalent of the unwritten constitution or the common law. We learn what is right through making choices, then reflecting upon them as a way of guiding future choices. We take action, or refrain from it, because we have learned from past action or self-restraint. Learning from, and building on, the past: this is how the Christian present grows in resilience, and this is how a Christian future is built.

Proper 7
Sunday between 19 and 25 June inclusive
(if after Trinity Sunday)

Continuous: Genesis 21.8–21; Psalm 86.1–10, 16–end [*or* 86.1–10]; Romans 6.1b–11; Matthew 10.24–39
Related: Jeremiah 20.7–13; Psalm 69.8–11 [12–17] 18–20 [*or* 69.14–20]; Romans 6.1b–11; Matthew 10.24–39

It is quite a while since I was a parish priest. But some things you never forget. Today's Gospel is one of them. The preacher that long-ago morning was Joan, then an ordinand, now a parish priest herself in this diocese of Ely. From the Gospel, she chose these words as her theme (Matt. 10.24–25): 'A disciple is not above the teacher, nor a slave above the master; it is enough for the disciple to be like the teacher, and the slave like the master.'

Why, out of all the sermons I have heard, that is one of the few that clings on tenaciously in my memory, I cannot say. But it does. I often remember preachers and the impact they had; their words have their effect, but in a different way. That morning, Joan's sermon helped this Gospel to 'speak' to me, as we Christians like to say. It was a revelation of divine love. I am still reflecting on it all these years later.

'It is enough for the disciple to be like the teacher.' The biggest impact came from the least significant words: 'It is enough'. Over time it has reduced further, like a simmering stovetop sauce: 'enough'.

'Enough' is one of those strange words that can mean very different things depending on the tone of voice used. It can indicate gross surfeit. Or it can sound the way I hear it here: reassurance. It tells me that there is no need for anxiety, striving, stress; that the work of a disciple (a pupil, in other words) is to find a point of similarity with the teacher. That is enough.

Jesus has not always been made known to seekers as a Good Teacher. Some people are introduced to him as a Judge, treading out the grapes in the great winepress of the wrath of God (Rev. 14.19; with Isa. 63.2). Then the hope of patience and gentleness can be swallowed in a storm of almighty fury. The message that we should fear him has been heard loud and clear down the years. There are still churches aplenty preaching it.

Against this, Matthew 10.24 is a whispered reassurance cutting through our self-doubt. Enough, it says; no more of fear and fury. It is enough for the disciple to be like the teacher. Not exactly alike, mind. We must not replace one guilty fear with another, interrogating ourselves constantly, 'Am I enough like the teacher?' All we have to do is find within ourselves that point of contact, a glimpse of likeness, catching the sound of that 'gentle voice calling' (echoes of another Welsh hymn, this time my grandmother's favourite – *Mi glywaf dyner lais*).

Jesus reinforces the word 'enough' by telling us to have no fear (10.26). We will always have reasonable reasons to be afraid. Serving Jesus will not insulate us against them, not even irrational or obsessive ones. The promise he makes is simply that we cannot be parted from our heavenly Father (10.29–31). Now 'enough' turns out to mean that what we have, and what we do, cannot set us apart from God, simply because of what we are. We are his children.

In the New Testament reading, Paul is warming up for that glorious paean of confidence in God (in Rom. 8.31–39), which makes the same point. Augustine once did a Bible study on that passage as a way of showing how God inspired the apostle (to Augustine, Paul is always 'the' apostle) to deliver his teaching with every power of persuasive speech at his command. The end of Romans 8 often brings solace and hope to Christians at funeral services; but it is today's passage from Romans 6 that touches those who have yet to hear the call of the Teacher's gentle voice. They hear it mediated through a poem of Dylan Thomas, that flawed, fabulous wordsmith, repeating over and over, 'And death shall have no more dominion' (Rom. 6.9). There it is, in the Good Book, in 'Bible-black' (and white).

'Have no fear', 'Do not fear', 'Do not be afraid', says Jesus. Where else can we find a clearer reassurance for the besetting pain of our humanity? I am glad to have found a Teacher who knows how to teach me, by example; and who is patient, and corrects me with love. Of course I want to be like him. Of course that is enough.

Proper 8
Sunday between 26 June and 2 July inclusive

Continuous: Genesis 22.1–14; Psalm 13; Romans 6.12–end; Matthew 10.40–end
Related: Jeremiah 28.5–9; Psalm 89.1–4, 15–18 [*or* 89.8–18]; Romans 6.12–end; Matthew 10.40–end

Most weeks I try to spread my observations across the readings, with an emphasis on the Gospel because everyone always hears it. But sometimes a verse is so challenging that it dominates completely. Romans 6.22 is one of those verses.

It reminds me of special offers: 'Buy life insurance and get a free pen'. You want one thing, but buy it because of another, because it is FREE. In this case, we choose to be liberated from sin. Then what? Surely some freebie is on offer too – a complimentary dove, perhaps, on our next visit to the temple. While stocks last.

We are guaranteed the thing we really want – 'freedom from sin'. But with it comes something we think we could do without – 'enslavement to God'. True, the enslavement has sanctification thrown in. Perhaps we shall become so holy that we will not mind being 'enslaved'.

I am not qualified to say how this verse is read by people today in whose lives the slave trade casts its shadow. Nor am I certain how it sounded to his original recipients. But I think most of us would rather not be enslaved. Enslavement in any language, in any time, means that we do not belong to ourselves. Whereas the autonomy of the individual has emerged in our history as a triumphant ideal, a goal for all right-thinking people.

Whether we find the language distasteful, and whether we accept this teaching or not, slaves is what we are, according to Paul. I do not feel entitled to disagree with him. Not until I have turned the idea inside out and striven for a way of making sense of it, rather than dismissing it out of hand.

In Bible days, slavery was just the way things were. Earlier in his ministry, Paul had written to Christians, 'you are not your own; for you were bought with a price' (1 Cor. 6.19–20). Put like that, it does not sound so, well, *slavish*. It makes us feel valuable, even precious. But that still may not be enough to detoxify the concept.

Two things suggest to me that Paul is right. One is that he was honest about inequalities in society; more, surely, than we are. The other is that his frankness about the nature of human existence is reassuring. All our life long, constraints of human obligation tie us to work we may not enjoy, people we sometimes find annoying, situations from which only money can liberate us (and sometimes not even money is enough). Just because our bonds are invisible does not mean they are not bonds. The more I hear the language of human autonomy and freedom, the more I become sensitized to what appears to be an ideal/reality gap.

Being God's slave cannot be attractive, admittedly, unless we accept that he is a just and kindly lord (though that still may not be enough to render it palatable). We did not choose to be born or to exist. We cannot feed, shelter or clothe ourselves apart from him (Luke 12.24). No, we are not our own, for he bought us. We belong to him.

I no more wish to be free of this bond-service to God than I wish to shrug off the ties that bind me to my family, my workplace, my many Christian brothers and sisters. None of this feels to me like a burden. I embrace it gladly, as the opposite of an enslavement, for I believe from experience that 'his service is perfect freedom'. I also trust in Paul's visionary promise of the 'glorious liberty of the children of God' (Rom. 8.21).

So are we lowly slaves, or beloved children? There is nothing divine about religious quietism, or robotic obedience. But however ingrained our love of liberty and autonomy, there are places where those hard-won blessings for human society do not reach.

Unless we are so allergic to hierarchy that we refuse to acknowledge our smallness in the face of almighty God, we have to admit that, unlike our earthly fathers and our priestly fathers, our heavenly Father always knows best. When Paul wrote of our enslavement to God, he did not negate the 'glorious liberty' that emerges from that enslavement. He 'enslaves' his body too (1 Cor. 9.27), but his body *is* him. He chooses this path. Not all service is servitude.

Proper 9
Sunday between 3 and 9 July inclusive

Continuous: Genesis 24.34–38, 42–49, 58–67; Psalm 45.10–17
or Canticle: Song of Solomon 2.8–13; Romans 7.15–25a;
Matthew 11.16–19, 25–end
Related: Zechariah 9.9–12; Psalm 145.8–15; Romans 7.15–25a;
Matthew 11.16–19, 25–end

I sometimes quote Matthew 11.30 to people who are exploring faith. 'His yoke is easy,' I tell them. 'His burden is light.' The point is that it may be human nature to make religion a complicated business of shared but secret knowledge accessible to the few, but true faith is about openness, simplicity. We should not feel weighed down by spiritual complexities. If our faith is burdensome, we cannot be fully trusting what it promises.

Some outside the faith might say that Paul has corrupted Jesus' 'easy yoke' and 'light burden', supposedly turning a 'good man Jesus' into a 'scoundrel Christ'. His words in Romans 6 will weigh on us differently depending on our individual experiences of faith, on how far we recognize ourselves in his theological tussling.

I take Romans 7.23 as pinpointing our need for liberation from the temptation of the 'purity spiral', a kind of moral arms race, in which different sectors within a group disagree over ideology, trying to outdo each other in scrupulosity and freedom from the taint of ideological error.

Obsessive effort will not, cannot, bring us closer to God. Those of us who are tempted by sanctimonious one-up-person-ship in our faith can also recognize ourselves in Paul's passionate outburst, his entangled desire and devotion. So we repent, and look instead for his 'more excellent way'.

Saying this much, though, is the beginning, not the end, of a longer exploration. For there is no denying that faith can feel onerous at times. We do not need to add another item to our long list of failures in faith by not being positive enough, by not being sufficiently holy to find the life of faith 'easy' or 'light'. The yoke is still a yoke. The burden is still a burden.

Looking for guidance from the Gospel, but finding it rather disjointed, I consulted a commentary and read a statement on Matthew 11.18–19 that cheered me up: 'Jesus seems to have had a habit of taking up his opponents' accusations and doing something positive with them.' Being a Christian suggests certain standards of behaviour and attitude: if we are accused of mingling with sinners, it is understandable to want to reply,

'Me? Never! I am pure in word, deed, association, and belief!' Thus the purity spiral starts to spin, as we lay ourselves open to scrutiny, imperfect beings inviting upon ourselves judgement by impossibly perfect criteria. Downfall and disgrace become inevitable. Recent examples of this in our public life, in politics and the media, are not difficult to find.

Jesus goes another way. He highlights the inconsistency of those who attack him and his kinsman, and at the same time refuses to offer any self-justification. This leaves his critics nowhere to go with their inquisition. Later in the Gospel, he will make his preference for sinners over the self-righteous even plainer (Matt. 21.31).

His concluding comment about wisdom being vindicated (11.19) comes in two equally puzzling versions: 'by her children' or 'by her deeds' ('wisdom' is grammatically feminine in both Hebrew and Greek). Both seem to be ways of saying what he teaches elsewhere (7.16): that we should judge people by the fruits of their actions. Some say that 'wisdom' is his way of referring to himself. But that cannot be entirely right, for what he says must apply both to himself and to John Baptist.

The Gospel passage focuses on the positive. It leaves out the 'woes' that Jesus pronounces like an Old Testament prophet (11.20–24). Instead it hurries on to thanksgivings (11.25–26); and to a statement about the relationship of Father and Son that is evocative of John's Gospel (11.27; also Luke 10.22). Any one of the disparate themes in this passage would repay further meditation. What draws them all together is Jesus himself, challenging illogical hostility, denouncing hard-hearted refusals to recognize God's acts of power, and laying claim to his unique relationship with the Father.

Matthew 11.28 is the antidote to purity spirals. 'Come to me, all you who are weary and are carrying heavy burdens, and I will give you rest.' That text is written, in Greek, above the altar in the chapel of Caius College, Cambridge, where I say my prayers day by day. But there is a tiny mistake in the Greek. I see this error as a *felix culpa* ('happy fault', a reference to the Fall). I like to think it embodies the truth that no Christian need fear falling short of perfection.

Proper 10
Sunday between 10 and 16 July inclusive

Continuous: Genesis 25.19–end; Psalm 119.105–112;
Romans 8.1–11; Matthew 13.1–9, 18–23
Related: Isaiah 55.10–13; Psalm 65.[1–7] 8–13; Romans 8.1–11;
Matthew 13.1–9, 18–23

Not every seed comes to fruition. The parable of the sower provides three possible places to lay the blame: the sower, the seed and the soil. We cannot blame the Lord, the sower. Nor can we blame the seed, which is the word of God; for it comes from God, and is distributed by God. The seed, after all, wants to grow. Growth is its nature.

The fault must be in the soil. And that means us, for whatever is falling short and failing always does stand for us. If the seed that is the word of God fails to grow, the fault lies not with that seed but with the soil into which it falls.

It is easy to answer that we are the problem. That is the default setting in Scripture. At this stage in Matthew's Gospel, though, before the Passion has changed our understanding of human sin and redemption for ever, we have to look back into the past to understand the ways in which humankind has been going wrong.

The Isaiah passage sings a positive message about the word of God. That word has gone out, and it is bearing fruit. All creation is celebrating along with human beings. Hills and mountains are singing. The trees of the field are clapping their hands. Lyrical visions of this kind (see Ps. 98.7–8) make it easy to see how one might come to imagine creation as a dance, in which mortals join in with everything else that God has made and called 'good'.

But there are passages in Isaiah, and the other prophets, that are anything but cheerful. In them, human hardness of heart, and contempt for God's word and commandment, repeatedly provoke God, and lead to suffering and disaster.

In the epistle reading, Paul holds these two extremes in tension: the singing hills and dancing trees, and the shadow side of creation. Flesh and Spirit, death and life: where do we fit in? What Paul is attempting feels like a task beyond the normal capacities of words to express our thoughts and feelings. If the letter to the Romans were as long as Genesis or Isaiah, it could hardly explain the tangle of principle and promiscuity, generosity and greed, decency and dishonesty, that makes up the interior being of every single one of us.

The key to hope and salvation is in that point I just made about the tangle of competing desires within us. Not because I have cleverly spotted something that escaped Isaiah, Paul and Matthew; but simply because I can write intelligible English using the first person plural. In other words, I can meaningfully say 'we' and 'us'; I am not confined within the boundaries of my own existence, stuck with always saying 'I', and 'me', and 'my'.

We have the capacity to imagine being one another, to act for the good of others as well as ourselves; and to feel compassion, not just relief or *Schadenfreude* ('malicious glee') for the sufferings of others. Paul could not make it clearer that everything that makes us who we want to be comes from God, from the Sower sowing good seed in us.

If we are soil, I want to know what soil is. Checking the Greek I find the word *'ge'* (from which we get 'ge-ology', 'ge-ography', etc.). It means 'earth'. That sets off scriptural resonances in my mind. If we want to understand how we are 'soil', we need to go right back to the beginning, and to grasp the fundamental lesson of Genesis: 'you are soil (*ge*), and to soil (*ge*) you shall return' (Gen. 3.19, Greek translation).

That statement puts it beyond doubt that the 'soil', or 'earth', or 'dust' is us. Rather than labelling ourselves 'good' or 'bad', we receive permission to think of ourselves as being in the wrong place (Matt. 13.5), or compacted and pressed down by countless travelling feet until we become rock-like, impenetrable (13.4). Then again, the seed may prosper in us, but so may other attractions – or rather distractions (13.7).

So the meaning of Jesus' parable of the sower is rooted in Genesis 3. Somewhere in these readings are clues as to why many (not all) are called, and few (not many) are chosen (Matt. 22.14). But for now we must be patient, and simply help each seed that comes our way to grow in us.

Proper 11
Sunday between 17 and 23 July inclusive

Continuous: Genesis 28.10–19a; Psalm 139.1–11, 23, 24
[*or* 139.1–11]; Romans 8.12–25; Matthew 13.24–30, 36–43
Related: Wisdom of Solomon 12.13, 16–19 *or* Isaiah 44.6–8;
Psalm 86.11–17; Romans 8.12–25; Matthew 13.24–30, 36–43

Not many Gospel passages in the Principal Service Lectionary have sequels. But here is 'Parable of the Sower II', 'The Enemy Strikes Back!' Last Sunday we heard how the Sower sowed seed that was good, and saw how it prospered or failed. This time, the focus is not on positive potential but on negative threat.

I wish verse 35 had not been cut. It says: 'Jesus told the crowds all these things in parables'. But if you then check the source Matthew is using (Mark 4.33), you find a slight but telling difference: 'With many such parables he spoke the word to them, *as they were able to hear it*'.

Matthew drops that little phrase because he wants to present Jesus' disciples as being in-the-know insiders, in contrast to the multitude who were still mystified by the parables. It is a small indication of how the retelling of the oral tradition about Jesus works, smoothing and streamlining the message as the first Christians went about doing what I am doing as I write this, and you are doing as you read it: namely, making sense of what Jesus Christ has to tell us.

The parable of the weeds and the Enemy is not as popular as the parable of the Sower. That suggests what we mostly intuit, that the gospel, to be fruitful, needs to be positive. We need to be *for* Jesus, not just against 'not-Jesus'. True, the Sower makes a great Sunday School theme. But I suspect that the Enemy would too: I can imagine children booing and hissing as they hear of the baddie sneaking about trying to undo all God's good work.

If this Gospel were read for Advent, it would be easier to unfold, for we could explore it in terms of the end-time, which is traditional in that season. But here, well into green time, the message reads slightly differently. Like Jesus himself, the Church gives us the good news first (the Sower, Trinity 6) and the bad news afterwards (the Enemy, Trinity 7). Jesus starts with what is positive ('Other seeds fell on good soil and brought forth grain, some a hundredfold, some sixty, some thirty'; Matt. 13.8). Then he tells us a *City of God*-style take on the parable: in this life, good and bad grow together, so no earthly institution, not even the

Church, can perfectly embody God's holy rule. Matthew wrote this part of the Gospel with one eye on fledgling churches under strain. He showed how Jesus was encouraging them to wait and keep the faith, because a time of vindication was coming.

The Gospel seems to envisage a separation of good people from evil people, a teaching that is even clearer in Matthew 25.31–46. There is a place of fire and punishment to which the wicked will be consigned, while the faithful and good take their places in the kingdom of heaven.

That is a straightforward interpretation of the passage, and Christians have taken comfort from it over the centuries, understandably so, for vindication is one of the sweetest emotional pleasures of this life. What a pity, then, that it is so often yoked to gloating. Micah 7.10 is a great example: 'My enemy will see, and shame will cover her who said to me, "Where is the LORD your God?" My eyes will gloat over her; now she will be trodden down like the mire of the streets.' It is as if all the positivity in the hundredfold fruitfulness of the good seed has shrivelled up into that creepiest of Christian sins, holier-than-thou-ness.

To those first Christians, this parable was a promise that they would be vindicated in time, even though it might seem as if their enemies were triumphing in the present. But who are our enemies here and now, in this land? Even if we can identify them – secularism, scepticism, atheism, media misrepresentation – I doubt that we want to see their perpetrators tormented for eternity. But we have enemies that are much more dangerous, because they are insidious. Inside of us.

Our inner enemies, our 'demons' we might say (consciously or unconsciously echoing Gospel language) are real enough. They damage us; they diminish us. There is a long list: idolatry, pride and selfishness are only the beginning. Against such enemies as these, the battle (in this life at least) is never done.

Proper 12
Sunday between 24 and 30 July inclusive

Continuous: Genesis 29.15–28; Psalm 105.1–11, 45b [*or* 105.1–11] *or* Psalm 128; Romans 8.26–end; Matthew 13.31–33, 44–52
Related: 1 Kings 3.5–12; Psalm 119.129–136; Romans 8.26–end; Matthew 13.31–33, 44–52

Five parables tell us what the kingdom of heaven is like: namely a seed, yeast, treasure, a merchant and a net. One person and four things. The seed is something insignificant that contains within itself boundless potential. For itself, it grows. For other living things, it provides shelter. As a sign of the kingdom, it is relatively straightforward.

Yeast (the old term for it is 'leaven') is more tricky. I have been reading a book by Augustine about how to study the Bible. He takes yeast as an example, to show how some Scripture verses need us to look at the context to interpret them correctly. In one way, the yeast is like the seed. It looks insignificant, but it has a life-enhancing effect even though it works imperceptibly.

Yet yeast is not always a sign of the kingdom. Elsewhere Jesus warns, 'beware of the yeast of the Pharisees and Sadducees' (Matt. 16.6). Paul uses yeast with a negative meaning too: 'Clean out the old yeast so that you may be a new batch, as you really are unleavened' (1 Cor. 5.7–8).

Yeast itself is neither good nor bad. Good yeast, like the kingdom, has power to be a blessing. Bad yeast also has transformative power, but it is corrupted and corrupting. To understand the meaning of yeast when it is used in the Bible to signify something, we have to think about bread-making and about human nature.

Augustine encourages us to look at different examples of a sign to help explain the one that is puzzling us. But it is not always straightforward. Here, seeing 'treasure' as a sign of God's kingdom can be difficult when other Bible texts deny that wealth is a sign of God's favour. Paul and Peter even refer to wealth as 'filthy lucre' (1 Tim. 3.3, 8; 1 Peter 5.2, AV).

In deciding what the treasure means, it helps to know about coin hoards in archaeology. In Bible times, or any times when war and danger threatened, people used to bury their money and other valuables in the ground. If the danger passed, they would come back for it. The more coin hoards archaeologists discover, the fewer people have survived a time of war or unrest in earlier years, and been able to return and recover their treasure.

In this parable, one person finds treasure that another person has hidden. Now we need to recall and compare the parable of the talents (Matt. 25.14–30). In that case, burying money is not the right answer. In the parable of the treasure, the person who discovers the abandoned hoard reburies it so he can go and secure ownership of it. The parable of the talents shows us what to do with money that we have not earned: for its original owner never benefited from it, and it was enjoyed instead by a stranger. The parable does not say what happened to the treasure next. But I hope that it was shared and put to good use.

The last two signs of the kingdom are the merchant and the net. The merchant is searching for 'fine pearls', plural. But he finds a single pearl, infinitely greater than the rest. All else is worthless in comparison. The meaning of the sign is a lesson about where value lies: not in quantity but in quality, and not in finding but in searching (Matt. 7.7). We need to seek out what we value, rather than sitting back and waiting for it to come to us.

Finally, the net. We need to picture a dragnet between two boats, catching everything in its way, good and bad alike. The kingdom draws us all. So usurping the angels' duty by dividing people into 'good' and 'bad' is something Christians should have no truck with.

Matthew 13 pictures seven parables spoken on a single occasion. They begin with human individuals as passive (being 'sown'). They end with us having choice and agency in our lives. When judgement brings the parabolic revelation to a close, Jesus asks the disciples if they understand. 'Yes', they blithely reply. Perhaps they do. But I think of parables as being more like 'anti-puzzles'. The more I look at a sudoku or crossword puzzle, the likelier I am to 'see' the solution. But the more I look at Jesus' parables, the deeper they take me into divine mystery.

Proper 13
Sunday between 31 July and 6 August inclusive

Continuous: Genesis 32.22–31; Psalm 17.1–7, 16 [*or* 17.1–7]; Romans 9.1–5; Matthew 14.13–21
Related: Isaiah 55.1–5; Psalm 145.[8–9] 15–22; Romans 9.1–5; Matthew 14.13–21

Jesus did many miracles during his ministry. The first Christians preserved them for future generations, for us. Their message is multi-faceted. Some are manifestations of his power, like walking on water and calming a storm (Matt. 14). Some are healings (the largest category) and exorcisms (casting out evil spirits that were thought to be responsible for some illnesses, mental or physical).

The feeding of the 5,000 stands apart because it is a 'corporate' miracle. The turning of water into wine at the wedding in Cana is another example (John 2). Effecting a miraculous change in an individual is one thing. Effecting such a change in a large crowd strikes us as much harder. Perhaps that is because we think of Jesus' power as a form of supernatural electricity: a measurable quantity of power has a measurable effect and scope. In other words, that power is still limited by its own nature in what it can do and how far it can reach.

There is a second reason why the feeding of the 5,000 stands apart. Think of the parable of the sower: that has a special significance because it is preserved along with a piece of secondary teaching. In other words, both the parable and the explanation of its meaning for the first Christians have been preserved in the Gospel text (Matt. 13).

By the way he has written it up, Matthew gives us his 'take' – to see the miraculous feeding in eucharistic terms – for it teems with resonances of the Last Supper. To us, this fact may be obscured because the meal consisted of bread and fish, not bread and wine. But in the early Church, the scope of what we call the Eucharist was less tightly defined. So there was a lot of variation in what the holy meal might include. Milk, cheese, honey and oil might be laid upon the altar. This was before Church councils had made rulings to define a distinction between food-offerings in general and the bread and wine of the Eucharist in particular (Matt. 26).

The word echoes between this miracle and Matthew's version of the Last Supper (26.20–29) are numerous: 'when it was evening'; 'taking bread'; 'he blessed'; 'he gave to the disciples'; 'eat'/'they ate'; 'all'. We could explain that these echoes simply reflect typical Jewish practices associated with food rituals in those times. But still the eucharistic impression persists. It is not only about parallels in what Matthew has said. It is also a matter of what he has chosen not to say, what he has left out. The question we need to ask is, 'what happened to the fish?'

Those fish matter, and not just because of the thoughtlessness of whoever brought a smelly fish-supper along with them, like a commuter on a packed train scoffing a tuna and sweetcorn baguette or an egg-and-cress sandwich. They matter because Matthew has made them disappear.

According to his version, Jesus 'took' both loaves and fish, but he 'blessed and broke' the loaves only. Possibly (the Greek does not make it any clearer than the English) it was bread alone that was shared among the 5,000; and bread alone that filled the 12 baskets. Matthew's main source for the miracle is Mark 6, but he has edited Mark's version, to make the eucharistic parallel stand out: Mark 6.21, for example, refers to the sharing out of the fish, but Matthew has cut that detail.

This does not mean that the fish do not matter at all. Bread and fish together are signs of the messianic feast that Jewish texts refer to with anticipation. We find traces of the feast theme in the New Testament too (Rev. 19.7–9), and in Matthew's Gospel (Chapters 22, 25). And, as most Christians know, the fish was an early Christian symbol, because the Greek word for fish formed an acronym for Christ: ICHTHYS (Jesus Christ, Son of God, Saviour).

A second-century African Christian called Tertullian looked to a miracle of the prophet Elisha (2 Kings 4.42–4), to help him make sense of this one. John's Gospel takes it as confirmation that Jesus was a prophet (6.15). Matthew, though, keeps his focus eucharistic: to confirm that the Lord's nurture of his people is something Christians do not merely commemorate, but also participate in. Sharing broken bread means sharing in Christ's sacrificial and salvific brokenness.

Proper 14
Sunday between 7 and 13 August inclusive

Related: Genesis 37.1–4, 12–28; Psalm 105.1–6, 16–22, 45b [*or* 105.1–10]; Romans 10.5–15; Matthew 14.22–33
Related: 1 Kings 19.9–18; Psalm 85.8–13; Romans 10.5–15; Matthew 14.22–33

One day I am in church, singing, 'Take my feet and let them be/Swift and beautiful for thee'. The next day I read Paul quoting Isaiah, 'How beautiful are the feet of those who bring good news!'

Feet are rarely anyone's best feature. Most of the year we hide them from view, neglecting them unless they become too painful to ignore. But on Good Friday, we kiss the feet of Christ crucified, as a token of our love. In this way we show that, though we cannot equal his abasement, we are willing to imitate it. By kneeling and kissing his feet, we real-ize our participation in his sacrifice. That is one reason to take feet seriously.

The enemy of wholeness, of body and mind alike, is compartment-alization. It can be a line of emotional defence. If trauma threatens to overwhelm us, we lock it away it in our mind, until we feel ready to tackle it. But we are not jigsaw-puzzle selves, not isolated elements click-ing together to form a flat image that looks complete but lacks structural integrity. We are three-dimensional, embodied: each element of us en-meshed with all the rest, each part of us capable of standing for us-as-a-whole (1 Cor. 12.14–26). Thus, every bit of us has the capacity to image the whole of us as made in the divine likeness.

I have pinched a grammatical term to challenge the compartmental-ization, or fragmentation, or dis-integration of the self: 'synecdoche'. It means 'understanding one thing with another'. Calling a car 'a motor' or 'wheels' is synecdoche. Paul referring to 'flesh and blood', when he means human beings (Eph. 6.12), is synecdoche too.

In Romans 10.15, beautiful feet are a synecdoche, encapsulating messengers in all their eager haste. Or we could think of God's 'hand', a synecdoche for his mighty power, for we find it easier to understand something that is concrete, rather than abstract.

Hands stand for power, and feet for haste. God's 'name' is yet another synecdoche. It stands for God's own being; that appellation by which he is uniquely known encapsulates his nature, his person. We often say that knowing a name gives us power over the one named. But we can also find that the name encapsulates the unbroken wholeness of another being: not click-together pieces, but the integrated self.

Jesus' feet do what ours do. They walk. But in this Gospel, they transfigure the ordinary laws of nature, by walking on the sea. If they are a synecdoche here, giving us, in one part of the self, an idea of the whole, they are telling us that when we are suffused with grace as he was, we too shall transcend our mortal limitations. Indeed, Peter proves as much, for when he asks to be commanded, so that he may walk on water as Jesus does, he begins by succeeding.

We should not rush to find the message of this Gospel only in Jesus' power contrasted with Peter's wavering faith. Peter showed both faith and lack of faith, and we are no different. We flit between the worlds of grace and condemnation, faith and frailty. The very fact that – even for a few moments – his feet found purchase on the restless waves is 'filled with messages' of hope, of faith in what we one day shall become.

God has many messengers, many ways of bringing us 'good news'. Paul is thinking of preachers and apostles like himself, travelling from place to place and telling the story of the Resurrection, and all that flows from it. We can probably think of clergy and other ministers who have done the same for us, bringing us to faith, encouraging us to persist in it, calling us back when we strayed.

But being God's 'swift and beautiful' messenger starts long before this. It comes first in the wordless language of a loving look, a smiling delight upon the faces of those who tend us in our infancy. It comes in the prayers we hear spoken over us with anxious care, and which we naturally learn to imitate. It comes in all who show us by example (not just by teaching) what true love and faith look like, and who make us want to be like them. Each good person of faith is, in their own way, God's synecdoche.

Proper 15
Sunday between 14 and 20 August inclusive

Continuous: Genesis 45.1–15; Psalm 133; Romans 11.1–2a, 29–32; Matthew 15.[10–20] 21–28
Related: Isaiah 56.1, 6–8; Psalm 67; Romans 11.1–2a, 29–32; Matthew 15.[10–20] 21–28

Principal Service readings from the Old Testament/Hebrew Bible are snapshots of a whole. Sometimes that means we lose something of the full message. Isaiah 56.1, 6–8 proclaims that God's welcome and protection are for everyone, not just for the children of Israel. Verses 2–5 make the same proclamation, but have been left out because they use the example of 'eunuchs' instead of foreigners.

There was a time when the Church interpreted the Mosaic law as meaning that persons with physical disabilities could not become priests. Deuteronomy 23.1 specifically mentions eunuchs: 'No one whose testicles are crushed or whose penis is cut off shall be admitted to the assembly of the LORD'. I have heard it argued that while the commandments of the 'moral law' remain binding upon Christians, those of the 'ritual law' are not. But just as our rituals need to have a moral component (being rooted in ethical principle), so too our morals need to have a ritual one (being rooted in habitual rather than occasional behaviour). That distinction is not biblical. Such teachings still matter.

Isaiah 56.1–8 taken as a whole reveals that human categories are not God's categories. Anyone once considered defective because their race does not conform to an approved human category has been declared welcome by God himself, speaking through the prophet. Now the same is true of those whose bodies are not conformed to human versions of a norm.

'The Law and the Prophets' is a phrase summarizing what God gives us by revelation, expressing his will. When we find law and prophet apparently at odds, as here, it is unwise to jump to the conclusion that one trumps the other. Instead, we need to consider the situations that they were addressing.

Isaiah 56 expands the category of 'the chosen' by thinking inclusively. We can do the same with Paul's teaching in Romans 11. Start with what is positive: God has welcomed gentiles within the covenant (before this lection). What is the next step, asks Paul? Is it a case of 'either Jews or gentiles', or 'both Jews and gentiles'? Once we accept that the gentiles are within the covenant, must we conclude that the Jewish people are now outside it? Paul's firm answer to this is 'no'. God is a 'both/and' God, not an 'either/or' God.

What enables Paul to take this incredible step forward for faith history is a God-breathed revelation that inclusion is better than exclusion, and that affirmation is better than condemnation.

If God's purposes do not, cannot, alter, there are two logical options for explaining such apparent changes of attitude. Either the past could be wrong (difficult), or an earlier understanding needs to be reprocessed by rediscovering (or reframing, or rebalancing) how the earlier teaching had previously been understood.

In the Gospel, a nameless Canaanite woman becomes a hero: to her people for not accepting that God values them less; to her daughter, whose life she saves through confronting a man so powerful that he can cast out demons; and to all Christians in every era (though perhaps women, as the supposedly 'second', 'weaker', sex, have a special claim on her) who have known themselves to be despised and rejected by the keepers of earthly versions of the heavenly kingdom. Perhaps God even chose her to show the full humanity of Jesus through her challenging him to change his mind.

If Christianity went on to persecute Jews, it was not the fault of Paul, still less Jesus. If it went on to reject minorities like those with disabilities, or to exclude foreigners, it was not the fault of Isaiah. All three proclaimed the messages God gave them. And in each case, human beings picked the bits of the message that they found palatable and sidelined the rest.

Our having only a partial vision and understanding is not wrong but inescapable. How can we mortals be anything else? The Church has lasted for millennia, the faith for even longer, while each of us that is born of a woman has so short a time to live that we deserve much more pity than we do blame. The partial nature of our vision of God is not wholly culpable, because it is not wholly avoidable. Perhaps the most important way for us to absorb the message of these readings is not to be hasty in judgement (Prov. 25.8).

Proper 16
Sunday between 21 and 27 August inclusive

Continuous: Exodus 1.8—2.10; Psalm 124; Romans 12.1–8; Matthew 16.13–20
Related: Isaiah 51.1–6; Psalm 138; Romans 12.1–8; Matthew 16.13–20

'Caesarea Philippi' is Christian shorthand for the moment when humanity recognized Jesus as the Messiah, the Christ. That visionary moment, though, is not straightforward. But we can ask Paul to help us make sense of it.

In Romans 12.2, Paul refers to God's 'perfect' will. He does not mean that God's will is 'perfect' in the sense of 'flawless' (though doubtless it is). He means that it is 'integrous', that it has a wholeness about it, a sense of purpose fulfilled, of will completed.

I have not invented 'integrous'. The Oxford English Dictionary records a single seventeenth-century example of it, an adjective to go with the familiar noun, 'integrity'. But Christian theology and devotion could both find space for a word so redolent of the Christian ideal, as we shall see.

As a preliminary to discerning God's will, Paul urges us not to be *con*formed but *trans*formed; and this transformation is a process as well as an event. Nowadays, when someone becomes a Christian, we refer to 'initiation' (from the Latin, *initium*, meaning 'beginning'). This beginning gets the lifelong process of transformation moving. Our inner reality may change to having an integrous quality 'in a moment, in the twinkling of an eye' (1 Cor. 15.52). But for our outer selves – those beings of flesh and blood that are flowers of the field one moment and fuel for the oven the next – a lifetime is not enough to achieve integrity, and all of us end our earthly lives still on the journey.

So we must not be deterred by the language of perfection. It is not there to remind us how unworthy we are of God's grace (*charis*) and gifts (*charismata*: Rom. 12.6). It is there to show that there is meaning and direction in our lives.

When Simon declares what he believes about Jesus, he does so because Jesus specifically asks him to. He does not recognize him as Messiah because he has perfect vision. His perception springs from weakness, not from strength. The sequence of events is vital to the Gospel's message here, but no single Sunday could include the whole. The order runs: (1) Simon's declaration; (2) the renamed Peter becomes keeper of the keys to the kingdom; (3) Peter's rebuke (when Jesus reveals the coming passion) rebuked; (4) Peter as witness to the transfiguration. We could summarize these steps as (1) vision; (2) honour; (3) error; (4) incomprehension.

God has a providential purpose. This is clear from the simple fact that Jesus has foreknowledge of the future, never mind Paul's more complex ideas about perfection and integrity and goodness in Romans. Jesus is not guessing at Simon's becoming the key-holder and the rock. He *knows* it, with all the divine clarity that comes from the Holy Three being outside of human time. For to God, everything is present, and nothing is future or past.

Peter may be a rock, and a key-holder, but he is 'only' a human being. Even with visions there come mistakes. The events that follow immediately after Caesarea Philippi witness to this non-linear (being polite), vacillating (being honest) quality about human striving for perfection.

I understand integrity as meaning 'wholeness', so 'integrous' means 'possessing the quality of wholeness'. Using logic, a philosopher might agree that Jesus can properly be called 'integrous'. A theologian might need to finesse this for the unity of the two natures, divine and human, in Christ. Both would find it hard to call Peter integrous, for vision has not perfected him. He remains flawed. In terms of strict logic, one cannot be a little bit integrous. Perfection can only be 100%.

The Gospel is not logical. It proceeds not by sequences of propositional reasoning but by chapters in a story. And every good story needs a plot, and elements of recognition, and changes of circumstance, and clashes of good with good, or evil with evil; all amid the stirring up of emotions of pity, fear and love.

Narrative truth is natural truth, in which Peter's imperfections are not off-putting but reassuring. We may not be able to call him 'perfect', but we can call him 'integrous': because he is growing in knowledge of his fractured nature, and wrestling with it to the end of his days. No wonder the words, 'love covers a multitude of sins' are to be found in the first letter attributed to Peter (4.8).

Proper 17
Sunday between 28 August and 3 September inclusive

Continuous: Exodus 3.1–15; Psalm 105.1–6, 23–26, 45b *or* Psalm 115; Romans 12.9–end; Matthew 16.21–end
Related: Jeremiah 15.15–21; Psalm 26.1–8; Romans 12.9–end; Matthew 16.21–end

I was so surprised when I read the second half of Jeremiah 15.18 that I had to read it again, and then set off in search of commentaries. A Jewish scholar confirmed that I had not misunderstood the meaning. He called it 'an accusation so bold and offensive that it cannot go unanswered'.

This reading is one of the passages known as the 'confessions' of Jeremiah. That label witnesses to the natural and human way in which the prophet converses with God: he speaks to God (prayer: 15.15–18) and records God's responses (judgement: 15.19–21). These confessions are a sometimes confusing mixture, combining language from the law court (pleas for God's justice) with lament and (as here) reproach.

We mortals had better be very sure of our ground if we are going to reproach God. The writers of parts of the Old Testament/Hebrew Bible have a different take on sin, and respond differently to what they perceive or experience as divine injustice. Reflecting on this confession of Jeremiah can enlarge our understanding of how to respond to suffering, so that we learn to offer something better than unquestioning submission to the evils that beset us, or misdirected criticism of God.

Jeremiah's prophetic experience helps with interpreting Romans and Matthew, for both these New Testament books call attention to the problem of suffering. Paul sets out a series of 23 commands in Romans 12.9–18. It contains only five that are phrased negatively ('do not'). That in itself expresses a truth of our faith. Like the old song says, we ought to 'Ac-Cent-Tchu-Ate the Positive' (and, conversely, 'eliminate the negative').

Among the positive commands, some are absolute, like the commands to love, rejoice, be patient, persevere. Paul does not make them interdependent with other people or external circumstances. These we have no option but to do our best to fulfil.

But they are not the whole picture, for there are positive commands that require more than an individual commitment or determination.

Associating with the lowly (Rom. 12.16) is such a one. What if the lowly do not wish to associate with us? Paul acknowledges the difficulty in 12.20, when he adds a clause to the command to live peaceably with all, 'so far as in you lies'.

It is often difficult to admit that we are ourselves responsible for discord or unhappiness within a group. Passive aggression (or 'pass-ag' in today's shorthand) is a useful human wheeze for sidestepping responsibility: '*I* have not changed; *I* have not done anything; therefore *I* cannot be at fault.'

For Christians, though, there are times when doing nothing is an action. To prevent us from justifying our tendency to negativity and obstructiveness, we have a moral category called the sin of omission. An obstacle to doing good need be no more than something, or someone, standing in the way of some positive thing or act. In other words, we do not need to be doing *something*, in order to be doing something *wrong*. Without moving a muscle or saying a word, we can be committing a sin or working against God's purposes.

Jeremiah tries to stir God to action (at least that is how I read the passage) by calling him a 'deceitful brook' and a dried-up water source. This must mean that God is not what he claims to be, namely a source of life and growth. It is a challenge to God to put right his omission, his failure to act. And it succeeds (15.19–21).

When it comes to the Gospel, this truth of human psychology is turned upside down. Passive aggression usually implies an obstructive attitude to change, or a refusal to engage with positive action. But when Jesus turns his face to Jerusalem, he declares an attitude of passivity, in which he must 'have many things done to him' (15.21, my translation). This marks a shift from active doer, teacher, healer, to the passive one who suffers and endures, the one who has things done to him. At this moment, Jesus turns negative suffering into a positive. In place of passive aggression, we, like Peter in the Gospel, find ourselves face to face with the very opposite: active peaceableness. The clunky phrase does no justice to so beautiful a transformation, but it is accurate, for all that. It teaches, paradoxically, that by doing nothing, Christ will 'make all things new' (Rev. 21.5).

Proper 18
Sunday between 4 and 10 September inclusive

Continuous: Exodus 12.1–14; Psalm 149; Romans 13.8–end; Matthew 18.15–20
Related: Ezekiel 33.7–11; Psalm 119.33–40; Romans 13.8–end; Matthew 18.15–20

The Gospel gives us guidance for living, but we may be surprised to find Jesus outlining a grievance procedure. It is specific to Matthew. Only the first verse of the passage is paralleled elsewhere (Luke 17.3).

Justice is a fundamental characteristic of God. So we expect Scripture to guide us about what it means and how it works in human society. Justice is not the same as the (human) law. Anyone involved in the law knows that it is a blunt instrument, unsuitable for managing everyday quarrels and disputes.

Whenever we hear of neighbours locked in a boundary dispute over half a yard of land, or children contesting a will in a struggle for an inheritance, we shake our heads at the folly of it, expecting that the operation of the law will consume the property and wealth that is being fought over.

Hard-wired in us is a thirst for the kind of justice we call 'fairness'. That is not abstract debate but everyday routine, depending on factors much more intangible than law. The 'greatest good of the greatest number', for example, becomes not a utilitarian principle obliterating the rights of the individual, but a shorthand for what works because most people will accept it. It is enforceable less through the courts than by common consent.

When applying a common understanding of fairness brings no resolution of a dispute, there comes an intermediate stage before resorting to the law for justice. That is what Jesus outlines here. Grievance procedures are part of modern employment culture, but they also work in other sectors of our common life. Safeguarding is a form of grievance procedure. It is a tried-and-tested method ('method' is crucial to a fair outcome) for making judgements about events where no independent witnesses may have been present, or where the wrong done may be of a subtle kind of oppression: a misuse of influence or a perversion of proper boundaries.

Jesus gives us a preparatory stage to his grievance procedure: a conversation between the two parties to a dispute (this will not be possible where there is an imbalance of power between them). We find it difficult to speak of being hurt or feeling belittled. Making such an admission is tantamount to putting ourselves in a position of weakness, making us feel even more vulnerable, not less. Some grievances can be overcome by such honest and well-intentioned conversations (Rom. 13.10).

For the next stage, Jesus recommends what workplace procedures also do: not to continue the conversation alone. This protects both parties from misrepresentation. Like the initial option of talking one to one, it requires courage: one reason why people are reluctant to let others in on a dispute is their fear of losing control of a situation that they are already experiencing in terms of helpless defensiveness.

Although giving other people insight into our secret difficulties can feel like weakness, it is really a form of self-safeguarding, for it prevents the damage done by the pain of suffering in isolation. Until we ourselves openly admit to a problem, we render relations, friends, colleagues powerless to support us through the sensitive business of finding a way forward.

Jesus uses the language of family when sketching his grievance procedure. The NRSV's wishful translation of the key word 'brother' as 'member of the church' obscures the fact that the gathering of faithful Christians is a gathering of family. Families in legal disputes attract the most opprobrium because it is within the family (whether of blood or faith) that we are supposed to learn good management of disagreements. If flexibility, together with enough self-knowledge and humility to admit from time to time, 'I was wrong', are not learned and reinforced there, it makes it much harder and more painful to acquire such skills later in life.

Even in this law-free grievance procedure, there is an ultimate sanction, and Jesus spells it out: expulsion from the community of faith (Matt. 18.17). An insoluble dispute leads to a parting of the ways. Human paths to fairness sometimes require sticking plasters on a wound, but at least plasters can prevent further pathogens from gaining access and festering. The healing that is divine justice may take centuries to effect (Ezekiel 33); Christians have still not dissolved all the divisions caused by the Arian controversy or the Reformation. But at least we no longer kill one other over them.

Proper 19
Sunday between 11 and 17 September inclusive

Continuous: Exodus 14.19–end; Psalm 114 *or*
Canticle: Exodus 15.1b–11, 20, 21; Romans 14.1–12;
Matthew 18.21–35
Related: Genesis 50.15–21; Psalm 103.[1–7] 8–13;
Romans 14.1–12; Matthew 18.21–35

Metaphor, you might say, is the last refuge of the exegetical scoundrel. When Christians encounter a hard biblical teaching, they need to have it explained. But too often the guidance they receive, from whatever source, seems more interested in explaining it away.

The point is beautifully made (among many other important observations on how religious people behave) by the film, *Monty Python's Life of Brian*. As Jesus delivers his Sermon on the Mount, many listeners are too far away to hear clearly. One mishears Matthew 5.9 as 'Blessed are the cheesemakers', and another responds, 'Well, obviously, this is not meant to be taken literally. It refers to any manufacturers of dairy products'. It is a great joke. So good, in fact, that it is easy to overlook the fact that 'peace' and 'cheese' do not actually rhyme.

Another example: I own a cartoon by Merrily Harpur, from her 'Unheard-of Ambridge' series. It shows Nigel Pargeter's mother asking the Bishop of Felpersham if he can exorcise the dry rot in her stately home. 'No,' replies the bishop, 'but you may find it helpful to think of it as a metaphor'. Decades later that still makes me laugh.

Alan Bennett's 'Life is like a tin of sardines' sermon from *Beyond the Fringe* is another exegetical joke, this time about clergy using ridiculous similes to illustrate platitudinous preaching. In all cases, the explanation that language is figurative is a way of diluting the seriousness of a message.

If it does nothing else, my short list of examples confronts us with how outsiders see our attitude to our own holy writings: we Christians are unable to face up to some starkly literal teachings, so diminish or redirect them. For today's Gospel, this is a timely warning, for the parable it contains is precious. It touches upon forgiveness, and something more – *forgiven* forgiveness. As such, it amounts to an exegesis of the Lord's Prayer.

This rather long-winded bit of self-justification on my part is necessary, for we absolutely must not take this parable literally. To grasp this, we can simply 'follow the money' (Matt. 18.24, 28). Giving an exact equivalent value in today's money is always difficult for Bible translators. But in this case, one of the sums involved is simply fantastical.

The 'denarius' (hence *d* in £.*s*.*d*.) was a silver coin weighing about 6g. Its name (but not value) is exactly like the English 'tenner'. It is roughly the equivalent of a day's pay at living wage level.

The denarius is not the problem. The problem is the talent. It too is a measure of precious metal (which is what all coins originally were: conveniently small units for fine-tuned payments). The talent is the largest currency unit in the ancient near East, says my commentary. Likewise, 10,000 is the highest numeral used in reckoning. So saying 'ten thousand talents' is like us saying (not billions or trillions but) 'squillions' of pounds.

Such an amount is imaginary, fantastical, such that no human individual, even working every day of their life, could ever come close to earning (never mind owing) so much. We should also remember that the man who owed the huge debt was a slave. He could not own property because he *was* property. Taking this parable metaphorically is unavoidable.

When the man's fellow slaves see that he has failed to learn from his master's generosity, and instead extorts a modest sum from another slave, they do the unthinkable: they grass him up (in the parlance of my Essex upbringing) or dob him in (in the cant of Australian soap operas). He has broken the camaraderie of the oppressed by behaving like a master instead of like a slave – and, what is worse, like an unjust master. Being a slave himself has not taught him to have compassion for the vulnerable. It simply encourages him to get his exploitation in first.

If we needed further confirmation that the message is not literal, the reference to torture (18.34) would provide it. As the amount of the debt is beyond imagining, the extent of the torture until it was repaid would necessarily also be unending. That cannot be the message.

But one of the parable's messages is perfectly clear: God's mercy towards us is meant to be a lesson as well as a gift. It teaches us first that forgiveness is possible, then that a forgiving nature begins with forgiving behaviour.

Proper 20
Sunday between 18 and 24 September inclusive

Continuous: Exodus 16.2–15; Psalm 105.1–6, 37–end [*or* 105.37–end]; Philippians 1.21–end; Matthew 20.1–16
Related: Jonah 3.10—end of 4; Psalm 145.1–8; Philippians 1.21–end; Matthew 20.1–16

Help for writing came from an unexpected quarter. Some Jehovah's Witnesses called, asking if I believed that suffering would ever end. They seemed remarkably cheerful, but I know how it feels when people would rather pretend to be out than open the door to you. I did not argue with them about their approach to the Bible, trusting instead that a warm welcome is a better witness to Christ than reluctance or hostility.

My answer to their question was 'yes'. I do believe that suffering will end. But like them, I set that ending in the distant (presumably) future glimpsed in Revelation 21. In this life, suffering is unavoidable.

The prophet Jonah was a missionary sent by God to the people of Nineveh. He went knocking upon doors with his gloomy message. And they responded, and repented, so God chose not to punish them after all.

This made Jonah furious. The missionary, who thought he was the expert, come to instruct the wayward, had lessons to learn. And he learned those lessons the hard way, through physical suffering brought on by his own stubbornness.

In Paul we see another face of mission. Despite all that he has endured, and is yet to endure, he sees faith as a 'win–win' situation: 'living is Christ and dying is gain.' In terms of personal holiness, he has moved far beyond the questioning that reflects an immature faith ('Is this fair?') and from an incomplete reliance on God.

It is not wrong to struggle with suffering, any more than it is wrong to argue with God. Jonah did not suffer the loss of the bush because he questioned God's actions but because he failed to see the value of the living creatures (both human and non-human) within the city. God's compassion for the people of Nineveh in their state of ignorance was something Jonah should have imitated. He ought also to have rejoiced that they had escaped divine retribution through their repentance.

If Paul reflects us as we ought to be, Jonah is probably closer to most of us as we are. His attitude is closely mirrored by that of the Gospel workers in the vineyard. In both cases they endure suffering and exhaustion, exacerbated by the heat of the day.

Jonah was ready (eventually, 3.1) to undergo hardship for God, provided that the ungodly got what they deserved, and that he could enjoy his moment of righteous vindication. The workers were likewise prepared to bear the burden and heat of the day for the sake of the wage on offer. But they resented working harder than other people who got the same reward.

Jonah and the workers have an immature understanding of divine forgiveness, and of the nature of the covenant between God and those who do his bidding and bear his message. The Gospel message is a 'hard teaching', for the parable challenges us on the level of instinct: we can easily see why the workers felt it was a swizz. In similar circumstances, we would probably feel disgruntled too.

If we want to take a positive message from the parable of the workers, all we need to do is re-read it, for we may have missed its most powerful point: namely, that in our lives as Christians we should not be measuring ourselves against other people. We should not fret ourselves that we are less holy than others, or less appreciated. Nor should we inflict upon ourselves the torment of envy, which (like the whine of an unswattable mosquito) seems impossible to ignore as it seeks a way to inflict biting sores on us.

Alongside the corporate dimension of Christian faith, which is so vital to our growth and development, there exists always that bare duality of the self and God. Alone, we take our stand before the judgement seat, knowing that nothing in the lives of others can justify the wrongs that we have ourselves committed.

Jeremy Taylor nails it with a prayer 'that I may never envy the prosperity of any one, but rejoyce to honour him whom thou honourest, to love him whom thou lovest … giving honour to whom honour belongs, that I may go to heaven in the noblest way of rejoycing in the good of others'. This would truly be 'living our lives in a manner worthy of the gospel of Christ' (Phil. 1.27).

Proper 21
Sunday between 25 September and 1 October inclusive

Continuous: Exodus 17.1–7; Psalm 78.1–4, 12–16 [*or* 78.1–7]; Philippians 2.1–13; Matthew 21.23–32
Related: Ezekiel 18.1–4, 25–end; Psalm 25.1–8; Philippians 2.1–13; Matthew 21.23–32

Jesus sometimes answers one question by posing another. This is not because he is sneaky, but because among rabbis it was a common way of arguing. In the next chapter, he will use the same method to avoid condemning himself ('render unto Caesar', Matt. 22.15–22).

The question put to him is not trivial, for sources of authority are a sensitive matter. Human beings learn to observe where authority lies in social situations, taking cues from the behaviour of an individual or group. The signalling of authority can be subtle (are others deferring to them?) or manifest: I recall a bishop's wife who regularly referred to her own husband as 'Bishop N'. James 2 is a recent lectionary example of how Christians ought (ideally) to make such calculations.

Naturally the religious authorities want to investigate the course content of Jesus' teaching. If he is promoting resistance to the Romans, the whole people will suffer for it. If his teaching about the law and the prophets is wrong, it could bring down divine judgement upon them.

Authority is at issue in Ezekiel too. This passage of the prophet is precious because it speaks of the new heart and spirit that are central to the Christian experience of redemption. It also denounces the belief that God makes people suffer for things that are not their fault. Corporate punishment for an individual sin, or a penalty laid upon offspring for the faults of parents, is not just. It forms no part of God's plan.

This is controversial stuff, because Ezekiel is challenging no less an authority than the Pentateuch (Ex. 34.7). Last week's Old Testament reading taught Jonah a lesson about God's sovereignty (his freedom to act as he wills) and his equity (the fairness of his judgement); both characteristics are foundations upon which trust in God's authority is built.

One of the lessons we can take from such passages is that there is nothing wrong with challenging someone (even God) to justify their behaviour or attitude. The chief priests and elders are not in the wrong because they question Jesus. They are in the wrong because the Gospel reveals that they are not motivated by a search for truth.

We may well ask how Matthew could know what the chief priests and elders said together. Otherwise we might assume that he has simply dreamed up some plausible words (21.25–26). On this point my commentary annoyed me by flannelling, 'The thoughts of Jesus' opponents are manifest from their deeds'. That disguises the difficulty. It is one thing to accept that they mistrusted the Nazarene and his motives, but quite another to treat the words Matthew reports as a verbatim record of what was spoken on that occasion.

Thus the first part of the passage, which is ostensibly about Jesus' authority as a teacher, also invites us to consider Matthew's authority as an evangelist. Why should we believe that he knows what he appears to know? Consciously or unconsciously we apply our different tests. (1) Does the Gospel 'hang together' as an internally consistent piece of writing? Yes. (2) Does Jesus display integrity and consistency in his words and actions? Yes. (3) Does the Gospel as a whole cohere with what we know of Jesus from other writings? Yes.

To this we should add a fourth point: (4) Is Matthew's account based on any extant source material? Again the answer is 'yes', for if we look at Mark (11.27–33), it is clear that Matthew has followed his account with only minor variations.

Once we are sure that the Gospel hangs together, that its picture of Jesus is convincing, that it is consistent with other evidence, and that it is based on a reliable source we can verify independently, where does that leave us? We still have no 100% certainty. If responding to Jesus our Lord with faith and love does not happen without proof, it is hard to see how a demonstration of his full identity would change hearts of stone to hearts of flesh.

However far back we go into the origins of the Gospel, we will never have 'enough' proof. Sooner or later we still have to take the leap of faith over the abyss of doubt and ignorance. But the voice of the one who speaks with authority, and not like one of the scribes (Matt. 7.29), fills us with courage to take that leap.

Proper 22
Sunday between 2 and 8 October inclusive

Continuous: Exodus 20.1–4, 7–9, 12–20; Psalm 19 [*or* 19.7–end]; Philippians 3.4b–14; Matthew 21.33–end
Related: Isaiah 5.1–7; Psalm 80.9–16; Philippians 3.4b–14; Matthew 21.33–end

Back when I was learning Hebrew, it took me weeks to read Isaiah 5.1–7. I had no time to compare versions in other languages. If I had, I might have learned that one version records a hilarious anti-climax: 'Let me sing for my beloved a song about my uncle's vineyard.'

Thankfully that version has not found favour with Hebrew scholars, so we can keep reading the passage as a love lyric. It begins as the song of a besotted lover. It ends as a condemnation issuing from a betrayed lover. The vineyard is not personified, but the 'beloved', who creates and tends it, reacts as if it owes him something in return for that nurture. At first, he treats it lovingly. But when it fails to reciprocate, in his anger he destroys it. In verse 5, the prophet makes it clear that the vineyard is more than a vineyard; it stands for Israel, or, to be more precise, faithless Israel.

The Gospel likewise focuses on a vineyard. But this time the betrayal is laid at the door of human characters in the story. Modern readers find this parable of the wicked tenants difficult to make sense of. We cannot see how the tenants' killing of their landlord's son would give them title to his property.

The explanation is sadly simple. No one knows the true origin of the saying, 'Possession is nine-tenths of the law'. But we can see how difficult it would be to claim back ownership of something that had been misappropriated. The Romans might have identified this as a case of 'property-that-ought-to-be-given-back' (*res repetundae*): restitution was the father's right, though he was in no position (Matt. 21.33) to enforce it.

Those wicked tenants are not just plotting the kind of theft or fraud that ought to demand restitution. They are conspiring to commit murder, and the pecuniary motivation increases their culpability. If the parable is to speak both to Jesus' listeners and to us, we need to know more about those wicked tenants. Who do they stand for? It surely cannot be us, because most of us (I would say none, except that even reading the *Church Times* is not an absolute guarantee of moral probity) are not plotting murder for gain.

Or can the parable, after all, stand for us? Another prophet, Jeremiah, declares bluntly that 'the heart is deceitful above all things, and desperately wicked' (17.9 AV). Murder is the grim pinnacle of the upward slope of sin, but, in one way, it is not essentially different from all the petty wrongs that go on in our society: the tax-evader, the expenses-fiddler; the grubby greed of a dishonest care assistant pilfering from a client's purse, or the shoplifter who justifies their thieving as a victimless offence, or the speeding motorist, or the cyclist ignoring traffic lights because rules are for drivers.

Every sin from the smallest to the greatest is some kind of failure to give other people their due. There is an interesting parallel for this in the world of social etiquette. Etiquette can be codes and norms indicating what to wear, how to eat, who to defer to. This is not restricted to the rich and posh. There is as much etiquette at work among spectators as a football match or shoppers in a queue as at the ballet or the opera. The conventions are different, but the authority they exude is not.

A simple rule cuts through the complexities of etiquette. It is a form of the 'Golden Rule' (behaving towards others as you would have them behave towards you). Use your imagination and intuition to behave towards the people you encounter with commensurate politeness, consideration and kindness. I would add in one further factor. Do not assume that if someone has offended you, they did so with malice aforethought. It could just as easily be from ignorance, shyness or misunderstanding.

In the parable, the owner of the vineyard is expected to assert his rights and punish the murderous fraudsters. When Jesus first told this parable, they stood for the entitled priests and Pharisees, with their counterfeit ownership of valuable property. As we hear Jesus now, verse 41 invites us to become those 'other tenants', who will act honestly by giving the landlord his due. Just because we can act without thought for other people, or for justice, does not mean that we should.

Proper 23
Sunday between 9 and 15 October inclusive

Continuous: Exodus 32.1–14; Psalm 106.1–6, 19–23 [*or* 106.1–6]; Philippians 4.1–9; Matthew 22.1–14
Related: Isaiah 25.1–9; Psalm 23; Philippians 4.1–9; Matthew 22.1–14

You can tell that I struggle with Matthew 22.1–14 by the number of references I make here to other people's opinions about it. My favourite comment observes that the parable of the wedding feast 'is enough to make any interpreter go weak in the knees'.

The last verse is the most difficult of all: 'many are called, but few are chosen'. One morning years ago (it must have been Trinity 20, when the BCP 1662 sets this passage from Matthew 22), I attended early Communion, and followed the readings in my prayer book. The priest stopped the Gospel reading at 'weeping and gnashing of teeth', leaving out 'many are called, but few are chosen'.

As a refusal to proclaim the Gospel, that shocked me. It implied that the priest knew better than Jesus and Matthew what it ought to say. But it did bring home to me how repellent even many Christians find these words of Jesus. Perhaps they evoke unhappy memories among those of us who were always last to be picked for the team in school games lessons (I count myself among them). It is not so much that the Gospel is arbitrary as that it suggests God will reject part of his creation. In particular, it highlights the theological conundrum of persons being condemned from the first moment of their existence.

The words themselves are plain enough, and both of the translations I have quoted are perfectly accurate. So where can we find some theodicy? How can God be defended against the charge of injustice, even cruelty?

The man without a wedding garment is a gate-crasher ('Friend, how did you get in here?'). He stirred up memories of my sister-in-law's parents, who years ago, while travelling right across America, ate well for free simply by walking into hotels and heading for the breakfast room as though they were guests.

The matter of the wedding-guest not having the right clothing compounds the problem rather than resolving it, for wearing the wrong clothing ought not to condemn anyone. This makes the king appear harsh. Matthew 6.25–31 seems to contradict 22.11–13 too, for in the Sermon on the Mount, Jesus teaches that we are not to worry about what we wear.

That could completely change the direction of the parable by implying that the guest who has the wrong clothing has the right attitude – though then we could no longer identify the king with God. The identification with God was problematic in any case, for having someone tied up and thrown into darkness is an excessive penalty for gate-crashing a party.

Commentators have naturally tried to detoxify verse 14. Among the possible defences of Jesus' words, one option with a long ancestry is to understand 'many' as if it were a synonym for 'all'; then to interpret 'few' as 'not all'. One scholar refers to an early translator's poignant take, 'all are called, *too* few are chosen'. To my mind, though, the added 'too' makes the verse more problematic, not less, because it sets up the evangelist's opinion against that of Jesus when he relates the parable.

Taking it as a reflection of the place of Israel among the nations, we might identify the 'many' with all the nations, but the 'few' with faithful Israel. As a solution this comes at a price of inconsistency with Jesus' teaching elsewhere, not to mention much of the rest of the New Testament. A further option is to read it in conjunction with parallel passages like 7.14–15, in which 'many' take the easy path, but 'few' the steep and narrow one.

The choosing out of groups who find favour with God from among humankind as a whole feels awkward. Even within the Old Testament, there are traces of an alternative approach: that God chooses individuals not nations; and that he chooses on the basis of character and behaviour, not ritual or blood or primogeniture (1 Sam. 16.7). When nascent biblical theories about predestination and election came to be worked out systematically and with theological rigour, the problems of privileging groups were not erased. Instead they multiplied.

If I could argue the problem of Matthew 5.14 away, I would by now have done so. The best I can do instead is to proffer some potential solutions. I hope it is not cowardice to take refuge in trusting to providence, combined with the comfortable words of Matthew 11.30.

Proper 24
Sunday between 16 and 22 October inclusive

Continuous: Exodus 33.12–23; Psalm 99; 1 Thessalonians 1.1–10; Matthew 22.15–22
Related: Isaiah 45.1–7; Psalm 96.1–9 [10–13]; 1 Thessalonians 1.1–10; Matthew 22.15–22

Reading this Gospel in isolation risks missing a fuller message. For in the sacrament of the word, the Holy Spirit liberates readings to speak to each other. It shapes messages in the spaces between them, as well as inside each one taken on its own. Isaiah 45 is paired with the story from Matthew 22: in both, God is expected to support only 'his' people, yet entrusts his will to people who have never heard of him, still less worshipped him.

Cyrus (in Isaiah) and Caesar (in Matthew) have much in common, though they come from different lands and eras. Cyrus ('the Great') founded an empire. Much later so did Caesar. They were territory-grabbers, asserting control, imprinting their personalities on the civilizations that they led.

The prophet says that Cyrus, a foreigner, is God's chosen one, his 'Christ' ('anointed one') to save God's people by restoring them after their exile. Prophetic messages often take us by surprise, perhaps because we have no equivalent institution. But such prophetic voices as we do have often suffer like their biblical forebears did. Today's mainstream and social media alike can have a prophet crucified on the Calvary of popular opinion in less time than it took Pontius Pilate to glance through the execution lists that first Good Friday morning.

But clergy are ordained, and some are also anointed, so surely they should have prophetic confidence to proclaim the Lord's message for all the people. Many of them avoid challenging the political status quo, though. They concentrate their energies on the priestly sphere. Just because the Bible brings the starkest, bravest prophets to the fore, we should not forget that there were plenty of prophets upholding popular views that supported the religious establishment (Jer. 23, 28; Ez. 22.28; Matt. 7.15).

Verse 7 of the Isaiah passage almost drove out all other thoughts and ideas from my mind. The oldest translations do its baldness justice: 'I make peace and form evils' (Septuagint Greek). 'I make peace and create evil' (Vulgate Latin, AV). In modern times, RSV replaces the high-calorie version with a low-sugar solution (sweetened by a neat alliteration): 'I make weal and create woe'. Other version plump for 'well-being and disaster', 'prosperity and doom', or 'prosperity and disaster'.

Only in the older versions is it clear what is really being said in the Hebrew: 'I make *shalom*, I create evil/calamity'. The only reason I can see why the RSV (followed by the NRSV) goes for 'weal and woe' (a ridiculous archaism in a modern translation) is to avoid the conundrum of God telling us that he creates, on the one hand, peace (no problem with that), but on the other calamity, even evil, (awkward, to say the least).

I used to admire how Jesus sidesteps the trap laid for him by the Pharisees in Matthew's Gospel. But now, helped by Isaiah 45, I have come to see that he does not *side*step the trap at all. He steps *over* it. The trap fails to ensnare him because Jesus is saying what the Pharisees themselves also think.

They hope that he will betray revolutionary opinions and be condemned for them. They are themselves tolerant of Roman imperial control. They accept giving to Caesar what is due to him: recognition (in the form of obedience) and tribute (in the form of taxes). In exchange for this, they get protection and the *kudos* of being part of the top team in the Premier League of nations.

In a premodern culture with rudimentary public order, many people might have seen Roman rule as a better path to a secure society than protection rackets and local mafias. The famous question (which was intended as rhetorical), 'What have the Romans ever done for us?', eventually produced this answer: 'sanitation, medicine, education, wine, public order, irrigation, roads, a fresh-water system, public health – and peace'.

Jesus tells the Pharisees that they are right. The only difference between them and him is their malicious intentions, for they are enticing him into collapsing the categories of religion and politics into one another, whereas he arranges them in a constructive parallel.

From the fourth century, Matthew 22.21 began to be interpreted as a proof text for the separation of religious and political powers. Jesus taught us to give respect to both. No wonder the Pharisees went away amazed, for the radical firebrand had just agreed with them.

Proper 25
Sunday between 23 and 29 October inclusive (Last Sunday after Trinity)

Continuous: Deuteronomy 34.1–12; Psalm 90.1–6, 13–17 [*or* 90.1–6]; 1 Thessalonians 2.1–8; Matthew 22.34–end
Related: Leviticus 19.1–2, 15–18; Psalm 1; 1 Thessalonians 2.1–8; Matthew 22.34–end

This Sunday can be either the last Sunday after Trinity or Bible Sunday. I am using the ('related') readings for the former to reflect on the latter, in order to illustrate a principle. There is a serious point to this. Any text of Scripture, for any date in the Church's calendar, can be an opportunity to reflect on how the Bible works in the life of Christians and of the Church.

So I ask: Do the texts speak with one voice, or are they challenging one another? How can they help people to hear the voice of God?

Leviticus 19 uses repetition of 'I am the Lord'. It looks merely formulaic. But it is more like the 'only' that we oldsters used to write on cheques to prevent changes or additions. 'I am the Lord' is really a full stop. It marks the close of each section of the Law. Since punctuation and layout are yet to be invented, words must do those jobs on their own.

When we read a Bible book, deciding what connects with what, and which words, sentences, or stories belong together, are reading skills as essential as learning the alphabet. We divvy up the Bible into sections (this can be called 'chunking'), either within books or across the whole Bible – and therefore across centuries, cultures and languages. Then we can see Psalm 22.1 talking across a millennium, to Matthew 27.46. Or Deuteronomy 6.4–5 speaking to Matthew 22.37. Or 1 Kings 8.27–30 to Revelation 21.

All 66 (at least) books can speak to each other, within or between the Testaments. Lectionary compilers help us to see this. They highlight this constant dialogue by deciding what and where to chunk. They draw on the wisdom of Bible translators and exegetes, experts who pour a lifetime of scholarship into working out where sentences begin and end, whether words should be capitalized (for example, does Matthew 22.43 mean 'by the Spirit' or 'in spirit'?), and how to arrange text on the page so as to help modern readers and express authors' meanings.

None of the visual aids we rely on, from upper and lower case, to ink colour(s), to chunking, to verse and chapter numbering, was commonly practised among the first copyists of our sacred writings. We do not know how blest we are to have our modern Bibles presented to us with such beautiful clarity and with every assistance for wise reading.

Every technology that helps the Bible to be read has been lavished upon us. Every 'jot and tittle' (Matthew 5.18) matters, because the word has to speak with equal clarity to the occasional visitor dropping in to church one Sunday, the hotel guest glancing randomly through the Good Book because sleep comes slowly in a strange bed far from home, the habitual churchgoer, the devoted lifelong Christian, and the suspicious but attracted 'outsider'.

In this case, the choice of Leviticus 19 to speak with Matthew 22.34–46 cannot have been especially difficult. But we will appreciate the message better if we hear the Old Testament reading in a larger chunk, as Jesus did. The words he quotes in Matthew 22.39 are shorthand for that fuller expression in Leviticus 19.17–18.

The full stop, 'I am the Lord', marks off the chunk of message. Jesus knew it as a unit. So should we. His summary is shorthand for the whole: do not hate, do not criticize, do not take vengeance or bear grudges – in a word, *love*. The teaching is clearly stated. Now we look in the Gospel for what calls forth that teaching, and hear how to apply it.

Matthew agrees with Luke that the question asked by the Pharisee lawyer is to 'test' him. That is not necessarily negative: Mark makes it a response to recognizing Jesus' wisdom, not the danger that he posed. In Luke, Jesus encourages the questioner to attempt his own answer first, as good teachers (Luke 18.18) often do. As we absorb one message from the readings, another chunk, not even part of this day's portion, resounds in our minds as an exegesis of the whole (Luke 10.29–37):

A lawyer asked, 'Who is my neighbour?' After the story of the Good Samaritan comes the lesson:

Jesus: Which of these three, do you think, was a neighbour to the man who fell into the hands of the robbers?'
Lawyer: The one who showed him mercy.
Jesus: Go and do likewise.

The Last Sunday after Trinity
(*if observed as* **Bible Sunday**)

Nehemiah 8.1–4a [5–6] 8–12; Psalm 119.9–16; Colossians 3.12–17; Matthew 24.30–35

This verse, 'Let the word of Christ dwell in you richly' (Col. 3.16), precedes instructions on singing in worship. So it attracts attention from people who want to learn about how early Christian worship looked and sounded. Perhaps reflections on singing distract us from focusing on letting the word of Christ dwell in us richly. But Bible Sunday it is a good day to reconsider.

If we think of the Bible as having authority over our lives, we may turn 'the word of Christ' too quickly into 'the word of Scripture'. But this verse tests our notions of authority. According to the canons of the Church of England, our doctrine (teaching) is 'grounded in the Holy Scriptures' because our faith is 'uniquely revealed in the Holy Scriptures and set forth in the catholic creeds' (Canon A5, C15). But where does the writer to the Colossians regard 'authority' as existing in his early church?

Two thousand years on from the New Testament's formation, Church authority is a given. If nothing else, it embodies the practical attitude encapsulated by the saying, 'He who pays the piper calls the tune'. The Church has authority because the Church has buildings, money, people, tradition, history, territory, control.

Where was authority to be found in that early church in Colossae? Not in buildings, money or territory. But it did have people, and was beginning to grow a tradition and a history, if we imagine it going on in time, past the era of its foundation by Paul and Timothy (Col. 1.1; 4.18). It was not a national territorial Church like the Church of England. It cannot have been a global Church like the Church of Rome. The concept of the 'catholic' (in the sense of 'universal') Church had not yet been born. What the Colossians did have in common with the communities of Christians in Rome, Corinth, Galatia, Ephesus, Philippi and Thessalonica, was allegiance to Christ.

Later in this same passage comes the teaching, 'just as the Lord has forgiven you, so you also must forgive' (3.13). I imagine it as inspired by the Lord's teaching on prayer, that forgiveness is a quality that descends from God, upon us, so that we can exhibit similar forgiveness towards other people. But that teaching is making explicit a principle about authority.

The Christians of Colossae are to base their behaviour upon Christ. He is the authority who defines what is proper for them. They have no Bible for it has not yet been written. They have no national or international Church. They have no forms of authorized ministry to ensure that God is taught and learned truly. But they do have the guidance of their founders, whether Paul and Timothy, or others.

They have learned that the imperative to forgive (without which no form of community, Christian or not, can survive long) descends from Christ himself, because they have been listening to stories and teaching, and receiving letters from those who first brought them the good news. Now they are reminded of another aspect of what they have been given: the word of Christ.

History tells us that it cannot yet be a written word. The words of Colossians 3.12 confirm the fact, for it is to 'dwell' in them. In other words, make its home with them. And ink and paper cannot be 'in' us.

The word of Christ, which dwells in us richly, is the ultimate authority for every Christian, not just then but now too. It transcends even the Scriptures themselves, because, to paraphrase a verse of Scripture, 'before Scripture was, the word of Christ is' (see John 8.58).

Now the pressure is well and truly on to work out what this fundamental 'word of Christ' is. It is not written, we know. It is not the Word who 'was in the beginning with God' (John 1.2). It is not explained in the text at all, for to the writers and to the recipients it must have been so obvious as to need no unpacking. I do not think it is the good news, or story, of Jesus either. That leaves something we might rephrase as 'the word spoken by Christ'. That word does not belong in a book. No human institution has authority over it. It is free. It abides in us. In this (the Word), in him (Christ), we trust.

All Saints' Day (1 November) or Sunday between 30 October and 5 November *if this is kept as* All Saints' Day

Revelation 7.9–end; Psalm 34.1–10; 1 John 3.1–3; Matthew 5.1–12

[CHORUS]   'Sweeping through the gates of the new Jerusalem,
           Washed in the blood of the Lamb.'

This Salvation Army hymn, written over a hundred years ago, was once popular enough to have been familiar to the fictional sleuth Lord Peter Wimsey.[1] I would be surprised if many of today's Christians have sung it.

It is one of a large class of hymns for which stirring music, designed for enthusiastic singing, triumphs over words that are theologically or aesthetically iffy. I can think of other church music too, which falls short on grounds of quality, but which I enjoy all the same.

In Noël Coward's *Private Lives*, Elliott put it snootily but accurately: 'Extraordinary how potent cheap music is.' The music of 'Sweeping through the gates' might indeed make for enjoyable singing, if we, like the characters in the play, could shrug off our inhibitions. Certainly the ideas in the words are extraordinarily potent (regardless of their quality). One day, they declare, we who stand 'beside the chilly wave, | Just on the borders of the silent grave, | Shouting Jesus' power to save' shall *sweep* (not amble, stroll or process) through the gates of heaven, because we have been washed in the blood of the Lamb.

Washing in blood is a monumental paradox. Blood is notoriously difficult to wash away, either literally (Bio Tex stain remover, now unavailable in the UK, once claimed to do so) or metaphorically (ask Lady Macbeth). How does something that of its nature stains and discolours ever come to be associated with cleansing? The logic evades us. But the connection of blood with life (Lev. 17.11), and the teaching of Scripture, are both undeniable.

Washing in blood came to be especially associated with Christians who suffered for their faith to the point of martyrdom. But it still applies to all of us. Blood is powerful. It can surprise the most phlegmatic of us into visceral physical reactions when we are shocked by seeing it outside its proper sphere (inside, invisible). We are so used to blood in the context of the Eucharist as to be desensitized to the command to drink it. But on All

---

[1] Dorothy L. Sayers, *Strong Poison*, Gollancz, 1930.

Saints' Sunday, Revelation 7.13–14 brings the blood of Christ insistently to mind.

Whatever the logic, blood washes away sin. It did so under the old covenant, and it goes on doing so under the new. The Lamb of God, who takes away the sin of the world (John 1.29, 36), is an icon of innocence, but a paradox too, in that – full of life and promise – his blood is shed for the salvation of others. Perhaps that old hymn, which revolts good taste and evades musical quality control, expresses with conviction how it feels to be saved by Jesus precisely because of the lack of inhibition required to sing it. Proclaiming faith is generally a disinhibiting experience.

Christians are used to paradox. The Gospel beatitudes (from the Latin word for 'blessings') include a number of paradoxes. Uniquely among Jesus' teachings, which commonly proceed by dialogue, discussion or parable, they have a liturgical quality. We must see past the gloss of familiar rhythmic phrases to the underlying structure of thought.

The first three blessings are paradoxes of nature: that poverty, sorrow and gentleness are all gifts from God. The fourth is a paradox of action: a striving against the lower instincts of human nature (and perhaps of morality over biology).

Blessings five, six and seven are the opposite of paradoxes. Statements of reciprocity, they affirm balance and proportion (responses to divine mercy, purity, peace). The eighth blessing returns to paradox: 'Blessed are those who are persecuted …'

All eight are third-person statements: 'Blessed are *those who* …' So the final beatitude comes as a real shock: 'Blessed are *you* when people revile *you* and persecute *you*'. The impact is like Nathan denouncing David (2 Sam. 12.7); or the condemnation of Judah and Israel (Amos 2.4, 6). Now is the time to 'rejoice and be glad', for only now are 'you' on the side of God's prophets.

Washing with blood is paradoxical, but then so are the blessings God gives us. When praying for blessings, we may get nothing that we have asked for, but we shall get everything that we need. That is God's way of sweeping us through the gates of the new Jerusalem, washed in the blood of the Lamb.

The Fourth Sunday before Advent

(for use if **All Saints' Day** *is celebrated on 1 November)*

Micah 3.5–end; Psalm 43 [*or* 107.1–8]; 1 Thessalonians 2.9–13; Matthew 24.1–14

Nobody wants to be made a fool of. It dissolves our self-respect (which may already be somewhat shaky), and it exposes us to other people's ridicule. I think of the unknown numbers of people deceived by phone and internet scammers. One subtype of such scams is known as 'romance fraud': people meet over the internet and part with large sums of money for the sake of someone they love without having met them in person.

The shame this creates arises from our fear of being thought stupid or gullible. But even when the rip-off is cruel and seems, to an outsider, an act of folly, it can still bear witness to human love and generosity. Not that this is ever uppermost in the mind of someone who has been deceived.

When I read this Gospel, it reminds me that the practice of preying on the vulnerable has always been a path some people are happy to tread. The centre of gravity of this problem is not the 'vulnerability' of the 'victim'. It takes courage to put your trust in another human being, and to make yourself vulnerable by acting on that trust. Similarly, it takes self-discipline to give up your past life, overlook the negative comments and perhaps the scorn of friends and family, and dedicate your life anew, by following a leader who claims to have the answers to your questions.

I first learned to turn conventional reactions around like this when I was giving up smoking. 'Do not think of yourself as weak-willed', went the wise advice. 'Only strong-minded people can keep it up despite the expense, the smell, the social unacceptability.' That showed me how to stop feeling helpless in the grip of an addiction and to redirect the power, the strength, of my determination.

In the light of such decidedly modern experiences as nicotine addiction and internet scamming, what are we to make of this Gospel? Well, first things first. Scammers are bad. No, scammers are BAD. Exploiting others has no excuse, no justification, perhaps even no mitigation. When we look at the details of Jesus' teaching here, his attitude towards deceivers tells us what our own should be: 'Beware' says the NRSV, rendering the Greek 'look out!' or perhaps 'be alert!'.

Scamming people can happen quickly, because scammers need to apply pressure to their 'mark' to take action instantly (rather than thinking things through). But it can also be a slow grooming process, a type of coercive control, gradually making another person dependent, afraid, hyper-vigilant and hyper-conformist. Another part of Jesus' warning in this passage is directed at the dangers of cults and their charismatic leaders. Indeed, it is hard to imagine a 'successful' cult without a charismatic leader.

The attraction for the leader, the false prophet, is not always money. Power too can be addictive, aphrodisiac, intoxicating. They mislead others, as Jesus warns, all the while making out that theirs is the safe path, while everything else, 'out there' in the wider world, stinks of corruption.

If we needed confirmation how wise is Jesus' warning against the wiles of false prophets, we find it in 1 Corinthians. Paul is horrified to find his new Christians have started asserting their loyalty to himself, or to Apollos, or to Cephas. 'No!' he exclaims. They should have one loyalty, and one leader, and that is Christ himself (1 Cor. 1.12).

But Christ no longer walks the earth. We have to trust someone if we want to learn about him. So how are we to recognize true leaders? Again Paul gives us the answer (2 Cor. 4.5): he does not preach himself; he preaches Christ crucified. This recalls the alcoholic vicar's wife in the Alan Bennett *Talking Heads* monologue, heartsick at her husband's delusive holiness and heartily sick of his fans 'thinking they love God when they just love Geoffrey'.

Two sayings of Jesus show us what to make of false prophets. One tells us how to discern what really matters: 'Where your treasure is, there will your heart be also' (Matt. 6.21). The other (Matt. 18.6) expresses the Lord's judgement on those who gain gratification and profit from exploiting others (my translation): 'If anyone causes one of these little ones who believe in me to stumble, it is better for him to have a big millstone hung round his neck and to be drowned in the depth of the sea.'

The Third Sunday before Advent

Amos 5.18–24; Psalm 70; 1 Thessalonians 4.13–end; Matthew 25.1–13

Remembrance Sunday is a time when churches honour war dead and pray for peace. But the Gospel looks forward rather than back: to Advent, the Second Coming, the Judgement. The Greek word for this is *Parousia*. Remembrance is easy to prepare for, because it comes round yearly, whereas we are still awaiting *Parousia*.

Christians have waited long for this *Parousia* (1 Thess. 4.15), an idea that combines elements of 'coming' (dynamic) and 'presence' (static). But our impressions of it are confused. The coming of Christ has been pictured as a last judgement, a sifting of wheat from chaff, a separating of sheep from goats (and what is wrong with goats, we may well ask?).

Poetry calls it a day of wrath. Paintings depict torture for those who fall into the pit. Music thrills us with cataclysmic drama. No one wants to be consigned to damnation; but when we look at the saved, wearing the uniform of salvation as they march robotically into light, we do not fancy being them either. Eternal agony or eternal boredom is not much of a choice.

Looking for something both sensitive and constructive in these lections, we may wonder how the *Parousia* is a helpful theme for Remembrance Sunday, if salvation is only for the righteous. The recent conflict in Ukraine has shown that war is sometimes an inevitable outcome of the clash of good and evil (though that take on Putin's fight may be simplistic). Not everyone is a Christian, never mind a good Christian. So not everyone sees weakness as strength, *pace* Paul (2 Cor. 12.10).

All war is bad, but not all war is wrong. That seems to me a realistic attitude, though others will disagree. I once spent several years studying battle narratives in the Roman historians, and I admire Julius Caesar's portrayal of the courage of his centurions, within his self-justifying 'Gallic War' commentaries. They contain truths about human courage, even if their main purpose lies more in directing Caesar's political future than in accurate historical reporting.

I also admire the very different reportage in Spike Milligan's war diaries (likewise, coincidentally, in seven books), which begin with *Adolf Hitler: My Part in His Downfall*. Boredom and chaos, we discover there, are as much a part of warfare as courage, loyalty and self-sacrifice.

In 1 Thessalonians 4, Paul explains how Christians will experience union with Christ. He does not describe the *Parousia* as a 'last battle'. Jesus, too, keeps it simple, giving no back story to explain why the foolish virgins had not kept their lamps ready, or why their error was so egregious as to shut them out from the party, when doubtless there were lamps aplenty on the other side of the closed door.

Our problem with interpreting today's Gospel in a context of remembrance is social, not theological. Why did the wise virgins not share their lamp oil with the foolish ones, in the way that soldiers whose rations are running low might do, to ensure that all had something rather than some having nothing? The message seems to be that the wedding banquet is for some, not for all.

It may be that our generation has something genuinely positive and fresh to add to the interpretation of this parable. For we have rightly become cautious about dividing people into 'good' and 'bad'. We recognize, too, that faith is not a badge of Christian superiority but a gift, and a gift, moreover, to which people have varying degrees of access and opportunity. We who have received the gospel are not necessarily better than those by whom it has been misheard, or not heard at all. Sharing the lamp oil would surely have been a better, more humane, response.

The key to creating mutual support and nurture – among soldiers, or Christians, or churches, or communities – is to foster in individuals a sense that their own wellbeing is interwoven with that of others within the group. One day, we hope and trust that this sense, for which the Bible term is *koinonia*, will extend to the whole human family rather than individual sections of it. However sincerely we intercede for 'the poor' or 'the oppressed' or 'the refugees' in war, our prayers will not take on a heartfelt (rather than a principled) quality until we learn to see them as our fellows, and see our own wellbeing as bound up with theirs.

The Second Sunday before Advent

Zephaniah 1.7, 12–end; Psalm 90.1–8 [9–11], 12 [*or* 90.1–8];
1 Thessalonians 5.1–11; Matthew 25.14–30

The second Sunday before Advent turns to the second parable in Matthew 25. Like the other two, it is an urgent warning that time is fleeting, pressing ever onward.

The idea that time is linear is so embedded in our minds that questioning its truth can seem silly. But not all cultures imagine time like this. Christianity pictures time as directional because it has a historical start point, or, strictly, two: 'In the beginning' (Gen. 1.1; John 1.1). Likewise it expects a culmination: 'the one who testifies to these things says, "Surely I am coming soon." Amen. Come, Lord Jesus!' (Rev. 22.20).

The sequential arrangement of the books in a Christian Bible reinforces a linear concept of time, which is further corroborated by a belief that the Old Testament prophets predict the future. Judaism focuses less on future-orientated aspects of prophecy.

The more we think about time, the harder it seems to grasp. Witness Augustine's struggle to show that 'the present' exists at all (in *Confessions* 11). He remarks that 'time does not go idly by nor flow to no purpose through our senses', and that 'it does strange things to the mind' (*Confessions* 4). Understanding time begins to look as difficult as the more obviously mind-boggling concept of eternity. Ford Prefect put it like this: 'Time is an illusion. Lunchtime doubly so.'[1]

Our perception of time has the power to distort happiness, at the same time generating anxiety. Perhaps this is because our understanding of it is so inadequate. When we are under stress or pressure, we put the blame on a lack of time. In reality, it is usually an imbalance in priorities, for anxiety distracts us from important matters by displacing our attention onto unimportant ones, which we feel better able to manage.

But our dreams confront us with what our waking minds refuse to see. For this parable strikes me as a form of anxiety dream. Almost all the dreams I remember on waking are anxiety dreams. I was late, I was wearing the wrong clothes, I forgot something vital. Whatever the circumstances, being condemned by those who witness our failure is what we dread – and therefore remember most vividly.

---

1 Douglas Adams, *The Hitchhiker's Guide to the Galaxy*, BBC Radio 4, 1978–80.

This parable focuses on the slave who gets just one talent to do something with. We know that he is in trouble because the first two slaves were praised for doing what he did not. So we intuit his dread, flinching at the bitter irony that his own fear is what has brought down upon him his master's wrath.

That slave, though, was in a lose–lose situation. The household's slaves would not all have been expert traders in stocks and shares: most of them would have been labourers, secretaries, cooks, and the like. Their master should have told them that, if they felt unable to take risks with his cash, they ought to put the money in the bank to gain interest. Instead, he virtually forces his less skilled, more cautious slaves to fail. Here is the essence of an anxiety dream: unavoidable failure, humiliation, condemnation.

Letting people down makes us feel horrible. I can see why Jesus wanted to discourage people from doing nothing with what God gives them, but why did he have to make failure (in this and the other two Chapter 25 parables) so terrifying? The fear of being condemned and humiliated does not encourage people to succeed; it makes them hide mistakes and bluster to disguise their weaknesses.

At this point I need to remind myself that this story is parable, not history. However we translate the Greek adjective ('worthless'? 'useless'? 'unprofitable'?), the label 'worthless slave' is oxymoronic, for in reality he would not have been thrown out of the house but sold.

The parable seems to teach that those who have something already get more, while those who have little get nothing. But I hope this is mistaken, and that God is not the 'master' (25.24), for then it is no true depiction of divine judgement, rather a nightmare distortion of it.

To avoid being just 'myself creating what I saw',[2] we could do with informed reassurance that divine judgement is mercy-full, pity-full. Thank goodness Paul gives context to Matthew's dark warning: 'God has destined us not for wrath but for obtaining salvation through our Lord Jesus Christ' (1 Thess. 5.9).

---

2 William Cowper, *The Task, a poem, in six books: Book IV: Winter evening*, 1785.

Christ the King: The Sunday next before Advent

Ezekiel 34.11–16, 20–24; Psalm 95.1–7; Ephesians 1.15–end; Matthew 25.31–end

With the last Sunday before Advent, Christ the King, we come at last to the parable for which previous weeks have been preparing us: the separation of the sheep and the goats.

I have often used Matthew 25.31–40 as a funeral reading for those who have lived lives of selfless service outside the Church. But it is only comfortable to do so when we omit verses 41–46, which link the salvation of the righteous to the damnation of the unrighteous. For some Christians, though, this very act of division is a key part of the parable's attraction.

From the Gospel, I turned to the reading from Ezekiel, looking to find help there. I did not find a way to make Matthew's message more palatable. What I did find was a different kind of help, as I absorbed the prophetic voice. Instead of analysing the content, I responded to the form. Formal textual analysis can be an arid exercise, but not in this case. For I do not think that I have ever seen a reading so crammed with verbs.

Going by the NRSV (rather than the Hebrew original), the passage contains 24 verbs by which God describes his own actions. The most prominent are 'seek' (four times), 'bring' (three times) and 'feed' (six times). They give the impression that Ezekiel's God is an intervening God, powerful and active. Of all the verbs used in this passage, though, the last one seemed to me to be richest in meaning and most replete with hope.

It is a verb that in many languages turns out to be old, complex and very meaning-full: the verb 'to be'.

The torrent of action verbs ('I will search/seek/rescue/bring/shepherd ...', etc.) comes to a sudden stop in 34.24: 'I, the LORD, *will be* their God, and my servant David shall be prince among them.' God stops being a direct participant. He shifts from doing to being, from action to existence. By raising up a prince among humankind, in the person of King David, God discloses his design for his creation. He calls this human being to take on the role of shepherd, binder-up, feeder, strengthener of his people.

Through the succession of human rulers, God reveals to us the impossibility of human rule embodying the divine will completely: even David and Solomon fall short. But David and his successors, set over God's people Israel to rule them, are not a failed 'plan A', obliging God to dream up a plan B; they are a stage in the progressive unfolding of a single divine purpose.

Thus the 'fullness' that had always been the objective is inaugurated through the Incarnation. God's Son will rule his kingdom, and his body will be the Church. This is revealed in that fullness for which Paul longed and we still pray: the birth of Christ, which ushers in the 'kingdom of the heavens' (Matthew's distinctive expression). God shifts from doing to being, as Ezekiel prophesied so long ago, to make possible the binding together of divinity and humanity, which otherwise would be entirely disparate, incapable of integrous communication. So came the revealing of God's own Son as the Good Shepherd, the Prince of Peace.

The commemoration of Christ the King celebrates an ultimate end, which is somehow the beginning of a new dawn too. God makes Jesus Christ his way of drawing humankind to himself for ever. What was initiated in Ezekiel is completed in the Gospel, because Jesus and all who follow him as their Lord begin doing and fulfilling the will of God, whose being is now known to them. The sheep from the Gospel are both the doers of God's will and its embodiment.

So we should not underestimate the verb 'to be'. Its noun-form, 'being', is not a wishy-washy, weedy word, lurking in the background but devoid of substance. It is the term we turn to, Sunday by Sunday, to express the foundation of Christ's kingship, when we proclaim that he is 'of one being' with the Father. The Nicene Creed turned to that word 'being' to express the ultimate reality of God, both Father and Son (and finally Spirit too). Christ's kingship is simply this: God's ultimate reality, his purpose fulfilled, a disclosure of the whole meaning not just of salvation history but all history, from 'in the beginning' to the 'ages of ages, Amen' (Eph. 3.21).

YEAR B (MARK)

The H. Scriptures I

OH Book! infinite sweetnesse! let my heart
   Suck ev'ry letter, and a hony gain,
   Precious for any grief in any part;
To cleare the breast, to mollifie all pain.

Thou art all health, health thriving till it make
   A full eternitie: thou art a masse
   Of strange delights, where we may wish & take.
Ladies, look here; this is the thankfull glasse,

That mends the lookers eyes: this is the well
   That washes what it shows. Who can indeare
   Thy praise too much? thou art heav'ns Lidger here,
Working against the states of death and hell.

   Thou art joyes handsell*: heav'n lies flat in thee,
   Subject to ev'ry mounters bended knee.

                    George Herbert (1593–1633), in The Temple *(1633)*

---

*handsell is an archaic word for prophecy or future fortune.

The First Sunday of Advent

Isaiah 64.1–9; Psalm 80.1–8, 18–20 *or* [80.1–8]; 1 Corinthians 1.3–9; Mark 13.24–end

The new Church year begins with the end of all things, as the universe crumbles away, and the angels gather in the faithful. In the passage of Daniel that underpins Mark's account (Dan. 7.13–14), the Son of Man ascends before the throne of the Ancient of Days. In Mark, the Son of Man descends instead, from the clouds to earth, and there he gathers his chosen.

'They will see "the Son of Man coming in clouds" with great power and glory' (13.26). Jesus foretells a time of destruction going beyond any plague, poverty or oppression – a glimpse of the end of the universe. Creation returns to what it was in the beginning. Primordial darkness. Formless, chaotic void. Not because God's sovereignty has failed, but because it is being fulfilled. Sun and moon are cast-aside creations for 'the city has no need of sun or moon to shine on it, for the glory of God is its light, and its lamp is the Lamb' (Rev. 21.23).

The reading from the end of Isaiah reveals the Advent experience as one of contrasts and mysteries. The Lord is powerful. So why do we not reverence him and turn to him? Even if we failed to do so out of devotion, you would think that fear of judgement might get us to the point of obedience. There is no simple tie-up between our individual sins and the cosmic judgement that is being pictured; we are one body (Rom. 12.5) as well as individuals, and relate to God in both those identities.

The technical word for justifying God to humankind is 'theodicy'. Everything else about faith depends on it. If God's dealings with us are anything but fully righteous, why would we want to serve him? No one wants a God who is just the biggest bully in the celestial playground. Isaiah is *longing* for God's coming (64.1), which makes no sense without a belief in God's mercy. It might even seem like God is responsible for our wrongdoing – we hid ourselves, certainly, but only because he was angry. Like little children who know they are in for a telling-off. Like my son who, when small, 'wanted to see what would happen' if he threw stones at the car window. He ran and hid, too. Being afraid of anger is like being afraid of pain. What really hurts, in both cases, is the fear.

Isaiah's remedy for such foolish behaviour is 'calling on the name' of the Lord. It is often said that knowing a name gives you power over that person. Even speaking a loved one's name can be an act of love, embracing your feelings for them and your appreciation of their qualities. It can also give you, to be frank, leverage. Look how much easier it is for scammers when they have found out the name and identity details of their target. In the case of God, too, there is leverage. We know his name because he chose to trust us with it. When we call on that name, we know he will not ignore us. That is why Isaiah reminds God of their relationship, a bond that even wrongdoing cannot break entirely.

When Paul writes to the Corinthians, he treads a careful path between praise and criticism. Like Isaiah, he sees the people of God as trying and failing; wavering between trust and control. He takes the same path as Isaiah and Daniel, encouraging his listeners (his letters were passed between congregations to be read aloud) in what they are doing well. He mingles praise and criticism so that they keep listening, and have the courage to face up to failures as well as recognize spiritual successes. This kind of balancing act is always part of the preacher's calling. Too much emphasis on failure, and people will give up. Too little, and righteousness shades into self-righteousness.

When Jesus warns us to keep awake and be on the watch, it could seem like he is recommending hyper-vigilance. It's a fine line between anticipation and anxiety. But like the servants, we take on that vigilance as a community. When the doorkeeper needs to sleep, another servant will take his place. Christians need not be always on the alert as individuals. It is as the Church that we keep watch. Which means that when prophetic voices say, 'Here he is!', we need to listen.

The Second Sunday of Advent

Isaiah 40.1–11; Psalm 85.1–2, 8–end [*or* 85.8–end];
2 Peter 3.8–15a; Mark 1.1–8

Mark's Gospel opens in stark simplicity. It continues in that same style right to the end. Or ends (plural), depending on what view you take of the longer version (from Mark 16.9 on). No poetry like Luke. No kingly origin like Matthew. Certainly no grand philosophical prologue like John.

I was about 20 when I first formulated for myself a truth that still frustrates me to this day. You can never read a book twice for the first time. Underneath the silliness of that statement is something serious. We can never undertake that first reading with a full appreciation of the experience we are about to undergo. And by the time we acquire that appreciation, we cannot go back and have the first-time revelation again. I do not remember when I first read Mark's Gospel, but I am aware of a gradual appreciation of its qualities, helped by the whole year of it which our three-year lectionary cycle treats us to.

When I review a book for the *Church Times*, it comes with a request to ensure that readers are not left in the dark as to what the book is actually about. Mark clearly had no such guidelines. He plunges straight in as if we definitely know already what a Gospel is: 'The beginning of the good news ['gospel'; in Greek, *evangelion*] of Jesus Christ, the Son of God'. For us, 'Gospel' (with a capital G) means a book of the Bible. Back then, I am sure that Mark thought gospel meant the act of telling good news. His words were written to people who were already making the gospel their own. He wanted to make sure they stayed in that state.

In the early Church, as men (mostly) fought over what was genuine good news and what was not, there was a real chance that the Hebrew Bible (which Christians call the Old Testament) would be chucked out, on the grounds that Jesus had made the old covenant redundant. Paul's delicate line between supersession and inclusion of 'God's ancient people, the Jews, the first to hear his word' was boiled down into a simplistic rejection. The destruction of the temple in AD 70 was proof that God, like a cuckolded husband (Hos. 1.1; 3.1) had traded in his old, unfaithful, people and found himself another. This new people, moreover, were not defined by race or language, nor by a common history, or a special building. Instead, they were defined by an allegiance to a person: someone they identified as the only-begotten Son of God.

These readings help us to see why it would have been a fatal error if Christianity had jettisoned the Old Testament/Hebrew Bible. True, God in the Hebrew Bible can be terrifying, angry, jealous, vengeful. Yet he is also a mother bird with nestlings, and a kindly shepherd. There is an element of us finding the God we go looking for, according to our taste or preconceptions.

We can only see God with the blurred vision of faulty humanity. God is not inconsistent; rather, our vision and understanding change and grow. Remembering the injunction to 'put on the gospel armour, each piece put on with prayer', I used a verse from Isaiah when I was first priested. As I put on my microphone I prayed: 'Through this channel of your truth, may I be a voice crying, "Prepare the way of the Lord".' I still try to be that voice. Preparing the way of the Lord was John's cry once. But it is our job now.

What John does ought to astound us. Would any modern leader with numerous enthusiastic followers, disciples even, see another leader emerge and think it was time to make way for someone greater? It is not mere modesty on John's part. It is sheer, beautiful honesty. He has the integrity to know that he is the Forerunner (as some Christian traditions call him); his function is to show people the Way to the Truth who is Life, and then to step back into obscurity. We want to know what happens next, after the baptism of water and Spirit. But it is not the Forerunner's concern. For that we turn to 2 Peter 3.11, to find out 'what sort of persons we ought to be in leading lives of holiness and godliness'. Conversion is a moment, but its consequences play out over a lifetime.

The Third Sunday of Advent

Isaiah 61.1–4, 8–end ; Psalm 126 *or Canticle:* Magnificat;
1 Thessalonians 5.16–24; John 1.6–8, 19–28

John the Baptist doggedly refuses to give in to the logic of his own success. 'Do you claim this grand title?' 'No.' 'What about that one?' 'No.' When asked *who* he is, he instead answers with *what* he is, and tells his questioners that he is the voice of one who cries in the wilderness. We cannot ask him what he meant when he spoke those words, so we have to deduce from the Gospel how John came to see himself as the fulfilment of Isaiah's prophecy (Isa. 40.3).

All four Gospels witness to John claiming this identity for himself. So their common witness confirms his claim. John's baptism uses water, the sign of the inward reality of the cleansed sinner. But John knows that the baptism of Jesus will be a baptism of the Holy Spirit and fire (Luke 3.16).

We can see what water is: we know its properties, its feel on our skin, the evidence of its presence, the way it refreshes us when we are thirsty. With the Holy Spirit, it is not so clear. Yet our baptism was a baptism with the Holy Spirit and with fire. Where is the evidence for both of these elements? It is easy to get stuck in guilt (Christians are so good at guilt!). The glow of the Spirit and fire is lacking in us. Other people seem not to notice it. But it is unhelpful to think this way. We risk confusing medium and message. The media by which we grow are the Bible, the sacraments and the Church. The message is that lived experience of the gospel when it touched us; that first vision of Jesus our brother, the friend of sinners, who overcame the sting of death 'and opened the gate of heaven to all believers' (verses from the hymn, *Te Deum*).

The gathering darkness of the dying year affects us all, whether we realize it or not. Advent is an opportunity to look into this paradox of light and dark. What must we do when our Christian faith feels like another job to do, another burden to shoulder? The challenge is clear from the New Testament reading: 'Rejoice always, pray without ceasing, give thanks in all circumstances; for this is the will of God in Christ Jesus for you' (1 Thess. 5.16–18). Paul is not trying to add to our burdens, or increase our guilt. His lived example as a man of faith proves that the yoke of faith should be easy, and the burden light (Matt. 11.30). If it is not so for us, we need to rethink. We may not have any outrageous sins to repent of, but faith carries with it always the need to be re-formed. The warning to the church at Ephesus is precious: 'You have abandoned the love you had at first. Remember then from what you have fallen; repent, and do the works you did at first' (Rev. 2.4–5).

Remembering our first love means rediscovering the person we were when faith was new, and love was easy and natural. Just like with other love affairs, when they settle into habit and routine, we may not be able to recover that freshness in its original form, but we can reappropriate it. We can remember why we started the journey of faith. The readings for today are an icon of this remembering and renewing. Isaiah had proclaimed, 'The spirit of the Lord GOD is upon me, because the LORD has anointed me; he has sent me to bring good news' (61.1). Jesus picks up this declaration (Luke 4.18), first spoken centuries before, and takes it to himself as something new.

Hidden away in Isaiah's prophecy is a way of thinking about salvation that will be renewed in the white robes of Christian baptism centuries later. It is striking that the prophet speaks in clothing metaphors: 'the mantle of praise ... the garments of salvation ... the robe of righteousness'. We may think of clothing as something that hides our true selves, or as something that expresses who we are and what we believe. But the truth is that uniforms, clerical collars, barristers' wigs, designer labels, football shirts, head scarves, and the like all do both things. As for faith, it is something we take on as initially external to us. But if worn well, it becomes an expression of who we really are underneath as well (Eph. 6.13–17).

The Fourth Sunday of Advent

2 Samuel 7.1–11, 16; *Canticle:* Magnificat *or* Psalm 89.1–4, 19–26 [*or* 89.1–8]; Romans 16.25–end; Luke 1.26–38

These readings begin with a conversation between God and his prophet, whose name, 'Nathan', is the root of two modern boys' names: *Nathan*iel ('God has given') and Jo*nathan*, 'the LORD has given'. They both express a conviction about God's nature and action , that he is a god who gives. God challenges Nathan to explain why his people want to give him a house to live in. He does not need it. He says so.

David sets his heart on building God a dwelling place (prompted by the concern that a humble tent might dishonour him, 2 Sam. 7.2). So even though he questions the naivety of that wish, God does not reject the instinct that underpins it. It is good for us to want to give (2 Cor. 9.7). The desire to give is one way in which human beings prove themselves to be truly made in the image of God. But when we try to give something to God, he turns the action back upon us.

In this case, he is giving his people a land they can belong in. It really matters to know where we belong, and who belongs there with us – as any migrant or refugee would agree. Migration is part of most people's identities; many nations know that at some point in their history they were migrants. The ancient Athenians saw themselves as special because they believed they were 'autochthonous' (always having lived in the same land). For now, the challenge of whether we regard God's gift as a cause for self-congratulation or as a blessing to be shared remains open. Either way, setting the act of giving at the heart of the conversation between God and humankind prepares us for the challenges of the next readings, and ultimately for Christmas itself.

The reading from Romans comes with a complication. Many editors see it as an addition by someone other than Paul, at the time when Paul's letters were being collected together. It is a doxology, the grandest of all those that conclude Paul's letters. Behind it we catch the echo of an early liturgy, ascribing glory to God forever, through Jesus the Christ. It fits perfectly with the Advent theme of revelation (the Greek word for our 'uncovering' is 'apocalypse'). It speaks in terms that make sense in this generation, when pious obedience has given way to sceptical questioning.

It also provides an explanation of God's silence, using the term 'mystery' as a virtual synonym for 'gospel'. Mystery preoccupied Paul. It recurred in many of his letters. He uses it for the knowledge, formerly hidden, of God's purpose, which has been revealed in Christ. But 'mystery' is a loaded word. For his readers, it would have evoked ideas about the mystery-cults of the ancient world, which people joined to gain access to truths kept hidden from non-initiates. The Christian mystery, though, is good news to be proclaimed openly, for all. Gnostic heretics claimed exclusive secret 'knowledge' ('falsely so called', 1 Tim. 6.20). The knowledge Paul declares is freely offered to everyone.

Both these readings prepare the ground, and make level the path, for the Annunciation. That is also a revelation of a mystery. For centuries after Christ, the sacraments of Christianity were kept as secret as any ancient mystery-cult. But like Paul, Luke reveals the mystery of God's Son for anyone with ears to hear. That mystery is the virginal conception.

Despite what some critics claim, it is not like the Greek and Roman myths surrounding the births of gods and heroes. There is no grandeur in the circumstances. Mary is just a young woman. Nor is there grandeur in the consequences. Life goes on as normal. What is astonishing (and this is obscured by too much familiarity with this Gospel passage) is how plain and simple it all sounds. Mary has 'found favour' with God. Here is a clear contrast with her Son, who was the eternal Word from the beginning.

There is something about Mary. She has 'found' favour. God has recognized her nature. That is why Christians should learn from her example of obedience, and her questioning. God has chosen her not for what she was 'in the beginning' (John 1.1), but because she has become a person whom he highly favours. That ought to direct our minds to the infinite possibilities of a life lived in tune with God.

Christmas Day (Set III readings)

Isaiah 52.7–10; Psalm 98; Hebrews 1.1–4 [5–12]; John 1.1–14

There are lots of ways of teaching Christianity, but two predominate – telling stories, and the reasoned discourse about God that is theology. Of the three sets of Christmas readings, this is the most theological, at least its New Testament lections are. The Isaiah reading is unapologetically anthropomorphic. Often in Scripture, God is said to have an arm that is 'strong' or 'outstretched', but only twice is it called a 'holy arm' (and it may have been introduced into Psalm 98 from Isaiah 52). The next chapter of Isaiah, 53, brings readers to the Suffering Servant; so for a Christian, the story moves from the might of God's holy arm to the vulnerability of holy arms outstretched on the cross.

Instead of accessible narratives featuring journeys, companions, get-togethers and a birth, the New Testament reading and Gospel provide propositions about God's nature and being, in a reasoned discourse. The Greek word for such discourse is *logos*. So John begins, 'In the beginning was the *Logos*'. He writes his extraordinary prologue with existing Christian communities in mind. But the words he uses suggest that he was also communicating Christian truth to the wider world. John quarries the philosophy of his day for ways to help Christian truth talk to 'pagan' ideas. In particular, he seizes on the Stoic idea that *logos* is the stuff that makes the world cohere and establishes patterns in nature and intellect. He identifies that *logos* with the being who 'was in the beginning with God'. Stoics thought that *logos* was a kind of stuff, not a kind of person. But John turns their idea inside-out, declaring that 'the Word was made flesh and dwelt among us' (1.14).

It has always been difficult to express theologically how God, being perfect, and 'dwelling in unapproachable light' (1 Tim. 6.16) could interact with the finite physical world of human beings. Multiplicity is one answer. Have a hierarchy of divinities, like the gods of Greece and Rome; or a system of intermediate beings such as angels, to bridge the divide between divine and human. Unity is another option. It has the virtue of clarity, but struggles to explain the complexity of the human experience of the divine, and of the fact of evil in the world. Early on (as both Hebrews and John bear witness) Christians dived into the centre of this problem and scattered it like water splashed from a pool. Their ground-breaking revelation was that God encompasses both multiplicity and unity. They explained this through what they called the Word's 'Incarnation' (a word derived from Latin: 'fleshification'). The Greek term *enanthropesis* means the 'humanification' of that divine Word or *Logos*. When John states that the Word became flesh, what he means is that he is really made of human 'stuff', that he has the same physical reality that other human beings have. An equivalent English idiom might allow us to say that the Word became 'flesh and blood' like us.

When John was writing, there was no such thing as capital and lower-case letters. He could not distinguish for his readers between 'the word' and 'the Word'. Nor could the author of Hebrews, whose name is unknown (in time past it was identified as Paul). Mostly the context makes it clear; but I haven't forgotten realizing, when reading radio listings in a newspaper, that the programme I thought was *Thinking Aloud* was actually called *Thinking Allowed*. New Testament books are documents for reading aloud and listening to. They are not meant to be read microscopically, with forensic attention to detail. What inspires and drives people, in all the Bible books, is the gists and impressions through which we encounter the details over a lifetime. It's not that details don't matter; rather that if they take precedence, they will obstruct, not communicate, the gospel.

Such ideas can be difficult to preach at Christmas. People who don't hear a sermon from one year's end to the next don't want their feel-good worship spoiled by Stoic materialist philosophy. Gist, impression and story are better ways to alert people to the infinite theological complexity and simplicity of God. This can mean that the right time to explore John 1 gets deferred perpetually. But Christmas will always be the right time for someone to hear why God's 'humanification' is reasonable as well as beautiful.

The First Sunday of Christmas

Isaiah 61.10—62.3; Psalm 148 [148.7–end]; Galatians 4.4–7; Luke 2.15–21

One sending begets another. Angels are sent to some shepherds to deliver world-changing news. Then the shepherds send themselves off to Bethlehem. There is not a trace of scepticism in their response to the angelic news; not even a polite inquiry about 'how?', such as Mary speaks to Gabriel in the previous chapter (Luke 1.34). It is characteristic of Luke to balance his story with people's reactions to it: when the shepherds spread the news, the reaction is general amazement. It is as if Luke, more than the other evangelists, is anticipating our responses and indicating the proper forms they should take.

One commentator on Galatians calls 4.3–5 the 'theological center of the entire letter'; and the idea it contains, of God's 'sending', the 'center of the center'.[1] It is true that the Sundays in Advent have prepared us for an act of sending. The patriarchs, prophets and, above all, John the Baptist were all sent by God to fulfil his purposes. Galatians 4.4 is as close as Paul comes to stating that the Son pre-existed his human birth. He may have believed that, but what he chooses to share with us is the other side of Christ's identity – that he was 'born of a woman'. The phrase is a way of saying 'human' or 'mortal', as Job uses it (14.1). Apparently, the first Christians had no particular difficulty accepting the divinity of Christ, but they may have struggled to make sense of his humanity.

The problem for us in a sceptical age is the other way round. In the novel *Robert Elsmere*, by Mrs Humphrey Ward, an idealistic clergyman becomes tainted by dangerous new-fangled European teachings on the historical nature of Christian dogma. Eventually he loses his faith completely. While the agonizing process of disillusionment is working out in him, his sermons become more and more emphatic about the human suffering and human goodness of the man Jesus. It is hard to imagine such a plot seizing the public imagination today; but back in 1888 it was a red-hot topic for discussion.

What would Robert Elsemere have made of Paul's 'born of a woman'? He would have emphasized it as a truth people could still hold on to, despite the seeming impossibility of a virginal conception. I think he would also have wanted to emphasize the reactions of Mary in this

---

[1] J. Louis Martyn, *Galatians*, The Anchor Yale Bible Commentaries, Yale University Press, 1997.

chapter of Luke. Twice we are told how she responded to other people's reactions to her extraordinary son. And she alone, of all the people who have ever lived, knew, rather than believed, that his virginal conception was historical fact.

In 2.19, Luke says that she 'treasured all these words'. A little later on, after the finding in the temple (2.51), she 'treasured all these things in her heart'. 'Words' and 'things' translate the same term in Greek; 'treasured', on the other hand, translates two slightly different words as if they were the same. I don't know why the translators chose to do so. But being a translator myself, I want to give them the benefit of the doubt. We need to take note of Mary's human, motherly reaction to what people say and do concerning her son. She treasures, or perhaps 'cherishes', them.

It is hard to read the Isaiah passage without thinking of Mary's response to God and, above all, of her Magnificat. That tends to divert us from the question of who 'I' is, historically speaking. Prophets more often speak God's words, not their own. The language is ecstatic; the vision is timeless. The comparison with the fertile earth and the blossoming garden tells us that both righteousness and praise are, in God's eyes, natural phenomena (61.11). At the heart of the prophecy is Zion's restoration. For Christians, it also reflects God's work of restoration in themselves: a rebuilding of the human individual broken by sin, and its remaking in the image of the Christ-child.

Looking back to Galatians, through the lenses of Luke and Isaiah, it's now clear that the epistle has a centre to its 'center of a center' – 'you are no longer a slave but a child' (4.7). When we think that our happiest memories of Christmas, whether they represent dreams or reality, cluster around the time of our childhood, we see that to be a child of God, at Christmas, is the most special thing of all.

The Second Sunday of Christmas

Jeremiah 31.7–14; Psalm 147.13–end; Ephesians 1.3–14;
John 1.[1–9] 10–18

No committed Christian reads a passage of the Bible only once. The life of faith rests upon repeated reading and reflection. In such a context, every interpretation we reach is at best provisional: 'This is how the passage strikes us *now*.'

The Ephesians passage looks first like a paean of praise, an ecstasy of adoration. But it is a sturdy theological stem with a vigorous root system. One such root is the word 'plan'. It's a dull word in English. The Greek is *oikonomia*, or 'economy.' For the first Christians, 'economy' was not about the science of money. It was a theological term expressing how God relates to the world he has made. It contrasts with who God is in himself. We tend to think that Jesus solved that conundrum through the Incarnation. But the first Christians were trying to understand it both rationally and biologically. When we ask questions about how the divine and human co-exist in the person of Christ, we too need to make intellectual sense of that according to the understanding of our own time. We can't just park the question in the category of mystery or spirituality.

In Scripture, God's 'plan' is sometimes explored theologically, sometimes in story form. When Jeremiah piles up images of return and homecoming in a fusillade of verbs – 'bring', 'gather', 'return', 'lead back' – he is referring to the liberation of God's people from their exile in Babylon. God is a king who goes into battle for his people; or a skilled negotiator who pays a ransom to buy back ('redeem') hostages. Taking hostages and then using them as leverage to get money was a standard tactic in ancient warfare. It still is – think of the kidnapping of hundreds of schoolgirls in Chibok, Nigeria, in 2014. They were pawns in a political game. Pawns tend to be expendable, in politics as in chess; but in the divine economy, God disagrees. He thinks it important to buy them back whatever the price.

Another term in Ephesians that needs a fresh look is 'the fullness of time'. Once again pedestrian English words cloak a buzz of questions. The Greek for 'fullness', *pleroma*, expresses the sense that life has a direction, towards a fulfilment of God's plan. It is not left as a pious mystery, which we can adore but not interrogate. This 'fullness' or 'fulfilment' will come about because of another action that looks ordinary in plain English: 'gathering up'. Still, sometimes plain words are best: *anacephalaiosis* in a mouthful in Greek or in its closest English equivalent, 'recapitulation'.

Just beneath the surface of this mystical language is a truth that we need to commit ourselves to by living in a way that shows we believe in it. History is not a meandering mass of meaninglessness. It's a journey with a purpose, towards an end point or fulfilment. That fulfilment will come about through the rethinking, reordering, restoration (all translations of *anacephalaiosis*) of the whole creation. In the beginning, God saw all that he had made and it was 'very good' (Gen. 1.31). So in the end, everything he has made will become as he willed it to be.

God rescues us, then, from wandering through life as though it has no meaning. The stories of the Jewish people's return from exile in Babylon, and the Exodus in the time of Moses, reveal a fundamental characteristic of God himself. Though human existence may be experienced as disintegration or pointlessness, God-centred living holds out the hope of integrity, restoring us to wholeness.

This contrast between divine action and human inaction is summed up in the Gospel: 'He was in the world, and the world came into being through him; yet the world did not know him' (John 1.10). For those who did know him, ultimate blessing was the result; they committed themselves to the story and the promises. God gives us stories to make sense of him in human time. But neither he nor the Son, the Word, are bound by time; hence the paradox as John the Baptist puts it: 'He who comes after me ranks ahead of me because he was before me' (1.15). History is faith in time; theology is faith drawn out of historical time. Gospel truth leads us beyond both: it's timeless, because it restores us to the fullness of grace and truth, as we learn to love the one who is 'of the Father's heart begotten'.

The Epiphany

Isaiah 60.1–6; Psalm 72.[1–9] 10–15; Ephesians 3.1–12; Matthew 2.1–12

Appropriately for the appearing of Jesus to the world and all peoples, at the heart of Isaiah's prophecy is a veritable orgy of giving. The glory of the passage is its positivity. Light shines. God's people become a source of light for other peoples. All the good things of earth and sea will be given as a willing tribute, a thanksgiving offering. My favourite among the gifts is the camels. I can't help finding unintended humour in the news that 'a multitude of camels shall cover you' (60.6). Picture this in your mind's eye and the result is hilarity. It reminds me of a dry observation made by the dramatist Sophocles: reflecting on Homer's beautiful description of dawn as 'rosy-fingered', he pointed out that if the goddess Dawn really had rosy fingers, she would look like a dye-worker, not a goddess. The gap between literal and metaphorical language was nailed for ever there and then.

A similar range of ways of reading a text is apparent in the Gospel for the Epiphany. If Bethlehem is a city, with all its buildings doubtless packed closely together, how could the wise men from the east tell exactly which one the star had stopped over? That precise point was sent up in the opening section of *Monty Python's Life of Brian*, and ever since 1979, we have been made to work a little bit harder to take the Gospel at face value. Our understanding of how the world works tells us that stars cannot change their course or stop moving. The text tells us that this is what the wise men observed; and we know they were experts in astronomy, because it was their noticing of this unusual phenomenon in the sky that prompted their journey in the first place. In other words, it struck them as odd too. So odd that they were prepared to face great difficulties: 'A cold coming they had of it at this time of the year, just the worst time of the year to take a journey … the ways deep, the weather sharp, the days short, the sun farthest off, in "the very dead of winter".' So Lancelot Andrewes described it in a famous sermon in 1622.

Beyond this, the Gospel cannot take us. If we want to understand the astronomy of the Epiphany, we have to look to science, not exegesis. I can't say I've ever been tempted to try that road, though commentaries on the Gospel are full of heroic efforts in that direction. For me, it's enough to know that this is what those present thought had happened, and what they carefully recorded so that we could know it too.

In Ephesians, Paul tackles Epiphany from a different angle. He continues his exploration of those key concepts of 'economy' and 'mystery', which describe the unfolding of God's eternal plan in human time. It is no accident that he returns repeatedly to 'grace' as the gift that spills out abundantly through the Epiphany, or appearing, of Christ to all peoples. Unlike camels, or gold, frankincense and myrrh, this grace is not something we can wrap and hand to a recipient. Paul tells us how he came by this understanding of God's grace at work. He didn't construct it for himself, or intuit it from creation, or find it in the law and the prophets. It came to him through revelation.

The Greek word for revelation is 'apocalypse', or 'uncovering'. God communicated to Paul by uncovering his divine hand at work in human affairs. The wise men's star was another such revelation. No one in Jerusalem seems to have noticed the star, or understood its meaning. That isn't surprising. Most Christians probably don't experience more than a few revelations (if that) in a lifetime. Most of the time, God communicates with us in straightforward ways: through seeing, speaking or listening. That makes an omission from the Gospel text all the more surprising. A word that appears twice in the Greek original, *idou*, has been left out of the NRSV. The AV translated it first as 'Behold' and then as 'Lo'. Omitting it implies that there is no modern equivalent. But 'Look!' or 'See!' would do fine. We should put this word back in, if only to prompt ourselves to us sit up and pay attention; and remind us that the gospel needs to be revealed, spoken, heard and seen.

The Baptism of Christ
(The First Sunday of Epiphany)

Genesis 1.1–5; Psalm 29; Acts 19.1–7; Mark 1.4–11

At first glance, camel's hair clothing and eating locusts sounds less like Scripture and more like a challenge on *I'm a Celebrity... Get Me Out of Here!* But anyone who's ever worn a camel coat or knitted with camel hair fibre will know what an indulgent luxury it is. Perhaps the Baptist deliberately chose only the scratchy guard hair on the surface of the pelt rather than the soft fluff beneath. At any rate his meals were kosher (Lev. 11.22).

John's baptism of Jesus marks the beginning of the Lord's ministry. It also shaped later Christian expectations of what a baptism should be. There must be water; then, on coming up out of the water, there would be the Holy Spirit. The picture in Acts is similar: those disciples were baptized in the Lord's name, but the Spirit came upon them afterwards, when Paul laid hands on them. Human action and divine response form a progressive sequence, rather than combining in a single moment.

What John predicted, and what baptized Christians now expect, is slightly different: not water followed by Spirit, but water baptism 'in' or 'with' the Spirit. Water alone is not enough under the new covenant. Nor is repentance (and the forgiveness of sins it confers) sufficient in itself. To be 'in Christ' we need to be baptized with, or in, the Spirit. That means the whole package of baptism into death and resurrection (Rom. 6).

In our eagerness to stress the difference between John's water-baptism and Christian Spirit-baptism, we tend to go straight to the superiority of Spirit-baptism. We ought to be noticing, though, that even Spirit-baptism requires water; it does not replace it. The descent of the Spirit upon Jesus comes after immersion in the Jordan. This is a proto-sacrament before sacraments became familiar in worship of God.

Christian Spirit-baptism, then, incorporates water-baptism. Luke does not tell us in the Acts passage whether Paul's Spirit-baptism of the Ephesian disciples used water. I suspect that it did. Not merely as a way to big up the experience for those being baptized, but because the pattern of symbol and referent (or 'meaning' and 'thing') is so ingrained in Bible thinking. Faith is about seeing the meaning under, or within, ordinary things. It is not about dismissing ordinary things, because God has chosen to work through them, not in spite of them.

Acts says of the disciples Paul baptized that 'there were about 12 of them'. That is a resonant number; it is not incidental. It signifies more than a quantity of units. That makes the 'about' that precedes it a bit peculiar. We could imitate modern colloquial speech by translating the Greek for 'about' (*hōsei*) as 'like', which would have Luke saying 'there were, like, 12 of them'. Tempting. But better not.

When we read them in order, the lections suggest a progressive disclosure about the Spirit from the beginning of time onwards. But it's not as certain as the NRSV makes this appear. In the opening verses of Genesis, what was 'the Spirit of God' in the AV (*ruach elohim* in Hebrew) is downgraded in the NRSV to 'a wind from God'. Spurrell's *Notes on the Hebrew Text of the Book of Genesis* (1887) dismisses this out of hand: 'Spirit of God' could never be anything as pedestrian as a weather report. I think it matters to Christians that the Spirit of God, not a wind from God, is moving over the waters.

The three lections have been chosen to reflect on one another. Yet it is not a progressive disclosure, from Old to New Testament, simple to complex, or surface to depth. It is an oddity of English education that study of the Greeks and Romans ('Classics') and study of Judaism and Christianity are generally taught in separate faculties, when the boundaries between the disciplines are quite porous. But while Scripture does not have much to say about its own nature, a 'pagan' scholar (we know him as pseudo-Longinus) spotted straightaway the sublime quality of this Genesis vision, when, in the first century AD, he wrote the first recorded 'pagan' reaction to a Bible text: 'The lawgiver of the Jews was no ordinary man. He had a worthy conception of the power of the divine when he writes, 'God said what? "Let there be light", and there was light' (*On Sublimity*, 9.9).

The Second Sunday of Epiphany

1 Samuel 3.1–10 [11–20]; Psalm 139.1–5, 12–18 [*or* 1–9];
Revelation 5.1–10; John 1.43–end

Each of these three readings is a call to vision. Visions are not the preserve of the mad or saintly (or both). They are for all Christians. The reason why not everyone gets them is (in part) because not all of us open ourselves to the possibility. Not having visions could be because we aren't looking for them (hence the angel's command 'See!', Rev. 5.6) or because we are looking but somehow not seeing.

Augustine thought that sight was the highest of the five physical senses, perhaps because he associated it with light. As Christians, we can use the word 'sight' to refer to ordinary seeing and 'vision' for a special kind of Christian seeing. The distinction isn't always clear-cut, but there's no doubt that all three of these readings are about vision in the fullest sense.

In the Gospel, Philip calls Nathanael to 'come and see', while Jesus has already 'seen' Nathanael, before he met him in person. John of Patmos is commanded to 'see' the conquest of the Lion of Judah. In the Old Testament/Hebrew Bible reading, by contrast, Eli's sight has grown dim, and that failing external sight is a symbol of his failing internal vision, as God turns from Eli to Samuel, the young boy who has heard the call and responded.

In both the Old Testament/Hebrew Bible and the New Testament readings, elements of the passages feel severe. Eli is punished for not rebuking his sons' behaviour. It is a reversal of the old 'sins of the fathers' problem, for which Scripture offers us two different ways of understanding the issue (Deut. 5.9–10 versus Ez. 18.1–4), and then we choose what prevails. But like the practice of Jewish sons saying Kaddish on the death of their father, their outward behaviour is a confirmation that the father fulfilled the obligations of his faith by bringing up his sons to reverence God. In this, Eli failed. The sin that can never be expiated strikes such fear into Samuel that he is afraid to speak God's words to Eli. But it seems that Eli knows the judgement is coming, and is content to accept it.

When it comes to the visions of John of Patmos, readers can struggle to make sense of strange creatures like a lamb with seven horns and seven eyes (Rev. 5.6); or feel surprise at how incense that used to signify prayer becomes itself the prayers of saints. Or is it vice versa? With John of Patmos, one can never be sure.

We also struggle (unless we see faith as for the chosen few) to match up his visions of restoration and healing (Rev. 21.1–7, for example) with his Christ of final judgement (Rev. 21.8). Our analytical instinct is to tidy up discrepancies. But the Scripture insists on keeping them, holding them in tension. The contrast between solving the problem and living with it, or between an imaginative approach to Scripture and a factual one, will be approached differently depending on our personality and character:

> 'You wicked thing,' said Lavinia, turning on Sara; 'making fairy stories about heaven.' 'There are much more splendid stories in Revelation,' returned Sara. 'Just look and see! How do you know mine are fairy stories? But I can tell you' – with a fine bit of unheavenly temper – 'you will never find out whether they are or not if you're not kinder to people than you are now.' (Frances Hodgson Burnett, *A Little Princess*, 1905).

The vision is true, and sure, but for some of us, as for Nathanael, it is not yet. 'You *will* see', says Jesus. And when Jesus declares what that vision will be, he does so in terms every bit as extraordinary as the visions of his namesake on Patmos. What you cannot tell from the English is that although Jesus is speaking to Nathanael, his words are in the plural, 'all of you will see'. The vision begins as for an individual in historical time. It becomes a universal vision. Whatever the precise meaning of Jacob's vision of the ladder (Gen. 28.12), we should remember that it was taken then as a promise of blessing to all the families of the earth (Gen. 28.14): a confirmation, if you like, of John 1.14, that between heaven and earth, where once a great gulf was set (Luke 16.26), there is now a connection: a bridge, a ladder, a way of passing over, in the person of the Son of Man.

The Third Sunday of Epiphany

Genesis 14.17–20; Psalm 128; Revelation 19.6–10; John 2.1–11

January is not a popular time for weddings. Not in northern Europe. But it looks like we are not in the world of 'ordinary time' in any case. Counting up the references to days in the first two chapters of John as if they marked a strict chronology just befuddles us. If we start from Bethany then Cana is the fifth day. At John 1.28–9, the Baptist is in Bethany; at 1.35: he calls Jesus 'Lamb of God'; at 1.43 Jesus talks with Philip and Nathanael. It can only be the third day if we start counting at 1.35. There is God's time, and there's government time, as a character in a novel once remarked.

The readings in the lectionary are usually chosen because they speak to one another in some way. But on this occasion, the tie-up is particularly close. Be it January or June, the focus is firmly on weddings – a sensitive subject in church at the time of writing. Among other challenges, there is the pressure of a built-up blockage of marriages in the sacramental pipeline caused by Covid-19. Those who have a 'high' doctrine of marriage as a sacrament will not like the image of sewers and drainage as a way of expressing the current situation of holy matrimony; but these readings preserve the sublimity, by pointing to a far higher understanding of what marriage can and should mean than any human could otherwise imagine.

In today's psalm is one of the loveliest family prayers in the Bible. But I had not previously noticed how well this psalm and Gospel go together. The psalm is a celebration of the blessings of family life. It ends with a prayer I use at every wedding I officiate at. It touches me, and likewise many of those present at every wedding, for whom the beginning of one 'new life together in the community' is an opportunity to look back on many choices and commitments made decades ago, for better or for worse. 'May you live to see your children's children', I pray for the couple; 'and peace [glossing here for the sake of a non-churchy congregation] upon God's people'. It reminds me once more of the Jewish tradition of saying Kaddish, a mourner's prayer that marks how the late parent now dead has brought up their child in the faith and fear of God. It joins the inward joy of family life to the outward joy of life in fellowship with others. One blood family, and one spirit family: in both cases, to live to see your children's children is to be richly blessed.

Weddings are not the only sacramental prefiguring in the readings. The Genesis reading, short as it is, fixes our attention on the single theme of kingly priesthood in association with (as Christians immediately identify it) the eucharistic offering of bread and wine. Salem is traditionally identified as Jerusalem. So one commentator observes that in this short section, we find both the racial and the geographical identity of the people of God together for the first time. What Abram is doing, recognizing the status of a foreign king, and receiving his blessing, is harder to understand. But the acknowledgement of the Hebrews' God by the rulers of other nations is a key theme in other scriptural texts, especially Daniel, which forms the daily preparation for Christmas, as this set of readings guides us in its aftermath.

The weaving-together of the themes of marriage and Eucharist continues in Revelation too. A bishop once remarked to me on how disappointing he found the liturgical version of Revelation 19.9, 'Blessed are those who are called to his supper'. He had a point. The 'marriage-supper of the Lamb' sounds far more exciting. When it comes to actual weddings, the theme of the Lamb and his Bride is rather too rich theological fare, when some plainer bread-and-butter truths are required, and are much more likely to make the necessary impact than a lot of church-speak. Where the 'marriage-supper of the Lamb' inspires deep reflection among those who are already Christian, a prayer that we may live to see our children's children (whether blood family or spiritual family) will surely touch the hearts of all. Because everyone is somebody's child.

The Fourth Sunday of Epiphany

Deuteronomy 18.15–20; Psalm 111; Revelation 12.1–5a;
Mark 1.21–28

Exorcism has acquired some unfortunate connotations. Very unfortunate, when you consider that every baptized Christian has been exorcized. Exorcizing someone means bringing them out of hell – or perhaps bringing hell out of them, as Jesus did with a legion of evil spirits in Mark 5.1–20. There is a powerful exorcism prayer in Holy Baptism:

> May almighty God deliver you from the powers of darkness,
> restore in you the image of his glory,
> and lead you in the light and obedience of Christ. **Amen.**

But the liturgy does not mention that the prayer is an 'exorcism'.

Christians have learned to counter the works of darkness by putting on the armour of light (Rom. 13.12) for protection. They trust that this protection is real, strong. But those who do not equip themselves with the armour of light may find those powers of darkness an insoluble burden. If we think that we in the developed world are free from that burden of fear, and that it is rooted in primitive instincts that we are too sophisticated to be troubled by, we should think again.

The face that evil wears may change, but its corrosive harm does not. It feeds on our fears for the present and future – climate catastrophe, war, populism, and the like. The term 'witch hunt' has become a label for any pursuit of someone we scapegoat for our terrors. Witchfinders General are at work in the twenty-first century on social media, hunting for lives to destroy.

If exorcism is now a whispered word in mainstream Christianity, then, it is not because evil is a problem that has been solved. The 1973 film, *The Exorcist*, has played a part in making exorcism a trigger-word for terror. It would be good to rehabilitate exorcism as a Christian objective, or at least to recognize that those elements of exorcism that persist in Christian texts and sacraments can be living blessings, not dead superstitions. 'Deliver us from evil' is one of the most powerful prayers we have.

The ministry of exorcism among Christians is also referred to as 'deliverance'. In this Gospel, Jesus does not see the evil as inherent in the man himself. It is an external power that has forced its way in, from which the man needs to be delivered. Jesus does not even speak to the possessed man. His conversation is with the unclean spirit he confronts. This makes me wonder whether we are seeing, in this apparently straightforward healing, a clue to Jesus' power to restore us to the state that God intended for us. Evil may be a corrupting presence, but it does not penetrate the essence of our nature, which remains what it has always been: made in the divine likeness, free from any taint.

The crowd is excited by a 'new teaching' (Mark 1.27). But what humanity has yet to learn, the unclean spirits already know – and they tremble (James 2.19). Still, it is too soon to be carried away with the benefits of exorcism. This Gospel shows that is it not a straightforward procedure. Like the disciples before us, we cannot have the complete command over spirits that Jesus does (Mark 9.28). And not every instance of exorcism or deliverance ministry practised in churches is beneficial: some Christian communities claim to 'heal' people who exhibit non-conforming characteristics that are judged unacceptable. Where this is directed at enforcing uniformity, or manipulating individuals, it is potentially devastating in its effects.

This is not to say that all Christian healing is suspect, or that all exorcisms target evils that are imaginary. Healing (not the same thing as 'curing') can be effected by prayer and laying-on of hands in accordance with biblical teaching and Church guidance. Exorcism can make a real difference to people who have been traumatized by experiences for which the only fitting word is 'evil'. We can understand this as the reintegration of the fractured self. In this Gospel, the unclean spirit is one, but speaks as both one and many: 'What have you to do with *us* ... Have you come to destroy *us*?' (1.24).

All four evangelists have their own 'take' on Jesus' ministry, which they highlight right at the start, so that listeners and readers can watch out for it. Mark's simple, straightforward Gospel has this truth to drive home to us: that one principal focus of Jesus' ministry is the driving out of evil.

The Presentation of Christ in the Temple (Candlemas)

Malachi 3.1–5; Psalm 24.[1–6] 7–end; Hebrews 2.14–end; Luke 2.22–40

On the surface, Candlemas is a simple initiation ceremony, primarily for the family, but with a social dimension as well, marking the child as belonging to a community. When babies are born, adjustments need to take place. Society makes room for the new person's existence; and recalculates the status of the parents, especially the woman who has given birth. In ancient societies, she moves into the special social and legal category of 'mother' – and in modern societies, some would argue, into a category of being in which everything she does is ripe for criticism and nothing that she chooses is good enough. In fact, every firstborn child creates two new beings – usually (and in Bible days always) a new mother and a new father. Like mothers, fathers have social expectations attaching to their new role (Matt. 13.55).

Luke's account points to deeper meanings. Most important is a double recognition: first, that this child is the long-expected saviour (2.30) sent both to the children of Israel and to the gentiles (non-Jewish races); and second, that a man and a woman (representing faithful Israel) have been waiting a long time to see this world-changing moment with their own eyes (2.26, 38). There has never been a better time than now to remember the importance of being present at certain family and social events, to fulfil ancient traditions.

All three readings touch on purification. In Malachi, God does the purifying, like a 'refiner's fire', which sounds powerful and positive; or like 'fuller's soap', which does not (a fuller is someone who cleans and felts grubby, greasy wool using harsh chemicals). In Hebrews, purification is effected through a double test, of sacrifice and suffering.

It does not take long to realize that this theme takes us into sensitive territory. Variations in the translation of the Greek hint at the need for care in expressing gender, whether in grammar, biology or exegesis. In Hebrews, the NRSV follows its standard practice of taking the Greek word for brothers (*adelphoi*) to encompass sisters too. But to justify this practice, we need to be confident that whoever wrote this letter was really thinking of women as well as men in the communities to which they were writing. It is not enough that we *wish* the term included both. Or that we decide that he *should* have meant both, and so adjust the meaning to fit.

No more than Hebrews does Luke's Gospel reveal Bible times as a paradise of gender equality; though his own positive attitude to women throughout his telling of the Gospel story is well-known. Here, trying to explain the law of Moses to gentiles, he either mistakes or simplifies the process. Full marks to the NRSV here for faithfully transmitting the statement that both Mary and Joseph came to be purified (2.22). The 1611 AV 'improved' the BCP 1552 by attributing a need for purification to Mary alone. The BCP 1662 followed the AV. Some ancient interpreters suggested that 'their' purification was a reference to Mary and Jesus, rather than Mary and Joseph. But this is to infect the Gospel with later ideas of baptizing infants for the washing-away of sin. Under the Mosaic law, Mary's purification would have been understood as physical, not moral or spiritual. The idea of babies needing purification would not have made much sense.

Through the blessing given by Simeon (2.34), Luke acknowledges the role of Joseph – an adoptive father is a real father, no question. Yet he still marked Mary out as *uniquely* (my eisegetical emphasis) filled with divine favour (*charis*: Luke 1.28, 30). By repeating the word 'favour' (2.40), he makes a verbal connection between her and her son a theological one too.

Purification of women after childbirth was once common in the Church of England. It had its own office (known as 'churching') in the BCP 1662. That faded away in the twentieth century, around the same time as 'all women labouring of child' was cut from the Great Litany (because it was felt that science left nothing for intercession to achieve?). Common Worship, thanks be, put that prayer back where it belongs.

To strengthen our understanding of God as purifier, we can return to Malachi, for he reveals purification as a moral and spiritual quality too (3.3): 'he will purify the descendants of Levi and refine them like gold and silver, until they present offerings to the LORD in righteousness.'

Proper 1
Sunday between 4 and 10 February inclusive
(if earlier than the Second Sunday before Lent)

Isaiah 40.21–end; Psalm 147.1–12, 21 [147.1–12];
1 Corinthians 9.16–23; Mark 1.29–39

My first intention, on reading up about this Gospel, was to go straight to Mark 1.31, 'she began to serve them'. Really? Only moments before, the poor woman, the mother of Peter's wife, had been seriously ill. Now she gets up and starts to serve those gathered in the house. At least five visitors were present (Simon, Andrew, James, John, Jesus and the sick woman) plus (probably) Simon [Peter's] wife too.

This verse is at least as annoying, in its way, as Luke 10.40, in which making life comfortable for everyone and putting their needs before her own gets Martha less credit from Jesus than her contemplative (or lazy?) sister. Should not Simon, Andrew, James, John, Jesus and Simon's wife have had the consideration, the gumption, to serve the poor woman instead?

The simple answer to this question is probably the correct one: her being well enough to carry out this work is meant to show that she is completely cured, as if she had never been ill. That is certainly in sympathy with other Gospel healings. People healed by Jesus are restored completely, not partially.

It is not in itself implausible that someone he had healed should become as if their illness had never happened. We could compare forgiveness: the pardon God grants to sinners is so complete as to render their wrongdoing as if it had never been. All the same, to the wrongdoer, appropriating God's forgiveness can takes time. It may never be complete.

Even in modern times this remains the case. Not all the wonders of modern medicine can make us as if our physical illnesses had never befallen us at all. For this reason, as well as others, it matters that the nature of her illness is specified: she has a fever. The illness is physical and potentially fixable.

Without the blessings of modern medicine, which offer us the possibility of living into a healthy and active old age, in Bible days both mental and physical illnesses were dangerous and distressing for patients and relatives. A scratch, a sniffle, a pregnancy, could kill. Epilepsy, depression and schizophrenia were known and feared as making people dangerous to themselves or others.

Without science, the only sensible option for treating a high temperature was symptomatic relief. I have to remind myself of this when I am annoyed by a lack of imagination in a period drama: someone falls ill, and without fail another character is set to dab their face with wet cloths. It is as indispensable as the sound-effect of a tawny owl's 'ke-wick' or 'wooo' telling viewers that the action is taking place at night-time (in case the lack of light failed to alert them).

Imagine watching a loved one struggling to survive, while equipped with nothing more curative than a wet cloth. In just this situation, such is Jesus' healing power that Simon's mother-in-law recovers well enough to serve his friends.

Just a couple of verses earlier (1.23–26), Jesus performed his first healing in Mark's Gospel, but it was not the curing of a physical ailment. It was an exorcism. Jesus ordered an 'unclean spirit' (a literal translation, *akatharton pneuma*, not a euphemism for 'demon') to leave a man who was yelling at him in the local synagogue.

I once asked a friend to stand in for me by taking the early service at the church where I was Rector. He later told me that it had been an 'interesting' experience. A young man with mental health problems, well-known in the village, had done what the spirit-possessed man in the synagogue did: bursting in and shouting, clearly troubled about something. I never established exactly what.

Between my friend, more capable and more experienced than I, and my churchwarden, a recently retired GP, all was made well. The young man was calmed and reassured, and the congregation departed having made their Communion without lasting trauma. I sometimes wonder how I would have handled it, either as one of the congregation or as the sick person. Disruption to worship can be shockingly unsettling.

Learning of a feverish woman, ill enough to be in bed, made well enough to assert her right (as she might see it) to be the dispenser of hospitality to honoured guests (and not merely a dogsbody or doormat) strikingly illustrates this mostly unknown new healer's power to change lives for the better.

Proper 2
Sunday between 11 and 17 February inclusive
(if earlier than the Second Sunday before Lent)

2 Kings 5.1–14; Psalm 30; 1 Corinthians 9.24–end; Mark 1.40–end

Here is a tricky passage where the Gospel says quite different things, depending on which version you are reading. The two modern translations most often used during worship in the Church of England are the NRSV and NIV: the former says Jesus was 'moved with pity'; the latter says that he was 'indignant'. These two readings are not different interpretations of a single Greek word. Behind them lie two different Greek words, one found in a minority of manuscripts ('indignant', or, more literally, 'angry'), the other in the majority ('pity').

In themselves, such differences should not trouble us. On the contrary, they are reassuring, for they show that the texts have not been seriously interfered with to streamline the narrative into one smooth storyline.

At first sight, pity seems a much more understandable reaction to the man suffering from this debilitating sickness. But if that is so, where has the troublesome word 'angry' come from? Is it there to show us a human side to Jesus, perhaps because he was feeling too grumpy for healing lepers that day? I hope not. Who might Jesus be angry with? Or what might he be angry about?

Looking at what Matthew (8.2–3) and Luke (5.12–13) have done with this story can help us to decide between 'pity' and 'anger'. They both omit the detail that Jesus became angry. But they both fail to mention his feeling pity either. If they have left out a word, it is much more likely that this was the awkward 'angry' than the sympathetic 'pity'. But no definitive solution is possible. If we go with 'angry' for now, we have to find a reason why Jesus might be angry.

This is the first time that Jesus has been asked to heal someone with a sickness that made them 'unclean'. This means a sickness that cut them off from table fellowship, common worship and every kind of social interaction with their fellow human beings. He has healed someone possessed and someone with a fever. But now he is being asked to heal someone who is a complete outcast.

This could be what makes Jesus angry: not the man's disease, but his being isolated and ostracized. In particular, he sees ritual laws intended for human wellbeing used to increase, not diminish, human anguish. So he responds to the man's plea, stretching out his hand and touching him, and saying to him, 'I do choose. Be made clean'. That moment of touch is like the fractional, universe-changing brush of fingertips between God and Adam on the Sistine Chapel ceiling. It is not just a moment of healing but one of creation as well.

That is a lot of theological power to invest in one disputed word. But sometimes exploring the Bible is like that. You can choose to take one tiny thing on trust, and suddenly you hear the sound of a lot of other things clicking into place.

Still, before we get carried away by Jesus' righteous anger, is there anything to be said for his feeling pity? Might that, even now, be the more probable original? It is never implausible for Jesus to feel pity, for this is the characteristic virtue of his compassionate heart. Anger, in contrast, he displays more rarely. When he does, it is because of some wrong done to others, often by those who are, in essence, liars: the kind of people who apply double standards, who exploit the vulnerable, pretending devotion to God while acting harshly towards others made in his image.

The leper shows a degree of faith in Jesus that is very striking at this early stage in his ministry. We do not find him asking for magic words, or potions, or elaborate rituals. One thing only effects the cure – Jesus 'wills' it to be so (I think the verb 'choose' sounds a bit arbitrary for this significant act). He could have healed the man without touching him at all, without even being at the same location (Mark 5.21–43). The act of touching is a gesture that accords dignity to the man with leprosy, but its wider purpose, I think, is to teach the crowd.

What we can say with complete certainty is that if human suffering arouses Jesus' emotions, it should arouse ours too, whether anger or pity. Again, if his emotions prompt him to take positive action, so should ours.

Proper 3
Sunday between 18 and 24 February inclusive
(if earlier than 2nd Sunday before Lent)

or Sunday between 24 and 28 May inclusive
(if after Trinity Sunday)

Isaiah 43.18–25; Psalm 41; 2 Corinthians 1.18–22; Mark 2.1–12

This Gospel looks straightforward. Jesus encounters someone in need, addresses that need and attracts trouble as a result. The person in need is described as a 'paralytic'. It is a Greek word that has come into English usage. I might have guessed this much. But I would not have guessed that 'paralytic' has the same *range* of meaning in Greek as it does in English. It can apply (in medical terms) to disabled or malfunctioning nerves, but also to the effects of excessive alcohol (loosening is the key idea). Medical 'paralysis' means that our nerves are not activating our muscles. Being socially 'paralytic' often means that our brain has stopped communicating with our mouth.

Those kind friends who went the extra mile to get the paralytic healed by Jesus get a good press for their efforts. 'See how they loved him', people might say (John 11.36). But their actions could be transgressive, especially among British readers: for this is the ultimate social sin – queue-jumping. I remember an occasion of 'till rage' in a Co-op years ago, when I and another shopper both thought we had been first to join the queue. Not that things became violent: rather, we strove to out-do one another in sanctimonious politeness: 'No, no, *you* go first, I can see you're in a hurry'.

How did all the other people in the 'throng and press' of the crowd feel about the paralysed man and his queue-jumping mates? Mark does not tell us whether Jesus kept on with his healing until all the broken, suffering people who had come to him that day looking for help had received what they needed. It is hard to imagine Jesus putting up a 'closed' sign and telling those last in the queue to come back tomorrow or after the weekend.

One clue to his attitude comes from the way he speaks elsewhere about the poor. His attitude is, as ever, compassionate. But it is also realistic. 'You always have the poor with you', he says in Mark 14.7. Matthew (26.10) and John (12.8) record this same saying, so it was probably a familiar aspect of Jesus' teaching. If this was also how he thought about the sick, and all people in need of healing, he must have realized that even he could not reach and heal everyone. Even if he had kept going that day until everyone in the queue had been healed, in addition to the man let down through the hole in the ceiling, the next day would bring more people, and still more again the day after that, as his fame grew, and the crowds' expectations grew with it.

Most people who read this story will never have experienced physical paralysis, yet it has a message that reaches everyone. For once, it is not action that matters the most but words. Somehow (we are not told how), he knows what the scribes are saying among themselves. They are suspicious of him. That is not surprising given that he is, as it were, trespassing on their territory: not by healing the man, but by showing a non-judgemental attitude towards his condition.

Mark says Jesus 'perceived in his spirit that they were discussing these questions among themselves' (2.6–7). Putting this statement after his own 'independent' account of their thinking (2.8), Mark gives the impression of having autonomously corroborated Jesus' perception. Not that it needs to be in any way supernatural: he may have been reading their body language, their defensive postures or dissenting gestures.

On other occasions, we shall encounter his opponents criticizing him for his actions (such as healing on the Sabbath, or picking corn to eat – see the Gospel reading, page 200 [Proper 4 Yr B]. In this case, the scribes evidently believe that words are easy and cheap (which, *per se*, is difficult to disagree with). Their 'prosperity gospel' sees human suffering and simply equates it with human sin – the paralytic man must have sinned to be afflicted with this ailment (the self-inflicted suffering of the other kind of paralytic is not in view here).

The sceptical scribes think that forgiveness is easy because it is just words. So Jesus adds a teaching to go with his healing. Are words easy and actions tough ('Which is easier ...', 2.9)? Well, he can do both with equal ease. In one stroke, he turns his compassion into action, and discredits the prosperity gospel once and for all.

The Second Sunday before Lent

Proverbs 8.1, 22–31; Psalm 104.26–end; Colossians 1.15–20; John 1.1–14

First, a word of warning: the NRSV, the BCP 1662 and the Hebrew all number the psalm verses for this service as 104.24–35. The CW Psalter numbers them from 26–37, so unless you are following that version, you will need to correct the reference, or else fall into the trap of setting verses that don't exist. Such discrepancies between the CW and BCP Psalters occasionally occur, with lectionaries prescribing according to CW and choirs (usually) singing according to 1662. It's a useful reminder that the Bible books did not originally have any chapter or verse divisions. Keeping it that way would not stop vain disputation (1 Tim. 6.5–7), but it might slow it down a bit.

From the trivial to the truly sublime – the opening chapter of Colossians is one of the few New Testament lections that can make an adequately exalted companion for the prologue of John (which we recently looked at in its Christmas context). Now it is Epiphany, the focus has shifted forward (especially if this Sunday is remembered as Sexagesima) and the Gospel has a different aim. In fact, all three readings have the same truth at their heart – the eternal pre-existence of the Word.

Proverbs 8.22 was a favourite weapon in the hands of Arian heretics in the early Church. They thought it proved that Wisdom (identified with the Word of John 1) was part of the created order, historically and hierarchically secondary to God the Father. The contending faction, which won the fight at a theological level (less so at the level of popular faith) argued that the emphasis belonged on Wisdom's presence with God in the act of creating, and hence co-equality. In our time, 1,700 years distant from the drafting of the Nicene Creed, it is not easy to convey the heat this generated. Nor is it easy to imagine modern Christians caring that much whether Jesus the teacher and healer existed before his conception in the Virgin's womb; even though our faith depends upon just that.

When Paul, or A.N. Other, wrote in Colossians that Christ is the Beginning (*arche*), he was not echoing John 1.1. Rather, both texts witness to a like understanding of the incarnate Word and his cosmic significance ('He is the *icon* of the invisible God'). This makes for creative tension with the infancy narratives of Matthew and Luke. Recently the word *arche* has come to wider attention through the Duke and Duchess of Sussex, whose letter for 2021 on their Archewell website urged us to 'build a better world, One act of compassion at a time'. They may not have had John's Gospel in mind, but there is no discrepancy with the Bible view that a world can be built, and rebuilt. After all, this world *has* been built. In the beginning. By God, together with Wisdom, his master-worker (Proverbs 8.29).

Many commentaries describe the Colossians text as a hymn. That can be mighty puzzling when it is not metrical and doesn't rhyme. There was no such thing as free verse in those days. If it is a hymn (or 'song'), then it must be modelled on the psalms. The closest familiar parallel is *Gloria in Excelsis* (from Greek) or *Te Deum* (from Latin). Only in the fourth century did hymns as we know them begin to be composed. The reason why Proverbs is set out like poetry in the NRSV is that it is written in a rhyme-free, metre-free poetic form like the psalms. It relies on balance and contrast to reveal its poetic nature. A glance at the texts of Isaiah, Jeremiah, Job and the like will show a similar distinction expressed by how the text is laid out in some versions. What is set out as verse is likely to be original; prose sections tend to be explanatory or connective texts. It's a rule of thumb; indicative, not diagnostic, but helpful.

One last thought: Proverbs 8.26 uses the phrase, '*bits* of soil'. The NRSV also applies this words to the metal gadgets for steering a horse, to food, to small particles and, once, in the phrase 'shattered to bits' (Amos 6.11). This reads very oddly in Scripture. Why not 'shattered to pieces', 'scraps', 'morsels'? NJB goes for 'the first elements of the world'. That is rather more like it. Mind you, if you want to say '*something*s of soil' it is hard to find a substitute for 'bits'. Suggestions?

The Sunday next before Lent

2 Kings 12.1–12; Psalm 50.1–6; 2 Corinthians 4.3–6; Mark 9.2–9

For the second Sunday in a row Christ is revealed as the 'image' (*icon* is the Greek) of God (2 Cor. 4.4). This is the measure to apply to all else that we learn about him. The lectionary reiterates the point to make sure we have grasped it – through Christ, God has given us the light of knowledge (*gnosis*), and it is to be found not in the 'essence' or 'identity' or any such abstract entity, but in the actual (real, physical) person of Christ. Rather like John the Baptist a few weeks ago, Paul goes against the majority inclination of grasping at status and power: 'We preach not ourselves,' he insists. It's the strongest possible counter to an egotistical culture: 'It's all about ME!' It's also a counter to a hierarchical culture: Paul could have said, 'I preach Jesus Christ, and I am his chosen mouthpiece'. Instead, the true preacher is lowest on the ladder of status: 'We are your slaves,' he tells the Corinthians.

The vision of the divine provided by 2 Kings 12 looks very different. Instead of transforming the meaning of being divine by revealing the exaltation of a human person, it transforms the meaning of being human by drawing a human being into the realm of the divine. It is a masterpiece of storytelling too – especially if we don't worry too much about the geographical logic of the journey Elijah and Elisha undertake.

One view of how to tell a story is to surprise an audience with unexpected plot twists. It is a staple of television serials like *Line of Duty*. Another looks more naive but is actually more subtle: to share with the audience the secret of what's about to happen. That is what the author of 2 Kings does. He makes a point of telling his audience that the day of Elijah's departure is at hand (2.2); then makes the players in the drama reveal it to one another (2.3, 5, 9, 10). The groups of prophets who confront Elijah and Elisha on their journey keep trying to put them off; they take it as a given that the day of one's death is something to be avoided.

On one level this is a story about succession. How does one prophet make way for another and ensure the continuation of that calling? Elisha assumes the mantle of Elijah, giving rise to an English expression familiar to many who have never heard of either prophet. Elisha's cry, 'The chariot[s] of Israel and its horsemen!' prompts a few questions, not least whether there is one chariot or several. Going by ancient Jewish scholars, it is an honorific title for Elijah as the protector of the nation. A modern commentator draws a parallel with Psalm 68.4, 17, where God himself, with his heavenly host of horsemen, is the 'chariot of Israel'. Elijah's flaming chariot and whirlwind mark the second bodily ascension into heaven in Judaeo-Christian history. Enoch was the first (Genesis 5.24), Jesus (Luke 24.51; Acts 1.9) and Mary (according to some traditions) are still to come.

The RCL sets the Gospel of the transfiguration for this Sunday to focus devotion on the true identity of Jesus. Not the good man only, or the divine Son only, but both. This is challenged by the scepticism of Bultmann and others, who argue that it is really a resurrection story, and so a transposition rather than a transfiguration. That is an uncharacteristically sophisticated, as well as presumptuous, thing for Mark to have done with his 'Good news of … the Son of God' (1.1).

Peter, James and John glimpsed a truth sufficient to sustain a life's discipleship (not without a few pitfalls). The rest of us see it through their eyes, with all the self-questioning that encounters with divine truth awake in us. It makes me think of a conversation, in *The Lord of the Rings*, between Gandalf and Frodo about the Elf-lord Glorfindel, in which Frodo's near-death experience has endowed him with clarity of vision: 'You saw him for a moment as he is upon the other side.' Whether or not this resonance was intended by Tolkein (who was a Roman Catholic), it shows us that we can only see people with the vision we possess at any given moment. We should never assume that what is on the surface is the 'real' or the 'whole' person.

The First Sunday of Lent

Genesis 9.8–17; Psalm 25.1–9; 1 Peter 3.18–end; Mark 1.9–15

Location, location, location. The settings of these readings really matter, particularly the exegetical problem of 1 Peter 3.19 ('he went and made a proclamation to the spirits in prison'). Various solutions have been proposed, the least convincing being to 'correct' the Greek. The text is what it is; our first duty is to make sense, if we can, of what stands written in Scripture.

In the third century, Origen saw it as an answer to the question: 'Where was Christ between Good Friday and Easter Day?' He suggested that Christ was descending to the dead to convert souls – embracing the dead, as well as the living, in the salvation of the Cross. If correct, this version of the harrowing of Hell points to a universalist view, that salvation will eventually embrace every human being without exception.

Calvin took a different line, downgrading the 'prison' to a 'watchtower' and having Christ preach only to the righteous dead, to uphold the principle that conversion after death was impossible. Others viewed Christ as descending to pronounce a final (adverse) judgement, not a gospel of salvation, regarding the 'prison' as metaphorical, a prison of ignorance. But the word 'proclamation' (*kerussein*) is about a positive message: good news, not bad.

Some scholars observe that 'to make a hermeneutical decision is to take sides'. They encourage us to work out the meaning by asking ourselves *how* the words of 1 Peter 3 bring comfort to suffering Christians in Asia Minor. If we ask what the text says to us now, we may find ourselves answering, after our experiences of lockdown, that not all prisons are visible. What's more, to be shut in a room, you must first go through a door; and if the door can be closed on you, then it can be opened again. That is surely a message of hope for those who have lost faith either in God or in themselves.

Christ was 'in the Spirit' when he proclaimed to the spirits in prison. The Spirit was responsible for another journey of his, less extraordinary but still perilous – his forty days in the wilderness. The Greek says 'desert' (*eremos*). In the Old Testament/Hebrew Bible, the wilderness is almost a mythic place (Hebrew *midbar*). That is not to imply that it did not exist, but that it encompasses more than mere location. It points to an experience and an encounter: the place where John proclaimed his baptism of repentance only a few verses before.

Mark does not give us any of the specifics found in Luke and Matthew's temptation narratives. This has been seen as evidence for the existence of a source document, Q, from which the other two evangelists quarried the material that Mark lacks. The fact that the Spirit is the agent who 'casts Jesus out' into the wilderness where he is tempted makes clear that this is not a place of punishment but a place of testing.

During that time, Jesus has two kinds of company: wild beasts and angels. The wild beasts are unique to Mark's version. This could be meant to represent Jesus as a second Adam in a primal paradise of harmony between man and beast. Much more likely is that those wild creatures represent the forces of chaos and satanic assault. This would mean that we should identify them with what the AV calls (translating the Hebrew very literally) the 'beasts of the field': wild animals, in other words, not domesticated livestock, and therefore neither open to human control, nor respectful of human safety.

Genesis 9 does not use the term 'beasts of the field' but talks instead of 'animals of the earth' and 'living creatures'. This passage really does make the case for the divine plan as a paradise of creation in harmony, for God's covenant is not just with human beings but with all living creatures (9.15–17). No wonder, then, that the rainbow sign of God's covenant with 'all flesh that is on the earth' has been chosen to embrace people once thought to be outside the covenant. Origen wouldn't be the last Christian teacher condemned in his own time but later found to have had a genuine insight into the divine will.

The Second Sunday of Lent

Genesis 17.1–7, 15–16; Psalm 22.23–end; Romans 4.13–end; Mark 8.31–end

Lent is a time for new challenges, and new beginnings. Christians see the change in Abram and Sarai's names as signalling a new beginning for them both; for the nation that will come from them; and ultimately for Christianity too. We follow Paul's complex exegesis, which relies on an etymology of Abraham as 'father of many nations'. Paul takes a fresh approach to salvation history, looking back beyond the giving of the law, and basing salvation in a relationship of mutual regard, rather than in 613 commandments, or *mitzvot* (a traditional numbering of the Mosaic law). Or, as we might say, in the wood rather than the trees; or the meta-narrative – the overarching theme – rather than the detail.

Paul has already made the point that Abraham was made righteous (Rom. 4.1–8) by faith, and that he was made righteous before he was circumcised (4.9–12). Some early Jewish exegetes argued that Abraham was righteous either because he already kept the law before it was revealed to Moses (Gen. 26.5); or on the grounds of his obedience in being ready to sacrifice Isaac (Gen. 22.9–10). The word for being 'made righteous' can also be translated as 'justified'. This latter is a compound of the Latin words for 'justice' and 'making'. 'Justification by faith' ('by faith *alone*' according to Luther) later became a corner-stone of the Reformation.

This linguistic forest risks obscuring the single tree. If Paul is right, then 'righteousness' is not to be found in behaviour (what we do) or in belief (what we think), but in something that God does to (and with, and in, and for, and through) us. In other words, it is the passive (*'was made righteous'*) that counts. Unfortunately, that passive that completes Paul's argument, *dikaiothentes*, is held over to the start of Romans 5, which will only be read at a Sunday principal service two weeks from now. We also have to bear in mind that 'faith' for Paul is not propositional, a checklist of correct opinions; it is a state of being, much closer in feel to our word 'trust'.

It can be hard to make sense of all this. Modern translations tend to say that Abraham was 'made righteous'. That way of translating the Greek emphasizes the inner, spiritual, ethical dimensions of right behaviour towards God; whereas 'justification', in colloquial English, sounds like making excuses and, in formal language, sounds legalistic. The division between outward observance and inner disposition is one of the most fundamental in Christianity (and doubtless in other faiths too). On the one hand, interior inclination is worthless without corresponding behaviour (James 2.18). On the other, outward observance, without the right motivation of the heart, is criticized repeatedly by Jesus (Matt. 23.23, 27) and the prophets.

Like many puzzles in Christian faith (the existence of evil; theodicy), this one, our 'righteousness' or 'justification', turns out to be a tension we have to live with. The puzzle itself is be God's gift to us, the only way for Christians to avoid the twin extremes of arrogance and despair.

We have another puzzle to tackle with this Gospel. Unless the eternal Christ is peeping out for a moment from behind the human Jesus, how does the taking up of a cross make any sense at all at this point in Jesus' ministry? Sceptical commentators may dismiss it as retrojection. To show Jesus as aware of what will befall him before it happens is one way to reduce the stigma of a shameful death. Centuries of art and worship have gradually anaesthetized that acute pain. But when the New Testament was being written, it was a slave's death, a sharp and fresh embarrassment.

The Lord's command to take up a cross is a response to Peter's rebuke of him for speaking openly of his death. It must have been a horrible shock for Peter, after he had offered words that were meant to reassure Jesus ('Don't be silly: of course you're going to be successful'), to hear himself addressed as Satan, 'the Adversary'. The warning Jesus then delivers only really comes fully into focus in Mark 14.66–72. Being ashamed of openly following Jesus, even when 'we believe and trust in him', may be understandable in a society intolerant of religious belief and ignorant of religious praxis. But it is still a challenge that Christians must confront, not wish away.

The Third Sunday of Lent

Exodus 20.1–17; Psalm 19 [*or* 19.7–end]; 1 Corinthians 1.18–25; John 2.13–22

Religions are among the longest lasting of all human phenomena. They can withstand exile, war, technology and time: but only if they are able to rethink, repackage, renew their essence. All the readings contain such a rethink. It is clearest in the psalm, when what began as a celebration of the sun becomes a revelation: the light of the sun stands for the wisdom of Torah, the Law. The great Baptist preacher Charles H. Spurgeon (who believed that David was the author) spoke beautifully of that message, 'the psalmist devoted himself to the study of God's two great books – nature and Scripture'.[1]

The delivery of the Ten Commandments (or Decalogue) also marks a shift. Between exile and homecoming, God tells Moses that the people need to be prepared, indeed *consecrated*, for what is about to be given to them. We might not think that a list of 'dos' and 'don'ts' is much of a gift. But the wonder of it is in the simple clarity. There may have been 613 commandments in total, but here is their distillation for God's people: when we seek guidance on how to live in accordance with God's will, such rules are wonderfully welcome.

There is another version of the Decalogue in Deuteronomy 5, and comparison of the two versions shows that (despite variants) the content of the message is remarkably stable – this is how one generation should entrust faith to the next. Some of the commandments may be flexible, according to context. 'Do not make graven images' might ban *all* artistic representation, or it might be a warning not to confuse images with reality. Others cannot. There is nothing ambiguous about Ex 20.12–17, unless one takes refuge in that last resort of essay-writers, 'it depends what you mean by adultery (etc.)'. Only one of the ten has no 'not' in it – to honour one's father and mother; and it is also the only one of the ten that carries a blessing with it, 'that your days may be long'.

One purpose of the Decalogue is to make the people righteous. But it is also there, Paul explains, so that they have no excuse when they do transgress. His indictment in Romans 2.17–24, directed at Jews, can nowadays apply equally well to Christians – who among us can honestly

---

1 Charles H. Spurgeon, *The Treasury of David*, London Metropolitan Tabernacle, 1866–85.

claim that they did not know they should love their neighbour as themselves, when failing in that duty?

In 1 Corinthians, Paul does not equate wisdom with Torah, but he does see an affinity between those two patterns for human behaviour. The danger for Christians is not just that they will fall into judgementalism by reformulating the old Law in Christian terms (based perhaps on behavioural codes in the letters to Timothy and Titus). It is that they will claim to be righteous merely because they have acknowledged Christ and the Cross. This is the mindset of the Pharisees whom John the Baptist criticized (Matt. 3.9), or the people Jesus debated with, 'If you were Abraham's children, you would be doing what Abraham did' (John 8.39).

It is shameful how often Christians condemn a form of Jewish legalism that actual Jewish people would see as a gross parody of their faith. Christians may boast of having the life-giving Spirit, not the freedom-killing letter of God's Law, following Christ directed by nothing but personal conscience. Though Paul seems to go along with race-based generalizations about Jews and Greeks, he then surprises us with a re-think of his own: racial background is now irrelevant. All that matters is following Christ crucified.

The last of these gear changes comes in the Gospel. It contains puzzles for those who like geography and history: it is disputed whether Jesus went to Jerusalem once (so the synoptics) or repeatedly (so John), at the beginning of his ministry (John), or at the end (synoptics). We can ask whether he cleansed the temple once or twice. His actions in the temple seem fine on the page, but a little meditation reveals how uncomfortable they are: violent, dismissive, condemning a whole class of people (who put bread on the table when the money-changers went home that night?). What they embody is a prophetic sign-action, Old Testament style. Its message is so vital that even good manners give way before it. Whatever else it may be, our relationship with God is not a financial transaction.

The Fourth Sunday of Lent ('Refreshment' Sunday)

Numbers 21.4–9; Psalm 107.1–3, 17–22 [*or* 107.1–9]; Ephesians 2.1–10; John 3.14–21

There is lot of sin in today's readings, and, despite the other traditional name of this Sunday (*Laetare* – 'rejoice!'), not a lot of rejoicing. At least, not at first glance. The Israelites in the wilderness admit that they have sinned against the Lord. In the psalm, people become sick with sin. In Ephesians, Paul goes one step further: they are dead because of their sins. Only the Gospel lacks the word. The closest it comes is to speak of evil deeds and evil-doers.

Another word Paul uses to pinpoint the phenomenon of wrong behaviour is 'trespasses'. In the modern version of the Lord's Prayer, 'trespasses' give way to 'sins'. But the Greek says 'debts'. This highlights a problem for readers of the Bible: how to make sense of a key idea when writers keep using different words to describe it. What is unacceptable to God can be a stumbling or going astray ('trespass'); or making a mistake ('sin'); or transgressing ('mis-step'); or failing in an obligation ('owe'). But Scripture draws us into an entirely different moral universe when it speaks to us of 'evil'. This is what lawyers used to call 'malice aforethought'. God is not troubled by mistakes and stumbles. But evil, that is another matter. Conflating mistakes and stumbling with real evil is misleading. It could even be dangerous.

These very different readings, reflecting on various human wrongs, offer an opportunity to refresh our examination of conscience (a traditional Lenten practice). In Romans 3.23, Paul claims that 'all have made mistakes and been too late for the glory of God' (my translation). There are Christians who are untroubled by a sense of personal unworthiness, but I doubt that they are in the majority. It is hard to draw near to the living God and *not* feel unable even to lift up one's eyes (Luke 10.13).

The wrongs done by the Israelites in the wilderness and after were repetitive to the point of boring. Again and again they forget God's steadfast love and blessings and so fail to trust him. Surely here we find ourselves, as this echoes our own most troublesome sins, the ones we go on committing year after year. Sin is often expressed as a state of separation from God; one that people may be feeling in the present time of crisis. The state of separation from God into which Paul writes and preaches is sometimes intensely personal (2 Cor. 12.9), sometimes a group experience, as here. But the habitual nature of human wrongdoing has not changed in the centuries since the Bible was written.

The effect of the readings leading up to today's Gospel is to leave nowhere for honest Christians to hide. Whenever I hear weasel words like 'mis-speaking' or 'being economical with the actualité' (as though telling lies were somehow less reprehensible in French than in English), it feels as if the speaker is trying to admit and downplay wrongdoing at the same time. That leaves little room for real repentance. The point is not the word we use to describe it, but the behaviour it describes.

Into this world of wrongs, the Son of Man speaks words of wonderful truth. He confounds any apprehension of the 'terrible voice of most just judgement', as the Prayer Book Commination puts it. In Ephesians 2, 'the world' is the place where 'trespasses and sins' abound. It is a place of the living dead: those who still have life and breath, and yet are dead to the true life that is for those who love and serve God (John 14.6). Jesus' words in John 3 turn this around. The world (*kosmos* is the Greek term) is not a place of alienation from God, still less a place where human beings are condemned or rejected. God loved the world. We can and should trust that he still does.

Not for nothing is John 3.16 one of the best-known, best-loved verses, proclaimed on countless church notice-boards, felt by generations as an individual promise. It belongs to each of us as if it was addressed to us alone. We might imagine ourselves, on Laetare Sunday, picking up our Bible, finding John 3.16, crossing out 'the world', and writing our own name: 'God so loved me ...' That might give us the encouragement we need to trust that God sent his Son into the world not to condemn it but to save it.

Mothering Sunday

Exodus 2.1–10 *or* 1 Samuel 1.20–end; Psalm 34.11–20 *or* 127.1–4; 2 Corinthians 1.3–7 *or* Colossians 3.12–17; Luke 2.33–35 *or* John 19.25–27

Literary scholars look at texts from different times and places, seeing how they 'talk' to one another. Rather than analysing each text in isolation, the intertextual method begins from context, interpreting the relationships of themes and books over time, and between languages, nationalities and religions.

Christians have been reading texts this way for a very long time. The readings for a Sunday Principal Service (usually a Eucharist) are a carefully curated selection, almost always from two languages, sometimes spanning centuries. It presupposes the intertextual method: readings are expected to 'speak' to each other, especially when the 'related' lectionary is chosen.

I have mentioned before (see page 124) how a Christian Old Testament differs from a Hebrew 'Bible', having the same books, but in a different arrangement. The Jewish order is thematic (law, prophets, writings); the Christian one is chronological.

Consider this arrangement in the light of the idea that changed nineteenth-century understanding of what it is to be human: evolution. It prompted Christians to think about humankind's relationship with God as something evolving in time, developing, refining itself from primitive drives such as anger, jealousy and pride, towards more enlightened principles of justice and morality.

Such a view makes it possible to see the Bible as a spiritual work-in-progress, a snapshot in time, as humankind evolves towards moral and spiritual perfection. Perhaps there is evidence for this in one of the highest and most beautiful expressions of the Christian ideal: the New Testament reading from Colossians 3.

But the cruder, less sophisticated forms of religion have not been left behind. Colossians 3.12–17 is an inspiring ideal, not a daily reality. Human history has not evolved spiritually away from the primitive: such passages are glimpses of what God calls us to, not morale-boosting evidence of having 'made good progress', like a school report.

Perhaps such a take influenced those who wish to write 'brothers and sisters' wherever the Bible says 'brothers', helping us to progress away from patriarchy, making division, injustice and oppression vanish into the abyss, renewing Paradise, in which male and female return to their non-hierarchical equality, as God's intention was from the beginning.

Or perhaps not. This chain of thought was triggered by 1 Samuel 1.20, a small detail. It reminded me how John's name was dictated by an angel (and Jesus' likewise); no one listened to Elizabeth when her husband was unable to speak his son's appointed name (Luke 1.11–13).

In contrast, Hannah – who has a husband, and Eli, and doubtless other patriarchal characters ready to dictate her baby's name – names her son herself. She calls him Samuel because she 'asked God' for him, and God gave him to her. That name reflects her circumstances and her son's. Is the Old Testament is more 'evolved' here than the New?

When Elkanah, her husband, Samuel's father, goes off to sacrifice to the Lord, Hannah chooses to stay behind. This is a decision that her husband accepts without argument: 'Do what seems best to you.' Once Samuel is weaned, she will offer him back to the God who gave him. And he will become the greatest leader of his people since the days of Moses and Joshua.

Like Joseph in the Gospels, good Elkanah recognizes the bond between mother and son for the particular miracle it is, steps back, respects it and honours his wife's decisions.

It is easy to see why, when Christians celebrate the motherhood of Mary, they think of Hannah. Both women have miracle babies, gifts from God against all expectation. But the fact of their two separate yet similar stories coming from opposite ends of the Christian holy book, cuts right across the idea of spiritual evolution from Old Testament to New.

We mortals are what we have always been. All that changes over time is the style in which we express the impulsive, instinctive aspects of our humanity (at one extreme) and our higher calling to be governed by faith, hope and love (at the other).

Hannah's life is contingent upon her status as a married woman and the sometimes unfair judgements of the men she meets. But she is her own person, with her own idea of what her purpose in life is and how she can live in relationship with God through asking him, and thanking him, and bargaining with him. Exactly as we all – male, female, in every human identity, parents or not – would wish to be today.

The Fifth Sunday of Lent (Passion Sunday)

Jeremiah 31.31–34; Psalm 51.1–13 *or* Psalm 119.9–16;
Hebrews 5.5–10; John 12.20–33

Psalm 51 sets the tone. If the readings are to do their work in us for Passion Sunday, we must begin with our side of a conversation with God – admitting what we've done wrong. The psalm has a superscription, pointing us to a pivotal historical moment when one man had a choice – and chose wrong, with catastrophic consequences for himself and others. He betrayed a wife's faithfulness, a husband's loyal service, and his own duty to God. He did so despite being God's anointed. That is what can happen when a mere human, even a King (David), is entrusted with sovereignty.

That story is coupled with another betrayal of marriage vows. Jeremiah adopts a theme in Hosea, showing God as the loving husband of Israel, his faithless wife. To understand this passage in Jeremiah, we have to be clear about his use of names: often Christians hear 'Israel' and 'Judah' as synonyms. In the same way, Jesus and Christ are taken as personal names for the Son of Man. But 'Israel' is the northern kingdom that was ethnically cleansed in the eighth century BC: it was long gone by Jeremiah's time. 'Judah' (which includes Jerusalem) is the southern kingdom, which was not exiled until much later, when Jeremiah was active as a prophet. Unlike the northern kingdom, it was later restored.

Jeremiah 30–33 makes such a contrast with the preceding gloom that it is known as the Book of Consolation. Within it, this passage is unique; the prophet refers to a new covenant and foreshadows a specifically Christian theme. The idea that our love for God is something to be located in the heart is strongly associated with the book of Deuteronomy and the school that produced it. What we may miss, distracted by the beauty of the promise, is the point that encourages us towards this Christian interpretation. The emphasis has shifted from repentance (the constant theme of the deuteronomists) towards divine forgiveness. God will abandon the old covenant of reciprocity, and chooses instead, by a sovereign act of divine will, to endow people with knowledge of his being and reverence for their relationship with him. This is something that human beings had constantly failed to accomplish for themselves.

The message of the prophecy is that where our relationship with God is concerned, teaching and learning are not, in themselves, enough. For human beings to flourish in relationship with God, they need his presence at the core of their being. And from this point on, that is what they are guaranteed. The deuteronomists had spoken for a religion of interior attitudes as well as external observance. Jeremiah moves the development a further step towards what Christianity was to become – a prophetic religion, as well as a priestly one, and one rooted not even on love for God, but on his prevenient forgiveness. It deepens our understanding of this section of Jeremiah to read it as an answer to Deuteronomy 6.6.

Hebrews provides the balance of the priestly to the prophetic Jeremiah; but 5.7 had me puzzled. What on earth is Christ's 'reverent submission'? The Greek word means 'discretion' or 'caution' – at a push 'reverence' or even 'fear'. I could put up with 'obedience', but 'submission' is an eisegesis too far. Still, whichever translation is used, the passage knits together two extremes of being in the incarnate Lord. What is more, the glory it reveals in Christ's high priesthood draws our minds towards the Gospel, which identifies the death of Christ as his access to that glorification (John 12.23). In Hebrews 5.7, Christ seems to be praying for others, not himself. But like Jeremiah and the author of Psalm 51 before him, he engages in a dialogue with God. They all talk to God in their own way, but every such conversation is real.

From conversations like these we learn how to talk to God ourselves, praying the words of Scripture, the actual verses, as if they were our own: 'Against you, you alone, have I sinned' (Ps. 51.4); 'Now my soul is troubled' (John 12.27). John's Gospel shows how quickly the conversation can escape from our control. We may, like the Greeks in that Gospel, say, 'we want to see Jesus'; but the response we get will not be a visual spectacle. He is not teaching us to gawp at celebrity, but to follow, and cleave to, the Son of Man.

Palm Sunday

Liturgy of the Palms: Mark 11.1–11 *or* John 12.12–16;
Psalm 118.1–2, 19–end [*or* 118.19–end]
Liturgy of the Passion: Isaiah 50.4–9a; Psalm 31.9–16 [*or* 31.9–18];
Philippians 2.5–11; Mark 14.1–end of 15 *or* Mark 15.1–39 [40–end]

In Isaiah, Christ has spoken in the person of the Suffering Servant, in a foreshadowing of the Passion. Neither retaliating nor resisting, he received from God strength to know his vindicator was near. That happened centuries before the earthly life of Jesus. Even in Jesus' own time, it was read as 'Scripture'. Like other parts of the Bible, it is always speaking of both the past and God's eternal 'now'. Isaiah for ever foretells our Lord whose prophesied coming is in our past; whose earthly existence is likewise past for us, and yet whose living being still speaks, suffers and is vindicated, in every generation. We learn through Scripture that he will endure in all the years yet to come (Hebrews 13.8).

When we enter upon the liturgy of Palm Sunday, we know what we are letting ourselves in for. We are going to encounter shame, violence and injustice – and rejection. It could be claimed that rejection is the cruellest blow of all. Whether it is family ('you're no child of mine!'), institutions ('the number of applications was very high') or relationships ('I like you as a friend'), it can eat away at our self-worth, a worm in the bud.

How this could happen? How there can be meaning in the suffering? These are questions we choose to ask ourselves each Palm Sunday. No one is forcing us to walk with Jesus the path to Calvary. No one forced him either, but he knew the path he had to tread, as do we.

To say that God gives us suffering to teach us something is no answer at all to rank injustice or unbearable pain. But if there were absolutely nothing to learn from the 'Passion' (from the Latin word for 'suffer'), Palm Sunday would be mere spiritual masochism. The New Testament reading and the Gospel of Mark both offer answers to this problem, but to understand them clearly it helps to have a bit of context.

Understanding the Passion is a lifetime's work, not to be squeezed into 730 words. But even one small point can help. Christianity has accustomed us to seeing vulnerability as something that deserves compassion (meaning 'suffering *with* someone'). It has not always been so. The Romans put no value on weakness. Theirs was a warrior elite culture driven by ambition, competition and prestige. The reaction of the soldiers to Jesus reflects that. He attracts their ridicule and contempt. Pilate's reaction is more that of a bureaucrat (or J. K. Rowling's Giants): let's kill him, 'jus' to simplify things'.

In the Passion, Jesus confronts opposition on two levels. Only one is evident on the surface: the level of ordinary human interaction. The other, cosmic, level is articulated by Paul, in Ephesians 6.12 and elsewhere, but here it is only a shadowy presence. Thus the responsibilities for wrongdoing, on every level, are located where they truly belong – with the human beings who commit them. Some are famous, like Judas, Pilate and (temporarily) Peter; others are nameless, like the chief priests, council, false witnesses, soldiers, crucified prisoners and the crowd.

One way of absorbing the Palm Sunday Gospel is to imagine it through a character in the story. To experience this most fully, we have to include imagining inflicting suffering as well as enduring it. Some people find it hard to admit their sins – their acts of vanity, cowardice or judgementalism – even as others cannot accept their own good qualities and intentions. We find both kinds of denial among the people in the Passion.

Mark's is the simplest of the four Passion Gospels. Like the other three, it comes at the end of years of teaching and healing for Jesus. Thus it represents the summit of a lifetime's formation for him, and the pivot point of human history for us. If we want to merge the human Passion with the cosmic Passion, we do not have to reinvent the theological wheel. All that is required is to turn to Philippians 2. There the Word is both Jesus and Christ; in the form of God and in human form, humanly humbled and cosmically graced with the name that is above every name (2.9). Here are words that show us how to move from passion to compassion – through fear cast out by love, and pain soon to dissolve in rejoicing.

Good Friday

Isaiah 52.13—end of 53; Psalm 22 [*or* 22.1–11 *or* 22.1–21]; Hebrews 10.16–25 *or* Hebrews 4.14–16; 5.7–9; John 18.1—end of 19

When we read any one of the Gospel passions, we bring to that reading all our other times of reading, hearing or singing them. Bible scholars mostly agree that they were the earliest parts of the Gospels to be compiled, and that their content (though not the final form given to them by the evangelists) became fixed and familiar among the first Christians at an early stage in the development of the New Testament.

Good Friday may seem like a time to put passion before scholarship. But in fact, the two strengthen each other. To get the most out of Good Friday, as we enter into the Lord's Passion, we need to be passionate ourselves, about every tiny scrap of information, every jot, every tittle. Something tiny but new has just jumped out at me. Not having noticed it before, I had obviously not thought about it before.

It is natural, when reading the Gospels devotionally, to merge the details into a single continuous story. The first Christians gave serious thought to merging the four Gospels into a single book. It is good that they did not. So here is my new observation, with apologies to any readers who noticed it years ago: of the four Gospels, only John says that both the scene for the betrayal and the scene for the Resurrection was a garden.

Mark, followed by Matthew, refers to a place called Gethsemane, on, or near, or most likely at the foot of, the Mount of Olives. Even today, the Mediterranean gives some idea of how it might have looked. In a dry landscape, olive trees are marvellously green. Oil from their fruit clinches their miraculous status. Surely most gardens near Jerusalem would have included olive trees and vines.

Mark and Matthew do not refer to Gethsemane as a garden. For them it is a place of refuge and struggle. There, shockingly vulnerable, Jesus wrestles with his Father's will and his own feelings about what is to come. Luke calls it neither Gethsemane nor a garden. For him it is simply, 'the place' on the Mount of Olives where Jesus went every evening at that time (21.37).

So John's insistence that it is a garden stands out. Saying that Jesus led his disciples to it 'across the brook Kidron' fixes its location more precisely. Christians soon connected the place by the Mount of Olives (Luke), called Gethsemane ('Oil Press': Mark, Matthew), with John's garden. The name was probably as self-explanatory as 'Mile End', Mill Street', or 'Brookfield' would be to us. The mountain's foot was the best place to gather and press the olive harvest.

Connecting Gethsemane with the garden is a guess, but a good guess. Next, John takes us beyond guesswork into the realm of cosmic meaning. His Gospel began by recalling Genesis ('In the beginning'). Important things happen to human beings in gardens, according to the Old Testament/Hebrew Bible. He evokes that primordial beginning, by explicitly locating Jesus' betrayal, and burial, in gardens. He also makes a garden the place where Mary Magdalene is first to witness Jesus' Resurrection.

John has one last thing to say about gardens as places where cosmic meaning is disclosed. It is another one of those details that look so simple but mean so much. While Peter is sneaking about hoping to see what is happening, a relative of the man whose ear Peter had cut off, asks him, 'Did I not see you in the garden with him?' (18.26).

In the garden of Eden, the man and the woman both transgressed by doing something God had commanded them not to do. If God saw that as a betrayal, he did not say so. A price had to be paid for the disobedience (Gen. 3.15–19); but God was still their protector, because he was first their creator. It is as if by the acting of creating humankind in the first place, God has made himself eternally responsible for our wellbeing.

Like the man and the woman in Eden, Peter has a chance to live up to the best that he was meant to be. Unlike them, he had even promised to do so (John 13.36–38). But he failed, denying that either Jesus or the garden were anything to do with him. In a garden, he is about to discover that failure is not the end of the story.

Easter Day

Acts 10.34–43† *or* Isaiah 25.6–9; Psalm 118.1–2, 14–24
[*or* 118.14–24];
1 Corinthians 15.1–11 *or* Acts 10.34–43†; John 20.1–18
or Mark 16.1–8

†The reading from Acts must be used as either the first or second reading.

In Acts, Peter warns that God shows no partiality; James confirms that we should not either (2.9). In 1611, this came out as 'God is no respecter of persons'. Knowing that God has no favourites is good news, for favouritism is something we are hard-wired to resent. What the Scriptures show is an equality so radical it ought to take our breath away. Anyone – yes, anyone – can be acceptable to God. There are only two necessary conditions: one is right understanding about God, and the other is right behaviour. Peter explains what the right thinking consists in: believing that God raised Jesus from the dead and made him Lord of all.

Suddenly we discover that being acceptable to God is more complicated than we were first led to believe. Peter's speech moves quickly into the details of what's involved: anointing with the Holy Spirit ('what on earth does that mean?', his hearers might have wondered). Resurrection (which is somehow not the same as being reanimated). Judgement of the living and the dead ('how?'). Forgiveness of sins ('without blood sacrifice?').

There is a fundamental rule in both teaching and selling. When you start, keep it simple. Do not cloud the message with caveats and complexities. Get people interested and leave the small print for later. But make sure you go back to the simple message at the end: 'everyone who believes in him receives forgiveness' (Acts 10.43).

Paul's approach is different. He is refreshing memories of earlier stages in the learning process, taking his Corinthian converts through the articles of belief that by now they have known for a while. So it is important to reassure those shaky believers that this may look like made-up religion invented yesterday, but it is authentic, traditional: 'handed-down', and 'in accordance with the Scriptures'. Religious movements come and go, but even the most radical and free-spirited need to claim the mantle of authenticity: when the product they're selling is the meaning of life, ancient and authentic become virtual synonyms.

What you cannot tell from the NRSV is that both Peter and Paul are talking about 'good news'. Acts 10.36 refers to 'preaching peace' – but the Greek says *euangelizomenos*, 'telling the good news of peace' – by Jesus Christ. The NIV is more faithful to the Greek here. (The word 'good news' in archaic English is 'God-spell', hence our 'gospel'.) It was a rare word in most ancient Greek texts, but it comes front and centre in the New Testament, encapsulating in a single term the whole Christ-event. Suddenly it is not what is ancient that speaks authentically of God, but what is unprecedented.

In John's god-spell, we may be hearing the voice of a third apostle, for Mary Magdalene is sometimes known as the 'apostle to the apostles'. Peter and John have had their say, and revealed the truths entrusted to them for their hearers and for us, their distant descendants according to the Spirit. Now as the liturgy of Easter Day unfolds, we turn to her and to the Lord himself. Mary discovers the empty tomb – a shell encasing earth and air that proves nothing and suggests everything. Unable as yet to recognize the truth we know, she resorts to the third-person plural, that repository for every wrong for which no wrongdoer can be found: '*they* have taken away ... *they* have laid him'.

Two verses of John 20 that attract less attention in the Easter story, 8 and 9, carry a powerful message of reassurance for us when we consider them closely. That other disciple 'saw and believed'. But he did not yet understand. If we see faith as a matter of accepting certain propositions about God, this can make no sense at all. If we keep reminding ourselves that 'faith' here really means 'trust', then the puzzle dissolves. We already know the experience of seeing and trusting without understanding. Most of our learning begins in this way, with those simple statements, like Peter's in Acts and Paul's in 1 Corinthians; they cloak complexities we are not yet ready for. But one day we will be ready, and we too will turn at the sound of the Bridegroom's voice when he calls our name, as once he called Mary's that first Easter Day, ready to learn from our Teacher whatever truth, old or new, he has to entrust to us.

The Second Sunday of Easter

[Exodus 14.10–end; 15.20, 21]; Acts 4.32–35†; Psalm 133;
1 John 1.1—2.2; John 20.19–end

†The reading from Acts must be used as either the first or second reading.

The evangelists rarely speak of their own writing. Luke 1.3 says 'I decided'. John 20.31–2 speaks obliquely, giving us a self-effacing 'these are written' rather than 'I wrote'. His final sentence gives us his unique first-person reaction to Jesus (21.24–25).

John has chosen his material to support our believing; that is his primary objective. He sets it out immediately after the story of Thomas, giving us courage to say 'My Lord and my God' without having seen yet for ourselves.

The fact that the evangelists rarely express their intentions should not stop us asking what their writings are trying to achieve. They are not mere reports, but exercises in persuasion; and our existence as living Christians two millennia later is evidence of their success.

When their intention is to persuade us that Jesus is the Son of God (1 John 1.7), or that he was resurrected from the dead (Acts 4.33), this is uncontroversial. Our acceptance of those beliefs goes with our discipleship. But in the reading from Acts, we enter sensitive territory. It is more than a rare statement, it is unique in the New Testament: namely, that among the first Christians, private ownership was dissolved into the holding of all property in common.

This is shockingly radical. Can we really be encountering proto-communism in Scripture? For the most part Christians have been happy to sidestep it with a shrug: 'That was then, this is now.' In terms of practical living, we do not dress, speak or think exactly as they did, so why should we coexist as they did? And anyway, they were the apostles, gifted with 'great power' and 'great grace', which made their acts of goodness more extreme than our ordinary ones can be.

That excuse will not hold water. The apostles in Acts are plainly giving us examples to imitate. So if relinquishing private property is a Christian goal, we should be doing it. Some Christians already are: men and women who are chosen by the religious life (as monks or nuns) are living that apostolic paradigm today. The rest of us? Not so much.

This may be the only clear example (Acts 4.32) of an apostolic teaching on common ownership, but it is reinforced by a cautionary tale: Ananias and Sapphira (in Acts 5). Ananias' punishment was fierce enough; but Peter and the others could have given Sapphira a chance to repent and save herself. Instead, they virtually entrapped her. The very existence of their story hints at misgivings concerning common ownership among some of the faithful. After this tale, the teaching fades from view.

When we turn to the first letter of John, Scripture and liturgy merge in verses familiar from the Book of Common Prayer daily office and Holy Communion (1 John 1.8, 2.1–2). These powerful verses challenge us to radical honesty, and give us a coping mechanism (confession of sin) without which the Easter faith could hardly have survived down the years. They could have been the solution for Ananias and Sapphira.

John the letter-writer is here inclusive, not exclusive. Christ's atonement is for the sins of the whole world, not just for believers. Set for this day, when we reflect on the outworkings of the Resurrection, his words encourage those who have been believers for some time, but struggle with their inability to live a perfect Christian life.

How do we take to ourselves the common holding of property in Acts? In truth most of us don't. It is written as a third-person statement, rather than a command, which seems to give us room for moral manoeuvre. But in 1 Corinthians 11.1–11, Paul orders women to cover their heads, though – unlike with male headship, for some reason – many Christians freely ignore him. If we want life-lessons from our readings, we can highlight that it's legitimate to set aside biblical examples for good practical reasons; that trust is best but Jesus doesn't condemn doubt or scepticism; and that our fellowship with one another is a necessary condition for our fellowship with Christ.

For a human family, or a Christian family, to live together in unity is indeed good and pleasant. But that does not mean that everyone has to be exactly the same in terms of what they own or how they behave. We do better to live by the principle that 'we're all different, and that's fantastic'.

The Third Sunday of Easter

[Zephaniah 3.14–end]; Acts 3.12–19†; Psalm 4; 1 John 3.1–7; Luke 24.36b–48

† The reading from Acts must be used as either the first or second reading.

In the Gospel, Jesus ate a piece of 'broiled' fish. This is not a spelling error or an archaism for 'boiled'. It means 'grilled'. It dropped out of British English usage (and would better have stayed out) in the nineteenth century, but survives in the United States.

The everyday act of eating opened people's eyes to the physical reality of Jesus' Resurrection, just as looking at his hands confirmed the reality of his suffering. Next, listening to his teaching opened their minds to the Scriptures.

Jesus was not doing this then only for the Eleven and their companions; he set an eternal standard. We should not decide Scripture's meaning without asking Jesus to open our minds, which he does. The readings from Acts and Luke are expressions of one man's understanding, reached by exactly this method. So it is not surprising that their approach is similar. Peter appeals to 'our' ancestral faith as he offers his hearers both a challenge and a reassurance. In the Gospel, meanwhile, Jesus continues the work he began at Emmaus, explaining how the Scriptures point to the Resurrection and to the meaning of that event.

Both the NRSV and RSV see Acts 3.19–20 as one continuous statement, but the lectionary cuts it in half, so that we hear the command to repent, but not the 'times of refreshing' that are to follow in consequence. This is unfortunate. When we share the Christian message, it is important not to let repentance for sin predominate over the blessings of faith.

Psalm 4 offers a constructive model. It begins with personal experience of God's help when in dire straits and ends with reassurance – not trivial – that faith in God enables us to sleep soundly. Many people struggle to sleep when pressured or anxious. In darkness we ought to find rest, but it is not always so. When darkness is a place of fear, we need reminding that God is the creator of that darkness (Ps. 104.20). Then we can balance our insecurity against the promise that all shall be well. I have learned from Phoebe, our beagle, that dogs have two ways of sleeping: one with an eye half open, able to wake in an instant; in the other, when they feel completely safe and protected, they close their eyes fully, giving off a wonderful 'sleepy smell' to signal to others that they too can 'lie down and sleep in peace'.

One of the things that makes Easter harder (in my opinion) than Christmas to put into words is that it urges us to take thought for 'the life of the world to come' (as the Nicene Creed puts it). If our faith is predominantly tied to this earthly existence, this is challenging. We need to develop confidence in the promises explored by John the epistoler, and to feel comfortable talking about that life of the world to come. John is frank about the gap between what we can and can't know: 'we are God's children now; what we will be has not yet been revealed' (1 John 3.2). This emphasis on our identity as God's children is touching. It is also heartening for those who are uncomfortable when Scripture speaks of 'men' as if it included women too. The Greek word is neither masculine nor feminine, but naturally inclusive.

As so often with Scripture, the beauty of an idea can distract us from the detail of a passage. 1 John 3.1 is a good example. If we are too quickly seized by the thrilling idea of being God's own children, we risk missing the epistoler's careful emphasis, reassuring us in case it all seems too fantastical. Yes, we can be called 'God's children', but he must repeat it, 'that is what we are'. In the next verse, even this gives way: it is wonderful to be God's child, but what lies in store is as yet unknowable, and that will be still more glorious. We shall see God. That promise, which later came to be called the beatific vision, is dependent on our growing into God's likeness.

During Lent, we worked on repentance. In Eastertide, we should work with equal commitment to growing in likeness to God, specifically through the example of Jesus who opens the Scriptures to show us the way, the truth and the life. And who – as he tells us in this Gospel – expects us to be witnesses to his Resurrection.

The Fourth Sunday of Easter

[Genesis 7.1–5, 11–18; 8.6–18; 9.8–13]; Acts 4.5–12†; Psalm 23; 1 John 3.16–end; John 10.11–18

†The reading from Acts must be used as either the first or second reading.

Two families square up to one another in Acts. One is a blood family. Based on kinship, sharing a similar outlook, they are unsympathetic towards those they judge. The other family has a kinship of obedience to Jesus. Treating people favourably or unfavourably depending on whether you see them as like yourself is understandable. But by reacting to external identity, we fail to see the whole person. It becomes harder to give outsiders the benefit of the doubt. Peter's words of judgement, 'there is no other name ... by which we must be saved' (4.12), do not encourage the high-priestly family to try. The healing at the Beautiful Gate (Acts 3.1–10) is given for a sign, but they cannot access such salvation because they do not think they need it.

The epistle goes further than the 'children' of last week's lection. This time it has a diminutive form, 'little children'. Like *bach* in Welsh or the '-lein' ending in German, it can instantly set an affectionate tone. Diminutives can also be patronizing, literally 'belittling' a person. In conversation with family or friends, context and intention are everything.

The epistoler is not dictating from on high to little people at the bottom. He speaks from their midst, understanding that they need reassurance, that their confidence falters without support. He shows that not everyone is called to the same kind of imitation of Christ. He laid down his life for us, but we may be called to different kinds of sacrifice (1 John 3.16). Meanwhile, we are not to fear the fact that God sees everything, because 'God is greater than our hearts'. His seeing everything turns out to be the very thing that sets our forgiveness in motion, because he understands us, in every particle of our being.

The faith community of John the epistoler is a united group. Not so the writer of psalm 23. He describes a personal, one-to-one relationship with his God who shepherds him. But shepherds do not usually have only one sheep. Sheep are not solitary creatures. To thrive, they need to be with other sheep. It is a sign that we can be authentic followers of our Threefold God both in our individual identities and as members of the body of Christ.

The idea of God as a shepherd, and his people as a flock, is familiar from the Hebrew Bible. John the gospeller highlights a fresh aspect of it, though, with this, the fourth of his 'I am' sayings. As well as the shepherd, other characters (the flock, the hired hand, the wolf) appear, playing different roles. The flock is the object of his care, whether this Good Shepherd is identical with God or identifiable with him in some less straightforward way ('I and the Father are one', John 10.30). The hired hand is a poor-substitute Good Shepherd, working for wages, not fulfilling an obligation out of love. The wolf could stand for Satan, or for one of the historical enemies of the faith.

As so often, familiarity blinds us to the freshness of the message. Jesus tells us that the relationship between us (both individual and group) and him is a reflection of that between him and God. To see the relationship between God and human beings either in terms of kinship or through similarity of nature is truly extraordinary. No wonder the first Christians were bowled over by the outpouring of the Spirit (1 John 3.24) and the 'newness of life' (Rom. 6.4) that came to them through faith in Christ.

The image of the Good Shepherd was one of the earliest expressions of Christianity in art. That was because anyone could look at it and see an image of nurture and goodness, regardless of whether they recognized its secret meaning for people of faith. Also, a shepherd makes for a more appealing picture than a stone rejected by builders or a corner-stone. It looks as if our God has a human face to help us relate to him simply and naturally. But it would be more accurate to say that we have a divine face to help us feel at home with God. Whichever way round we put it, it is because, through Christ, we are God's kin that we are drawn to him. It is also the reason that we have an innate capacity to grasp some tiny fraction of the divine mind.

The Fifth Sunday of Easter

[Baruch 3.9–15, 32—4.4 *or* Genesis 22.1–18]; Acts 8.26–end†;
Psalm 22.25–end; 1 John 4.7–end; John 15.1–8

† The reading from Acts must be used as either the first or second reading.

Not everything about the Bible is difficult. When Scripture speaks straightforwardly, we sometimes shrink from the plain sense, like St Bernard reading the Song of Songs as depicting the love between God and his Church. 1 John 4.12 is as clear as it gets: '... if we love one another, God lives in us, and his love is perfected in us.'

Calling God a 'vine-grower' (NRSV) or 'husbandman' (AV) suggests that he is like a farmer, typically (because, being God, he has to be in charge) a landowner. RSV is more cautious, translating as 'vine-dresser' (a 'dresser' is employed to tend crops). The Greek word *georgos* (our name 'George') means someone who works the soil: possibly still a farmer, but definitely one who is prepared to get his hands dirty. This tells us that God, like his creation Adam (Gen. 3.18), knows what hard work is. A Hebrew Professor pointed out in long-ago lectures the oddity of Genesis 1–3, in which human beings lounge at their ease while God does all the work.

Repeatedly in the Old Testament/Hebrew Bible, God's people are pictured as a vine or vineyard. Wine has not changed its character that much from then to now, although it was common in the ancient world to drink it diluted with water. It is still an everyday miracle, changing plain fruit into a substance that 'maketh glad the heart of man' (Ps. 104.15, AV). There is a parallel with the mysterious leaven which turns flat bread into a lighter, tastier food. In fact, we find a trinity of mystery in these miraculous blessings of our existence, as psalms 104.15 and 4.7 bear witness (depending on the version): for oil, yielded by a tree (the olive), is also a mystery defying understanding.

John's Gospel lacks standard parables, but in the seven 'I am' sayings of Jesus, we encounter parables in a new guise. Exegetes will talk of 'symbol' (a pearl, a mustard seed) and 'referent' (the kingdom of heaven; faith). In the 'I am' sayings, the symbol varies (one is human, six are not) but the referent is always the same: it is always Jesus.

Not that John the gospeller is making the same mistake as the legendary Sunday school teacher, whose every question had the same answer (it was always Jesus). The 'I am' sayings begin with Jesus, who is the referent

('I am') and work their way back to symbols ('the True Vine') which help us understand him. If Jesus is the True Vine, that means that he stands for fruitfulness, happiness, community and (to believing Christians) communion.

With teachings like the True Vine and the Door, we come close to that prophetic mode of behaviour that we know from Old Testament/Hebrew Bible, which characterized John the Baptist and sometimes Jesus, in the New Testament. This is a way of teaching that reveals divine guidance in things as mundane and unglamorous as grubby underwear (Jer. 13.1–10).

Every such image has its limitations, though. The branch of an actual vine, unlike us branches of the True Vine, does not have a mind or will to choose to blossom. Nor is it responsible for its own fruitfulness. Jesus says, 'No good tree bears bad fruit, nor again does a bad tree bear good fruit' (Luke 6.43), a saying that the late Jim Cotter put to prophetic use 40 years ago in his little book *Good Fruits* (1981).

The Acts reading is a rare opportunity to encounter a person of minority sexual identity (albeit not one they chose for themselves) in Scripture. Some argue that 'eunuch' is a synonym for 'homosexual', but this is wishful thinking, not exegesis. When I visited Egypt and the Sudan, decades ago now, I remember the pride with which Coptic Christians identified the Ethiopian eunuch as the founder of their Church. If we needed reminding that Christianity is an identity we must accept for ourselves, rather than passing on through offspring, here it is.

1 John 4.21 must be the measure of all our Christian actions: '… those who love God must love their brothers [and sisters] also'. We could apply that measure by making baptism easy and welcoming, not a hoop-jumping exercise: 'Do you believe in God? Do you accept the good news about Jesus?' The next step would be immediate: 'Look, here is water! What is to prevent me from being baptized?'

The Sixth Sunday of Easter

[Isaiah 55.1–11]; Acts 10.44–end†; Psalm 98; 1 John 5.1–6; John 15.9–17

†The reading from Acts must be used as either the first or second reading.

The key to the New Testament reading is its last verse: '... the Spirit is the one that testifies, for the Spirit is the truth' (1 John 5.6). That is easier to understand than the verses that equate love with obedience, or see faith in terms of conquest. Liturgically, it points us forward to Pentecost.

These readings contain chicken-and-egg puzzles. Which came first: Jesus who is the Truth (John 14.6 narrates events before the time of this epistle), or the Spirit who is Truth (1 John 5.6)? Jesus appoints his disciples to bear fruit (John 15.16) before they have even become apostles. This contrasts with the synoptics. John uses the term 'apostle' only once (13.16, not a reference to the Twelve), but the cognate verb, 'send out', is present throughout his Gospel (there is no commissioning of the Twelve as such). This is how John the gospeller handles the Eucharist also: by way of allusion, not definition.

What we decide about the puzzle in Acts may affect how we understand sacraments (as they later came to be called) and the grace that underpins them. In the case of baptism, our default setting is 'baptism → Holy Spirit'. It is the same with confirmation and holy orders: the pattern is 'laying on of hands → Holy Spirit'. Here, though, the descent of the Spirit upon faithful people may precede sacramental washing, or the declaring of the Lord's name.

What does it mean that, while Peter is still preaching and expounding, the Holy Spirit is 'blowing where it will' (John 3.8). Clearly, the Spirit takes no account of what is 'proper' in human processes and priorities. Preachers may be dismayed to have the Spirit distracting 'their' listeners by speaking across lovingly structured arguments. But it reminds all Christians that the Spirit speaks to us 'through' the proclamation of the word, not just by instructing us – clarifying what was once opaque – but by making proclamation a moment of receptivity to the divine will. Instead of being busy, we are attentive and open to the Spirit. This should be true of preacher and congregation alike.

What about the puzzle of love and obedience? Both Johns make reference to it. In 1 John 5.2, loving God means obeying his commandments. This is hardly surprising in a patriarchal culture. In the case of Roman society, that cultural power was also an absolute legal right. But when patriarchy ('father-rule') becomes a slur, there is a problem. Even apparently loving fatherhood can be seen as toxic control. One person's 'guidance' can be another's 'coercion'.

Christians are not free to jettison the concept or reality of obedience to a heavenly Father. For those whose earthly fathers have fallen short (sometimes very short indeed), John 15.14 at least gives us a positive alternative. Rather than completely rejecting obedience as a Christian virtue, we can focus our obedience where the image for God we are using speaks most purely and positively to us. In this case, there is a safe refuge for many in those words, 'You are my friends if you do what I command you'.

Psalm 98 too encapsulates a puzzle, one of great antiquity. In verses 5–6 people praise God with whatever they have – voice, lyre, trumpet and shawm (a kind of oboe). When we turn to verses 7–8, we find that God's creation (made by him, just as we are) is doing the same thing. Side by side with human voice and musical instruments, the sea roars, the floods clap their hands, and the hills are joyful. Ascribing human emotions to inanimate things is known as 'pathetic fallacy'. That does not mean that it is a rubbish deceit. Rather, it is the ascribing of a capacity to feel emotion to things usually considered to be inanimate. In the psalmist's vision, both we and the world have characteristics of the divine written into us: most importantly of all, the capacity to respond to God.

There has long been a division in Christian thought between 'natural theology' (seeing all that has been made as expressive of God's reality) and 'revelation' (seeing only the supernatural divine disclosure to human beings as carrying divine truth). In this psalm (one of many such), that false dichotomy must fall. And a good job too.

The Seventh Sunday of Easter (Sunday after Ascension Day)

[Ezekiel 36.24–28]; Acts 1.15–17, 21–end†; Psalm 1; 1 John 5.9–13; John 17.6–19

† The reading from Acts must be used as either the first or second reading.

Luke says that there were 'about one hundred and twenty persons' listening to Peter; he sounds (not for the first time) as if he is being both vague and precise at the same time. Peter declares that the number of the Twelve must be 'filled up', to pass on Judas' share in their ministry. That share is allotted to Matthias. It could not be clearer that the Twelve stand for something fundamental. Their number, depleted by Judas (Matt. 27.5) needs to be restored; and ten times twelve are there to witness it. Peter's speech is addressed to 'men and brothers' (using the Greek word for adult males, not the generic term for human beings), but the NRSV disguises the gender specificity, 'friends'. So does the NIV, 'brothers and sisters'.

Having prophecies that were fulfilled (Acts 1.16) made Christianity attractive to many people. Life seems unpredictable to us at present; but that is nothing compared to Bible times, when everyone, rich or poor, was at the mercy of weather, and disease, without any of the scientific resources with which we protect ourselves. No wonder that when the first Christians read the Old Testament/Hebrew Bible, and found passages predicting events in the life of Christ, they saw the its books as a USP for the new faith. Prophecy fulfilled could tame the unknown future.

When we read the passage of Acts alongside the epistle, it is easy to miss the connection. Both speak of witnessing (Acts 1.22, 1 John 5.9–11), but the epistle obscures this by translating it as 'testimony'. The Greek word for someone who offers testimony is 'martyr', but it is not yet a label for those who are faithful to the point of death. For now it is a less extreme objective: simply declaring the truth about Jesus, based on personal experience of him. In this sense, we should all be martyrs.

In Acts, Matthias was suitable because he was there with the others following Jesus from the beginning (Acts 1.21–22). In the next chapter of the story, even before Peter and the others have realized that this criterion of theirs for witness and leadership has a very limited shelf life, the solution has been provided. The Holy Spirit will become the criterion of authentic Christianity for all the generations yet to come, including ours.

Christian faith is sometimes criticized for offering, instead of good things in this life, 'pie in the sky when you die'. That phrase comes from a song attacking preachers who promised blessings in heaven rather than fighting for human rights on earth. John the epistoler takes a different tack, telling us three times in three verses that, for the faithful, eternal life has already begun. We are living life eternal right now (1 John 5.11–13). We need to remember that, and act accordingly.

The Gospel comes from Jesus' farewell discourse, or 'high-priestly prayer'. The language is solemn, ranging back and forth over the meaning of Jesus' life. I find it difficult to keep my grip on Chapter 17 (unlike most of John). The words of the prayer are like a sparkling surface of water in sunlight, each flash gone in a moment, but leaving a trace of transcendence in our minds. This is different from how Jesus teaches his disciples to talk to his Father (e.g. Matt. 6.9–13). Verse 10 reminds me of wedding vows, which signal a 'mystical union' symbolized by the sharing of persons and property; the relationship of Father and Son is certainly that.

Jesus asks his Father for protection, unity, joy and finally, repeatedly, consecration (also translated 'sanctification') for us. Consecration is a divine gift. It does not turn the thing that is consecrated into something completely different, but makes it the best and truest version of itself. We are waiting for the descent of the Holy Spirit to fill the void left by Christ's Ascension. As we do so, we need to remember that we are not our own (1 Cor. 6.19). Like Christ, we are consecrated (John 17.17, 19). Our experience of consecration tells us that what God does in us changes us – and not only in our imagination or will; it becomes an objective truth about us. This is how we come to be a 'kingdom and priests' (Rev. 1.6; 5.10), who are promised a crown of glory (1 Peter 5.4) and a crown of life (Rev. 2.10).

Pentecost (Whit Sunday)

Acts 2.1–21 *or* Ezekiel 37.1–14; Psalm 104.26–36, 37b
[*or* 104.26–end];[1] Romans 8.22–27 *or* Acts 2.1–21[†]; John 15.26–7;
16.4b–15

[†] The reading from Acts must be used as either the first or second reading.

John 16.4-15 is a harder Pentecost Gospel, I think, than those set by the lectionary for Years A and C (A, John 20.19-23; C, John 14.8-17). It is a moment of anxiety, sorrow. The disciples are (as we sometimes are) terrified of the unknown, and – understandably – reluctant to let Jesus go. He exposes the negative thoughts underpinning their silence, '… none of you asks me, "Where are you going?"' (16.5).

They probably respect him too much to argue with him. But he perceives the thinking that they dare not speak. What he offers them, they do not understand and therefore do not want. Plainly, they would rather not let him go. This air of reluctance compounds my annual difficulty: I find it hard to put my thoughts on Pentecost into words (oh, the irony). But another preacher is available to help. Not that he can take my place in the pulpit. He has been dead for almost 400 years. In the centuries that lie between us, preaching fashions have changed. In place of his two-hour-long addresses, I usually have 12 minutes. But his sermons contain a depth of detail that is imaginative and intuitive rather than a boring compilation of facts and cross-references. So I make the most of them. I hope he would approve.

On Whit Sunday, 12 May 1611, Lancelot Andrewes preached before the King at Windsor. The start of his Pentecost sermon captures the festival with perfect simplicity: this is the day when the 'promise of the sending' turns into the 'sending of the promise'.

Andrewes spends his entire sermon on John 16.7, interpreting the exchange that Jesus insists on in this sentence. Something that is familiar (our Lord in his earthly being) must give way to something that is unfamiliar (the indwelling Spirit). Andrewes knows that trying to keep things as they are does not prevent change. Earthly existence is nothing but change. It is fear, rather than love, that drives their sorrow. Jam tomorrow (the Holy Spirit) is an insufficient inducement for giving up jam today (Jesus).

---

1 Psalm 104.26–36, 37b in Common Worship equates to 104.24–34, 35b in BCP and NRSV.

Jesus persuades the disciples that it is better for them that he go away, so that the Paraclete can come. Yet this is not a matter in which he could have been dissuaded from fulfilling the divine plan. We have all been in situations where we need to convince someone that initial pain will give way to something better. It can be a hard sell, especially to those who, like children, live perpetually in the present rather than calculating rationally. Andrewes imagines the disciples' response: 'The Comforter will not come? Be it so; let Him not come. We desire no other Comforter (than you, Jesus).' Then he suggests another step in their attempts at persuasion:

> Why may not Christ send *for* Him, as well as send Him? Or, if He go, come againe with Him? ... Are they like two buckets; one cannot go downe, unlesse the other go up?

Christ's work was truly finished on the Cross, as he himself confirmed (John 19.30). But salvation is the Holy Trinity's business, not Christ's alone. Andrewes uses another striking image, this time a will, to make his point. Christ is the *Word*, the written substance of the document. But the Spirit is the *seal*. Paul confirms this, referring to 'the Holy Spirit of God, with which you were marked with a seal for the day of redemption' (Eph. 4.30).

Trust is at stake here, as much as obedience. Jesus is making his disciples a promise. Every promise calls on the faith of those to whom it is made: do they trust the one doing the promising? If someone owes me money, and promises to leave now, fetch it and return to pay me, how confident am I that I will see her, and my money, again?

If the disciples had held on to the Jesus they knew, rejecting the Spirit that they had yet to recognize, would Jesus persist on earth like a creature out of time? That must not, could not, be. They did trust, and accept, what they could not yet understand, so that we, their successors, *would* understand and so find our eternal Advocate.

Never again, from the moment of that first Pentecost, will Christians be without their Lord. True, he is not before our eyes. But only because (Andrewes again) he is now in our hearts.

Trinity Sunday

Isaiah 6.1–8; Psalm 29; Romans 8.12–17; John 3.1–17

'Well-intentioned but theologically inadequate' is one commentator's verdict on Nicodemus' approach to Jesus. He saw Jesus as a teacher ('rabbi'), but showed no inkling of the teacher's identity as incarnate Word. So the Teacher teaches Nicodemus, taking him through the process step by step.

He begins with being born 'from above'. In the AV this was rendered, 'born again'. That gave rise to a subgroup within the faith consisting of those who claim to have been 'born again' in conversion experiences. 'Born from above' is closer to the Greek but lacks one particular aspect; think of English phrases like 'starting *over*' or 'from the *top*' and you get closer to the meaning, to a sense of being 'born over'. This is not a matter of conversion experiences but a statement of fact. Becoming Christian is a new life, a new beginning. Nicodemus doesn't understand. But how could he? This is Trinity Sunday; it comes round every year, and still we Christians do not fully understand it either.

These lections are our best clue to the triune nature of the God we believe and trust in. Isaiah gives us divine multiplicity with the threefold repetition of 'Holy'. Then he reveals unity and multiplicity together: 'whom shall *I* send?' and 'who will go for *us*?' The psalm begins with the heavenly court of divine beings offering worship to the Lord and closes with the peace that is his gift to his people on earth. One commentator with an ear for liturgy remarks, '"Glory to God in the highest" is the beginning, and "peace on earth" is the end'. The overall impression given by the psalm is the awesome power of God, both in himself and as God-with-us.

Romans draws out the indivisibility of God and Spirit, but not before it has delivered a warning. Christians may be no longer indebted to the flesh, but only while they put to death the deeds of the body (another way of describing 'the flesh'). For this, the Spirit is indispensable. To many Christians down the centuries, this has pointed to living lives of severe self-denial. That option is always present; but for most of us Paul is commending a life lived in cooperation with the Spirit, in full recognition of what is due to God. In such circumstances, there is no body or flesh to put to death. Rather, body and flesh fade in importance because there is less and less self-centredness for them to feed upon. It is a high ideal that Paul sets before us – not one we can attain to by what we strive for or achieve through effort, but one that emerges naturally from a Spirit-filled life.

Paul's writing about the death of the flesh, and life in the Spirit, opens up the subject of Christian baptism. The same theme is also present in the Gospel, in the reference to being born of water and the Spirit. When it comes to the details of the passage, especially John 3.5, there is plenty of argument among scholars. The most important thing to take from such disputation is not a single right answer out of many possibilities, but a golden thread of connection. We find woven together water, birth, Spirit and new life. Taken together, they express the Christian practice of baptism, which is no mere ritual washing but a slaying and resurrection that unite the believer to Christ for ever.

After we have combed these four passages for clues to the meaning of the holy and undivided Trinity, what have we learned? One thing stands out: the trinitarian nature of God is woven into the fabric of Scripture; it is not plonked into it like the Decalogue in Exodus 20. It is becoming clear that God has no intention of providing us with a mission statement; or terms and conditions; or aims and objectives; or a teaching summary. What we do with these four readings is what we must always do with questions of faith: tease out the truth woven into the text (the word 'text' comes from the Latin word for weaving). We have to make do without perfect clarity or monumental definitions. Instead, we must learn to work with glimpses, fragments, signs and symbols. God does not entrust us with certainty – probably because he knows how we behave when we think we have all the right answers on our side.

Proper 3
Sunday between 24 and 28 May inclusive
If this follows Trinity Sunday, Proper 3 is used (see page 160).

Proper 4
Sunday between 29 May and 4 June inclusive
(if after Trinity Sunday)

Continuous: 1 Samuel 3.1–10 [11–20]; Psalm 139.1–5, 12–18;
2 Corinthians 4.5–12; Mark 2.23—3.6
Related: Deuteronomy 5.12–15; Psalm 81.1–10;
2 Corinthians 4.5–12; Mark 2.23—3.6

I have a lot of questions when I read this passage. Some are points of information: What is the 'bread of the Presence'? (Answer: weekly sabbath offerings of bread in the sanctuary of the temple.)

Who are the Herodians? (Answer: no one really knows.) Other questions are more interpretative: How can Jesus be angry and grieved at the same time?

As they are walking along, the disciples begin to pluck grain and eat it. They do so despite the fact that Mark has already drawn attention to the day of the week – it is a sabbath. So the disciples are doing something they knew was 'wrong'. Jesus did not tell them to do it. If he had done so, we might have to conclude that he was engineering an opportunity to denounce his opponents for their legalism.

So the disciples commit this apparent sin all by themselves. But then, like a supportive friend, Jesus takes their side. He acts as their leader, taking responsibility for their actions as well as defending them. The Pharisees acknowledge as much when they complain to Jesus instead of directly to the disciples. After all, Mark has not told us that Jesus too ate the grain.

But Jesus defends them by quoting Scripture, and the way that he does this confirms that he is taking responsibility for their actions. Perhaps he has been teaching the disciples what he now declares to the Pharisees, that 'the Son of Man is lord even of the sabbath' (2.28). Perhaps he has chosen this very moment to put a principle into practice.

Now that the issue Jesus is confronting has been identified (breaking the sabbath, Ex. 20.8), Mark moves on to a second event. Reading his account is like encountering a series of prophetic 'sign-actions' (look at Jeremiah 19 or 27–28, for examples). First, we must accept that Jesus is the Son of Man, a title he first claimed only a few verses before (Mark 2.10).

The term 'son of man' is used in the Old Testament/Hebrew Bible to mean 'human being'. Isaiah and Jeremiah both use the phrase a couple of times, whereas Ezekiel uses it frequently. So when Jesus says to his critics that 'the Son of Man is lord even of the sabbath', he could perhaps be referring to human beings in general having the right to apply the sabbath law to suit themselves.

Whatever we make of the term 'son of man' in the prophets, Mark is using it to identify one individual, namely Jesus. By making this claim, Jesus is encouraging his critics to react to himself and his ministry.

Christians believe that Jesus was (and is) the Son of Man, and therefore has the right to forgive sins; so he is justified in making this claim and demonstrating it by his power to heal. But it is still surprising that he claims it so frankly. It seems odd when set beside the constant theme of the 'messianic secret', Mark's ever-present warning to the few not to share the Lord's wonders and signs with others, with the many.

Having staked a claim to be Lord of the sabbath, Jesus now proceeds to reveal a little of what that means in practice. The man who has a withered hand will still have a withered hand the following day unless somebody, somehow, helps him. So there are really two questions in the little story. First, why does Jesus heal the man? Second, why does he heal him there and then, instead of waiting until the sabbath was over?

We should not confuse Jesus' emotions with his reasons. Yes, he is both angry and sad because the Pharisees cannot explain their attitude but still cling to it. But the reason why he heals the man is not to make a theological point but to set a fellow human being free from suffering. This is Luke's view too, when he tells of a woman who has been crippled for many years: '... ought not this woman, a daughter of Abraham whom Satan bound for eighteen long years, be set free from this bondage on the sabbath day?' (13.16).

Jesus is not interested in making people wait until they have suffered enough, or until they 'deserve' healing. He reacts immediately, not letting laws that were designed as a blessing for humankind become instead a burden.

Proper 5
Sunday between 5 and 11 June inclusive
(if after Trinity Sunday)

Continuous: 1 Samuel 8.4–11 [12–15] 16–20 [11.14–end];
Psalm 138; 2 Corinthians 4.13—5.1; Mark 3.20–end
Related: Genesis 3.8–15; Psalm 130; 2 Corinthians 4.13—5.1;
Mark 3.20–end

After the 'divided tongues' of Pentecost, this week we are back with serpents as we know them best – the baddies. In this, the first of three 'curses', a single serpent is condemned (Gen. 3.14–15), and transmits that condemnation to its entire species, thereby providing a blueprint for the mechanism of 'original sin'. Here begins an eternal warfare between snakes and people. Literal-minded commentators who worry about how a snake can 'bruise' someone's heel have probably never seen a snakebite wound.

We are accustomed to thinking that three Christian virtues are enduring: faith, hope and love (1 Cor. 13.13). But the Gospel for today touches on a darker kind of eternity: the 'eternal sin' that is against the Holy Spirit. What agonies of scrupulosity this must have evoked over the years! And with good reason. Christianity is built upon forgiveness; the kind of forgiveness the psalmist celebrates with confidence (130.4). If that is withheld from us, we are lost in terrifying territory.

This Unforgiveable Sin (it seems to beg for capital letters) has been variously identified as presumption, impenitence, envy and, most often, despair. Suicide was a criminal offence in England until 1961. The belief that it is sinful persists and underpins some opposition to assisted dying (1 Cor. 6.19). To a non-Christian, it may seem absurd and cruel to turn human desperation into something to be punished. The temptation to revert to legalism is always with us, but we need to look within. That will explain the logic, and explain away the terror, of the Unforgiveable Sin.

Jesus' comment is triggered by people saying that he had an unclean spirit. His reaction suggests that he was aware that they knew he was in his right mind, but that they were unwilling to accept the consequences of that knowledge (Mark 2.17), so they took refuge in lies.

We human beings have the terrifying freedom even to reject our Maker and refuse to hear his voice. There are people, both inside and outside churches, who put themselves, and keep themselves, beyond God's forgiveness. This makes them literally 'unforgiveable'; because they refuse to respond to him, they harden their hearts against the call to turn and begin anew with him. This is not a matter of external observances (reading the Bible, church attendance, saying prayers); it is about the command to confess that God *is*, with all that flows from that confession. It is no sin to be ignorant of that. Or to refuse it based on a misunderstanding of what God is. But truly to know and still refuse? That really is Unforgiveable.

One of the things that stops people confessing the truth about God is family pressure. We see that pressure at work in today's Gospel. What other people think has a powerful influence on us; and breaking through it to follow truth and conscience is never going to be easy, not even for Jesus. I wonder if his mother and brothers were hurt by his words (Mark 3.34). Probably they were; but suppressing the truth out of shame or fear (even fear of hurting someone's feelings) is a dangerous path, as we have seen already.

The stories in Genesis and the Gospel are both about beginnings: the beginning of humankind, and the beginning of a ministry. In 2 Corinthians 4–5, we are carried to the other end of the human story, to our ultimate end. I would express 4.16 as 'the person that we are externally is crumbling, but the person that we are within is being renewed'. That is Christian fundamentalism of the good sort. Our inner renewal is not visible to most people. God can always see it; we can sometimes feel it; occasionally those closest to us intuit it too.

Early in my experience of funeral ministry, an elderly woman in my congregation chose this reading for her husband's funeral. But it doesn't seem to appeal to non-churchgoers in the same way. I think of it as a reading for Christians. The earthly tent we live in (our bodies) can be destroyed. Not so the 'house not made with hands', which is our eternal abode in heaven.

There is temporary, changeable us, and there is eternal us in newness of life. Eternal glory and an eternal home are our birthright. Just so long as we don't doom ourselves to lose them.

Proper 6
Sunday between 12 and 18 June inclusive
(if after Trinity Sunday)

Continuous: 1 Samuel 15.34—16.13; Psalm 20;
2 Corinthians 5.6–10 [11–13] 14–17; Mark 4.26–34
Related: Ezekiel 17.22–end; Psalm 92.1–4, 12–end [*or* 92.1–8];
2 Corinthians 5.6–10 [11–13] 14–17; Mark 4.26–34

Gardening is never only about gardens. If we try to help a plant grow, we are changing the course of nature (for the better, we hope). Whenever we do so, we are imitating God's action in creating the world, setting birth and growth in motion. We are aligning ourselves with his purposes and even with his nature. Of course, we may also be making a living; or expressing ourselves; or keeping up with the Joneses. There is no single point of view when it comes to growing things. One person's exotic orchid is another's monstrous triffid; one person's wildflower paradise is another's weedy wilderness.

In the tough new world that follows the Fall, cultivating land is a battle against the hostility of nature (Gen. 3.17–19). It takes unrelenting, backbreaking effort and the painstaking acquisition of skill and knowledge. The curse of Adam is how the Bible explains why the earth is no longer yielding food in plenty of its own accord, as it once did in the garden of Eden. This is not only a Judaeo-Christian insight into creation; it is shared with other cultures in the ancient Mediterranean.

It is hardly surprising that Bible readings are full of references to the natural environment, when that environment was, for most people, the chief source of food for survival and the chief means of generating income. Oil from the olive tree was a staple of ancient economics, used for everything from lighting to healing. Wars were fought over territory because land for growing corn was the most valuable resource for food.

What is more surprising is the way these readings speak about trees. The cedars of Lebanon are not food plants; Ezekiel uses them (2.13) as a symbol of pride, alongside oak trees, mountains and towers built by human hands. The psalmist takes another tack, describing their great bulk and the extensive shade they provide as making them symbolic of the righteous person, growing strong and flourishing. Trees, like people, grow upright and, with a little imagination, can suggest the human form. Strong growth, which leads to fruitfulness, is virtually synonymous with goodness.

When Jesus speaks in parables about a mustard plant, he uses it to explain the idea of fast growth from a tiny seed – a strong contrast with the cutting from a cedar, which takes a long time to reach full maturity. Botanists can speculate as to which member of the mustard family is meant. But all of us can meditate on the mystery by which one thing becomes something else. After Jesus, grains of wheat metamorphosing into bread became a potent symbol of the Resurrection for Paul and those who learned Christ from him (1 Cor. 15.36–38).

Equally important is the way in which such parables express the idea of purpose. It is not random chance or chaos that makes a fallen grain germinate and grow into a plant. The seed has a direction to its existence; we might even call it a teleology. As do human beings. Our lives move in a direction: either towards God or (seemingly) away from him, but either way we are going somewhere. Gardening is one of many ways in which human beings align themselves with the nature of their Creator. Having children is another. There are good and bad ways to garden and to parent; but being a gardener or a parent can help us to understand God through imitating him.

This is no reason to become arrogant. Everything that we create is merely a pale imitation of his creation. Paul tells us that we are not just God's creation but his *new* creation (2 Cor. 5.17): that we who come to be 'in Christ' really do begin again, as fresh and new as everything else made in the first six days, which were so important to the early teachers of Christianity that they gave them a special label, the 'Hexahemeron'. This new identity bestows fresh insight: the Jesus who was a beloved friend of those first disciples has come to be known in a greater and better way (2 Cor. 5.16): as the Christ who redeems the world.

The 'love of Christ' (2 Cor. 5.14) urges us on to share him with others. That includes our love for him and his for us – for the Greek, in providential ambiguity, encompasses both.

Proper 7
Sunday between 19 and 25 June inclusive
(if after Trinity Sunday)

Continuous: 1 Samuel 17.[1a, 4–11, 19–23] 32–49; Psalm 9.9–end;
or 1 Samuel 17.57—18.5, 10–16; Psalm 133; 2 Corinthians 6.1–13;
Mark 4.35–end
Related: Job 38.1–11; Psalm 107.1–3, 23–32 [*or* 107.23–32];
2 Corinthians 6.1–13; Mark 4.35–end

'Gird up your loins like a man' is a difficult verse (Job 38.3) now that concepts of masculinity are fraught with sensitivity. Things were simpler in Bible days. There are several words for 'man' – just as English can say 'chap', 'fellow', 'guy', as well as 'man'. Here the Hebrew word *geber* suggests strength, courage and righteousness; these qualities make someone a 'man'.

I discovered, while teaching Latin, that some students had no idea what 'girding up your loins' meant. Loins, I explained, are the area of the body from waist to hip, a place of strength. Think of yourself wearing a long robe with a belt (the 'gird' bit of 'girdle'). You bend down, grasp the back hem, pull it through your legs and tuck it into the belt at the front. Instead of legs being swamped by material, they are free to move, turn and run. Girding is preparation for work or battle.

Back then, battle was a man's job. To most of us, it is now an alien concept, but we still speak the language: we battle temptation, debt, disease. God has a battle of words with Job, challenging him, in an alpha-male sort of way. Perhaps this is God as people in Job's time imagined him, rather than as we believe he is. If we get past the squaring-up, we find a divine decision to curb infinite power and establish boundaries to make the world comprehensible instead of chaotic. This is not bluster; it is blessing.

Paul reminds us, in 2 Corinthians, that life as a Christian is still a battle. He returns to the idea repeatedly. Verses 4–8 contain a list we may be tempted to skim over ('hardship, sufferings, peace, love, yada yada yada'), but it cloaks complexity. It begins with tough stuff: horrors that Christians can expect to endure, based on Paul's own experience. But then it changes, without explanation. In the Greek, Paul commends himself 'in' each one of his sufferings; and the list continues, with no change, into 'in' purity, knowledge, and the rest. Unlike the NIV, the

NRSV obscures this, marking a shift which we feel should be there to flag up the change of subject: '*by* purity ...' and so on. But that shift isn't there.

What this suggests is two parallel aspects of Christian discipleship. On the one hand, we are 'in' painful challenges that take us to the limit of our endurance. Negative goodness, if you like: the resistance of cruelty, a refusal to meet force with force. On the other hand, we are 'in' virtues and blessings, which, if we live our faith aright, are as unavoidable as the sufferings. We do not strive to achieve them; we are already 'in' them. This is positive goodness: immersion in all the favours that surround the true disciple.

The Gospel explores the difficult territory of our expectations of the Saviour. Saviours are strong. They conform to a familiar type of masculinity. Every other movie seems to feature a saviour figure, powering through to victory whatever the cost to him- (it usually is) -self. Jesus doesn't behave like a hero or claim heroic status. All through Mark's Gospel he avoids it. The conversation between him and the disciples in the boat shows a gap on both sides between expectation and reality. They are surprised that he isn't aware of the danger they are in; but then they are amazed because he has power over wind and waves. He questions why they are afraid, as they should have understood by now (have they 'still' no faith?).

When the disciples got into the boat, 'they took him with them ... just as he was'. It seems like an unimportant aside, but anyone who has ever been moved by the hymn 'Just as I am' will intuit that it may not be so. Mark reminds us that Jesus has been acting all day as an ordinary person, a teacher, who uses parables to express truth in a way that silences the 'aha, but' of the enthusiastic logic-chopper. The crowd, hungry for teaching in a time when education was not free, saw and valued him thus. His true identity, we were reminded earlier in Chapter 4, is only shared with the disciples. Confronted with their own mortality, they cry for help. And he provides it. But he is unsurprisingly surprised that they didn't know his help would always be there for them.

Proper 8
Sunday between 26 June and 2 July inclusive

Continuous: 2 Samuel 1.1, 17–end; Psalm 130; 2 Corinthians 8.7–end; Mark 5.21–end
Related: Wisdom 1.13–15; 2.23–24; *Canticle:* Lamentations 3.23–33[†] or Psalm 30; 2 Corinthians 8.7–end; Mark 5.21–end

[†] Lamentations 3.23–33 may be read as the first reading in place of Wisdom 1.13–15; 2.23, 24

It is not only concepts of masculinity (as last week) that are currently fraught with sensitivities. We must also wrestle with what it means to be female. The Gospel presents two women: one is at the age of burgeoning fertility, and hence marriageability, according to Jewish tradition. As for the other, we may suspect from the 'uncleanness' (Lev. 15.25–28) of her bleeding, that her fertility is rapidly diminishing. It is no accident that the two are set side by side. The older one, after bleeding for 12 years, was surely ill from anaemia, if nothing more. Perhaps she prayed as her hand reached out, 'there may yet be hope'. The younger, meanwhile, has for 12 years been developing, to a point where she begins to be constrained by her fertility. She might have been told, 'It is good for one to bear the yoke in youth' (Lam. 3.27, 29).

To die before one has the opportunity of bearing children was, in Jewish tradition, a matter for lamentation, as Jephthah's daughter reminds us (Judg. 11.37). This may add an extra layer of suffering for Jairus the Jewish synagogue leader. It is unusual for Mark to give a name to such a character in his story, which suggests that he wants us to pay close attention to Jairus. He shows a father's distress at his child's suffering, asking Jesus to restore her health; there is no hint that he is anxious about his own posterity.

Modern-day contraception, by disconnecting sexual intercourse from childbearing, has created a gap that was unknown in Bible days between female sexuality and female fertility. It is shocking to twenty-first-century Western Christians to think of girls marrying at puberty, around the age of 12. We treat adolescence, roughly the years from 12 to 18, as a time for learning and maturing, needing protection. The perception that biology is destiny, that women's fertility dictates their life choices, leaves a grim trail of exploitation of the immature and vulnerable behind it. Still, standing up to that perception leaves us with ethical and practical issues that did not trouble Jesus, or Jairus, or Jairus' 'little lamb'.

The message of this challenging Gospel story is not wholly clear on a first reading. But at least it doesn't have the uncomfortable subtext of the epistle. If there's one thing guaranteed to make us uncomfortable in church, even more than the wrong sort of hymns, or Bible stories about women bleeding, it's too much talk about money. Or 'filthy lucre' (Titus 1.11), as the Bible calls it. Or the 'root of all evil' (1 Tim. 6.10) as the Bible is said to call it.

My favourite Bible verse about money comes from this letter. It came to life liturgically when I started celebrating Holy Communion according to the BCP 1662. In 2 Corinthians 9.6–7, Paul reminds people that 'God loveth a cheerful giver'. Which may be bad news for people like me who can always think of something fun to spend money on. More yarn. Another orchid. Tickets for the football.

There must be a reason why this lection begins at verse 7. But the only one I can see is that instead of starting with the Corinthians needing to open their purses, it begins with a bit of ego-massage ('as you excel in everything'). Then it starts urging them to be generous. The Greek says that they should abound in *charis*, which encompasses 'favour', 'gratitude' and 'gift'; the dominant meaning here is 'generosity'.

Last time the question of money came up in the Sunday readings, it was about the apostles holding everything in common. It didn't feel odd to me, as a teenager, that at the moment when a collection was taken in our big Baptist church, the treasurer read out the total for the previous week's giving, and we were told whether we had given enough, or whether there was more to be done to pay the bills. But that would be shocking in most parish churches.

One answer to Paul, and to Jairus, and to the unnamed older woman, lies in the beatific poetry of Lamentations. Suffering and poverty are not intentionally imposed on us by God. So when we endure them, as sometimes we must, we should do so knowing that help will come, and that our hope is not in vain.

Proper 9
Sunday between 3 and 9 July inclusive

Continuous: 2 Samuel 5.1–5, 9–10; Psalm 48;
2 Corinthians 12.2–10; Mark 6.1–13
Related: Ezekiel 2.1–5; Psalm 123; 2 Corinthians 12.2–10;
Mark 6.1–13

Ezekiel is exceptionally careful about claiming that he has encountered God. Unlike Isaiah, who was plain and direct (6.1), he avoids definite statements as far as he can: 'something that seemed like a human form ... something like gleaming amber ... something that looked like fire, and ... splendour ... this was the appearance of the likeness of the glory of the LORD' (Ez. 1.26–29). The truth emerges without a definitive statement that the being he encounters is the Lord himself, when God confirms that his people have been rebellious against him (2.3).

The prophet's visions of wheels within wheels, and the four living creatures, have become part of the iconography of Judaism's daughter faith, Christianity. The four creatures were, much later, identified with the four Gospels: Matthew with the human, Mark with the lion, Luke with the ox and John with the eagle (1.15). This is not the world of reasoned theological discourse and debate; it is a world of vision and dreams, the God whom we encounter when we are least prepared, not the one we purposefully go in search of Sunday by Sunday.

It is frustrating to be given glimpses of heaven, but no more. Isaiah provides us with a certain amount of information, but only what is strictly relevant to his prophetic call. Ezekiel gives a little more, but the visions are visions sent specifically to him. He can be guided by them, but we cannot enter into them fully – at least not by merely reading about them.

In this contrast between experience and observation, there has always been a dilemma for individual Christians and whole Churches alike. There is an element of our experience of God that comes to us corporately, through liturgy and sacrament, and through the ministry of the word. But there is also a dimension of spiritual experience that remains stubbornly personal. It cannot be subjected to official scrutiny (though church authorities have tried), because it is not intended for general consumption. It is unalterably individual. No wonder we can struggle to make sense of it when someone does try to put their spiritual encounters into words.

Ezekiel's spiritual encounter has raised questions of authority and authenticity. When we turn to Paul, we find different influencing factors. Paul does not say that this was his own vision, for he relates it of somebody else, 'I know a person' (2 Cor. 12.2). This has not stopped most commentators ascribing the vision to Paul himself. Certainly, there is a logic about his distancing himself personally from the experience he relates. He is trying to draw the gaze of the Corinthian Christians away from the miraculous and exciting. Instead, he wants to fix it to the earthy and earthly realities of their discipleship.

Instead of boasting of his close encounter, or broadcasting the insights gained from it, Paul remains cautious. He is not sure (12.2), he cannot say (12.4), he must not reveal (12.6). In writing like this, he is not being stingy. Rather, he is treading a fine line (one that often exercises preachers) between expressing this personal dimension of the life of faith and seeming to claim credit for it as therefore being somehow 'special' or 'chosen'. 'With great power comes great responsibility', he might have said, if he were Spiderman and not the apostle to the gentiles.

If we want proof of the wisdom of the line Paul has taken here, we find it in the Gospel. What happens when people encounter the charism of vision and divine truth? 'Where did this man get all this?' (Mark 6.2) The wisdom? The powers from his hands? Note that it is 'powers', plural. This is language describing the miracles of a wonder-worker. It is not the recognition of 'power' singular, that quality inherent in the person himself that marked him as God's anointed.

When they ask where he got these powers from, it is tempting to shout an answer to their questions: 'From God, you morons, isn't it obvious?' But it was not obvious. Not to them then, and not to most people now. It is obvious to us because we have already experienced that encounter for ourselves. Perhaps not as spectacularly as Paul, but then Paul teaches that spiritual encounters are not always dramatic. A vision need be no more than a moment of clarity or a recognition of reality. Not even a thorn in the flesh can weaken its lifetime hold on us.

Proper 10
Sunday between 10 and 16 July inclusive

Continuous: 2 Samuel 6.1–5, 12b–19; Psalm 24; Ephesians 1.3–14; Mark 6.14–29
Related: Amos 7.7–15; Psalm 85.8–end; Ephesians 1.3–14; Mark 6.14–29

John the Baptist was not known for his tact. If his view of marriage had prevailed, it could have changed the course of English history, for Henry VIII might never have married (and then divorced) Queen Katherine. Here is a useful reminder that none of us can ever know the ultimate ramifications of our choices and decisions. Best to 'tell the truth and shame the devil', as the Baptist did.

The story of his beheading sits in the Gospels as a digression, unconnected to what precedes and follows it. It was important to record it, for the story of the Baptist matters to all Christians, and not just because of his kinship with Jesus (recorded only in Luke, 1.36). His role in the scheme of salvation is unique: because he was the first to recognize the true identity of Jesus (Luke 1.41), and because he died a martyr's death, witnessing to the truth, albeit before salvation was effected through Christ's death on the Cross.

The story of Herod's disastrous birthday party follows a theme found in other traditional stories: the unforeseen consequences of a rash promise. It is a familiar enough theme for Ecclesiastes to issue a warning against it (5.2). Such rash promises are more than casual remarks: in the Gospel, Herod first suggests one, and then confirms it with a solemn oath. The message could not be clearer: that we do not understand what we ask God for, or foresee the outworkings of our desires. How could we? But the partial nature of our understanding makes us prone to do things that have no ill intent about them, but which put us in the genuinely tragic position of having to choose not between good and evil but between one evil and another.

The story gives us pointers to what to do when we find ourselves trapped by our own rash promises. It would be hard to argue that what Herod did was 'right'. But for him to have broken an oath to God would have been disastrous too. This was a world in which dishonouring God could have consequences beyond the fault of the individual concerned. Jonah, for example, imperils an entire crew by his attempt to resist God.

One of the keys to a right interpretation here is in Mark 6.26. Herod feels constrained to execute John because of his 'oaths and his guests'. I do not think that he is merely afraid of being criticized if he breaks his vow. To commit such an act would be monstrous, a blasphemous evil to inflict on people he had invited to his feast.

Herod put himself in a position where he could not 'do the right thing'. That left him choosing to condemn a human being in order not to offend other human beings, or God. We might choose differently in his position and risk offending God instead. But if we did, we would have to take the consequences of shame and dishonour upon ourselves.

We may never find out how we would respond, but surely at least some of us would take the easy path, telling ourselves that John had brought this upon himself. This is often how people who prefer the quiet life tidy uncomfortable truths out of sight.

Amos did not shrink from the challenge to uphold truth, however uncomfortable or risky. God had given him a part to play and he accepted it, realizing that the gift of prophecy overrode his previous life and family identity. God is the master builder, whose wall, built with a plumb-line (the ancient equivalent of the spirit-level App on my phone), is perfectly upright. He will test his creation by this means, and whatever falls short will be destroyed. 'Passing them by no more' in 7.8 is a way of saying that he will withhold forgiveness.

There are five visions in Amos. All of them are everyday things suddenly charged with visionary meaning. When we turn to Ephesians, that visionary world is to the fore – heavenly places, election, adoption, inheritance – the images come thick and fast. One that ties this letter to the other readings is 'mystery' in 1.9. The word does not denote secret rites or sacraments; it points to what once lay hidden but now has been revealed, namely God's loving purpose, summed up in his Son. Here at last is a vision all can share.

Proper 11
Sunday between 17 and 23 July inclusive

Continuous: 2 Samuel 7.1–14a; Psalm 89.20–37;
Ephesians 2.11–end; Mark 6.30–34, 53–end
Related: Jeremiah 23.1–6; Psalm 23; Ephesians 2.11–end;
Mark 6.30–34, 53–end

This is a shepherd-heavy Sunday. It brings challenges for those who are less familiar with shepherding than people in Bible times. Bishops are required to be 'pastors' (the Latin word for shepherds), remembering that the shepherd stands for God in the Old Testament and Christ in the New. What the Jeremiah reading reveals, though, is that not all shepherds are good shepherds. Scholars argue whether this condemnation opens with criticism about the bad shepherds (so the NRSV here, 23.1) or directly addresses them ('you shepherds'). Either way, the condemnation of the shepherds is probably a general reference to the kings of Judah, rather than to the weak king Zedekiah specifically.

Ambivalence about having human kings to rule God's people has been evident from the beginning, for not even Saul, David and Solomon were free from error and sin. When human shepherds have failed (not surprisingly given that God himself is the agent of the exile, 23.3), God pledges to step in. The immediate reference is to a return from exile in Babylon; but time has given it a deeper significance, referring to the end of time, when the faithful are shepherded together after their dispersion. This holds a promise for Jews and Christians alike.

Calling people 'sheep' is not a compliment now. Sheep are silly. They can eat themselves to death. They walk in front of cars when roaming free. They startle at the slightest thing. They follow a leader unthinkingly, which is a behaviour no human being wants to be charged with. Yet many of us secretly prefer to be followers rather than leaders. It brings a certain freedom, despite the risks if you put your faith in the wrong person.

When Jesus has compassion on the crowd, we are told that he sees them as 'sheep without a shepherd' (Mark 6.34). The truth is that hitherto they may have been just that, but right now they are certain that they have found their shepherd. They are determined to follow him, even when he is (to put it politely) somewhat evasive.

Their plight elicits a reaction, as it ought: *esplanchnisthe* says the Greek – he 'had compassion' on them. That sounds like he is regarding them sympathetically. But the Greek follows the physicality of Hebrew emotion, for *splanchna* are 'guts', and that is where compassion hits us. The canticle Benedictus tells us that God too has *splanchna* of mercy (Luke 1.78). True compassion is something we feel in our inmost selves, where our heart beats faster and our stomach churns as we react to the needs of others. It is a godlike response to weakness or vulnerability, the opposite of Nietzschean superiority and contempt. It is a sign that the crowd have judged correctly that when their determination to reach the Good Shepherd enables them to find him, despite his (and his disciples') need for solitude, he does not turn them away.

Standing somewhat apart from the other lections is the reading from Ephesians. It is not about God or Christ as shepherd. There is no trace of the nomadic, pastoral lifestyle so important to God's ancient people that it persisted as a symbol into a time of settlement and agriculture. Instead, we have an image from that time: a building made by human hands for God. To honour one's god with a monumental building was so ubiquitous in the ancient world that it must have seemed natural: Egypt, Greece, Rome and Persia all built massive architectural structures to induce awe in those who saw them. The Israelites followed suit with the Jerusalem temple, similarly monumental and awe-inspiring.

Waves of invasion and destruction in Jerusalem over centuries meant that buildings came to seem inadequate symbols for the steadfastness of God. They were a temptation to put trust in what seemed strong and stable, rather than what was invisible and (apparently) less reliable. Ephesians combines aspects of both these attitudes, by exploring the idea of a building not made by human hands, but consisting of human beings. The foundation is apostles and prophets. The corner-stone is Christ. These are not dead but living stones, for they grow (Eph. 2.21; see also 1 Peter 2.5). Indeed, they grow together. God's temple is the place where he dwells; and under the new covenant, who are the living, growing, stones from which that temple is constructed? We are.

Proper 12
Sunday between 17 and 23 July inclusive

Continuous: 2 Samuel 11.1–15; Psalm 14; Ephesians 3.14–end; John 6.1–21
Related: 2 Kings 4.42–end; Psalm 145.10–19; Ephesians 3.14–end; John 6.1–21

Twenty-one verses of John's Gospel is an ambitious dollop for a Sunday morning. Unsurprisingly, the Gospel ends up as a game of two halves: (1) the feeding of the 5,000; (2) Jesus' walking on water. They are both 'signs', though only the first is explicitly called so (6.14). It takes place in the sight of a huge crowd, whereas the second is a 'private' sign for the disciples, and (arguably) with no benefit or blessing to any of those who witnessed it.

There are various well-tested strategies for interpreting such signs. One is pietism: 'It is not for the likes of lowly mortals like ourselves to question how this happened. The more supernatural it appears, the more we must accept it as a miracle.' The other is scepticism, which likewise affirms the truth of the miracle, but in a way that robs it, as far as possible, of any supernatural component. Thus the 5,000 all received a token fragment of the broken bread and fish. The disciples, in their panic, thought Jesus walked on the surface of the water when actually there was a solid footing just below the surface.

There is a third way, but it is not an option for Christians: outright rejection of any miraculous element in the signs. In this case, the feeding of 5,000 men, women and children is an outright fraud. It was a sharing of scanty resources made out to be something altogether different. The walking on water was also a lie. It never happened; or Jesus tricked the disciples into thinking they saw him do this; or the disciples exaggerated an experience of Jesus' having come to them at a dangerous moment into a cause-and-effect saving of their collective bacon.

Seeing a trick or fraud exposed can be emotionally as well as intellectually satisfying. When I read the Dorothy L. Sayers detective novel *Strong Poison* (which I warmly recommend), one of the characters deployed techniques of charlatan spiritualism to extract information from another character. I enjoyed learning how such tricks were done. After finishing a more recent crime story, I turned to Google to find out how some of the tricks, like levitation, might have been done.

I mention these by way of contrast, because I cannot see a single shred of evidence pointing to the fact the Jesus, or any of his disciples, or John the evangelist, was trying to deceive anyone, either by inventing such stories or by 'improving' them to make them more extraordinary.

There is a feature that I have learned to look for in any narrative that asserts as fact something that I cannot reconcile with my understanding of how the world works. That is the introduction of what I think of as the 'strategic doubter'. There are a few such characters in Scripture, and in other early Christian writings like the *Protevangelium of James*, which introduces us to a sceptical midwife. Unconvinced that Mary had given birth while still preserving her virginity (for that virginity is conceptualized in physical rather than moral terms), she inserted a hand to check the birth canal. Her hand shrivelled up, until Mary's prayer restored it.

Another example comes from Matthew's version of the Passion (27.63–64). The evangelist anticipates sceptical attacks on the fact of the Resurrection, by bringing forward, as his strategic doubters, the 'chief priests and the Pharisees' to demand that a guard be set beside the tomb in which the Lord's body was laid. This 'independently' reassures readers that there can have been no hocus-pocus with the tomb or the corpse.

No single explanation will reassure Christians about every one of the miraculous signs that Jesus did. Some, such as his calming of the storm, need have been nothing more than good luck and fortuitous timing (Mark 4.35–41). I find pietist explanations worthless, as they virtually demand the switching off of our God-given human intelligence. Minimizing explanations get rid of the problem, but throw out the salvific Lord with the miraculous bathwater.

One detail in Jesus' walk on the waves gives me confidence to trust: namely, that the disciples are terrified by what they see (John 6.19). If the story had been written to pull the wool over our eyes, they would have been confident, triumphant. Their terror is our reassurance: that Jesus our brother and friend is also the eternal Son of God.

Proper 13
Sunday between 31 July and 6 August inclusive

Continuous: 2 Samuel 11.26—12.13a; Psalm 51.1–13;
Ephesians 4.1–16; John 6.24–35
Related: Exodus 16.2–4, 9–15; Psalm 78.23–29; Ephesians 4.1–16;
John 6.24–35

John does not describe the instituting of the Eucharist on the night Jesus was betrayed. To be precise, he does not take the reader through a narrative account of it. For he does allude to flesh that is real food, and blood that is true drink, beginning before Jesus' birth, and continuing into the future life of believers (John 1.13, 19.34; 1 John 5.6–8).

Within this passage are two characteristic Johannine elements. One is the 'I am' saying, 'I am the bread of life'. Together with six others it forms a gallery of images that reveal the full identify and truth of the Christ. The clue to this is in the verb 'I am', which links the human Jesus to God himself (Ex. 3.14). The listening crowd speedily identify the divine nature of the claim being made, and suddenly the mood changes (6.41, just outside the lection for this day) from enthusiasm to outrage.

The other expression is the distinctive doubled 'Amen' that Jesus uses. This 'Amen Amen' phrase occurs 25 times in John's Gospel. In the synoptic Gospels, Jesus introduces key teachings with only a single 'Amen'. What might not attract so much notice, though, is the fact that Jesus' use of it is unique in all four Gospels. 'Amen' is elsewhere a concluding formula. It was used in his time, as in ours, to end a prayer or affirm support for one.

Jesus states the truth before the teaching itself ('Amen' indicates that a statement is 'confirmed' or 'supported', and that it is therefore 'true'). Even the most sceptical commentator would find it difficult to deny the authentic voice of Jesus in this. What a shame, then, that so many Bible translations render that doubled 'Amen' as 'very truly' or 'I solemnly assure you', or the like. For that simple repetition takes us as close as anything else in the Gospels to his actual speech, and doesn't even need to be translated, for we ourselves pray using the same word.

We tend to skate over the literal meaning in the term 'bread of life', making straight for the figurative one. This obscures the fact that for most people, most of the time, the job of a strong leader or of a powerful divinity is to secure material prosperity (including food security) for their servants and followers. When the Israelites received manna in the wilderness, it was first not a spiritual gift but a practical one. The manna seemed to form physically like the frost that it resembled (Ex. 16.14). It came up as dew, not down like falling snow.

Moses had a role in the miracle of manna: God conversed with his servant and explained his reasoning to him, so that he could make sense of it for the people. That 'bread from heaven' was part of the Exodus story in the ongoing life of Judaism, as the psalm bears witness. It was a physical substance with a spiritual grace attached to it. In other words, what we Christians would identify as a 'sacrament'.

Moses did not live for ever. He went the way of all flesh, replaced in the life of God's people by others who could carry on his work. Without a way of passing such roles on to new generations, Judaism would have disappeared from history. Without a way of authenticating those to whom such a role was assigned, Christianity could not have survived either.

This is where Ephesians comes to the fore. It weaves together the doctrine of God and the place of baptism in the Church (4.4–6). It describes the ideal shape of a Christian community (4.11–12). Essential to that community is the idea of the body of Christ, which (like the fullness of the Trinity) is both one and many (4.4, 11). Some roles would be familiar from Judaism (prophets), others unique to Christianity (apostles).

All these limbs of the body of Christ, described in Ephesians 4.11, were needed to share out the work of nurturing the Church, ensuring that no single individual became indispensable. The Christian faith may be named after the risen Christ, but it is not hero worship. Rather, it was, and remains, the opposite of what we would now call a 'cult'. The job of its leaders is not to glorify themselves but to guide other to 'the measure of the full stature of Christ' (4.13).

Proper 14
Sunday between 7 and 13 August inclusive

Continuous: 2 Samuel 18.5–9, 15, 31–33; Psalm 130;
Ephesians 4.25—5.2; John 6.35, 41–51
Related: 1 Kings 19.4–8; Psalm 34.1–8; Ephesians 4.25—5.2;
John 6.35, 41–51

I recently mentioned 'guts' as the place where we, and God, feel compassion (see page 215). Being 'well gutted' as Ephesians puts it (4.32, my translation) is not Essex-speak for disappointment, but Scripture-speak for 'tenderheartedness', a quality Paul encourages, urging the Christians in Ephesus to be kind to one another. That kindness becomes something richer when we understand that the Greek word also implies being 'useful'. Christianity is love expressed in action.

When Paul urges the Ephesians to 'be imitators of God', he is commending something not found elsewhere in the Bible. Scholars point to Old Testament/Hebrew Bible passages about 'following' God, but that is hardly the same as modelling oneself on God, attempting to emulate his characteristics.

We come closer through the New Testament command to imitate Christ, which appears in two other letters of Paul (1 Thess. 1.6; 1 Cor. 11.1). This is not a dominant strand in Paul's thinking, but it is part of the proper understanding of the Christian life.

'Imitating' God does not only mean 'following' him. Paul is a Hebrew in race and thought, but he is also a skilled speaker of Greek, writing in Greek, to Greek Christians. For Greeks, the term 'imitation' more often meant that derivative process we call 'copying'. Read Ephesians 5.1–2 as a unit, and we see the imitation of God by Christians as dependent on the mediating person of Christ. But Paul's blunt command should not be minimized. Like 2 Peter 1.4, it is a precious reminder of our high calling.

The simplest message of the readings taken together, and following on from last week, is that food is a gift from God, and (if we needed reminding) a necessity of human existence. One of the most surprising things Jesus does after his Resurrection is to eat and drink, thus revealing his ongoing humanity. God, we know, does not eat the sacrifices burned for him (Ps. 50.12–14), though he enjoys the smell of them (Eph. 5.2). He has no need of food, unlike the gods of ancient Greece who, according to the poet Homer (roughly contemporary with Isaiah of Jerusalem), ate 'ambrosia' and drank 'nectar'.

The fact that we have reached a situation where part of humankind is starving for the lack of food, while another part is getting more and more sick from a surfeit of it, only shows how far we, the human race, are from any kind of success in imitating God. When Elijah makes ready to die under the broom tree, an angel appears, offering food (a cake) and water. This is miraculous. It is also strategic, for the angel first encourages him to eat, and only when he speaks for the second time does he couple encouragement with a *quid pro quo*. Elijah's rescue is for a purpose. He has more to do, a journey to make, a calling still to fulfil.

I remember a childhood story about a king who announced a competition: all the best chefs in his kingdom were to make their (as we would now say) signature dish for him. Elaborate and fussy confections appeared, until the king was sick of all the rich food he tasted. Last he came to a child, who had baked a loaf of bread for the king. The king enjoyed that bread so much that he declared the child the winner. This fairy tale sits comfortably beside today's readings, which commend what is wholesome and straightforward rather than complex and mystifying.

In fairy tales, it is fine for one person to win, while others lose. Like psalms, they are often told from the point of view of a single individual who faces enemies beyond their apparent strength. Either by noble effort or by supernatural intervention, the individual hero wins through. Usually.

The story of Christianity is *not* a fairy story, not even one of the morally improving kind. Tucked away in this Gospel are two clear pointers to the universal nature of God's love for all that he has made: in John 6.44, the Father is the enabler who draws people towards Christ; and in 6.45, every person who is so moved by God will come to him. This teaching absolves us of any guilt at our failures to inspire and convert others, and their 'failures' to repent for themselves. The first task of every Christian is to follow Christ.

Proper 15
Sunday between 14 and 20 August inclusive

Continuous: 1 Kings 2.10–12; 3.3–14; Psalm 111;
Ephesians 5.15–20; John 6.51–58
Related: Proverbs 9.1–6; Psalm 34.9–14; Ephesians 5.15–20;
John 6.51–58

Some people are never satisfied. You might assume that witnessing the miraculous feeding of the 5,000 (John 6.1–14) would be enough to convince the crowds that Jesus was, at the very least, a holy man, and perhaps even the Son of God. But no. One miracle is not enough. They want more.

Jesus does not give them what they think they want. He gives them what he knows they need. That turns out to be a full explanation of that sign. Indeed it is so detailed that the Church cannot fit the whole episode into a single Sunday's Gospel. It takes up 71 verses, the whole of John 6. We have to take it piece by piece, while reminding ourselves that this section, 6.51–58, is a part of a bigger picture.

When they start making their demand ('More!'), the crowd give Jesus his opportunity. They are not completely lacking in insight. They have enough knowledge of their nation's history to make the connection between this feeding of the 5,000, which has just taken place, and the ancient miracle of manna in the wilderness (Ex. 16). Perhaps some of them have recognized that by asking for signs, they are being unreasonable, even greedy. God does not deserve such mistrust.

Jesus answers them (still outside this lection) with words that tell them what they claim to want to know: that 'the bread of God is that which comes down from heaven and gives life to the world' (6.33). In other words, the answer, he explains, is right in front of them, for they are looking straight at him, the 'bread of God', who has indeed come down from heaven. We already know this, from Chapter 1. Yet although they look, they do not see.

John's Gospel, with its complexity of thought, is surprisingly close here to Mark's supposedly simpler 'version': 'Do you still not perceive or understand? Are your hearts hardened? Do you have eyes, and fail to see? And do you not remember? When I broke the five loaves for the five thousand …' (Mark 8.17–19).

Then Jesus speaks with perfect clarity: 'I am the bread of life' (John 6.48). Again, a few verses later, 'I am the living bread (6.51). Surely by now the crowd must have understood? But we must remember that it is not as obvious to them as it looks to us. We have had two millennia to develop interpretations of the Last Supper, as it has grown to become the central way of experiencing the risen Christ in our lives.

At this point in the story, the Last Supper is yet to happen. And at the scene, the moment, when it does happen, John will tell us nothing about it. This is not because he does not know of it. Some passages in his Gospel, like this one, are saturated with eucharistic thinking. It is hard to be sure, but the likeliest explanation is that the bread and wine of Communion were part of Christian practice from earliest times, but for committed members of the Church only. John would not reveal details reserved for believers.

Like the other three evangelists, he writes for communities that are already Christian. But his greater purpose is mission: to share the gospel, and bring more people into this new and living way of faith. In 1.14, John declared that 'the Word was made flesh and dwelt among us'. Now we learn that as well as living as one of us, this Word-made-flesh will also feed us.

If Jesus' language, talking about eating flesh and drinking blood, makes for uncomfortable reading, we should not be surprised. At the time when John wrote, people felt so awkward about the shameful physical realities of crucifixion (which went on being used as a judicial penalty) that they looked for ways to repackage it in more acceptable terms. Some argued that because Jesus was the Messiah, the Son of God, his sufferings were somehow not real. What saves us from repeating their error is John's plain, straightforward language about 'flesh'.

The English word 'meat' once meant 'food' in general. The word 'flesh' in the Bible can encompass everything that is material and physical. When we eat the bread and drink the wine of Holy Communion, we are reminded of Christ's physical sacrifice, of course, but also of his being embodied (as we are): of his Incarnation.

Proper 16
Sunday between 21 and 27 August inclusive

Continuous: 1 Kings 8.[1, 6, 10–11] 22–30, 41–43; Psalm 84;
Ephesians 6.10–20; John 6.56–69
Related: Joshua 24.1–2a, 14–18; Psalm 34.15–end;
Ephesians 6.10–20; John 6.56–69

At the end of John's chapter on the Eucharist, we reach a turning point. Jesus speaks of his flesh being eaten, his blood drunk (6.56). Some disciples, shocked, exclaim, 'This teaching is difficult; who can accept it?' (6.60). 'Difficult' is a weedy translation. The NJB nails the offensive quality: 'This is intolerable language. How could anyone accept it?'

We must not dilute the Lord's teaching to minimize offence. It will always be shocking. It did make me think, too, about Jesus' absolute certainty about God's will. In his commentary, Raymond Brown remarks that 'while Jesus himself is said to "know God", he is never said to believe in him'.

The moment I read that, my thoughts flew to Plato. When I studied Plato as a student, I found him annoying. He adopted the persona of his teacher Socrates, as a way to explore philosophical questions, from justice and goodness to politics. Ideas were tested through conversation, on the grounds that dialogue is the best way to truth.

That bit, I had no grumble with. But the abstractness was often frustrating, and without knowing how to label the tricks he used to make his points, I felt that I was being cozened into agreement.

Understand Plato a little better now, I have nothing but respect for his teaching us that when we explore the nature of truth and reality, we must always take care to distinguish between what we *think* and what we *know*. I may have a lot of opinions, and many of them may happen to be true. But I cannot always claim to 'know' the truth of them. And yes, you saw it coming: God is like that. We do not 'know' God in the sense in which Plato used the term. We have opinions about him. They are based on good evidence. They are confirmed by history and our own experience. But they remain opinions, not knowledge.

This matters, both for John's Gospel and for my commentator's point, because Jesus does not need to believe in God. If we want a Christianized version of Plato's perception, here it is. Belief, as a religious phenomenon, goes into Plato's 'opinion' category. It may rest on good evidence, and be confirmed by wide and long experience, all of which shape the intuitions guiding faith-full Christians. But it cannot yet be knowledge.

1 Corinthians 13 has been in my mind recently, because it is wedding season. Some couples' wedding choices make clergy hearts sink ('All things bright and beautiful'; 'One more step along the world I go'). Others we never tire of, however many times we hear them sung or read. 1 Corinthians 13 is like that for me. Now I 'know' in the ordinary sense in which people use the term, says Paul (*ginosco*); one day I shall 'come to an understanding', or 'recognize', or 'know fully' (*epiginosco*).

Believing, or having faith (Plato's 'opinion'), is the way God has chosen to disclose himself to us. Christ needs no such disclosure, because with him all is knowledge, not opinion. We do not need to immerse ourselves in platonic dialogue to drive home this point. It is here in the Gospel, when Peter makes a connection akin to what flesh and blood could not reveal to him at Caesarea Philippi (Matt. 16.17).

The setting is sombre, for many of those who had been following Jesus are beginning to turn from him. They seem to be doing so because Jesus has not love-bombed them, guru-style, with flattering estimations of the place they will have in the coming kingdom. Instead he warns them: 'I have told you that no one can come to me unless it is granted by the Father' (6.65).

Asked whether he too wishes to leave Jesus, Peter makes a passionate declaration, which is also a pointer to the hope in which we share: 'Lord, to whom can we go? You have the words of eternal life. We have come to believe and know that you are the Holy One of God' (6.68–69). For him, the time of choice and decision is over, so the verbs are in the perfect tense, 'We have come to believe', he says, 'and we have come to know'.

In the recognition of Jesus as Messiah, *Logos*, Word, Peter comes as close to true knowledge as any earthbound mortal can. And for that, we honour him.

Proper 17
Sunday between 28 August and 3 September inclusive

Continuous: Song of Solomon 2.8–13; Psalm 45.1–2, 6–9 [or 45.1–7]; James 1.17–end; Mark 7.1–8, 14, 15, 21–23
Related: Deuteronomy 4.1–2, 6–9; Psalm 15; James 1.17–end; Mark 7.1–8, 14, 15, 21–23

Whenever I come to the letter of James, I think of Martin Luther. I remember how Luther disliked this letter because of its emphasis (as he saw it) on justification (or 'being made righteous') by works. Paul's letter to the Romans? Rock solid. James' 'catholic epistle'? Iffy.

This has left me, paradoxically, always glad to find how interesting James' text can be. Perhaps this is because if I found myself in trouble, I would rather be met with the practical help of James than the noble theology of Romans. In this lection, we have a piece of intricate theology, expressed in 1.17–18. It ties the writer's practical charity to an exalted encapsulation of God's being. That deserves our serious attention.

Alongside it we have to set the message of the other readings. If they have a common theme, it is living out life in God by doing what is right and good. We are given a variety of pointers to what that might mean. The simplest is in the psalm. It is not a favourite of mine, for the simple reason that it seems to equate divine favour with good behaviour. If this were the whole of Christian truth, rather than a tiny crumb of it, we would all be in trouble. One line redeems it, though: the praise of those who keep their word 'even to their hurt'. It matters that goodness costs us something, rather than being either a mere habit, or a passive omission of wrongdoing.

When we turn to Deuteronomy, the theology is again troublesome. We have to encounter sensitivities over land ownership that cast a long shadow down the millennia. But as always with Scripture, something comes to our rescue: in this case, 4.6 is invaluable. What is the point of keeping the Lord's statutes and ordinances? In addition to the effect it is to have on families and individuals, it must have an effect that is international: keeping God's law is to evoke the response, 'Surely this great nation is a wise and discerning people!'

What a difference it might make if we were to set this aim at the heart of our national life, either in the United Kingdom or in the individual nations of which it consists. We would not then go bragging about our world-beating institutions, our sporting successes and commercial influences. Our ambition would reach no higher than to seek, at a national level, what Solomon asked of God at the individual level: to be wise and discerning. This would not be a matter of boastfully claiming greatness, then, but one of making that greatness evident to all through excellence, through wisdom and, above all, through sheer unfashionable goodness.

The Gospel has been filleted for us like a supermarket shrink-wrapped fish. The careful sequence of argument picked out by the lectioneers is not really there; its teaching is broken up by asides and reflections. It would be a mistake to conclude, from this Gospel about what defiles a person, that Jesus was uninterested in what we do with our bodies.

In one of the discarded verses, he expresses his frustration with a particular way of being religious that he sees as mistaken, perhaps even dangerous: 'Then he said to them, "You have a fine way of rejecting the commandment of God in order to keep your tradition!"' (Mark 7.9). Thus he draws attention to a behaviour or attitude that is extremely common in the life of faith, but which, like the offence of 'stalking', we can't really understand until we have a label for it. The label we need here is 'scruples'. In some of its modern manifestations, we may know it as obsessive-compulsive disorder.

In *The Simpsons*, Ned Flanders badgering Reverend Lovejoy with nit-picking moral questions is a good example of scruples. They can afflict anyone who is eager for boundaries and limits to behaviour, or eager to apply the principles of faith to every aspect of their lives. Attention to detail is good, but scruples are an empty tomb; we will never find God there. Gospel goodness is not about obsessive behaviour. It is about remembering James' words that every act of giving of ours comes through us from the Father of lights. Since we are not the givers of our own gifts, striving for control or completeness is the deadest of dead ends.

Proper 18
Sunday between 4 and 10 September inclusive

Continuous: Proverbs 22.1–2, 8–9, 22–23; Psalm 125;
James 2.1–10 [11–13] 14–17; Mark 7.24–end
Related: Isaiah 35.4–7a; Psalm 146; James 2.1–10 [11–13] 14–17;
Mark 7.24–end

The readings that go with this Gospel in the 'related' lectionary track all make reference to changes in human circumstances. We might once have said, unembarrassedly, that these changes went from 'worse' to 'better'. In Isaiah, impairments in sight, speech, hearing and mobility are done away, though the lectionary omits the start of the passage (35.3). Perhaps the compilers have not experienced arthritis: 'Strengthen the weak hands, and make firm the feeble knees.'

Awareness is growing of new ways of thinking that encourage people to accept themselves as they are. In this case, that means accepting deafness as an identity, not a state of loss. Not for the first time, *Monty Python's Life of Brian*, with its 'ex-leper' whom Jesus cured, proves prescient: 'One minute I'm a leper with a trade; next minute my livelihood's gone. Not so much as a by-your-leave!'

Putting satire to one side, a serious point is being made. It can be risky to presume that we know what is best for another person (though in the case of parents of young children, it goes with the territory). If that person is (in the old way of speaking) 'deaf and dumb', they may be unable to express their wishes or to insist that they are heard. It is also potentially problematic that Jesus uses touch in his healing miracles, for that is a practice to which we have all become super-sensitized through our safeguarding training. Still, touch continues to be indispensable in the rites of the Church – anointing, confirming, ordaining, consecrating, blessing.

Years ago, before praying the office in church, I happened to mention that I had a bad headache, and suddenly found my clergy companion jumping up and laying his healing (so he supposed) hands on my head. It was not improper, but it was presumptuous of him to behave as if he knew what was best for me; and as if my consent to his ham-fisted healing effort went without saying. No, my headache did not get better.

I think back to that moment when tackling a Gospel like today's. We cannot say or think that Jesus was in any sense 'wrong' to use touch.

Consciously following his example, I see it as sometimes necessary in my work. Words alone are not always enough. James 2.15–17 shows them as a means of evading practical action. Covid-19 restrictions have given us a taste of what words-only faith might be like. It was not a pleasant flavour.

Jesus took the man away from everyone else – another danger signal, yet sometimes a pastoral necessity for those who sit beside other Christian souls in the darkest explorations of their journey. This does not undermine safeguarding. Proper safeguarding is a web consisting of both of rules and principles, and careful attentiveness. Checklists are not enough. We should aim to trust, but we must also verify.

No wonder Jesus did not want people to see or hear about this healing. Unlike leaders of cults and movements, the kinds of guru and charlatan who in that generation and in our own turn out to be 'wolves in sheep's clothing' (Matt. 7.15), he did not seduce his followers from malicious motives. His unease about people being attracted by signs and wonders was well-founded; his disciples had to love and serve God first and foremost (Matt. 4.10).

Tales of trickery are so common when it comes to faith healings that 'trust but verify' must never be denigrated as a negative, a 'hermeneutic of suspicion'. In this Gospel, the ultimate proof of both cure and healing is in the change from silence to sound. The point, after all, is that the man whose speech and hearing had been impaired is visibly cured.

Ephphatha has become a word of power, encapsulating the essence of a life lived in tune with God. But it was not originally such a word. Its preservation, an Aramaic word in a Greek text, suggests to us that Jesus really said it, and that people really remembered it on the occasion of this cure (and perhaps others too) – and that they believed that it mattered. Mark's Greek-speaking readers, like us, encounter *ephphatha* as a foreign, magic, word of mysterious power (like *avada kedavra* or *expelliarmus*, or *lema sabachthani*). But to Jesus, and to the man he cured, it was boringly normal and reassuringly, gloriously, ordinary.

Proper 19
Sunday between 11 and 17 September inclusive

Continuous: Proverbs 1.20–33; Psalm 19 [*or* 19.1–6] *or*
Canticle: Wisdom of Solomon 7.26—8.1; James 3.1–12;
Mark 8.27–end
Related: Isaiah 50.4–9a; Psalm 116.1–8; James 3.1–12;
Mark 8.27–end

There is a form of confession in Common Worship that goes, 'We are sorry and ashamed, and repent of all our sins'. To be ashamed, or feel shame, is normal, so perhaps encouraging people to confess it corporately is no bad thing. A few people, untroubled by criticism of their behaviour or morals, lack the capacity for shame. But for most of us, shame is a fundamental emotion.

Unlike guilt, it is not something we experience mainly internally. Guilty persons judge themselves in terms of boundaries transgressed or standards unmet. Shame is more instinctive. An evolutionary biologist might say that shame exists among complex mammals with social hierarchies to underpin cooperation and altruism, on which the success of the group depends. Guilt, though, is a human phenomenon, associated with values and motivations. For example, we do not feel guilt if our attraction to someone is found out, but we may feel shame at the fact of having our feelings exposed. Guilt, on the other hand, attaches to the wrongness of whatever triggers it; it is a value-judgement upon oneself.

Both these emotions regulate social behaviour. Both can become destructive to an individual, or a society. In the RSV and AV, Isaiah 50.6 is rendered, 'I hid not my face from shame and spitting'. The spitting comes from outside upon the Suffering Servant; the shame too is a cruel conduit between his sense of self, his 'integrity', and other people's adverse opinions of that integrity. It represents a perfect storm of negativity, triggered by the scorn of others, that tempts him to lose confidence in his calling, and even perhaps in his God.

Why would the preaching of Jesus evoke this emotion in those who heard him, in that 'adulterous and wicked generation'? The evangelist does not look into the inner dispositions of Jesus' adversaries and discover their guilt. He looks at the outside, at their behaviour, their attitude (or, we might say, their 'affect'). Their sense of shame at Jesus suggests that they see him as threatening the cohesion of their society, challenging its self-image. This must be because they know that his extraordinary holiness exposes the weakness of their religion, as hearers – but not doers – of the truth, substituting birthright for righteousness.

One of the more mysterious forms of shame is the third-party kind. We can feel shame for ourselves or for other people, for our actions or for theirs. Many teenagers go through a phase of being ashamed of their parents. It looks like a converse of the times, years before, when parents blushed as their toddler offspring misbehaved in public. In this latter case, they have good reason; it is easy to criticize a parent who fails to stop a child screaming in public or kicking the back of the seat in a bus or train or plane. But who looks at the misbehaviour of a parent and then judges their offspring harshly? Yet the emotion is painful and real. Here is evidence that human beings are a social species, dependent for their wellbeing on the good opinion of others, towards both themselves and those close to them.

Jesus suggests that shame can be a two-way process, and this offers some hope to any who are struggling with their conscience and their sense of shame about admitting to being Christian. Can we imagine the Son of God standing in the presence of his Father and experiencing shame for the failure of us, his brothers and sisters, to cleave to him? Perhaps we need to widen our interpretation of 'ashamed' to include 'refuse to acknowledge a relationship with'. There is surely at least an element of that here in this Gospel.

James says that 'all of us make many mistakes' (3.2). Such 'stumbles' (another translation) often cause us shame. In the end, being ashamed of someone or something is, if we act in response to it, a form of rejection. Our ultimate fear must be that God will be ashamed of us, that we will be 'weighed in the balance and found wanting' (Dan. 5.27).

If shame is the mirror-reflection of the altruism that is true love, then love can help us to understand it. To do as God wills for us, we must love with the perfect love that casts out fear (1 John 4.18). That includes the fear of other people's judgement and contempt.

Proper 20
Sunday between 18 and 24 September inclusive

Continuous: Proverbs 31.10–end; Psalm 1; James 3.13—4.3, 7–8a; Mark 9.30–37
Related: Wisdom of Solomon 1.16—2.1, 12–22 *or* Jeremiah 11.18–20; Psalm 54; James 3.13—4.3, 7–8a; Mark 9.30–37

All the readings except the Gospel reflect on being made to suffer by enemies. In Wisdom and Jeremiah (whichever is chosen), the theme is the unrighteous and their hatred for the righteous. In the psalm, a specific historical event is flagged up in the title: David hiding from Saul (1 Sam. 23). This is not comfortable reading for Christians who eschew judgement as indistinguishable from judgementalism.

The readings pit righteous against unrighteous, one group against another, but James offers a solution that is still helpful for those Christians who make a place for the psalms in their daily prayers. For James, the fight is against enemies, but enemies that are internal, such as manifold temptations, the 'cravings that are at war within you' (4.1).

Not for the first time, I wonder why a lection has been filleted. In James' case, the omission (4.4–6, 8b) cuts the exclamation, 'Adulterers!' (too old-fashioned?). James goes on to condemn forms of sin that have no direct connection with adultery. It looks like the accusation is really a general form of abuse, like 'bastard!', which has lost almost all its vituperative specificity in modern English invective.

More problematic than calling his reader an adulterer is James' reference to God as jealous. This is undoubtedly awkward for us, attuned as we are to jealousy as a sin (akin to coveting) or as an aspect of coercive control. But the price of the omission is too high if we lose James' reference to God opposing the proud but giving grace to the humble.

The Gospel, in contrast, reflects on a human instinct related to the theme of shame, which was touched on last week: '… they did not understand what he was saying and were afraid to ask him' (Mark 9.32). The disciples had been singled out by Jesus, trusted with a ministry of preaching and exorcism (Mark 3). Given this bond of trust between them, why were they afraid to ask Jesus what he meant? We cannot be sure, but every possibility we explore points to human beings dreading being exposed for stupidity or ignorance.

Years ago, I spent a month learning German at a Goethe-Institut in Bavaria. My teacher was very talented, but I remember her frustration with a group of *'japanische Mädchen'* ('young Japanese women') who would not speak out when they did not understand. To admit incomprehension, in their mind, seemed to amount to a criticism of the teacher. So they smiled a lot and said they were fine.

I have come across this reaction to ignorance or incomprehension many times as a teacher of Latin and Greek. The relationship with students, managed fruitfully, is one in which the student takes pleasure in learning and has no fear of admitting puzzlement. The greatest pressure on this is the student's perception of judgement by their peers. It is the job of a good teacher to banish fear right from the start and encourage students to 'catch' their own enthusiasm for the pleasure of attaining understanding. I use my own forgetfulness to encourage them. 'You don't know what this word means? What this verb form is? Nope, me neither. Let's look it up.'

Switching from teacher to pastor, there is another truth of human nature in this Gospel. Jesus took the disciples aside to teach them the hardest truths about himself: that he was to suffer and die. They were not ready for this; they could make no sense of it. It's not surprising. It would probably be like trying to explain the emotional cataclysms of puberty to a five year old.

They knew enough, though, to be sure that they did not want to go where his words were taking them. They were not yet ready even to imagine his future suffering. Like children who fear the loss or death of a parent, they were only able to absorb the lesson, and be changed by the new reality it brought, when they were dropped in at the deep end and given no choice.

As long as following Jesus is a mere lifestyle-choice, we would-be disciples cannot really know the meaning of that step. But once the balance tips and we find ourselves drawn, unable to resist, compelled to choose life in all its fullness (John 10.10), then we are truly ready to become what God would have us be.

Proper 21
Sunday between 25 September and 1 October inclusive

Continuous: Esther 7.1–6, 9, 10; 9.20–22; Psalm 124;
James 5.13–end; Mark 9.38–end
Related: Numbers 11.4–6, 10–16, 24–29; Psalm 19.7–end;
James 5.13–end; Mark 9.38–end

The readings from Numbers and the Gospel go together today because they apparently pose the same problem and answer it in the same way. Should people who act apart from the body of the faithful be accepted or prevented? The answer is that anyone who acts on the Lord's behalf is on the Lord's side. It is not stated whether their intentions in acting as they do are 'correct' or 'pure', only that they are acceptable.

The message in Numbers needs some work to come across clearly. The complete text would not only be too long, it would force us to tackle two interwoven stories at once (one positive, one much more difficult). That's fine for people reflecting privately on the Sunday readings. But it's a big ask in a ten-minute sermon. In the second story (sidestepped by the lectionary), the Lord hears his people's complaints about eating manna and gives them meat to eat instead, 'for a whole month – until it comes out of your nostrils and becomes loathsome' (11.19). This was because their complaining amounted to a failure of loyalty. They were given the bread of angels, but grumbled because they missed their Maccie Ds and KFCs. No wonder God was offended. His reaction made me think of the *Super Size Me* documentary of 2004 about the effects of a fast food diet.

All this is tidied away, to highlight the story of Eldad and Medad prophesying in the camp, instead of by the tent of meeting with everyone else. This too has its lesson, one more palatable than the food fiasco of 11.7–23. The fact that they are not doing the exact same thing in the exact same way as the rest of the elders turns out not to matter at all to God, or to Moses, his wise prophet. The fact that it did bother some people is still useful, though, because it reminds us how anxious we can become when other people don't conform to our expectations of correct behaviour. It hints that the problem may be ours, not theirs. It also underlines how important the lesson is for the Church as an institution. She is every bit as divinely graced as the children of Israel, but also every bit as likely to go astray, misunderstanding messages and even, sometimes, shooting the messengers.

When we turn to the Gospel, it looks at first like a simple authentication of this truth. The disciples panic when they find someone from outside their group who was healing people in Jesus' name. Then Jesus reassures them: 'Whoever is not against us is for us' (Mark 9.40). If that were not enough, we might refer to Luke 11.50, where Jesus gives exactly the same ruling on the matter. But there is a problem, and it illustrates perfectly why proof-texting is not only dangerous but also misleading. In the very same chapter of Luke, at 11.23, Jesus had just said, 'Whoever is not with me is against me, and whoever does not gather with me scatters'. And Matthew had confirmed that teaching too (12.30). The only safe way to interpret the words of Jesus is to look at each context that calls forth his teaching.

That reminder about the dangers of divorcing teachings from their context could not be more timely. It is immediately followed (and, unlike with Numbers, here we are made to encounter the rough with the smooth) by some of Jesus' hardest sayings. Cutting off hand or foot? Tearing out an eye? These are the actions of a person deranged with self-disgust and what we would call 'body dysmorphia'. But take the teaching literally, and we discover that it cannot be meant so: how can one eye offend without the other? Where one eye looks, the other eye looks too (thanks to Origen for pointing this out). This is not an answer to what Jesus' hard teaching here means. But it does narrow down the options by excluding what it cannot mean. And that is a start.

Challenging sin does not require us to mutilate ourselves or others. Saving those who lose their way, according to James (5.20), 'covers a multitude of sins'. In 1 Peter 4.8, love does exactly the same. We could do worse than apply a (Rabbi Lionel) Blueism to this: 'A righteous person looks after his own soul and other people's bodies. A hypocrite looks after his own body and other people's souls.'

Proper 22
Sunday between 2 and 8 October inclusive

Continuous: Job 1.1; 2.1–10; Psalm 26; Hebrews 1.1–4; 2.5–12; Mark 10.2–16
Related: Genesis 2.18–24; Psalm 8; Hebrews 1.1–4; 2.5–12; Mark 10.2–16

The psalmist asks God, '… what are human beings that you are mindful of them, mortals that you care for them?' (8.4). Each reading contributes something to answering that question. No less a student of the human condition than Hamlet has a stab at it, exclaiming, 'What a piece of work is a man!' It could be punctuated as a question.

The readings tackle the question via indirect routes, not logical method. The author/editor of Genesis uses a story. When God has made the first human, he declares, 'It is not good for man to dwell alone', and makes a 'help meet', another being to fit, or suit, him. The NRSV translates the word *'ezer* as 'helper', as if the creation of male and female is designed to be complementary, one leading, the other assisting. An exegesis by Phyllis Trible skewered this approach back in 1978.[1]

In order not to be alone, the human whom God has made needs to find something that is both like and unlike itself. And so it has been ever since. Two are joined together and become one flesh. In our liturgy, we call matrimony a 'holy mystery', and rightly so: for matrimony exhibits some of the qualities we associate more readily with the mystery of the Trinity. It brings about a 'new life' in which the two are truly two, but also truly one. Whoever the author of Genesis may have been, we can be sure he was not an English lawyer. Yet his understanding of the bond between the man and the woman in the garden is not dissimilar. God is the creator of them both, but they effect their own marriage bond between themselves.

It is unsurprising, therefore, that Christianity has held out so tenaciously against accepting the splitting into two of what had been made one. Only something as harmful as the unholy trinity of an adulterous liaison could bring about such a fissure. We do not need to be told how damaging and painful divorce can be, necessary though it sometimes is. Either by experience or by observation, all of us are well aware of the fact.

---

[1] Phyllis Trible, *God and the Rhetoric of Sexuality*, Fortress Press, 1978.

One answer to the question, 'What are human beings?', has been found by looking at the creation of humankind. We are made for life, but life together, not life in isolation. This model is not a prescription binding on every person; but it is a pattern that millennia of use have authenticated as a good way to live life with integrity.

The author of Hebrews answers the question another way. The psalm had referred to 'the son of man', meaning humanity in general. In Hebrews, it appears to be a specific prophecy about the (only-begotten) 'son of man'. As a result of a small discrepancy between the Hebrew and Greek, this messianic meaning is emphasized; instead of humankind being made 'a little lower than God', now the 'son of man' was made lower 'for a little while'.

So Hebrews begins with the culmination, not the origin, of humanity. Paul had shown the way when he contrasted the first man, Adam (*adam* in Genesis was a noun meaning 'human being', which came to be read as a personal name), with the last man, Christ (1 Cor. 15.21–22; Rom. 5). Hebrews gives a solemn assurance that God's Son is 'the reflection of God's glory and the exact imprint of God's very being' (1.3). The Son is 'glory … glory … glory'. What we might not have expected is that the Son is bringing us to a glory like his own.

Like and unlike God. And like and unlike one another. Such is our humanity. It is not good for us to dwell alone, so those who marry create a different kind of One. Yet the glory that awaits us will not come to those with distorted understanding of that 'oneness', who obliterate the otherness of those they love, cajoling, coercing them to suppress their true selves.

One final thought comes from the Gospel. If you have made your life a quest for independence and autonomy, outgrowing the need for others, think again. Think what your adult life has been focused on outgrowing. You have been trying to make yourself – in Hamlet's words – a 'quintessence of dust'. So stop. Take back the 'you' that you have been sloughing off, and learn to be that person once again.

Proper 23
Sunday between 9 and 15 October inclusive

Continuous: Job 23.1–9, 16–end; Psalm 22.1–15; Hebrews 4.12–end; Mark 10.17–31
Related: Amos 5.6–7, 10–15; Psalm 90.12–end; Hebrews 4.12–end; Mark 10.17–31

A dark thread runs through the readings. But we must not equate darkness with evil (Isa. 45.3). Amos sets the tone with his reference to wormwood. Most readers are probably unfamiliar with this plant, a type of artemisia. But we know what it means because of the way it is used in the text, always with reference to bitterness, causing illness. The great star Wormwood in Revelation (8.11) makes water poisonous. It is no great leap from there to draw a contrast with Christ, who provides us with living water (John 4.14; 7.38). Perhaps all this was in C. S. Lewis' mind when he had Screwtape address his letters to the 'junior tempter' called Wormwood.[1]

Bitter justice is an oxymoron, for justice goes with waters that are sweet and life-giving (Isa. 45.8). It is administered by the elders of the city at the gate (Deut. 22.15), where justice can be seen to be done and where all can access it. Amos prophesies that those who hear him should establish justice 'in the gate', so that, 'perhaps' (NIV: 'it may be that' in the NRSV), God will relent in from punishing. 'Perhaps' is one of those words that children learn not to trust on the lips of adults. Have we got a deal here, or haven't we? We want justice, we think, not perhapses.

There is an element of the same contest in Jesus' Gospel warning that many of those who are first shall be last, and the last first. Perhaps (!) it is a way of expressing factual truth: that those who have borne the burden and heat of the day, or taken years to feel ready to commit to God, will come to the kingdom later in their own lifetime than those who find faith quickly (Matt. 20.12, 16). It could also be that in both Gospels, Jesus is acknowledging the truth that infuriates children and which, even as adults, we find it tough to accept: that life is not always fair. Many people find it difficult to see the point of worshipping a God who apparently does not reward their loyalty.

Hebrews is a letter that causes a lot of readers trouble, because of its interwoven theology of the old and new covenants. This reading, though,

---
[1] C. S. Lewis, *The Screwtape Letters*, Geoffrey Bles, London, 1942.

is not directly theological, but has more the character of a spontaneous outpouring of adoration, an exclamation of wonderment at the divine Word. It falls naturally into two sections, both of them equally precious, both of them sure to make the hairs on the back of my neck stand up whenever I read them. They are so full of poetry. In saying this, I do not mean that they are said in flowery, elaborate language. I mean that they are singing words, words to stir the soul and make the living flame burn bright.

At first, this passage from Hebrews does not look like a text to turn the heart of a non-believer to Christ. There is no inspiring example of goodness in action. No straightforward answer to those problems of darkness and injustice. The passage starts with a 'treasure of darkness', which is made explicit later, at 10.31: 'It is a fearful thing to fall into the hands of the living God.'

In Greek, the impact of the passage is still greater because of the word order. The authors has written, 'Living is the Word of God, and active, and sharper than any two-edged sword ...' If you doubt the power of word order to affect readers, think of Tolkien's description of the battle at Gondor: 'In rode the Lord of the Nazgûl ...' It would not have had the same impact if Tolkein (a master wordsmith) had written: 'The Lord of the Nazgûl rode in.' The words of Hebrews are darkly terrifying: who does not quail at the idea of being pierced by the cleaving blade of divine judgement? Who does not fear their body being laid bare to scrutiny, and, still more, the innermost thoughts of their heart?

And yet. And yet. With the terror comes the promise. Jesus sympathizes with our weakness because he shared it. We are not to approach the throne of grace with trembling but with boldness. We have nothing to fear from 'nakedness or peril or sword' (Rom. 8.35), for these things can never separate us from the love of God in Christ Jesus our Lord.

Proper 24
Sunday between 16 and 22 October inclusive

Continuous: Job 38.1–7 [34–end]; Psalm 104.1–10, 26, 35c
[*or* 104.1–10]; Hebrews 5.1–10; Mark 10.35–45
Related: Isaiah 53.4–end; Psalm 91.9–end; Hebrews 5.1–10;
Mark 10.35–45

Hierarchy is problematic for us. Whenever people are bound together by blood or ideology, why do some end up mattering more than others? In ancient societies, telling people how grand your forefathers were would get you elected. To us it is at best irrelevant, at worst nepotism, a form of cheating.

Criteria change, but hierarchy persists. Egalitarian in principle, we are also acutely sensitive to our place within a pecking order. In meetings of ministers, there are sensitivities at the boundaries, whether between stipended and self-supporting, or lay and ordained. If we say that status does not matter in today's Church of England, we are kidding ourselves.

The Christ of Hebrews seems a long way from the carpenter of Galilee. Hierarchy here is unmistakeable. High priests are more than 'ordinary' priests, but less than one who is high priest 'once for all'. Of all the paradoxes bound up in the Christ-event, none is more shocking than today's: that the Son of Man came not to be served but to serve. Even a self-evident good like 'service' is not always uncontroversial. Some think in terms of 'responsibilities and duties … come with a life of public service', while others take the view that 'we can all live a life of service. Service is universal'.

Whenever we read our Bible, we should be asking ourselves what category of service is being referred to. It is a particular issue in Jesus' parables, where often the word translated into English as 'servant' should in fact be 'slave'. That is, in Greek, a *doulos*: someone who does not have the rights of a human person but is legally a piece of property. Conflating these categories must once have made the hierarchies of domestic service seem divinely instituted.

Human beings are not all created equal. Some are born into a life of servitude or enslavement. Others are born free from every anxiety about food, shelter, clothing. Hierarchies are harder to define now that we pay lip service to the equality of all, but it seems we cannot help creating and recreating them.

In the New Testament, slaves and slavery are mentioned more than other kinds of servants and service. In this Gospel, Jesus is not talking about slavery. A slave has no choice, no right to an opinion or feelings. A servant (*diakonos*) on the other hand, can refuse, argue terms or, in the last resort, walk away.

The first New Testament reference to this kind of service is in Mark's brief account of Jesus' temptation. When we think of the fuller version in Matthew, verse 12 of today's psalm jumps out at us, for it is the verse quoted by Satan when he tempted Jesus (Matt. 4.6). But Mark alone records that after his temptation, angels came and 'ministered' to Jesus. This 'ministry' (or 'service') is not slavery; it is *diakonia*.

So when Jesus makes his statement about the Son of Man, we can be certain that he does not choose the way of the Cross because he has to. He had called attention to a likeness between himself and the Suffering Servant of Isaiah 53. It could not be clearer that he expects his chosen path to lead him to ignominious death (Isa. 53.12). His circumstances, upbringing, sense of self and duty: all these may have influenced his choices. But they are still choices. Here he chooses to serve rather than being served. Ever since his choice was validated through death, resurrection and ascension, we have been responding to that act of supreme service by serving him in return, with worship.

This is not about logic, but it is about love. Being loved makes us want to be loving. Some of us, not born with kindly hearts or charitable instincts, learn to serve others because we learn first that Jesus loves us, and that our greatest joy is loving him. Love teaches us to be servants of one another.

The author of Hebrews makes a point of saying that even high priests have to atone for their own sins before they manage the rituals that neutralize the sins of others. The key thing about the service Jesus undertakes as Son of Man is, once again, that it costs him something. He could not have ransomed and redeemed us through being our servant in his spare time.

Proper 25
Sunday between 23 and 29 October inclusive

Continuous: Job 42.1–6, 10–end; Psalm 34.1–8, 19–end [*or* 34.1–8]; Hebrews 7.23–end; Mark 10.46–end
Related: Jeremiah 31.7–9; Psalm 126; Hebrews 7.23–end; Mark 10.46–end

Mark's Gospel does not, at first glance, appear to have much in common with one of the other greatest tales ever written, *Treasure Island* by Robert Louis Stevenson. But both are adventure stories, in which the principal character sets out on a journey of discovery and self-discovery. And both include references to people with disabilities, though neither is sensitive about how they refer to those disabilities. Blind Bartimaeus in the Gospel and Blind Pew in the story are both defined by their disability to such an extent that it becomes a part of their names.

In the novel, Blind Pew is one of the 'baddies'. His disability evokes more fear than compassion. His voice is 'cruel, and cold, and ugly', his actions sinister and violent. Not so Blind Bartimaeus, who sits by the roadside and cries out to Jesus only for mercy (Mark 10.47). But both are beggars, their regular work is getting money from people, by evoking compassion, guilt or fear. Pleading or threatening, they exercise their powerlessness to their advantage, because they have to in order to survive.

The public perception of physical disabilities has changed a lot in recent decades. It is no longer socially acceptable (or legal) to treat people with disabilities less favourably than the able-bodied. But such protection as they do have comes through legislation because sometimes compassion and principle make an insufficient safeguard. In previous centuries, it was seen as an impediment to ordination to have a physical disability, perhaps on the grounds that disabilities implied divine disapproval. The author of Hebrews may be thinking of the injunction that those with physical impediments cannot serve as priests (Lev. 21.16–23) when he remarks that Jesus is a high priest who has been 'made perfect forever' (7.28).

Blindness and lameness are top of the list of levitical no-nos. Robert Louis Stevenson made a lame character in his novel, the one-legged pirate and ship's cook John Silver, into the first children's anti-hero and one of the most morally ambiguous characters ever devised. To the reader, it begins to feel as if Silver's disability is a warning in itself (and this is reinforced by the drunken dread of Billy Bones).

Blind Bartimaeus has two elements to his story (described not in a novel but in a mere seven verses) which make him stand out amid the many healings that Jesus effected in his years of ministry. The first is that his is the final healing of that ministry. Immediately after it, Chapter 11 of the Gospel recounts Jesus' entry into Jerusalem. The second is that Bartimaeus alone, out of all the people Jesus healed in Mark's version of his ministry, responds by following Jesus on the way. Perhaps this explains why his name is recorded, when 12 earlier healings of individuals are not.

There had been another blind man (unnamed) whose sight Jesus restored (in Bethsaida, Mark 8.22–26). He did not get the same message as Bartimaeus, nor did he respond like him. Bartimaeus begins with an insight into the identity of Jesus ('Jesus, Son of David, have mercy on me!', 10.47). He asks for his sight to be restored, calling Jesus 'my teacher'. I think this is why his healing takes the form it does. Jesus does not say, 'therefore I heal you'. He says, 'your faith has healed you'. I take this to mean not that we can 'cure' ourselves through willpower or sheer determination, but that we can find healing through recognizing the truth about ourselves and Jesus; in this case, through having faith in the one who is Truth (John 14.6).

Unlike Jesus' one-way journey to Jerusalem, the journey described by Jeremiah was a journey home, consisting of former outcasts and refugees, and including those with disabilities and women who were pregnant or in labour. There could be no more vulnerable people in such circumstances. But they were not a nuisance or inconvenience for whom costly special provision must be made. They were the Lord's particular delight, his dear children, to be comforted and shepherded (Jer. 31.8–9).

Blind Pew was trampled to death by horses in a skirmish. John Silver's end is not recorded. Blind Bartimaeus' story did not end with his moment of prominence in the Gospel. It flowed onward, into the ocean of disciples who followed Jesus on the way, most of their names unremembered, but equally the Lord's particular delight. Just as we are.

The Last Sunday after Trinity
(*if observed as* **Bible Sunday**)

Isaiah 55.1–11; Psalm 19.7–end; 2 Timothy 3.14–4.5;
John 5.36b–end

What Bible teaching could be more familiar than 'the love of God' (John 5.42)? Our faith depends on it. If we surveyed the notice-boards of churches displaying posters with Scripture verses on them, John 3.16 would probably come out top: 'God so loved the world that he gave his only Son, so that everyone who believes in him may not perish but may have eternal life.'

The old Prayer Book calls these 'comfortable words', and indeed they are. But 'the love of God' suffers from the limitations of the English language. It can mean two different things, either 'God's love for us' or 'our love for God'. We must look at the context to decide which it is.

In this instance, both options make sense. Jesus' opponents may have no personal love for God in their hearts. Or they may not have accepted God's love for them and taken it to heart. Both possibilities are present within the one phrase. This is still encouraging, because it confirms that a reciprocal relationship between God and his children is at least possible.

One of the powerful attractions of Christianity in the early days was that it taught people that they mattered. Not because they were of noble birth, or possessed great wealth and high status, but because each one of them was God's beloved child. When that teaching was joined with the insight that the love-relationship was reciprocal – that people could love God back, rather than concentrating their energies on fearing or appeasing him – no wonder Christian belief spread so fast into every region and among people at every level of society.

We are so used to thinking of God in terms of love that speaking of fearing him, which is common in the Old Testament/Hebrew Bible, has come to seem off-key to us. 'The fear of the Lord is the beginning of wisdom' says the psalm (111.10). The book of Proverbs takes the same line, connecting the 'fear of the Lord' with wisdom, and even treating it like a refrain, repeating it over and over.

Fear can have positive connotations (awe, reverence). Love can have negative ones (craving, promiscuity, prurience). But one thing ensures that our understanding of the love of God and the fear of the Lord does not go astray: our deep-down conviction that above all else, God is good (Ps. 73.1).

'God is love', John insists (1 John 4.8, 16). It is easy to love him, because he loves us. So when Jesus accuses his opponents of not being within this love-relationship, what he says may seem fierce, even unkind. How I wish that John had chosen a different shorthand phrase for the opponents of Jesus in place of 'the Jews'! If we look in detail at the whole Gospel, it turns out that 'the Jews' is John's shorthand for 'the Jewish authorities'. But posterity has taken it at face value, and this has led to the general persecution of God's ancient people. In the wake of this have come attitudes that shame whole nations, including our own.

Jesus is not angry with his own people, the Jewish people. But he does mean to speak against individuals who claim the sole right to determine what God's message in Scripture means; who condemn anyone whose view differs from their own; who reject anyone whose national identity is 'other'; and who, finally, dictate to God what he can and cannot mean.

Jesus reproaches those who 'search the Scriptures' with the aim of proving their right to 'eternal life'. Familiarity with the holy writings has not made them wise; it has made them arrogant and judgemental. They manipulate Scripture to justify their sense of superiority.

It sounds shocking, but one meaning of this warning from Jesus has to be that too much emphasis on Scripture can lead us astray. Yes, Christians are a 'people of the book'. Yes, some of us search the Scriptures looking for eternal life, because we want to know God's love for us and to feel our own love for God begin to grow. But we are also brothers and sisters of our living Lord Jesus, and children of God – his living Father and ours. If we search the Scriptures for God on the page, but ignore the living God, God's love (both senses) will continue to elude us. There is always time, though, to turn back and repent.

All Saints' Day (1 November) or Sunday between 30 October and 5 November *if this is kept as* All Saints' Day

Isaiah 25.6–9; Psalm 24.1–6; Revelation 21.1–6a; John 11.32–44

According to James Bond in Ian Fleming's novel, we only live twice: once when we are born and once when we look death in the face. Today's Gospel shows that it is possible to die twice too. Lazarus' ontological essence (a grand phrase for what kind of a thing he was) after his first death is unique. How he felt about being revived from death is not recorded. How he felt about dying the second time around is not either.

The ontology remains mysterious. Not so the exemplary quality of Lazarus' first death. The story shows the power Jesus holds over life and death, and that is important because it suggests he himself could have chosen not to die. But there is also a deeper message about the nature of the Resurrection life. If we want to understand that message, we have to turn, despite All Saints' being the lightest and brightest of festivals, to darker matters.

When Paul writes about what is corruptible or perishable (1 Cor. 15), he is talking not of moral decay but of decomposition, the disintegration of the physical body. In Bible times, this was a process apparent to everyone. They might not have had modern science to explain the biology or chemistry or physics of the process, but they knew what it looked like.

Thus it is not a random embarrassing detail of the scene that Martha (like a disinhibited elderly relative) says aloud at her brother's tomb what everyone present must have been thinking. The Greek is exactly translated by the AV with 'already he stinketh'. The NRSV faces this courageously by having Martha speak of a 'stench'. The NIV is more euphemistic, offering 'bad odour'.

The historical point of her frankness may be partly to confirm that Lazarus really was dead, thus anticipating doubts about the fact from sceptical critics of the faith. But the theological point is more constructive. John is trying to teach us (here negatively; in Chapter 20 positively) about the Resurrection life. The physical unity of Lazarus' earthly body, what Paul calls 'the flesh', is crumbling. Jesus has the power to call that physical stuff back into the unity it had formerly been. Lazarus' resurrection body, like Christ's, like everyone else's, would not be like that. John has no more interest in the physics of human stuff than this. Only speculation and revelation can take us further.

Providentially, r/Revelation is exactly what we get today, to sit alongside the Gospel message. It is a perfect pairing of a text appointed for the epistle with its Gospel for the day. At the end of time and history, Revelation 21 envisages the death of death. A similar vision had once inspired Isaiah (25.7), as it still does us. In the prophet's mind, food and drink were not pointers to moral indulgence. Instead, they were (like the resurrection body) transformed into icons of divine generosity, of the life that is promised to those who keep the faith.

This can only be because human physical disintegration has come to an end. Instead, in those words of promise to which we cleave amid trauma and bereavement, Christ will 'make all things new', in the new Jerusalem where, as John Donne said in 1627, there will be 'no ends nor beginnings, but one equal eternity'.[1]

Reflecting on the resurrection of the body is out of fashion. Before the visible processes of dying were kept at a distance by hospitals, care homes, hospices and undertakers, people used art and poetry to explore death (think of Herrick's 'Gather ye rosebuds' or Holbein's *Ambassadors*). Church monuments drove home the message that death is all around us and that there is never a bad time to remember that in the midst of life, we are in death. But on All Saints' Sunday, we remember that in the midst of death, we are in life as well.

Christians have only one way to access 'the victor's crown of gold', together with that great cloud of witnesses who Christ 'by faith before the world confest'.[2] Earthly light withers with the dying of the year. Yet Christian hope burgeons, preparing us for life eternal, when we shall 'carry up our affections to the mansions prepared for us above, where eternity is the measure, felicity is the state, angels are the company, the Lamb is the light, and God is the portion and inheritance'.[3]

---

1 John Donne, 'Bring us, O Lord God, at our last awakening', prayer, 1627.
2 William Walsham How, 'For all the saints who from their labours rest', hymn, 1864.
3 Jeremy Taylor, *Holy Living and Dying*, 1650/51.

The Fourth Sunday before Advent
*(for use if **All Saints' Day** is celebrated on 1 November)*

Deuteronomy 6.1–9; Psalm 119.1–8; Hebrews 9.11–14;
Mark 12.28–34

Matthew and Luke draw their accounts of this story from Mark. But they do what we all tend to do when we read Bible stories: they hear the whole, but pick out what they need, what seems to them to speak most powerfully within the fabric of the whole.

Years went by between the writing of Mark's Gospel in the 60s AD, and the writing of Matthew's (between AD 80 and 95) and Luke's (around AD 80–85). In that time, more source materials kept coming to light, and more work went on in the long process of Christian discernment about Jesus. The two later evangelists read this passage from Mark as a clash between Jesus and one of the opponents who were trying to expose him as a fraud and discredit his teaching authority. What they find here, in other words, is what they unconsciously expect to find: a would-be challenger weighing Jesus in the balance in order to find him wanting (Dan. 5.27).

Another possibility is that Matthew and Luke read Mark, but thought, 'No, this cannot be right, the scribes are the Lord's enemies, so this man must have been trying to trick Jesus!' So they *consciously* changed the way they told the story to reflect more of a 'goodies vs baddies' Gospel.

Mark tells his tale his way. His version takes the form of an encounter, rather than a contest. 'One of the scribes', he reports, approaches Jesus to ask him a question. Picture the scene, and the message of the story comes into focus. This is not a tale of Jesus defeating his enemies. It is more nuanced than that and much more effective.

This scribe has come across a theological discussion going on. He belongs to the groups of religious experts who were learned in the Torah, the Law, and who had the authority to write legal documents. But in this story, he does not speak as a standard representative of this group. Instead, he is a human individual who has been attracted by Jesus' message of 'good news'. He draws near, intending to listen in. Then his curiosity, and his own inner questioning about the nature of God and human relationships with him, bursts out. Once he is sure that Jesus is not a charlatan, he asks his question. I get the impression that it has been bothering him for a long time.

Jesus gives him more than he asked for. He answers the question, 'which is the first commandment', by telling the scribe which are the first *and* second commandments. In doing so, he cannot have known that he would be providing posterity (i.e. us) with what we sometimes refer to as 'the Lord's summary of the Law'. This summary is familiar to Christians from its place in older Communion liturgies; it encapsulates all 613 commandments of the Torah.

Jesus has answered with an interpretation that is creative, for it brings two texts of the law into conversation with one another. They come from different times and different books (Deut. 6.5; Lev. 19.18). Jesus fuses them into a single great commandment, by connecting the love of God (whom we cannot see) with love of our neighbours (who are always around us, 1 John 4.20). So he makes all our human love-relationships versions of the love we have for God.

With this simple story, Mark has bequeathed to Christians a spiritual portrait of the questing soul, as it moves from curiosity, then questioning, to an important (and for his fellow scribes surely a controversial) acknowledgement. That searching scribe gives Jesus the recognition that he believes, and we know, to be his due: he calls him 'Teacher' (12.32). Gospel 'recognitions' are always a powerful moment, when we see a character's path come to its proper culmination, as they realize what we too have accepted for ourselves.

Mark's original version of this story contains another unique detail. It is a text that we can call to mind in the presence of any form of goodness that, though it is not explicitly built on a Christian foundation, has a positive nature that is evident to all. Jesus looks beyond the man's role as truly as he did with Zacchaeus the tax-collector. He looks at the man's heart, and his love for the Lord, and tells him, 'You are not far from the kingdom of God' (12.34).

The Third Sunday before Advent

Jonah 3.1–5, 10; Psalm 62.5–end; Hebrews 9.24–end; Mark 1.14–20

In worship, we read the Bible selectively. We grumble if bits are left out. We grumble if too much is put in. But the Bible itself is always there for us to go back to. Whenever we leave worship wondering how the readings fit into their context, our guardian angels must be cheering us on to 'come and see' (John 1.46, etc.).

All today's readings depend on us remembering their context. Two begin with words that show that they are stages in an unfolding story: '*For* Christ ...', and '*Now* after John ...' They only make sense if we keep that bigger picture in mind. We need some background to make sense of Hebrews 9.26. (Disclaimer: other theological interpretations are available.) Two Greek words are applied to the sacrificial death of Jesus throughout Hebrews: *hapax* and *ephapax*. Both mean 'once'. The NRSV phrasing, 'once for all', emerges in eucharistic prayers to tell us that his death was a unique event that cannot be said to be re-enacted or real-ized (for example through the Eucharist, as some denominations believe).

Translating *hapax* and *ephapax* as 'once for all' sounds as if it means the death was 'for everyone', referring to people – something all-embracing. That is a fair reading of the death of Jesus, but not of the Greek of Hebrews, where the sense of the original is expressed better by the NJB's view of it as a pivotal moment, 'once and for all'. Hebrews is about a unique moment in time, not the inclusion of all humankind.

Scrabbling our way to a meaning is not always so tough, or so tendentious. The Gospel is mercifully clear, and the author has done his best to make it so. We hear Jesus calling people to 'believe in the good news' (Mark 1.15). That echoes the very first verse of the Gospel, 'The beginning of the good news of Jesus Christ, the Son of God'. By the time Jesus speaks directly of the good news of God, Mark has twice (1.1, 14) prepared us for the content of his preaching, making us receptive to that good news and encouraging us to trust him.

In a similar way, simple repetitions guide our absorption of the lakeside scene. 'Follow me ... they followed him'. 'He called them ... they followed him'. Two weeks ago, Blind Bartimaeus became Mark's last example of one who responded to Jesus by following him. Today, we are right back at the beginning of it all: Simon (Peter) and Andrew left their nets, James and John left their father Zebedee. That act of leaving prepared the ground for Jesus' teachings about letting the dead bury their dead (Luke 9.60; Matt. 8.22), or setting one's hand to the plough and not looking back (Luke 9.62).

Whatever mistakes the disciples made later, they began with an act of outstanding faith and courage. Letting go of what we know is never easy or painless. Sometimes the familiar, even when it encompasses suffering or abuse, feels more reassuring than the unknown. 'Better the devil you know' is a piece of folk wisdom with persuasive psychology behind it. We instinctively understand why Abram's departure from Haran was such a world-changing journey in the divine plan for humankind.

We can also sympathize with another person whom God sent on a journey, a man whose reaction was not world-changing, though it made for an unforgettable tale. This man, Jonah, did not want to go where God sent him or do what God told him. He ran away and tried to hide from God (not a plan that was ever likely to succeed, Gen. 3.10). Then he got angry with God for making him look ridiculous (Jonah 4.1).

This tiny prophetic book covers fewer than four pages of my RSV study Bible. Yet its message is every bit as important as that woven into the story of Abraham. For if we read the whole book (it only takes a few minutes), we discover two messages. One is that God is persistent when he calls us, and that if we do not respond at once, he will simply keep calling until we give in and respond (see also 1 Sam. 3). The other is as truly a foreshadowing of Jesus' sacrificial death as anything in all Scripture: that it is God's divine prerogative to show pity, even upon people who, in our opinion, do not deserve it.

The Second Sunday before Advent

Daniel 12.1–3; Psalm 16; Hebrews 10.11–14 [15–18]19–25; Mark 13.1–8

Peter, Andrew, James and John were the first disciples to follow Jesus. Here they are with Jesus in the final phase of his teaching ministry. When he warns all his followers about the end-time, the four ask him for a further explanation, looking to go deeper than the rest. Jesus takes their appetite for understanding seriously. In private, he talks about what following him is going to mean, and what will happen as this world draws to its close. We hear his words as eavesdroppers: for his disclosure was not originally meant for the many. It is easy to see why.

Jesus' hard teachings only became endurable in the light of the Resurrection. It is no accident that the reading from Daniel is the first passage of Scripture to articulate, unambiguously, the resurrection of the dead. It offers hope, but does not neutralize suffering of the kind Jesus knew his coming to Jerusalem would entail (Matt. 23.37). So it is surprising that he tells the four not to be alarmed. After all, he is predicting the coming of war.

We cannot now reconstruct exactly what that prediction might have meant to the four. But at the very least they must have anticipated terror, bereavement, hunger, homelessness, violence, pain and slaughter. How then are they to obey his command and remain unafraid? He does reassure them that war is not the ultimate end (13.7). But the short-term future threatens a time full of disasters both natural (earthquakes) and human-made (famines).

It gets worse. Jesus does not say that the suffering will be momentary (2 Cor. 4.17). Instead, he tells them, this is the 'beginning of the birth-pangs'. Why choose childbirth as a metaphor for this suffering, when not one of those present at this conversation could possibly know what giving birth was like? Not because Mark is a proto-feminist, or because they were meant to explore their feminine selves. Quite the reverse. His words about birth pangs are terrifying because they speak of a pain that the four will often have encountered in others, but never had to experience for themselves. How often the fear of pain is worse than pain itself – whether for schoolchildren queuing to be vaccinated, or patients in the dentist's waiting-room, or women about to give birth for the first time! If the four had heard the women of their families crying out amid the birth pangs, but been excluded, as men, from everything to do with childbirth, no doubt it would seem more frightening than it does to the many who had faced it and (even in those dangerous times) survived.

This sombre tone is all very different from the light, bright reassurance provided by the prophet Daniel. He declares that a warrior prince, Michael, will appear to fight for God's people. That name is a rhetorical question: 'Who is like God?' The answer is 'no one'. For some, battle will mean anguish, but not for those on the right side. Instead, they will be saved. The wise, and those who lead others to righteousness, will be bathed in the light of heaven and become like the stars of heaven.

Just such a vision animates the author of Hebrews, as he tries to express the inexpressible and put gospel glory into words. He urges his hearers to goad one another to beautiful deeds (the word 'provoke' in the NRSV, 10.24, translates the Greek *paroxysm*, which means a prod with something sharp). True, sometimes we need a sharp poke to make us strive to do beautiful deeds for God. And more: sometimes actions that begin in unrighteousness (Luke 18.1–8) can themselves teach us about the value, indeed the beauty, of doing good deeds.

There are places in the Bible that seem to suggest that when people suffer, it is because they deserve to; because, somehow, they have sinned and fallen short. In other places, though, Scripture offers us a more profound insight into the mystery of suffering: as when Job rebukes his wife, 'Shall we receive the good at the hand of God, and not receive the bad?' (2.10); or when he refutes his so-called comforter, 'I would even exult in unrelenting pain; for I have not denied the words of the Holy One' (6.10). In the light of this vision, we can find enduring comfort in the words of Hebrews (10.23), that 'he who has promised us is faithful'.

Christ the King: The Sunday next before Advent

Daniel 7.9–10, 13, 14; Psalm 93; Revelation 1.4b–8; John 18.33–37

In twenty-first century Britain, monarchy and stability go hand in hand. With one brief interval, a monarch has ruled over first England, and latterly the United Kingdom, for the best part of a millennium. Stability is a major factor in the appeal of monarchy, though no British monarch reigned as long as our previous sovereign, Queen Elizabeth II. There are relatively few citizens left who remember the time before her reign. This may suggest to us that the link between monarchic sovereignty and political stability is a causal one, even inevitable.

Stability through time brings valuable benefits. If something does not change, we regard it as dependable and, above all, predictable. In Bible days, life was far less predictable than it is now. We can rely on His Majesty's government to act as a safety net in times of plague or war or natural disaster. Back then it was not so.

In ancient Israel, the monarchy was a source of glory. But it was also an icon of spiritual failure. God's people had the Lord himself as their shepherd. But they wanted to be like everyone else and have a human being to rule over them. So like a wise father he gave them what they clamoured for and let them find out for themselves how it worked out. Saul was not a success. David brought both achievements and failures. After Solomon, the nation fragmented, and parts of it were lost forever.

It is not a good thing to split a kingdom. The Old Testament bears witness to this. The tragedy of King Lear also explores the danger of splintering a whole into pieces. One nation, it seems, is better off when it has one ruler. That was certainly one factor motivating Constantine to end the system that divided the Roman Empire between four rulers, and to make himself sole ruler of his world. But it would be naive not to see his desire for absolute power as an equal influence on his actions.

We ask first what these readings reveal about the kingship of Christ. It is natural to ask next about the relationship between heavenly and earthly kingship. This should equip us to understand God's kingdom better. None of this is going to be uncontroversial in an era when we pay lip service, at least, to equality rather than hierarchy.

The quality associated with the kingship of Christ that the readings set front and centre is that of lasting through time. Again and again, the texts speak of what is 'everlasting', 'never-ending', 'eternal', or 'for ever'.

Twice John of Patmos reveals that God the Father is the one who 'is and was and is to come' – another aspect of the eternity that is ascribed to Jesus Christ in Hebrews 13.8, which declares that he 'is the same yesterday and today and forever'. In his excellent commentary on Revelation, John Sweet points out that a closer rendering of 1.4 would be 'the coming one', indicating that God is dynamic, not static. This would link up to 1.7 where he is 'coming with the clouds'. Incidentally, clouds are the proper way for God to travel, as we know from Exodus 13.21.

The kingship of Christ has not stopped earthly monarchs from doing stupid, selfish or ruinous things with the kingdoms entrusted to them – not even the ones who were Christians. From Constantine on, the temptation has been there to slide too easily between what is good for the nation and what suits oneself, either financially or in terms of satisfying vanity or wounded pride. All too often, 'our earthly rules falter', with the result that their 'people drift and die' (G. K. Chesterton).[1]

Daniel was a prophet, but also a visionary. What he sees in the night is the coming of one who was appointed a king for ever (Ps. 110.4). This Ancient One is surrounded by fire, the element that accompanies deity, being a source of both light and purification. The closest Jesus comes to declaring himself a king is in John 18.36. He cannot talk about 'my kingdom' if he is not a king. But with breathtaking verbal dexterity, he avoids stating that kingship as a political fact. No doubt this is because he knew that Pilate, a Roman working for an emperor who was king is all but name, could never understand the powerless power of the Lamb of God.

---

1 G. K. Chesterton, 'O God of earth and altar', hymn, 1906.

YEAR C (LUKE)

The H. Scriptures II

OH that I knew how all thy lights combine,
   And the configurations of their glorie!
   Seeing not onely how each verse doth shine,
But all the constellations of the storie.

This verse marks that, and both do make a motion
   Unto a third, that ten leaves off doth lie:
   Then as dispersed herbs do watch a potion,
These three make up some Christians destinie:

Such are thy secrets, which my life makes good,
   And comments on thee: for in ev'ry thing
   Thy words do finde me out, & parallels bring,
And in another make me understood.

   Starres are poore books, & oftentimes do misse:
   This book of starres lights to eternall blisse.

George Herbert (1593–1633), The Temple *(1633)*

The First Sunday of Advent

Jeremiah 33.14–16; Psalm 25.1–9; 1 Thessalonians 3.9–end;
Luke 21.25–36

It takes a brave religion to begin its yearly cycle with darkness and destruction. But Christianity is just such a religion, finding meaning in the murk. A new Church year is a new birth, from lightless primeval waters into sense and form, colour and life.

Jeremiah's vision is appealing from the liturgical and spiritual point of view. For scholars, though, it remains a puzzle. The three verses of the lection have 'no point of contact with the verses which precede them' (1–13).[1] Their message is at odds with the situation of gloom and disaster in which God's people found themselves at that moment. The hope they offer is for the future, perhaps a very distant future.

We can see why the first Christians identified this passage as a prophecy about the Messiah. The Branch (surely a branch of the tree of Jesse, Jer. 33.15; cf. Isa. 11.1) is the one who is rooted in the Lord, but called to grow into ruling over humankind. Such a foreshadowing of the Incarnation, still hundreds of years in the prophet's future, must have been thrilling. Like any good ruler, this righteous Branch will execute justice: that will mean people reaping what they have sown. And he will establish righteousness, which requires that the people's inner dispositions must come to match their outward observances.

One of the fun things about being a Christian from a liturgical Church, observing times and seasons, is juggling two different time patterns as the year unfolds. On the one hand, Advent is a beginning. It builds to a primary climactic moment, the Incarnation, on 25 December; then it develops momentum to another through the life, death and resurrection, before settling into green or growing time. This is a time of consolidation (in contrast to the acute form of learning that is the Promise of his Glory, or Lent, Holy Week and Easter).

On the other hand, Advent is a time of endings, specifically the Last Judgement, which once dominated Christian thinking and which still has power over us today. It is a time in which all that humankind has achieved, from the garden of Eden to the fortification of Jerusalem, to the birth, death and resurrection of the Messiah, seems suddenly to be under

---

1 William McKane, *Jeremiah: A Critical and Exegetical Commentary*, T&T Clark: London, 1986.

threat. It is the end time: the time of the four horsemen (Rev. 6) who signal the end of the world as we know it.

When we look at Jesus' words in Luke's Gospel, the second pattern is to the fore. The world is not being remade; it is being broken. The lights of heaven will blaze like beacons warning of impending violence. The seas, which represent primal chaos, will become stormy and destructive. It is hard not to identify the signs of climate change as part of this undoing of creation. At this end time (Rev. 21.1), the design and architecture of the world, its order and pattern (which once had given reassurance of God's hand at work in creation) will crumble to dust. Heaven and earth will pass away (Luke 21.33).

The Son of Man is coming, bringing a cosmic judgement upon the world, a macrocosmic counterpart to the microcosmic judgment upon Jerusalem that Jesus has just related (Luke 21.20). For Christians, this does not mean breath-stopping terror (21.26). They should be confident, with heads held high; not idle, asleep or caught unawares (Eph. 5.14). The moment these signs appear, as easy to read as the unfurling of new leaves in spring, they are to stand, ready to follow their leader.

Jesus had urged his hearers not to be heavy-hearted, meaning, perhaps, 'dull-witted' as much as 'downcast'. Paul recasts this message as a prayer for blessing, summing up a season in a sentence: 'may [God] so strengthen your hearts in holiness that you may be blameless ... at the coming of our Lord Jesus' (1 Thess. 3.13). From within the faith, this is the time to enter heaven, where (as John Donne expressed it at the end of a sermon) there shall be, 'no foes nor friends, but an equall communion and Identity; no ends nor beginnings, but one equall eternity'. He concluded that sermon with a perfect Advent prayer we too can use: 'Keepe us Lord so awake in the duties of our Callings, that we may thus sleepe in thy Peace, and wake in thy glory.'

The Second Sunday of Advent

Baruch 5 *or* Malachi 3.1–4; *Canticle:* Benedictus; Philippians 1.3–11; Luke 3.1–6

This is a short Sunday Gospel, only six verses. But three of the six are a quotation from Isaiah. A scant three verses carry the message for which Isaiah provides the confirmation.

At first glance, they are not promising. One and a half verses deal with historical dating. That leaves a verse and a half to provide spiritual sustenance for the week ahead (Luke 3.2b–3):

> ² ... the word of God came to John son of Zechariah in the wilderness.
> ³ He went into all the region around the Jordan, proclaiming a baptism of repentance for the forgiveness of sins ...

This is the fourth time Luke has given John's name. It came first through the angel to Zechariah, then to his wife Elizabeth; then Zechariah wrote it down. The scene in which people gather and ask Elizabeth what the child's name is to be (Luke 1.60–63), reminds me of the cartoon by Riana Duncan showing a board meeting at which the only woman present has just spoken. The caption reads: 'That's an excellent suggestion, Miss Triggs. Perhaps one of the men here would like to make it.'

Elizabeth's word is not good enough. Zechariah has to write his agreement for her direction to be taken seriously. But in the end, the right result is reached. God's will is done. The baby boy is named 'John'.

For the majority of Christians in the UK, the land of Jesus' birth and ministry is more myth than reality, a place of imagination, not experience. Only a small proportion of the faithful make a pilgrimage to visit it, perhaps because pilgrimage does not now bestow automatic spiritual credit in the way that it once did.

In that holy land of truth and meaning, the wilderness looms large. It is more than geography; it is a place of encounter and testing, across both Testaments. Luke does his best to orientate us within this strange setting, to help us make sense of John's ministry, because John is the first human to make a paradigm-response to the Christ-child: joy, retreat, spiritual wrestling and action in the world.

John is in the wilderness when the 'word of the Lord' comes to him. We can imagine why he went there because we know the story of God's ancient people, in which the wilderness is a desert, hostile and bleak, where various privations reveal true character.

Wildernesses are found all through the Old Testament/Hebrew Bible, and all are places of this kind. The four Gospels likewise mention the wilderness, but of course use the equivalent Greek word. It is still a desert, but unlike the Hebrew *midbar*, a testing refuge for fleeing Israelites, the Greek *eremos* (which in English becomes 'hermit') highlights its loneliness and isolation.

The wilderness is a place of spiritual mystery, experienced by Jacob, Elijah and David, confirmed by John and Jesus, and even the 'woman clothed with the sun' (Rev. 12.14). That place of desolation can also be a place of self-discovery. This is where God's chosen ones prepare for their calling in the Lord's service.

John proclaims himself to be a voice 'crying in the wilderness'. Yet what could be more futile, a greater striving after wind, than to cry aloud God's message, as a prophet, to the vast emptiness of that wilderness? No one can hear. No one will respond. Scorching sunbeams and chilly dewdrops test the prophet to the utmost, but his proclamation is not so much to inform as to embody, in the style of the prophets of old.

Encountering the Advent wilderness with John, we too are supposed to prepare for our task of embodying the kingdom. Here, Luke formulates one of the main themes of his writing in both this Gospel and the Acts of the apostles: the breaking down of human barriers. Jew and Greek must speak to one another. The commemorative writing of ancient Greece (with its emphasis on historical time) stands side-by-side with the timeless record of a prophet speaking the Lord's words to the Lord's people (3.1–3).

During this Church year, Luke will go on revealing how the good news breaks down barriers between Jew and Greek (ruler-chronology, prophetic inspiration), and male and female (men and women alike are named, they matter, they are participants, not mere observers, in the drama of salvation). Finally, through angels, a virginal conception and an infant Messiah, heaven and earth will become as one.

The Third Sunday of Advent

Zephaniah 3.14–end; Canticle: Isaiah 12.2–end [*or* Psalm 146.4–end]; Philippians 4.4–7; Luke 3.7–18

When it was first proclaimed, the message of Isaiah addressed the immediate future for God's people, specifically God's removing his adverse judgement upon them. This was not because they deserved it; it was a sovereign act of divine will. Judgement brings home their human vulnerability, but God's rescue will turn their shame into praise.

Centuries later, John the Baptizer came with a prophecy of impending judgement, but this time the focus was on individuals, not a whole nation. Correspondingly, the proper reaction to his prophecy was also individual, rather than corporate. Each person must repent for themselves. Individual or corporate, though, repentance did not mean an act of will but a change of attitude and behaviour.

If you were to ask people at random what a winnowing-fork is, they might have some difficulty explaining. But thanks to Google, a single image clarifies all. Someone digs a big fork into a pile of wheat, lifts it high and shakes. The wind blows the chaff (another tricky term in a post-agricultural church) away, while the grain, which is heavier, falls to the ground to be gathered. It must have been a familiar image, perhaps even comforting, in Bible times. But John uses it as an image of separation and decision. It's time to make a choice: who is on the Lord's side?

If Advent as a whole is about judgement, this Sunday is about the consequence of judgement, namely the division that must then take place. Winnowing-forks mean separation, but if division is followed by condemnation, the aftermath of separation could mean, for some people, pitchforks instead.

Unity is a powerful idea in Christian minds. So divisions between people can be troubling, even when sanctioned by Scripture. There is the axe ready to cut down any tree that does not bear good fruit. When we add in the idea of an unquenchable fire for burning up the chaff, the sense of threat increases. Even baptism, which for Christians is the sacrament of welcome, of inclusion, takes on a frightening aspect as John the Baptizer warns the crowds that Jesus will baptize with the Spirit – and fire.

John the preacher has his arguments ready, and like any performer seeking to win over a crowd, he anticipates objections to his message and deals with them, before any hecklers can sway the crowd in another direction. He is not a stranger, bringing a missionary gospel to foreign peoples. This makes it easier to tailor his message appropriately. In fact, he knows exactly what stands in the way of their taking him seriously, and he goes straight for it: 'Do not say, "We have Abraham as our ancestor"' (Luke 3.8). They cannot hide their individual sins behind a faceless corporate identity.

In a stable society, there are established mechanisms for shifting wealth and status within kinship groups from one generation to the next. But when established norms crumble, power is up for grabs by the person with most strength and skill to impose their will. Something like this may be in the back of John's mind when he voices the crowd's self-satisfied defence in order to knock it down. He himself has no time for claims based on status. Instead, he pictures for them the God on whose protection they are self-satisfiedly relying, and reminds them what he is capable of.

There could be no clearer proof of the sovereign will of the creator God than his ability to take stones and make them into children of Abraham. He had already created a woman from the rib of a man (Gen. 2.21). Not to mention creating everything that exists – and not by turning one kind of stuff into another, but by making something that exists out of non-existence. That is majestic divinity.

In complete contrast to this awe-inspiring divine judgement, John's message on how to prepare could not be more ordinary. Help other people. Share. Don't be greedy. It fits well with the message at the end of Philippians (4.6–7), which a kind Christian friend once gave to me printed on a green leather bookmark ahead of my first undergraduate exams. It did not stop me being anxious. But it did remind me comfortingly of the bigger picture of which I am part: that God rejoices over me with gladness, and that he will renew me in his love.

The Fourth Sunday of Advent

Micah 5.2–5a; Canticle: Magnificat *or* Psalm 80.1–8;
Hebrews 10.5–10; Luke 1.39–45 [46–55]

In his commentary on Luke, C.F. Evans makes a big claim for this passage from the Gospel, calling it a 'linchpin from both a literary and theological point of view'.[1] He is right that Luke does not give us this glimpse of Jesus' family background simply to add a bit of context or help us feel that we have a hero with an emotional hinterland. Nothing that Luke tells us here is mere decorative detail.

What unfolds through the encounter between the two pregnant women is a fusing-together of their stories and of the stories of their two sons. One is angelically announced to his father; the other to his mother. One is conceived through a minor miracle (but not one unknown in Scripture: 1 Sam. 1.1—2.10); the other through a unique one. One, it will emerge as their stories unfold, may be senior in time; but the other will be infinitely senior in status.

We cannot know for sure, but it is interesting to speculate whether Luke was trying to establish a hierarchy of divine inspiration. When Jesus appeared to be baptized by John, at the start of his years of ministry, it might have seemed as though, at most, Mary's son could only be an Elisha to John the Baptist's Elijah. Certainly all four evangelists, in different ways, insist that John himself understood his own position to be that of a forerunner. He was a holy man in the old style: a prophet like Micah looking forward beyond the difficulties of the present (this would be clearer if Micah 5.1 were included in the lection) to a time of peace. Jesus would turn out to be something, someone, altogether different.

So much we can glean from looking at how the story is constructed and from comparing it with similar texts (Evans' 'literary point of view'). Now we turn to the theology. What have Christians reasoned from this passage? The first thing that comes to my mind may not be the most obvious, but it matters to me because I took the name of John-Baptist at my ordination, to ally myself with the saint whose calling it was constantly to speak the truth.

John's leaping in the womb of his mother Elizabeth is a normal part of later pregnancy. It's fun to watch your child's head roll from one side of your swollen belly to the other. Yet the Church has made even more

---

1 C. F Evans, *Saint Luke* (New Testament Commentaries), SCM Press, 1990.

of this movement than Elizabeth could have done. For her, it was a sign that her own son had recognized Jesus, not only as kin but as Lord. For later generations of Christians, that leap of joy came to be the mark of the Holy Spirit at work in John. This prenatal gracing with the Spirit is – for him alone save for Mary herself among the saints – the reason why Christians celebrate his nativity (24 June) rather than his death as his principal feast. And it is why white is the colour of that feast.

In such theology, meaning accumulates over time. Layers of faith and reason are laid down like the deposits of sediment that time and pressure turn gradually from mud into rock. From a practical point of view, it also does away with what might otherwise have been a problem: that John died before the salvific death of his Lord. Another solution for that difficulty emerged later as a way to incorporate other righteous people in John's position: the harrowing of hell. But that was not adequate for John's unique place in the story. In the history of Christianity, he had earned his interstitial place, one foot in the Old Testament world of the prophets, the other in the New Testament world of the Church.

Sometimes, we need to think outside the realm of the familiar to make sense of people who don't fit neatly into our categories. We can see the author of Hebrews using what he knows about sacrifice and priesthood to make sense of how he, a Christian, experienced the death of Christ. We should notice that when the old categories of sacrifice and priesthood are not adequate for the task, he does not reshape Christ to fit the categories. Instead he redefines the categories in order to be true to God's Son as he encountered him then – and as we still do today.

Christmas Day (Set I readings)

Isaiah 9.2–7; Psalm 96; Titus 2.11–14; Luke 2.1–14 [15–20]

After writing my column about the lections for a year, I became aware that people read it for different reasons. Ministers looking for sermon material are not the whole picture. But they deserve sympathy, for at Christmas preachers can feel most frustrated. At the moment when we celebrate the Incarnation, the right time to explore the fullness of incarnational theology never comes. It always loses out to the family-friendly, simple and, above all, short homily. There is a meal to be prepared, presents to open. We cannot afford to linger. Those short homilies, though valuable, do not always reach into the corners of the soul in the way that the Incarnation suggests they should.

Luke Chapter 2 is the first Bible reading that I ever remember. I must have been seven, and my older sister was reading it at a school carol service in St Mary's Church, Great Baddow. I expect lots of people have similar memories of that Gospel. Chapter 2 of the letter to Titus, in contrast, is probably top of very few people's list of favourite Christmas readings. But over the years it has become one of mine.

The highlight in this Christmas Day feast, for what Augustine called 'the ears of the heart', is that glorious moment when 'the grace of God has dawned upon the world' (Titus 2.11). Scholars may think that this translation is not sufficiently close to the Greek, but I believe it is best at expressing the power of it. It comes from a Bible version that has fallen out of fashion, the New English Bible (now the Revised English Bible), and that is how I always hear the words, regardless of what is read or printed out for Christmas Day. If we only pay attention to the NRSV and NIV, both of which use a rather dull verb (the grace of God has 'appeared'), we will miss the triumphant tone of the good news.

So we can declare that the grace of God has 'dawned upon the world'. The Greek verb is vivid; it needs the English to be vivid too. It is the same verb as Zechariah used in his Benedictus (Luke 1.79). But we know it better through its associated noun – 'epiphany'. Perhaps 'the grace of God has been made manifest' is a fair compromise: that ties in with verse 13 of the Titus reading, where the writer refers to the 'manifestation of the grace of God'. There it is again: the word 'epiphany'.

On Christmas morning, crisp and bright if we are lucky, we make our way to church, and the dayspring has only just arisen in the east. Then, in a harmony of soul and body comes a dawn in our hearts to match the dawn in the physical world.

We hear the prophet's proclamation that the people who walked in darkness have seen a great light. Once, when God had walked with his people, they had a pillar of fire by night to light their way. That confirms that 'walking in darkness' is a state of separation from God. Almost all of us, whether or not we call ourselves Christians, have some experience of such a state.

At Christmas, the veil between people of faith and those outside it is at its most translucent. Something about this light in the darkness, a bright beacon at the time when natural light is most scarce, draws people in, regardless of mistakes they have made, or what they think about the identity of the baby. Without being clear what God's grace may be, or what a manifestation is, for that matter, people feel a deep and powerful pull.

What is this 'manifestation of the grace of God'? To come back to the simplicity of the Christmas story, it is exactly what Luke makes plain in his Gospel. A baby wrapped up warm and sleeping is a familiar sight that all of us can understand. It is reinforced by the Christmas crib in church, and perhaps by the babies and children in church with us on Christmas morning. Before the eyes of our mind (Augustine again) lies the sleeping infant. We tread carefully so as not to wake him. We watch him in all the beauty of his vulnerability and need. And with perfect clarity, the very grace of God dawns in our hearts and in our world once more.

The First Sunday of Christmas

1 Samuel 2.18–20, 26; Psalm 148 [*or* 148.7–end];
Colossians 3.12–17; Luke 2.41–end

For a second time this Christmas, Mary 'treasures' her memory of an event (first, Luke 2.19). The resolution of a family crisis ultimately makes the memory happy, for relief washes away the imprint of anxiety.

Memories build up our sense of self, for we learn to see ourselves through the lens of past events. They also form us socially, within family and kinship groups, and within our church family and other communities to which we belong.

Memory and self are inseparable. The cruellest part of dementia, for carers and loved ones, is the loss of a shared pool of memory. This is partly something we experience as observers of a loved one's decline. They themselves diminish; their capacity to meet our gaze with attention and understanding dwindles. We also experience it internally, as their diminishing diminishes us: bits of us that are bonded to the one we love, and are losing, break off and vanish.

There is a third element in our experience of memory loss and cognitive decline: how it affects us in terms of human empathy. We may doubt ourselves, as we struggle to make sense of offering love, devotion, respect, as well as mundane physical care, to those who are disappearing before our eyes, sometimes in a gentle fading, sometimes amid hurtful frustration and paranoia.

Memory is a fabric, woven from the stuff of our unique experiences and of those we repeat regularly. Christmas belongs in both categories, for each one is different, even if we try to recreate a perfect formula. As we grow older, the fabric becomes more complex in composition. If it were a garment, the label would surely say 'mixed fibres: wash with care'.

Every year works changes in our feelings about Christmas. Every birth and death, every adolescent blooming and elderly decline in the year now passing witnesses to the frailty and toughness of our humanity. Like Virgil's 'tears of things' (*lacrimae rerum*), the truths of human mortality press insistently upon our minds.

In this Gospel, the message is not hiding behind parable and mystery. It lies on the surface, a paradigm for family interactions. Parents do not understand their children. Because they have learned to read them so well in one way, they fail, time and again, to read them as the child moves on, grows up, becomes independent.

That process can be as traumatic as a bereavement for parents. Like God with Adam and Eve in the garden, they strive to keep their little ones in the paradise of childish innocence, even as those children scramble to leave it and go in search of new ways of being who they are.

But the fault runs in both directions. If this Gospel had only one lesson to share, it would be this: even supposedly perfect parents and children misunderstand each other. How, then, can we expect always to get it right ourselves, either as parent or as child?

Part of becoming one's own person is shutting out the voice and claims of parents, resisting the pressure to concede and conform. It is as if, having discovered that parents are not perfect and do not know everything, the child behaves as if those parents are flawed to the point of utter failure and know nothing about anything.

Parenthood is an education. It teaches us that we are not the centre of the universe. It makes carers of the cared-for. It puts us in a position where we observe the unfolding life-stages from childhood to adulthood, after having undergone that process ourselves. With understanding born of that observation, and from empathy, it becomes humbling indeed to realize what patience, what restraint, what sheer force of love our parents must have exercised when (for example) we were at our adolescent worst.

This Gospel comes from a stage in Jesus' life some 12 years after his Nativity. But Christmas can be a time when the combat between image and reality is locked in a Manichaean stalemate. Then this Gospel's lesson about family life and love is most timely. The greatest lesson we learn from being a parent to our own child is the same as we hope for in every child's nurturing: that even without being perfect as our heavenly Father is perfect (Matt. 5.48), parent and child alike will find that the love we know, and the love we give, both teach us the truth of God.

The Second Sunday of Christmas

Jeremiah 31.7–14; Psalm 147.13–end; Ephesians 1.3–14;
John 1.[1–9] 10–18

The second Sunday of Christmas is an oddity. In some years, it does not happen at all. But when it does, what a strange opportunity we are presented with! In the middle of Christmas, the Gospel is actually doing the groundwork for the Holy Trinity.

At Christmas, we often hear John 1.1–14. This passage links the beginning of the world to the beginning that is the Word ('in the beginning': Gen. 1.1; John 1.1). In its final verse, 1.14 (the moment of Incarnation), the truth in the text is so holy that many people bow their heads or kneel: 'the Word was made flesh and dwelt among us' (AV).

For this Sunday, the first nine verses of John 1 are optional. This puts the main focus on 1.10–18 as a unit. If we set aside 1.14, and the parenthesis about John that follows it, the core of the lection is this (1.16–18):

> From his fullness we have all received, grace upon grace. The law indeed was given through Moses; grace and truth came through Jesus Christ. No one has ever seen God. It is God the only Son, who is close to the Father's heart, who has made him known.

We have a natural instinct, as Christians, to assume logical coherence in these words. But the truth is that they read as a bit of a jumble, their logic hard to tease out. The best sense I can make of John's train of thought here is to see him preaching these words, rather than writing them. In such a setting, each verse has a powerful impact: imagining one fact after another tumbling from the evangelist's lips creates a crescendo that makes the words easier to receive.

On the page – or the screen – of our Bible, we still have to wrestle with the sequence of ideas. What connects each verse to the next? If only John had explained what he means by 'fullness', for it is already a key theological term in Paul's letter to the Romans (written before John's Gospel) and in Ephesians. But here it is mentioned only to vanish; John never refers to it again.

Next, John jumps forward to another complicated theological concept, 'grace'. Grace, we discover, is a fertile thing, for it begets itself in an emanation from that mysterious fullness: grace brings more grace into being. The idea is easier to grasp, for Christians and non-Christians alike, if we think instead of 'love', for love does beget love, as those who show or receive love know well. While it is true that Christians often experience grace in this way, it would still have been helpful to know more of what John means by it.

The jumble goes on being a jumble, for mentioning grace prompts John to jump to a contrast between law and grace. One writer has described this as 'the whole Christian revelation', with 'law' standing for the old covenant and 'grace' for the new. We should not assume that the one supplants the other, that law falls away where grace comes. God chooses his agents carefully: the law that came 'through' Moses was God's law. So too the grace and truth that come 'through' Jesus Christ are God's grace and truth.

Perhaps the meaning is that law provides the structure and framework for a life of faith, the body, we might say; whereas grace provides the spirit and inspiration. It is a churchy way of saying that grace is more than being nice and kind to people, and law is more than blind obedience or cold rigour. This 'take' does seem to do justice to John's words, while still preserving the unique revelation that is the Incarnation.

The last part of the Gospel takes the reader or hearer away from Christmastide Incarnation, into a proto-revelation of Trinity. Again, the sequence of thought is not smooth, but the ideas are powerful. John is talking directly to us here. He explains, like a preacher (rather than unfolding the narrative sequence of Jesus' life): first, an unarguable fact – no one has ever seen God (mentally we add 'fully', given the exalted access Moses was granted, Ex. 33.11). Then a fact accessible only by faith. And here we must read with care, not making assumptions: not 'an only Son', as in John 1.14, but 'God the only Son'. And this, centuries before the Nicene Creed was even thought of.

The Epiphany

Isaiah 60.1–6; Psalm 72.[1–9] 10–15; Ephesians 3.1–12;
Matthew 2.1–12

The festival of Epiphany preserves its Greek name in the Western Church. By the second century, it was beginning to be kept as a feast on 6 January. It is one of the earliest elements in the liturgical year to find its fixed place in the calendar.

In those early days, the Baptism of Christ (which comes next week) was included as part of the Epiphany. It took two more centuries before the Nativity began to be celebrated. That came from the Western Church, as its Latin-based name suggests. It was tied to what was then the midwinter solstice. So the 'light shining in darkness' became an image embodied in the festival of Christmas.

The Nativity feast spread to the Eastern churches as the Epiphany did to those in the West. But the Baptism of Christ (more on that next week) was left unclear, which caused some confusion and discontent in Eastern churches. Meanwhile, by refusing what seemed best to the godly wisdom of anyone but themselves, the old Puritans known as 'Donatists' refused to celebrate the Epiphany at all, whatever name it was called by. They were always eager to be against things.

The word 'epiphany' (or its cognates) appears in the New Testament, but not in Matthew's account of the coming of the Magi. Rather, it is applied to appearance of Christ signifying divinity. The closest parallel in any other New Testament text comes in the hymn known as 'Benedictus' (Luke 1.79), which refers to a light that will 'appear' to those 'who remain in darkness and in the shadow of death'.

So light, the means by which things become clear and perceptible, is at the centre of the meaning of 'epiphany', while the theological label was chosen after the event, to describe what had happened on the occasion described by Matthew. If we use the term 'epiphany' more generally, to indicate moments of clarity and recognition concerning the divinity of Jesus, then it stands second in the Gospels' historical sequence, with the Nativity itself coming first. Further 'epiphanies' are to follow: at the baptism (to all those who witness it), at the presentation (to Simeon and Anna: Luke 2.27, 38) and, later, on the mountain of transfiguration.

From this list, to which more could be added, we can see that epiphanies need to have an audience. They are always directed 'at' someone. Even the transfiguration, a very select epiphany, required the presence of four of the disciples, to act as witnesses. That is one more than the traditional number of the Magi (Matthew does not mention the number three).

The BCP gives both the traditional title for the festival on 6 January and a description based on a theological 'take' on the event concerned, calling it, 'the Epiphany: or the manifestation of Christ to the gentiles'. From this theological take on the scriptural event, we are shown that the manifestation, made first to a few specific gentiles, grows into something greater. Either through the personal witness of the 'three Kings from Persian lands afar'[1] or through the repeating and treasuring of the event itself within the community of faith, it becomes a manifestation to all gentiles.

By the time Matthew was writing of the journey of the Magi, Paul had been embodying the fruit of that manifestation, by carrying the gospel message – specifically the message of Christ's divine nature – to many gentile communities around the Mediterranean, in years of missionary activity. We, his successors according to the Spirit, are still doing our best, imperfectly, with that same calling, responding to that same light.

Finally, I want to add a word about one key phrase in this Gospel (1.11):

'… they knelt down and paid him homage' (NRSV)
'… they bowed down and worshipped him' (NIV)
'… and fell down, and worshipped him' (AV)
'… falling to their knees, they honoured him' (CEB)

I was doubtful whether many of today's Christians would understand the concept of 'homage' (NRSV). That prompted me to look further. The most literal translation would be 'falling they prostrated themselves to him'. Translators are resistant to saying what the Greek says in scenes like this. They avoid mentioning 'falling down' in worship, or 'prostrating'. The Common English Bible even finds 'worshipping' of the child Jesus unpalatable: 'they honoured him', it substitutes. To my mind, prostration before God is natural. Joyful. But 'honour' is a poor substitute for 'worship'.

---

[1] Peter Cornelius, trans. F. Corder, 'The Three Kings' (*'Die Könige'*), from *Weihnachtslieder* (*Christmas Songs*), Op. 8, 1856.

The Baptism of Christ
(The First Sunday of Epiphany)

Isaiah 43.1–7; Psalm 29; Acts 8.14–17; Luke 3.15–17, 21, 22

What's in a name? After Jesus has been baptized the Holy Spirit descends on him 'like a dove'. Or is it a pigeon? Nature makes no firm distinction between them: both are members of the same bird family. The Bible agrees, making doves and pigeons interchangeable as sacrificial offerings. So why are doves beautiful, where pigeons are a nuisance?

Partly this is a question of familiarity breeding contempt. Collared doves were once a rarity in the UK; and turtle doves (which are summer migrants) are becoming rare. But we are never short of pigeons. The countryside is full of wood pigeons, and towns are full of feral pigeons. In both cases they can be a common nuisance. The same word, *yonah* in Hebrew, usually refers to both birds in Scripture. Occasionally, the Hebrew word *tor* is used: this makes the bird easy to identify, by its call, as the turtle (*tur-tur*) dove.

When I think of the Holy Spirit descending on Jesus 'like a dove', I want it to happen delicately, gently. Yet when pigeons and doves take flight or land they are clumping, noisy. I imagine this baptismal dove/pigeon doing what no real-life bird of its kind has ever done, and hovering above Jesus' head. This we see in many an artistic image.

If hovering were authentic, a kestrel (also known as a windhover) would have done better. But kestrels are birds of prey, they divide flesh and spirit (Heb. 4.12); whereas Jesus is not yet even a dainty falcon, never mind a mighty eagle of divine truth. Besides, birds that are killers do not fit the brief. The Holy Spirit is described in terms more akin to a vegetarian than a carnivore (Isa. 65.25), as befits its pacifist credentials (Gen. 8.11).

It may be that our technology-dominated existence has blunted the sensitivity of our imagination here. The key thing about doves/pigeons is that they fly. This realm of movement was unavailable in Bible days. For us, anyone can do it who can afford a plane fare. The ability to fly links earth and heaven, bridging the gap between the realms of the divine and the human. A dove may have been the form chosen to describe this unique descent of the Holy Spirit simply because it is a species pleasing to God (an acceptable sacrifice, Luke 2.24), and especially associated with heavenly good news (the first confirmation that the flood was ending, Gen. 8.12).

The order of events in this scene is more than usually important. According to Luke, the baptism (in water) takes place first. Immediately, Jesus responds by praying – perhaps merely as one among the many who were baptized there. Then something happens that singles him out. After his water baptism, the heaven opened, the Spirit descended like a dove, and the voice sounded from heaven.

So we are invited to imagine a crowded, buzzing scene, a high pitch of spiritual excitement. Next, sudden stillness, and maybe silence, allowing the voice from heaven to be heard by all those who, up until that moment, had been talking excitedly of their own baptism. Then the revelation of the true identity of the seeming-nobody: 'You are my Son, the Beloved; with you I am well pleased' (Luke 3.22).

It is a conversation between Father and Son, which those who were at the waterside fortuitously eavesdropped on. Or so I once thought. But a little reflection convinced me that they too were chosen, to be witnesses: witnesses not only of a relationship of affection ('beloved', 'pleased') but also of kinship ('my Son').

A Gospel so rich in detail leaves little room for other texts. But there is space enough to note that the Isaiah passage puts God's name front and centre (43.1, 7) in the salvific process. In Acts, moreover, baptism is effected specifically in the name of God's Son (8.16); it is incomplete until, through apostolic invocation, the Holy Spirit is given to those who 'accept the word of God' (8.14). How then, shall we know if people have been fully baptized, with water, the divine name and the Holy Spirit? Paperwork and eyewitnesses should guarantee the first two conditions. The descent of the Holy Spirit may be felt by the persons receiving it; but the only sure test for this mark of the disciple is a life lived for God.

The Second Sunday of Epiphany

Isaiah 62.1–5; Psalm 36.5–10; 1 Corinthians 12.1–11; John 2.1–11

For the second week in a row, the richness of the Gospel demands almost all the attention, while I find myself wondering, 'What's in a name?' Matthew, Mark and Luke all refer to the mother of Jesus by name as Mary. John never does so, despite the high profile he accords her at key moments.

Insight into the story comes to us from meditation, for there are many details we would like to know, yet only a few have been imparted. Like many a family story, the actual event has been streamlined to highlight essentials, instead of giving every moment, every angle.

The scene in our mind's eye focuses on the relationship between mother and son. Mary, who was so quick to understand Gabriel's message, was quick also to sense the shameful situation in which the groom's family found themselves. (It was tradition to escort the bride to her husband's house where festivities would begin.)

You do not have to be an expert on first-century Palestine to understand the family plight that Mary intuited. It is still a cause for shame to invite people to eat and drink with you, but not to provide enough to satisfy them. In my own family, every get-together is over-catered – and I'm sure we are not alone in this.

Her realization leads to a conversation that at first glance looks disconnected. We need imagination, as well as exegesis, to make sense of it. She tells her son (I picture an urgent whisper) what's gone wrong, and clearly expects some kind of reaction from him. But to begin with, he shrugs it off. It is not his problem. The next part of the conversation ought to surprise us, logically if not emotionally. Mary does not respond to what he says, but to her knowledge of his nature. She knows, in other words, that regardless of what Jesus has replied, he will not leave the family comfortless (John 14.18). So she tells the servants to carry out his orders.

In what happens next, it is reasoning, more than prayer or exegesis, that helps us to come to an understanding. If there were six huge water jars standing there ready for the 'Jewish rites of purification', why were they all empty? They held between 15 and 25 gallons. How long might it have taken to have them all filled?

My conclusion from all this is not plainly stated in the Gospel as Bible truth, but it does make sense of how the story is told. The servants had to fill the jars up with water there and then, because it mattered for everyone who witnessed this beginning of signs to know that the jars had not contained wine from the outset. There must be no chance of trickery or sleight of hand. Beyond any doubt, the guests must be seen to be blessed, not deceived.

I hope the bridegroom, taking the undeserved credit for super-spoiling his guests (John 2.10), had the sense to enjoy the blessing that had befallen him, instead of fretting about the whys and wherefores, or wasting precious seconds of his life on being embarrassed. For him and for his kinsfolk, something else important was unfolding: the beginning of a 'new life together in the community' was also creating a new family in their midst.

This first sign, at Cana, is a reminder that God's love shows itself in generosity and protection. Hand in hand with overflowing generosity is the refuge he provides for all his people, 'under the shadow of his wings' according to the psalmist (36.7), who also declares that 'You give them drink from the river of your delights' (36.8). It is no accident that a wedding is the place chosen for this sign from God's Son. Isaiah 62, like the verses that precede the lection (and other prophetic passages), uses marriage, which creates family, as a symbol of God's love: his rescue of Jerusalem is like a marriage of one who had once been unloved, rejected (Lam. 1.1) – a reversal of unfruitfulness.

God calls his people Hephzibah and Beulah. These two female names are descriptions of a present identity and pledges of a promised future. Hephzibah means 'my delight is in her', and Beulah' means 'married'. The parameters of marriage may be debated, but its God-given potential to be one of the best blessings of human existence is not, I hope, in doubt.

The Third Sunday of Epiphany

Nehemiah 8.1–3, 5–6, 8–10; Psalm 19 [*or* 19.1–6];
1 Corinthians 12.12–31a; Luke 4.14–21

Ignorance is bliss, goes the saying. Ignorance giving way to knowledge, on the other hand, can be painful. In retrospect, former opinions or actions may look shameful or ridiculous. Just think of gender and racial stereotyping in classic books, films and television series. Society and ethics move on, but the texts and images go on saying the same thing for ever.

If 'bliss' means freedom from painful realities, then often 'bliss' really means 'lost bliss': a state of being that is only recognized when it is no more. For Adam and Eve, Eden was not bliss until they were deprived of it. Before their expulsion, they experienced discontent, temptation and shame there.

The same irony applies to Christian unity. Unity seems to be the original bliss of the first Christians before heretics and schismatics spoiled everything. When a group of Christians separates itself, it often claims to be the true church. So the word 'unity' might come to be applied to smaller and smaller subdivisions of the body of Christ.

If unity meant insisting that those who worship and think differently from ourselves were not proper Christians, Churches would soon vanish in a puff of self-righteousness. The fact that this has not happened, even after two millennia of splits and subdivisions, tells me that real unity is still present in our midst. When Paul wrote that 'there are varieties of gifts, but the same Spirit; and there are varieties of services, but the same Lord' (1 Cor. 12.4–5), I doubt he had ARCIC or the World Council of Churches in mind. He was talking about small groups of Christians valuing one another.

Understanding Christians as members of one body is at the heart of the Church. It is an appeal to every member to make their contribution according to their God-given gifts. Paul's explanation of how the body of Christ works challenges our fascination with status and hierarchy. 'The members of the body that seem to be weaker are indispensable', he reminds us (12.22): people are needed to lay tables for a harvest supper, as well as for a Eucharist; and to raise the parish share, as well as spend it. He wants to enable people to move beyond their social or intellectual comfort zone, so he urges them to believe that they may have more talents than they realize: 'strive for the greater gifts' (12.31).

Instead of making 'unity' our sole ideal, we could look at the context of Paul's exposition. Why talk about it at all? We talk about unity because we fear that we may not possess it. Yet it is a mistake to idealize one half of the argument, unity ('one body', in Greek, *hen soma*) and downplay the other ('variety' or 'diversity', in Greek, *diairesis*). There needs to be a positive value for diversity and difference, as well as for sameness. It helps that 'one body' sounds more concrete and achievable than the abstract English word 'unity'.

When we turn to the Gospel, Jesus is not the oldest or grandest person present. When he stood up to read, though, others saw that he was filled with the Holy Spirit (Luke 4.14), and that he was a young man of remarkable wisdom (4.15). Perhaps the person who handed him the scroll of the prophet Isaiah had heard that he had been teaching in other synagogues and wanted to encourage him.

The names of the men who stood beside Ezra when he read the law, and the names of those whose calling it was to teach it to the people afterwards, have been cut from the Old Testament reading. This may be in kindness to the readers who would otherwise have to pronounce those mouthful monikers in church. But mentioning Mattithiah, Maaseiah, Hash-baddanah, Akkub and the rest by name could remind us that we too can bestow honour upon our name simply by dedicating to God whatever job we are called to do.

We should value multiplicity. After all, it is not something we can escape from. Our other task, learning to be one body, need not conflict with this. Think of today's psalm, its final verse adapted so often by those whose gift is preaching: 'Let the words of my mouth, and the thoughts *of all our hearts* (pluralizing what was singular), be now and always acceptable in your sight, O Lord, our strength and our Redeemer' (Psalm 19.14).

The Fourth Sunday of Epiphany

Ezekiel 43.27—44.4; Psalm 48; 1 Corinthians 13; Luke 2.22–40

Luke has a way with words. In the Gospel, 2.35 stands out: 'a sword will pierce your own soul too.' We recognize that poignancy in our own close relationships, in which every beginning of joy, such as a 'child born into the world' (John 16.21–22), brings with it, one day, an inescapable letting-go, a final parting, and the grief that comes with loss.

But wait a minute. Whose poignancy is this? Luke's, or the translators'? Both the AV and RSV put the phrases in the order of Luke's original Greek. If the NRSV (and NIV) did likewise, 2.34–35 would read like this: 'This child is destined for the falling and the rising of many in Israel, and to be a sign that will be opposed – and a sword will pierce ['go through' in Greek] your own soul too – so that the inner thoughts of many will be revealed.'

If Mary's pierced soul stands as the final phrase of Simeon's speech, pain (as the price of human love) becomes the culmination of his prophecy. That is misleading. But the pierced soul could also be misleading if we leave it in the middle, as in the Greek. I had to punctuate carefully to show that it is a parenthesis (a remark logically separate from the rest of the sentence). Luke means the phrase, 'so that the inner thoughts of many will be revealed', to come straight after opposition to Christ. The revelation of inner thoughts is not a consequence of the soul-piercing sword. The child, not the sword, exposes those thoughts.

This is the third time Luke has associated Mary with prophecy. There was the single angel, Gabriel (1.30–32), then a heavenly host (2.16–17), and now a Spirit-filled human individual, Simeon. It has cost the mortal man Simeon something to be the agent of this prophecy. Costly obedience seems to be God's preferred way with human beings who speak his words (Jer. 20.2; 40.1; 1 Kings 22.24, etc.).

Simeon had waited into old age, but God had no need to make him wait at all. He could have given Simeon his revelation on the day of purification itself. Yet there is a 'stature in waiting', as W. H. Vanstone once put it: Simeon's recognition of Jesus is a blessing to himself, as well as to Christian posterity.

What about the sword? Luke uses the term *rhomphaia*. A *rhomphaia* is a bladed weapon with a single edge, not a double-edged sword, *xiphos*, or a *machaira*, which could have a single edge for cutting, or a double edge for thrusting and piercing.

It seems odd that Luke writes of a single-edge sword, when a two-edged blade would be a more effective weapon for piercing. I wondered about the ragged wound left by such a weapon, pointing, perhaps, to human pain as being more haphazard than surgical. But that 'take' is imagination, not exegesis. In any case, he could simply be using *romphaia* as a general term, like 'firearm'.

There is still the matter of that 'also' in 2.35. Looking for an answer across the Gospels as a whole, we might detect a parallel between the suffering of the Son on the Cross, and his mother at its foot: thus 'also' would mean, 'your soul will be pierced as Jesus was pierced'. But the piercing of Jesus' side, and Mary's presence where it takes place, are details found only in John (19.26, 34). Luke does not include either fact in his account of the Passion, so it is unlikely that he is alluding to them here.

Help comes if we turn once more to that single-edged cutting blade, the *romphaia*. Hebrews 4.12 gives the clearest image: this sword is not a stabbing weapon, for piercing a hole like the lance in John's Gospel. Rather, it symbolizes an act of division, as in Solomon's famous judgement upon the baby (1 Kings 3.24–25). It is for cutting things in two, for *cleaving*, 'dividing soul and spirit, joints and marrow'. Luke's 'going-through' (a literal version of the Greek) is not horizontal, but vertical: picture the blade coming down from above, not thrusting forward, when it 'goes through'. The sword is to cleave Mary's soul – and ours also, as Hebrews 4.13 completes the truth: 'Before him no creature is hidden, but all are naked and laid bare to the eyes of the one to whom we must render an account.'

The Presentation of Christ in the Temple (Candlemas)

Malachi 3.1–5; Psalm 24.[1–6] 7–end; Hebrews 2.14–end; Luke 2.22–40

Luke could not have known what we would do with his story. Neither the glitzy gewgaws of Christmas nor the Lord's carefully timed Nativity feast were part of his good news back in the first century AD. Yet it is Luke who links up the two ends of Christmas, turning the Lord's Nativity into a season, rather than a moment. The first mention of Jesus as Messiah, *Christos*, comes when angels announced good tidings of great joy for all the people to some shepherds (2.11). The next mention of that title comes in this Gospel, at 2.26, where we learn of the Holy Spirit's message to Simeon that, before dying, he would see the Christ.

Although more than a month separates these two Gospels in the Church's liturgy, a mere 15 verses separate them within Luke's Gospel. There, proof follows promise with remarkable rapidity. What is more, the causative factor at work in apparently humble human affairs – the Holy Spirit – is woven through both. We can trace the action of the Holy Spirit right from the Incarnation (Luke 1.35), and we learn that even from Mary's womb, the Christ-child has an effect on individuals through the Holy Spirit (1.41).

Now, on 2 February, comes Candlemas. It is also known as the 'Presentation of Christ in the Temple' and the 'Purification of Saint Mary the Virgin'. That range of titles offers a lot of potential themes for a commentator: blessing (of candles for the year), a temple epiphany and (more sensitive because of the implication of 'uncleanness') purification.

Rather than explaining how this layering of remembrances arose, or trying to cover too much, 'like butter scraped over too much bread' (in Tolkien's memorable expression), I am highlighting two pieces of the whole that jumped out at me as I was reading, and demanded to be investigated. (As an aside, that verb, 'investigate', is a favourite of mine. It sticks in my memory as a light-bulb moment when I first learned Latin, for *vestigium* means 'footstep', so 'investigate' means tracking something or someone's footsteps. Equally, I enjoy the enlightening of English conferred by knowing that *supercilium* is the Latin word for 'eyebrow'.)

My two highlights feature in 2.25 and 2.38. The first is 'the consolation of Israel'. The second is 'the redemption of Jerusalem'. Reading both phrases, we may not think twice about the linguistic shorthand that allows us to say that a nation can be consoled or a city redeemed. Such wording need be no more than a convenient way of referring to a whole people (Israel) or a whole population (Jerusalem). It goes without saying that not every single one of the children of Israel must be consoled, any more than every inhabitant of a city must be redeemed. That fact of group versus individual identity was long ago shown up by Abraham (Gen. 18.23–33).

Can I pull a etymological rabbit out of a metaphorical hat to cast light on the meanings of 'consolation' and 'redemption'? Perhaps. I have referred before to the word 'redemption' as meaning 'buying back' (see page 142 [Christmas 2 Year B]). It can mean a price paid for the return of hostages, which is topical as I write – though, please God, events have moved on by the time you are reading – or the release of a debtor after payment of a penalty.

We have confidence in Anna's prophecy that this baby will 'ransom' or 'redeem' his people, because it is a corroboration, from a completely different source, of what the song of Zechariah proclaimed in the previous chapter (1.68). Ransom and redemption are financial transactions, so the language helps to show a concrete judgement being made, rather than a vague tone set, as one thing of value is exchanged with another.

What about 'consolation'? In Greek it is *paraclesis*; but the term is not alien, despite its ancient origin, for many Christians are familiar with it. This becomes clear the moment we realize that someone who effects *paraclesis* is called a 'paraclete'. Versions of John 14.16 from the Roman tradition (Vulgate, Douai-Rheims, New Jerusalem Bible) retain this Greek word, 'Paraclete', for the Holy Spirit. Reformed translations tend to vary between two words to encapsulate its meaning: either 'Comforter' or 'Advocate'. Thus the 'consolation of Israel' embraces powerful blessings, namely comfort and defence, and a third shade of meaning should be factored in: encouragement. Simeon's song says that encompassing all three will enlighten Jew and gentile alike.

Proper 1
Sunday between 4 and 10 February inclusive
(if earlier than the Second Sunday before Lent)

Isaiah 6.1–8 [9–end]; Psalm 138; 1 Corinthians 15.1–11; Luke 5.1–11

As soon as the 'L' word (Lent) appears in our calendars, a change of gear takes place. Church will be darkly different for the next two months. In a strange counterpoint, the world around gets brighter and warmer, while we move towards the chill of shame and shadows. In northern Europe, this seasonal counterpoint does the work of exegesis for us. The end result of the Christian Lent will be an opening, a warming up, of life.

All the same, the price to be paid for that light and warmth of life is a high one. We must look at our own lives in the light of Jesus' Lenten journey, and when we do, we have to confess how far our lives fall short of his example. After acknowledging that, the next task is to decide what we are going to do about it.

There is a time for focusing on Jesus as a 'sacrifice for sin', more than an 'ensample of godly life', as the Prayer Book collect puts it. Christ as a sacrifice, made once in place of all on the Cross, belongs to Passiontide. But Jesus the healer, teacher and friend of sinners? He belongs to Lent and to these strange transition weeks we enter on today.

During his active ministry, before he turned his face to Jerusalem (Luke 9.51), Jesus gave us an example and a call to follow. This Sunday, as we prepare for Lent itself, we look at beginnings. We must reflect on three stories of the start of discipleship, that moment we often refer to as a 'call' or 'calling'. We shall find out what three people made of being given such a calling.

Isaiah's response to his vision of God enthroned upon the cherubim is truly that of an inspired prophet. He speaks first for himself ('I am a man of unclean lips') and then for the nation to whom his words of power must be spoken ('a people of unclean lips'). His reaction to being in God's presence is intense awareness of being 'unclean'. This is not a matter of physical dirt but a condition that demands distance between the person or thing, and God, who is not simply holy, but thrice holy.

Paul's reaction to being called takes place the best part of a millennium later. Yet it is markedly similar. His first reaction is also dismay. Where Isaiah was conscious of being an 'unclean' person from an 'unclean' people, Paul draws a narrower contrast, between himself and the other apostles. Among them, he is last in sequence of time, and least in status, because of his failure to perceive God's purposes, which led him to persecute the 'church of God' (1 Cor. 15.9). When he likens himself to an aborted foetus, we catch a bitter tone of self-disgust. He is describing himself as being unformed, premature and lifeless (15.8).

By the time we reach the Gospel, we are well-prepared for Peter to follow a similar path. But Simon Peter (Luke calls him by both names here) manages to surprise us. In a single word he sweeps us aloft from the humbling prospect of Lent by addressing Jesus as 'Lord': that is a title that the evangelists usually ascribe to him only in the time after the Resurrection. Peter often gets it wrong in the Gospels. Here, though, to his credit, he does not think to himself, 'Here is a powerful man who can work miracles: I must stick by him'. In a single short sentence, he acknowledges Jesus' true nature, and in the same breath confesses his own.

Peter could have stuck by Jesus the wonder-worker for his own advantage. Instead, he lets his weakness and terror show. Confronted in different ways with divine holiness, all three – Isaiah, Paul, and Peter – know their unworthiness. Jesus has seen beneath Peter's sense of shame, to expose the fear that has driven all three men's reactions. They feel (and admit to) woe and worthlessness. They feel shame for their misdoings. But shame should not be an abiding home; it is a point of transition, as we learn to turn regret into resolve.

In the beginning, fear and shame were Adam and Eve's reactions too. Yet they did what we must now do: shoulder the burden of our broken self, walk into the wilderness and search for our promised land.

Proper 2
Sunday between 11 and 17 February inclusive
(if earlier than the Second Sunday before Lent)

Jeremiah 17.5–10; Psalm 1; 1 Corinthians 15.12–20; Luke 6.17–26

This Gospel is a counterpart to Matthew's Sermon on the Mount, for Luke gives us instead a Sermon on the Plain (6.17). Both evangelists have drawn on similar material, but they use it in ways that highlight their own theological priorities.

For Luke, the coming of Christ is good news for the poor (4.18). Unlike Matthew, he does not spiritualize this poverty ('Blessed are the poor in spirit', Matt. 5.3). The poverty that Luke's Jesus refers to is straightforwardly material. In the same way, he proclaims a blessing on those who endure actual hunger and thirst, rather than a hunger for righteousness (6.21; Matt. 5.6).

Comparison of these two sermons of Jesus is fascinating, but there are plenty of commentaries to help us explore the details. One element that sometimes gets neglected is worth picking out here. Matthew, the supposedly Jewish gospeller, gives us only beatitudes. But Luke, the evangelist to the gentiles, chooses a more traditional prophetic form, by balancing his blessings with 'woes'. Matthew mostly saves his 'woes' for the scribes and Pharisees in the later part of his Gospel.

Woes are a special category of prophecy. They are found on the lips of prophets, crying out at impending evil or suffering, and they begin with an exclamation of distress, the Hebrew word '*oy*'. Even modern versions translate it as 'woe', though no one nowadays uses the word in that way: but then translators have little choice ('alas'? 'oh dear'?). So 'woe' remains in our Bibles despite sounding archaic. The linguistic jury is out on whether the Yiddish expression '*oy veh*' (also used for lamenting evils) comes from Hebrew 'woe', or from German ('*o weh!*').

It is unwise to accept prophetic blessings while ignoring prophetic woes. Both are declarations of the divine mind. Luke's account of the Sermon on the Plain shows Jesus preaching that the blessings and woes had to be received together. But when we look closer, we have to modify that picture somewhat. At first glance, the four blessings are reworked to show their opposite: four woes. But the second and third woes lack the power of the first, being little more than statements that the associated blessings will one day be undone. The fourth strives for a parallel where no true parallel exists: being spoken of in positive terms is not really a woe unless one engineers the (tenuous) connection with false prophets of old.

The first one, in 16.24, does have the full force of a true prophetic woe. In this case, Luke give voice to powerful conviction, also heard in the extended parable of the rich man and Lazarus (16.19–31). This is where Luke's theological priorities lie: this is what his Jesus really cares about. We ought to be thinking back to Epiphany 3's Gospel, especially 4.18: 'The Spirit of the Lord is upon me, because he has anointed me to bring good news to the poor.'

In 1 Corinthians, Paul does not balance weal and woe. Instead he sets truth against untruth. We could almost say that here is the purest distillation of the gospel, for our whole faith depends upon this one fact. If Christ has not been raised, then our preaching is lies. We have even misrepresented God, and our hope is void. And not only our hope but the hoped of loved ones who have died already. But if Christ has been raised, his Resurrection is a 'first fruits'. This means the first and freshest of the new harvest, which gives an indicator of the quality of what has not been gathered yet. Christ's quality should be the guarantee of our own.

If the Resurrection were a lie, or a fantasy, we would be trapped in sin, unable to escape. Then we would deserve pity. The contrast for Paul is between a vigorous, plentiful crop full of goodness, and a failed harvest yielding nothing. Jeremiah and the psalmist both think along the same lines as Paul, though without Paul's understanding of the Resurrection. They see water and strong growth going hand in hand: those who trust in God are fruitful. That Old Testament view of goodness as a simple reciprocity of goodness between God and mortals provides encouragement. But it is in Paul and Luke that we find the higher mystery, of woe and blessing bound together, that is the life of faith as we experience it every day.

Proper 3
Sunday between 18 and 24 February inclusive
(if earlier than 2nd Sunday before Lent)

or Sunday between 24 and 28 May inclusive
(if after Trinity Sunday)

Genesis 45.3–11, 15; Psalm 37.1–11, 40–end [*or* 37.1–7];
1 Corinthians 15.35–38, 42–50; Luke 6.27–38

Reciprocity is the moral law of mutuality. It encompasses primitive principles such as the *lex talionis* ('an eye for an eye and a tooth for a tooth', Ex. 21.23–27); and more 'civilizing' principles, like, 'as I have loved you, so you must love one another' (John 13.34).

Reciprocity means that we have a expectation of 'fairness' in how we are treated, whether as siblings (all getting presents of similar value at Christmas, for example) or as employees (all being paid the same amount for doing the same work, regardless of differentiating factors like sex or race).

The principle of reciprocity is present in divine–human relationships too. The psalmist sums it up perfectly (116.12–13): 'What shall I return to the Lord for all his bounty to me? I will lift up the cup of salvation and call on the name of the Lord.'

Where almighty God is concerned, it makes sense to err on the side of generosity. But in this section of the Sermon on the Plain, Luke is mainly concerned with human-to-human interactions. What we find in this passage is that Jesus turns normal rules of reciprocity into something qualitatively different.

The old way was to be generous and helpful, so that others would respond by doing likewise. There was a fundamental principle in ancient Greek thought: 'nothing to excess' (we might paraphrase, 'nothing should be too one-sided'). It expressed how there is a natural balance in human affairs that can be stabilized or destabilized according to how people behave.

Writing around the same time as prophets such as Amos, Hosea and Isaiah, the Greek poet Hesiod (who tells the story of Pandora's box) said, 'Invite your friend to a banquet but omit your enemy'; 'get a full measure from your neighbour and repay him in full ... so that if you fall into need in the future you will find him dependable'; 'love the person who loves you ... give to anyone who gives and do not give to anyone who does not give'.

To most people this still seems like a fair approach to life. Yes, it is fine to take the initiative in showing generosity, so as to induce a like generosity in the other person. But it makes no sense at all to keep showing a self-denying generosity when there is no reciprocity at all.

Senseless it may be. But it is undeniably Christ-like. Jesus drives home this message: that goodness is an end in itself for one who loves God. Such a person expects no reward 'save that of knowing that I do thy will', as the old prayer puts it. Jesus' commands in 6.27–30 go way beyond the 'golden rule' of 6.31. We could sum it up as: 'Do unto others far more than they are ever likely to do for you.'

If reciprocity encourages generosity that is really about improving one's own situation rather than anyone else's, that is not in itself a bad thing. But Jesus is telling his disciples, who must have been listening in astonishment, that they will be held to a much more demanding standard.

The principle 'nothing to excess' took two-sided generosity as part of the natural equilibrium of human affairs. To put all the weight on one side of the scale would overturn that equilibrium. Jesus' teaching advocates what is not only unbalanced, but actually risky to anyone who follows it. If an escaped prisoner asked for your coat, you would surely be assisting an offender if you offered your shirt as well. And who turns the other cheek to an enemy like Vladimir Putin?

Three of Jesus' teachings in this passage stand out because he repeats them (6.27, 34–35): love your enemies, do good to them, and lend to anyone who asks without expecting a return. They turn reciprocity into something different. In additional to the simple 'do-as-you-would-be-done-by' type ('do not judge, and you will not be judged'), Christians must make room for the counter-intuitive, morally outrageous demands of Christ-like love. Loving people who would harm you is as unbalanced as a life principle can be. Only in the topsy-turvy world of Christian values does it make sense. For we guard a deeper wisdom. That wisdom recognizes the execution of an innocent man as the means of rendering all that is worst in us powerless to separate us from the love of God.

The Second Sunday before Lent

Genesis 2.4b–9, 15–end; Psalm 65; Revelation 4; Luke 8.22–25

The so-called miracles of Jesus can be difficult for twenty-first century Christians to understand. The term 'miracle' suggests an event contrary to scientific fact, or confounding probability. This sits oddly beside the Jesus who criticizes those who ask for a sign (Luke 11.29). Luke's Gospel contains more than 20 such stories and actions. So we ought to tackle the issue, and not be tempted by fig leaves of pietism ('Who are we to question?') or minimization ('There must be a natural explanation, embellished later').

Up to this moment, the Gospel has been filled with calling, healing and preaching. From Chapter 3 on, Luke elaborates a crescendo of revelation. The calming of the storm is a further step in Jesus' journey to disclose his divine identity, as he moves in incremental stages from 'simple' wisdom, healing and teaching, into realms that associate him not only with royalty (as in 6.1–5), but (as here) with divinity itself.

As Luke tells the story (he is recasting an episode in Mark 4.35–41), we observe at almost the same moment Jesus' humanity and his divinity. First he falls asleep, probably exhausted by days of teaching. Then moments later, he rebukes the wind and the waves, and a calm ensues. The ability to calm storms is characteristic of God himself, as Psalm 104.6–7 declares.

It is more than usually difficult to make sense of this episode in isolation from its context. It is followed by the healing of the man with the legion of unclean spirits. Those spirits acknowledge Jesus as Son of God, but the man's reaction after being healed highlights a deeper truth of the Son's relationship with the Father: 'Jesus sent him away, saying, "Return to your home, and declare how much *God* has done for you." So he went away, proclaiming throughout the city how much *Jesus* had done for him' (8.38–39, emphasis added). That is hardly a slip of the pen.

I doubt that the reading from Revelation was chosen for this Gospel simply because it mentions 'flashes of lightning, and rumbles and peals of thunder'. This is not intended to be a storm-themed Sunday. There is a connection, though, because throughout Revelation, and indeed in the Jewish texts that inspired it, elements of stormy weather are reminders of the primal chaos back when God created the world. Loud noise and blazing light stimulate awe and fear, the appropriate response to being close to the throne of heavenly majesty. God has these elements under control, but no other being can wield a like power.

Genesis 2 contains no lakes, storms or heavenly epiphanies. What we do have is an aspect of the divine nature that appealed to those who wrote our Scriptures, and still appeals to us who read them. That is the imprinting of order upon the creation, to make it meaningful and explicable to us. It is the man's task to begin this, under God's direction. The man's giving of a name to each creature was a sign of the governance role over creation with which humankind was being entrusted (2.19–20).

In Eden before the Fall, there was no hierarchy, for God created them, male and female, in his image (Gen. 1.27). The man's act of naming the woman does not create dominance or control between them, for he and she are the same flesh, the same substance: unashamed because as yet they had nothing to be ashamed of. Our hope for a 'help meet' (2.20, AV) of our own is just the same: if it is to prosper, it must eschew hierarchy, for the two ought to be one flesh.

The disciples knew that they and Jesus were not alike in the sense of being equals. He had powers that they did not possess. When they feared for their lives, they cried out, 'Master, Master, we are perishing!' (8.24). The word they shouted is *epistata*, 'captain', 'commander'. Jesus our captain is not our hierarchical 'superior': he is not our captain because he is the most assertive, ambitious or alpha; he is our captain because he alone can save us from the storms of chaos that may sink even the most secure existence.

The old *English Hymnal* contains a hymn, with a tune by Vaughan Williams ('White Gates'): 'Fierce raged the tempest.' Singing it this Sunday would link Luke's Galilean tempest to our stormy lives better than any newspaper column.

The Sunday next before Lent

Exodus 34.29–end; Psalm 99; 2 Corinthians 3.12—4.2;
Luke 9.28–36 [37–43a]

Veils are controversial things nowadays. But if debates about freedom of religious expression, and potential oppression, are complex, the theology of Paul in 2 Corinthians is more complex still.

For those who already know what they think about God's covenants with the Jewish people, Paul's words here can be a simple affirmation of their own belief in 'supersession': in other words, that Christianity has annulled Judaism by replacing it with something better. In his longest letters, Paul tries to give full expression to the 'newness of life' (Rom. 6.4) that is the Christian gospel, but without treating his past religious life as worthless or meaningless. Yet some Christians insist that Judaism is a legalistic religion that belongs in the past.

When we read with close attention, that view has to be adjusted. Paul is trying to put into words what defies description. That is hardly surprising given that his subject matter is the glory of the Lord. Like the Jew he is, he takes a text from the Law (Ex. 34.33) and applies it to his current situation. Words that seem like a factual statement shade into a visionary experience.

None of us has seen a veiled mind. But we know what Paul means, because we have all experienced, at times, a barrier between ourselves and God. It could be distracting thoughts. Or our physical selves with their clamour for attention and indulgence. Or it could be the claims of others upon our time.

Paul does not suggest that the physical veil of Exodus was a bad thing. On the contrary, it was necessary to protect the Israelites from a sight they were not ready for. Any worshipper may find themselves in such a situation at any time. The experience of distance, 'seeing through a glass, darkly' (1 Cor. 13.12, AV), is set alongside a precious spiritual experience, and a rare one: clear vision. Language almost fails him as he tries to explain what he means: 'freedom', 'glory of the Lord', 'transformed', 'from one degree of glory to another'. Even in the new creation that is Christ (2 Cor. 5.17), the glory is seen reflected in a mirror. Mirrors in the ancient world would often be made of polished metal, giving imperfect images, so we know that he is still describing partial, not complete vision.

Where Paul gives us an exploration of the vision of glory, Luke records a concrete instance of it, at the time when Jesus turns his face to Jerusalem. That instance, the transfiguration, is reassuring and terrifying at the same time (Heb. 10.31). Just like last week's Gospel, it should be read with an awareness of the healing that follows it. This time there is not a herd of pigs but an epileptic boy. The glory that shall be cannot yet to be divorced from the needs of the body.

It is possible to read Luke's version of the transfiguration in a supersessionist way. Moses and Elijah appear, but then depart to leave Jesus alone. That might suggest that the 'old covenant' (2 Cor. 3.14 is the earliest record of this expression for God's relationship with his chosen people) has been annulled. Yet Moses and Elijah (standing, we are often told, for the law and the prophets, though in Judaism, Moses is one of the prophets) appear 'in glory' (Luke 9.31). It is not certain that their glory was obvious to Peter and the other disciples, for the evangelist notes that the disciples 'saw his glory and the two men who stood with him' (9.32).

When talking of, or thinking about, or praying this miracle of the transfiguration, I often identify with Peter's eagerness to be saying something, anything, to fill the moment, which he experiences as awkward instead of awesome. This almost made me miss the important detail, that Peter does recognize, without being told, who Moses and Elijah were. Perhaps that recognition was a moment of visionary revelation gifted to him.

It is also possible that Peter knew their identity because he heard what they were talking about with Jesus. Only Luke witnesses to the substance of this conversation, in 9.31. In Greek, it is clear that we have come to the fullest understanding of what was described in the Exodus reading, for this is the time when Jesus turns his face to Jerusalem (9.51): and the subject of their conversation? Jesus' 'departure' – in Greek, *exodus*.

The First Sunday of Lent

Deuteronomy 26.1–11; Psalm 91.1–2, 9–end [*or* 91.1–11];
Romans 10.8b–13; Luke 4.1–13

Barbara Pym is out of fashion as a novelist, but she sketches a marvellous moment when a grumpy clergyman is selecting books for the bedside table of a house guest. Out of spite he chooses a grammar of Icelandic. His comeuppance is swift: the next day his unwelcome guest enthuses about how much he enjoyed reading it.

Some people love words and cannot get enough of etymologies and linguistic nuances. Other people find them intimidating and opaque. I have always enjoyed languages, whereas numbers fill me with a leaden awareness of incompetence. Luckily, today's Gospel is a contest of words.

Instead of enigmatic parables, we have a straightforward story, a form of combat between Jesus and the devil, between good and evil. This is not the only time in Scripture when a human being strives against a supernatural one. In Genesis 32, Jacob wrestles with a being variously described as man, God, and angel (Hosea 12.3–5). Sometimes our contests with those who seem to be our enemies turn out to be the means of bringing us to fresh insight or deeper understanding.

In this story of the temptation, the form of the verbal exchanges between the two principal characters is an important clue to how to understand the story. But it is also a pointer to underlying eternal truth about the natures of divine and diabolic, and the great gulf between the two.

Jesus uses what linguists call the indicative mood. This means a form of words pointing to ('indicating') definite statements: these can stand on their own and make a sentence. He responds: 'it is written … it is written … it is said.' The devil makes conditional statements (things that depend on something else, another statement, before we can say that they are definite). All three of his challenges to Jesus are framed in the same way. Each statement about Jesus' true identity is conditional. It cannot stand on its own, but requires corroboration to be definite.

By structuring his attacks on Jesus in this way, the devil is trying to undermine Jesus' sense of self and purpose, just at the moment when he is both physically weak (he has fasted for 40 days) and spiritually vulnerable (tempted, in the reality of his human nature, to prove to himself that his Sonship is real). The contrast could not be greater with God as we encounter him in the reading from Deuteronomy, who acts 'with a mighty hand and an outstretched arm, with a terrifying display of power, and with signs and wonders' (26.8).

As a piece of verbal combat it is brilliant. The devil attacks Jesus on his own ground. He does not engage in theoretical questions about the nature of evil. Instead, trivial human weakness is his specialist subject, whether that takes the form of appetite, or vanity, or the endless quest for enough reassurance that we matter.

In the olden days when, if you wanted to find a Bible verse, you had to turn actual pages of an actual book, I once searched the New Testament for what eventually turned out to be Romans 10.9: 'If you confess with your lips that Jesus is Lord and believe in your heart that God raised him from the dead, you will be saved.' I had heard the verse quoted as the key to everything, a 'faith in a nutshell' teaching. I did not know what being 'saved' meant, but I knew that I wanted it.

Going by most of Paul's letters, his newly founded churches did not understand properly what being 'saved' meant either. He would not waste time writing letters of guidance to churches that were sticking to the plan. Or if he did, they have not survived. Most of the ones we have are to churches that were going astray, which skews our understanding of his teaching as a whole. Romans 10.9, though, is an exception. I am convinced that it was part of his original 'good news' to the communities he evangelized, not least because it still works for that purpose today. It is pure good news, shorn of historical and theological argument. Our belief in him may be conditional, but his reality is definite.

Paul understands what some preachers forget: keep it simple and keep it positive. Jesus is the Son of God: indicative, not conditional – or, in non-specialist language, no ifs, no buts, no maybes.

The Second Sunday of Lent

Genesis 15.1–12, 17–18; Psalm 27; Philippians 3.17—4.1;
Luke 13.31–end

Repeated words in Scripture always catch my attention. Few are more powerful than Jesus' threefold repetition of the name of the holy city (Luke 13.33–4). We might assume he is addressing some inanimate body. Cities do not have feelings, their stones do not cry out. But in Luke, the stones of Jerusalem do exactly that (19.40).

Jesus talks to Jerusalem as if the city were one of his close family. His repetition of her name has a beseeching tone, as if he must call out her wrongdoing, yet his reproach is a mere droplet, dissolving into nothing, in the ocean of his limitless love. He yearns for her like a mother hen with an instinct to nurture her offspring. For Jesus, the utterance of her name is an expression of his love. Each time he speaks it, he strengthens the impression that Jerusalem is not buildings, or geography, or society, but a single being, composed of countless individuals. This is akin to Paul's conception of the body of Christ: the city as both collective and individual.

My reaction to the sight of a city spread out before me is not like Jesus'. Looking from above I see cities as scabs on the skin of this beautiful planet. To my mind the sight of my own (modest) garden is more beautiful than any cityscape, however impressive or historic; for gardens are living, growing things, changing their mood and clothing daily.

But Jesus is not exclaiming at the beauty of the city either. He is thinking of the inhabitants. And they are wonderful and lovely, together or individually. It a hard thing to make sense of in human existence, that though we like to think of ourselves as autonomous individuals, most of us behave, most of the time, in extremely predictable ways, in accordance with our background, education and location. Seeing the city's people as a whole, Jesus wants to nurture them. But they – again, as a group – do not want his nurture, so they reject him, as he foresaw they would.

He never attracted enough followers to change the political reality in occupied Jerusalem, even if that had been his aim. But the movement that sprang up after his Resurrection changed history – and it is united not by ideology but by a citizenship that we might say is, 'out of this world' (Phil. 3.20). In a similar way, the children of Abram, an old man and his old wife, have outnumbered the offspring of many other families apparently more blessed.

Hebrew speaks of 'cutting' covenants: with Adam, Noah, Abram. This is probably the meaning underlying the dividing of the animals in Genesis 15. The cutting points to the consequences of breaking the covenant. The smoke and fire that passed between the pieces in Abram's vision tell us that God's very presence is validating the covenant (Ex. 13.21). The theophany is darkly terrifying.

A covenant is not a contract. God makes a covenant with Abram, who does not pass between the pieces (the ritual equivalent of 'signing on the dotted line'). Instead, cutting (in the form of circumcision) expresses his acceptance of the covenant as God has decreed it (compare Genesis 17.1–14 for a different angle). This is a one-sided declaration of God's commitment to his people. They can choose to cooperate with it or not. It is a remarkable act of love from our God, who is often oversimplified as angry and judging in the Old Testament/Hebrew Bible. Abram here is first an individual, but he also stands for a collective entity, a nation yet unborn.

Not all the repetition in today's readings happens within the passages themselves. Two texts have been lifted out of their place within the readings, and used for liturgical repetition. Philippians 3.21 is worked into the funeral prayer we hear when bodies are committed to earth or flame. It declares that 'our Lord Jesus Christ will transform our frail bodies that they may be conformed to his glorious body'. Luke 13.35 is lifted from the Gospel to take its place beside the Tersanctus ('Holy, holy, holy', Isa. 6.3) at the Eucharist. When Jesus repeats the name 'Jerusalem', the very word is a love song. When we partake in liturgies built from segments of Scripture, we repeat them often because repeating the words is one way for us to declare, as Jesus did, 'I love you'.

The Third Sunday of Lent

Isaiah 55.1–9; Psalm 63.1–9; 1 Corinthians 10.1–13; Luke 13.1–9

Today's Gospel and epistle mention events in salvation history that can be difficult to interpret. We happily sing, 'Types and shadows have their ending' in a hymn,[1] but it helps to know what the term 'types' means when we find it in the Bible. It is a Greek word (for a change!) that means a mark made when you strike something. When minting a coin, for example, you strike your original image onto a blank disc of metal, and the image produced on the disc is called a 'type'.

Paul uses episodes from the exodus – cloud, sea, manna, miraculous water – as types: this means that they are imperfect images of a perfect original. First, we meet the image produced, the type (Moses here, with Adam in Romans 5.14); later, the original (Christ). Through these types, Paul encourages his readers to see stories of the past as illuminating their own faith in Christ. He even brings in a Jewish legend from outside the Bible that a rock miraculously followed the Israelites in the wilderness. The rock that stands for God in the Old Testament God morphs into Christ the rock (*petra*) in the New Testament. It is also the name Jesus gives to Peter (*Petros*).

When we come to the Galileans killed by Pilate while they were offering sacrifice, it is not clear who they were or why he killed them. Sometimes, not knowing the historical background can be a drawback: Barabbas, for example, is mentioned in all four Gospels, but with varying details and no corroboration from other sources. We know nothing else about these Galileans, but no matter. Luke shows people using them purely as a moral example to get at Jesus' real thoughts. The point of mentioning their killing, in other words, was to discover Jesus' view of the relationship between crime (or sin) and punishment.

The common view that they seem to be alluding to, and which Jesus challenges, is one that works back from event (those Galilean sacrificers were killed) to cause (they must have done something wrong). This is confused thinking, but it is common enough, then and now. In the examples of those murdered while sacrificing and those killed when a tower fell on them, the questioners appear to make no allowances for what is chance or random. Their approach mixes up 'what happens' with 'what God wills

---

[1] 'Now, my tongue, the mystery telling', words by Thomas Aquinas (trans. Edward Caswall, 1849).

to happen'. Admittedly, this is sensitive theological territory for those who have a high doctrine of divine providence at the individual level.

Jesus does not affirm or deny the possibility that a divine judgement is being enacted. What he does is to remind the questioners that they are not safe from such judgement, because they are no less sinners than those who died. All stand in need of *metanoia* or 'change of mind', which we know as repentance (Luke 13.5; with Isa. 55.7).

Ever the wise teacher, Jesus next tries a more oblique tack. Those whom a direct challenge leaves unmoved may be stirred by a parable instead. I have a fig tree in my garden, growing vigorously year after year. But, like the one in the Gospel, its fruits never ripen. The owner in the parable could have ordered the gardener to cut his fig tree down and give a different plant its chance. But he does not. First he asks the gardener's opinion. I think he does this because he is looking for reasons to put off the moment of giving up on the tree. On the gardener's advice, he lets it have another year to show itself as fruitful.

Perhaps this is not the first 'one more chance' he has given it (Luke 13.7). It may not even be the last (13.9). The gardener commits to putting in the literal spadework, digging and manuring to give it the best chance. But the message is clear: the owner's patience, however great, is not infinite.

The ultimate fate of the fig tree is not recorded. But that does not matter. What we take away from the story is a truth which we also remember from Genesis (18.16–33): that God and his servant both do all they can to avoid consigning any living thing to destruction.

If this scriptural interpretation is too fiddly and abstract, there is a much shorter, but equally powerful, lesson for Lent in this week's readings, from 1 Corinthians 10.10: 'Do not grumble.'

The Fourth Sunday of Lent ('Refreshment' Sunday)

Joshua 5.9–12; Psalm 32; 2 Corinthians 5.16–end; Luke 15.1–3, 11b–end

The parable of the prodigal son, or 'lost son', is thronged with meanings, too big to tackle as a whole. So details must suffice. My first detail, though, is conspicuous by its absence. I have always considered Luke 15 to be about forgiveness. But unlike the shepherd and the housewife, the father in the third parable does not search. And unlike the sheep (15.4) and the coin (15.9), the son is not lost.

Perhaps we need to think instead of Luke 15 as the chapter of lost and found things. With that possibility in mind, I re-assess. Now, what strikes me first is the punchline quality of the father's final words: 'This brother of yours was dead and has come to life; he was lost and has been found' (15.32).

Fact: the son did not die. So the first part of verse 32 is metaphorical, not literal. Christians naturally latch on to its death/life antithesis. In the son's return we find an example of what has been called 'the joy of repentance', and a beautiful foretaste of the Resurrection.

As for the second statement in the father's final words, it is echoed, centuries later, in the lyrics of a well-loved Christian song. 'I once was lost but now I'm found' goes the song, inspired by this very Gospel. In 2022, I was at a Prom concert at the Royal Albert Hall celebrating Aretha Franklin, when the artist Sheléa sang 'Amazing Grace'. Afterwards my Welsh sister said to me, 'I've never understood why people like that song so much. I do now'.

The right singer, the right venue, the right performance, all make a difference to how the song affects us. But only because the words (John Newton) and the notes (William Walker) are right first. I was lost. Now I have been found. The popularity of 'Amazing Grace' somehow proves that the father's words are indeed a punchline. They contain the key to the parable of the father and his sons. They tie all three parables in Luke 15 together. They are forever telling us what we are.

A pair of verbs confirms that this is indeed the key message of chapter 15. 'Losing' (*apollumi*) and 'finding' (*heurisko*) are the antithesis that governs the chapter. They exemplify the life of faith at its most basic: we are lost until God finds us. How close this is to Augustine's famous confession: 'You have made us for yourself, and our heart is restless until it rests in you, Lord.'

The sheep is lost and is found, likewise the coin. Not so the son. His role is not purely passive ('*was* lost'). Students of Greek will know the verbal voice, part-way between active and passive, called (unimaginatively) the 'middle'. It can refer to things people do for or to themselves. Nobody 'lost' the son; he lost himself. But the final word, 'found', is a true passive. The son could not 'find himself'; the father did the finding. This interpretation confirms that human free will gives us the power to refuse our Father.

The father's final words carry this idea further. From his perspective as the loving but powerless parent, his son 'was lost/lost himself' but 'has been found'. The son seemed to be exercising human free will to make choices. But the father sees deeper, into the truth that the son has no power of himself to help himself.

This parable does not endorse the contrary behaviour of the older son. For he does not represent superior moral choice, only a calculating refusal to take risks. The impulsive folly of the younger sibling is far more appealing to most readers of this Gospel than the mean-spirited jealousy of the elder brother.

If I had been Luke's editor, I would have urged him (knowing how painful it is for authors to rethink their cherished texts) to put the coin first, before the sheep. Start with what is inanimate. Work your way up, via what is sentient, to the 'crown of all creation' as the eucharistic prayer calls humankind. If Luke had good reason for putting the three parables in the order he did, I cannot see it. What I can see, for absolutely certain, at the very end of the parable, is that the father's words to his son are my Father's words to me, active now, instead of passive: 'I have found you.'

Mothering Sunday

Exodus 2.1–10 *or* 1 Samuel 1.20–end; Psalm 34.11–20 *or* 127.1–4; 2 Corinthians 1.3–7 *or* Colossians 3.12–17; Luke 2.33–35 *or* John 19.25–27

We shall soon hear today's Gospel again, when Holy Week unfolds the Passion for us once more. Jesus' active ministry – three years in which he was accompanied by many disciples both male and female – is over. Usually the men were at the forefront: arguing with Jesus, and being taught, sent or rebuked by him.

The only male follower who is mentioned as being there at the foot of the Cross is the beloved disciple. Some scholars question this, given that none of the synoptic Gospels records any male disciple as present. It is possible, though, that the Fourth Gospel comes from a community that preserved the disciple John's recollection of the Passion: naturally, he saw events from his own particular angle.

In all four Gospels, a number of women keep watch close by Jesus in his final hours. But John the evangelist draws our gaze to Mary his mother, who not only sees her son suffering terribly, but also knows that it could have been different, if he had chosen autonomy in place of obedience.

The situation of both is pitiable. Enduring suffering is painful, true. But it is not so painful as watching the suffering of someone you love while being unable to help them – like Mary. The situation of Jesus is yet more pitiable, for he has to look on Mary's suffering, knowing that he could have chosen to stop it and that, by refusing to avoid his calling, he was compounding her grief.

Quite a lot of human relationships end up in tangles of unanswered need, even if the consequences are purely personal instead of world-changing. One thing helps people to form close relationships is a sense of mutual understanding and appreciation. But for most of us the sense is only partial. When the relationship is tested, our unspoken longings may escape the notice of our beloved. That can lead to disillusionment.

When Paul writes to the Corinthians, 'just as the sufferings of Christ are abundant for us, so also our consolation is abundant through Christ' (2 Cor. 1.5), he is describing his own ministry of endurance. The sufferings *of* Christ have become, in Paul, sufferings *for* Christ. This connection between the Christian and the Lord is direct, unmediated. Our sufferings are his, and our consolation is him.

Paul states this fact with a simplicity that leaves no doubt: this was his lived experience of Christ, not 'merely' his intellectual interpretation of Christ. It is a reality that every Christian can receive likewise. In 1.7, Paul reveals this chain of consolation binding Christians together, past, present and future: 'we know that as you share in our sufferings, so also you share in our consolation'.

That mystical conviction that we are not alone, abandoned, forlorn in our sufferings may be something beyond the power of words to represent. Lived reality, though, is justifiably part of our evidence for the fact that Christ consoles those who suffer. This is neither delusion nor fantasy.

Exodus 2 prefigures the Gospel scene, but in a surprising way. It is not a Hebrew who offers divine compassion, but an Egyptian. But for the tender heart of that Egyptian princess, Moses might not have grown up to be a prophet and lawgiver to his people. His own sister played a key role too – and like the women in the synoptic accounts of the Passion, she too 'stood at a distance'.

'In Johannine thought, the Beloved Disciple can symbolize the Christian'. So says the Bible commentator Raymond Brown. If we remember to be on the lookout for that idea in the fourth Gospel, this episode from the Passion can be interpreted afresh, becoming a direction for every Christian life. The dying Christ commands us to treat the vulnerable (in which category the widow and the orphan are biblical archetypes) as members of our own family.

At the same time, he commands the vulnerable (a category that embraces every honest Christian) to do likewise with those who reach out to them. Here is a lesson from the Passion to coax us away from fixating on the physical suffering of Christ and the theological intricacies of atonement. Perhaps if he had had breath and strength enough to emphasize the meaning of his command in John 19.26–27, he would have turned his eyes upon us, and said, 'Go, and do likewise'.

The Fifth Sunday of Lent (Passion Sunday)

Isaiah 43.16–21; Psalm 126; Philippians 3.4b–14; John 12.1–8

One commentator describes Isaiah's vision as an 'ecological transformation'. Jackals and ostriches are not creatures chosen at random. They stand for the ruin of what we might once have called 'civilization'. After humans have fled, or been driven out, streets and buildings revert to a wilderness state, where 'beasts of the field' (wild creatures) wander undisturbed.

Two approaches do battles in the womb of our minds (Gen. 25.22). One sees the buildings and fortifications of cities as protection from external threats. The other sees cities as places where God is forgotten. God declares that cities will not remain waste without inhabitants (Isa. 6.11): he will rebuild access (making roads) and secure the water supply without which nothing can live.

Recent events in Europe are a bitter reminder that civilizations are only a thin crust over the churning magma of human sin. In the passage from Philippians, Paul does not explore the universal dimension of sin; he focuses on the individual dimension, speaking from experience of what religious transformation is like.

He starts where sin begins. 'All sin is pride', it has been said. This puts pride in a category of its own, although in the traditional list of 'deadly sins', pride is merely one of seven, nothing unique. Thomas Aquinas offers a more acute perception: 'pride corrupts every virtue and every mental capacity.'

Paul calls pride in his Jewish ancestry, 'confidence in the flesh'. His life has been virtue-filled: he is 'zealous' and 'blameless'. Looking at virtues and vices, and assessing them according to a canon (the word originally meant 'measuring stick') of propriety is not how God judges. The Lord looks on the heart, the place where our attitudes and motivations come from (1 Sam.16.7). And for God, intentions matter. It is not enough to 'do the right thing'. We must do the right thing for the right reasons. That is why Paul reminds us that he is a persecutor before he points out that, according to the Law, he is blameless (3.6).

The passages from Isaiah and Paul guide us in making sense of the Gospel. Some who listen to this Gospel will be in instinctive sympathy with Judas, even though they know that such sympathy is not the 'correct' interpretation. Even giving to the poor can sometimes be the wrong answer.

There is already a difficulty for scholars in deciding how many women anointed Jesus on how many occasions. Mark, Matthew and John describe an anointing in preparation for burial (Mark 14.3–9; Matt. 26.6–13). Luke (7.36–38) describes a woman who is a sinner anointing him.

Such questions do not stir my interest as much as wondering why she (or they) used hair to wipe the perfume off. I cannot think of a less absorbent material for removing an unguent. But if wiping with hair is not practical, it must be telling us something at another level. It may not be practical, but it is intensely personal. Even sensual.

Another clash of practicality and symbolism: why wipe it off as soon as it has been poured on? True, the perfume, made from an aromatic plant, would have been (for want of a better word) 'gunky'. And a 'pound' is a lot: a couple of packs of butter gives us a fair impression. It would have been dripping off Jesus. Again, why did she pour the perfume six days before the Passover when Jesus tells us that she bought it to keep 'for the day of my burial' (John 12.7).

I have no scholarly answer to such questions. My answers come from imaginative prayer. She wanted to make a dramatic gesture, like Babette's feast in the film of that name. Not a parsimonious one like a bishop I once saw baptizing someone by dipping his thumb in the font and touching it three times to the candidate's forehead. Only something spectacular would do to express her feelings. As for the anointing happening six days before the Passover, if the woman took the opportunity to offer her gift, and show her love, earlier than she had planned, she would not be the first gift-giver who simply could not wait another moment.

Finally, a words about verse 4 of the psalm. God does not always give us what we want, exactly when we want it. To see what an answer to prayer after a long wait looks like, go to YouTube: https://youtu.be/bMm8wWNo7cA.

Lent 6 Palm Sunday

Liturgy of the Palms: Luke 19.28–40; Psalm 118.1–2, 19–end [*or* 118.19–24]
Liturgy of the Passion: Isaiah 50.4–9a; Psalm 31.9–16 [*or* 31.9–18]; Philippians 2.5–11; Luke 22.14—end of 23 *or* Luke 23.1–49

Philippians 2.5–11 carries a gigantic weight of scholarship. It is almost a hundred years since the prevailing view – that the text was about the historical Jesus, giving an ethical blueprint for Christian living – gave way to an insight that has been refined since, but never overturned. As a result, modern Bibles set the passage out in verse form, as a hymn exploring the universal, mythic meaning of Christ. At the same time, the case was made that it is a pre-Pauline fragment: part of the teaching Paul received about Christ before he began his missionary work of teaching others.

It is significant, then, that the picture moves straight from humiliation (from the Latin *humus*, 'ground', so very close to our word 'lowliness') to glorification. 'Resurrection' and 'ascension' are not even named. Instead, they are swept up into the movement of God's 'high exaltation' of his Messiah. At the name, 'Jesus', everyone must kneel (Phil. 2.10). This underlines his divinity, which is attached not to any of his titles (Son of Man, Christ, *Logos*) but to the personal name that belongs to his incarnate self. The exalted meaning of the Incarnation for human beings is thus revealed. In the following verse, the scope of the worship he merits is expanded a little, to include both his personal name and the title for him which came to predominate over all the others, 'Christ' (2.11).

A sharp challenge, though, comes right at the start of this passage, for Paul introduces the hymn with a command: 'Let the same mind be in you that was in Christ Jesus' (2.5). But he is not urging us to turn ourselves into mini-Messiahs. The Greek is something closer to 'Have this attitude among yourselves'. Willingness to accept humiliation rather than asserting status will resurface time and again both within the New Testament stories of Christian beginnings and in the subsequent history of the Church. It is a key criterion by which others will judge how genuine our faith and discipleship really are. After reading Philippians this Palm Sunday, we should be in no doubt which of the two ways of living is divinely affirmed.

Luke's account of the Passion stands apart from the other Gospels in several respects. One of the most noticeable is 22.24–7: a contest about which disciple was the greatest apparently intrudes into the narrative of the Last Supper. No one can be sure whether Luke was telling the story as he had received it, or whether he chose to insert the contest story as a commentary on the Passion theme of lowliness leading to exaltation. One thing that nudges us toward the less sceptical reading is how close Luke's account of the contest is to the message we find in John's account of the foot-washing (13.2–11).

If we enter into the Last Supper through meditation, it is instantly apparent that none of the Gospel accounts of it is complete in every detail. They all sketch their own key moments in a few sentences. Yet Jesus and the Twelve had all evening to eat this Passover meal, and share the cup, bread, and cup again (another detail specific to Luke: 22.17, 19–20). It is not difficult to believe that a lot happened that night that has not been recorded; or which only one source preserved, to be used later by one evangelist but not the others.

In Isaiah, the theme of humiliation emerges first, in a form that came to be seen as prefiguring Christ (50.6). But that gives way to an assertiveness we do not find in Jesus' Passion. Isaiah is forthright in asserting his innocence and his certainty of God's vindication (50.7–9). This contrasts with Jesus' enigmatic answers to Pilate when questioned about his kingship (Luke 23.2–3).

Resorting to the old theological stratagem of assigning marks of 'strength' to the divinity, and 'weakness' to the humanity, of Jesus is not enough to forge an exact parallel between the prophet and the Saviour. But this does not matter to Isaiah, who knows that he is called to be both learner and teacher (50.4: like Paul, who learned his hymn and taught it in turn). Isaiah passes on to Jesus, and Paul, and us, words that still resonate with anyone who clings to faith in dark and dangerous times: 'It is the Lord GOD who helps me; who will declare me guilty?'

Good Friday

Isaiah 52.13—end of 53; Psalm 22 [*or* 22.1–11 *or* 22.1–21];
Hebrews 10.16–25 *or* Hebrews 4.14–16; 5.7–9;
John 18.1—end of 19

West of Cambridge there is a place which, according to road signs and maps, is called Caxton. But locals refer to it as 'Caxton Gibbet' – and a gibbet still stands at the crossroads between Ermine Street and the Cambridge to St Neots road.

That careful positioning reminds us that in times we think of as less enlightened, it mattered that punishment was not only done, but was seen to be done. Gibbeting was a disgusting penalty, hanging the body of a malefactor from a hook or in an iron cage to decompose and disintegrate. In England, the death penalty ceased to be a public spectacle in 1868, but in some parts of the world, public executions continue to be the norm. Justice is a matter that concerns all a nation's citizens, so there is logic, if not much compassion, in such a practice.

There was never a chance of the Roman authorities turning a blind eye to insurrection. The moment they were convinced that Jesus might lead an insurgency, he was sure to be condemned. It is easy to condemn the fickleness of crowds who less than a week ago had cheered his entry into Jerusalem. But in our time too there exist regimes in which guilt consists not in what protesters do, but in what they may do if not crushed at once. Once again there is logic, but no compassion.

Jesus was crucified in public, no doubt with the aim of deterrence, but not at a crossroads. Instead, it happened at a place called (in Aramaic) Golgotha, meaning 'the place of a skull' (John 19.17). Latin translated by the word *calvaria*, which simply means 'skull'. Christians soon concluded that this name indicated a place that was domed in shape – a hill, in other words. This cannot be proved, but the importance of making executions as visible as possible certainly points that way.

Between John and the other Gospels there is a key difference of detail. The synoptics all affirm that the cross was carried by someone called Simon, who bumped into that pitiful procession on its way to Calvary. Yet John insists that Jesus carried it. Ingenious solutions have been proposed that rely on the cross being in two pieces, or being carried by two men. But neither can be harmonized with John's insistence that Jesus carried it 'by himself'. That does still leave the option that he did so for part of the way, but that Simon carried it either before or afterwards.

Such details are the bread-and-butter of New Testament scholars, a gift to opponents of the faith, and often an irrelevance to worshippers. On a day such as Good Friday, how can such (relative) trivia be important? In truth, detail is never unimportant when the USP of your faith is that it is historical fact. So when evidence is discovered corroborating the Passion, it is treasured. The marble inscription found at Caesarea Maritima in 1961, bearing the name of Pontius Pilate, is just such a piece of evidence. Christians take it for granted that Pilate was as real as the emperor Augustus; but until that inscription was found, there was no early evidence to prove it apart from the Gospels themselves.

We have another inscription within the Passion. All four Gospels mention it as giving the substance of the charge against Jesus. All four refer to Pilate recording Jesus' crime in Roman terms, not Jewish: revolution, in other words, not blasphemy. All four give different wording for it – ammunition for sceptics who would empty the Passion of theological truth, claiming that it is a story designed to explain away the 'failure' of the Jesus movement.

But look at the matter from another angle and the reverse is true. Yes, each one is slightly different. But what the four versions have in common is much more powerful than what distinguishes them. The man being crucified is labelled 'the King of the Jews'. Pilate refuses to change the inscription to suit the Judean authorities, tacitly refusing to collude in their vendetta against Jesus, while at the same time doing his duty to Rome by crushing all challengers. The studied ambiguity of his attitude (a mirror, perhaps, to that in John 18.37) is encapsulated in his famous question, 'What is truth?' The man Pilate crucifies does not speak the answer. He is the answer – 'I am the Truth' (John 14.6).

Easter Day

Acts 10.34–43⁺ *or* Isaiah 65.17–end; Psalm 118.1–2, 14–24
[*or* 118.14–24]; 1 Corinthians 15.19–26 *or* Acts 10.34–43⁺;
John 20.1–18 *or* Luke 24.1–12

⁺The reading from Acts must be used as either the first or second reading.

The Resurrection of Jesus Christ is a historical event. And a process being renewed daily in the lives of Christians. And a prophecy of what their eternal end will be. All these elements of the Easter mystery are present in the readings for 'this day, the first of days'.

Messengers from God are familiar characters within the books of the Bible, so we are not surprised that they play a part in explaining the Resurrection to mortals. Some of those messengers are human beings – Peter in Acts, for example, preaching his great Easter sermon. Or his brother apostle, Paul, who reveals the Resurrection as an event with consequences, demanding a response from everyone who learns of it.

Other messengers, though human in appearance, are not of human origin. That is the case when the group of women (Luke 24.4) have a strange meeting as they arrive at the tomb: '... suddenly two men in dazzling clothes stood beside them.' The dazzling clothes and the sudden appearance give the clue to the true nature of these messengers. The Greek word which defines them, *andres*, simply means men or 'males', but their bright and sudden appearing points to their being supernatural messengers: in other words, 'angels'.

But then 'suddenly' turns out not to be sudden at all. That translation is found in respectable version like the NJB and NIV as well as the NRSV. The AV sticks closer to the Greek, with an archaic word, 'Behold!' The difference may seem petty, but 'suddenly' refers to time, whereas 'behold' or 'look' emphasizes vision. Unlike a mere adverb ('suddenly'), 'Look!' is a command from the storyteller (Luke) to his listeners – us. Like all the evangelists, he speaks to audiences before he turns the good news into text. Here he orders us to turn our gaze upon these two figures in white. Their message to the women is a message for us.

The term 'angels' comes from the Greek word for 'messengers'. When Luke refers to them, he mingles divine and human detail. Though they are described as two 'men', they know, without being told, what the women plan to do. They even know some of what Jesus has taught the women.

We learn about the Resurrection, then, from God's messengers, both human and heavenly. But we cannot always be certain which are which. The idea of encountering angels in daily life is exhilarating but also intimidating. Scripture tells us that meeting angels unawares is a risky business (Heb. 13.2). The writer of Hebrews warns his readers how important it is to offer hospitality to strangers, not only because it is a time-honoured custom, but also because any stranger may turn out to be of divine origin, and require respect and care as such. Perhaps this was what lay behind Peter's blurted-out offer of hospitality at the transfiguration.

Peter and Paul's voices speak to us from the distant past, but with present, urgent clarity. The voice of the risen Christ had made Mary Magdalene realize who was the stranger she was talking to (John 20.16). It helped the disciples to recognize him after his Resurrection, and soon after that brought a cry of recognition from Thomas that went a step further, 'My Lord and my God!' (John 20.20, 28). It was the same voice that had cried to Paul, 'Saul, Saul, why do you persecute me?' (Acts 22.7). Many of us will identify with the shame and self-reproach Paul felt at how slow he had been to accept Christ.

Peter's sermon ties the human Jesus to the risen Christ, showing us – as we listen to it – that we too can have an encounter with the Lord's Anointed. We too can let go of fear and trust in Paul's assurance that Death, the last enemy, will in time be emptied of power. Angelic encounters are unlikely ever to be a routine part of our faith experience. So it is just as well that we need not depend on them as a way to develop our relationship with God. We receive Christ through our indwelling faith, through what we hear and read, and through the sacraments of baptism and communion. All these ways of meeting him are straightforward, tested, reliable and open to all. If we reach out our hands for his broken but life-giving body, we do not just hope that we shall receive it, we *know* that we shall.

The Second Sunday of Easter

[Exodus 14.10–end; 15.20, 21]; Acts 5.27–32; Psalm 118.14–end *or* Psalm 150; Revelation 1.4–8; John 20.19–end

†The reading from Acts must be used as either the first or second reading.

I think of Revelation as a book that belongs to Advent, for it speaks of the life of the world to come, the consummation of all things. Within it, we do not encounter the Resurrection in the same way as in the Gospels, where the foundation of the Easter message is rooted in historical time.

Anyone who reads Revelation notices that John of Patmos was fascinated by numbers. Some are used symbolically: there are seven churches and seven spirits (1.4). He weaves rhythmic numerical patterns into his writing. Twice there comes a triplet: the one who 'was and is and is to come' (1.4, 8). Jesus Christ has four characteristics (obscured by translating 'the faithful' as an adjective): 'witness', 'faithful', 'firstborn', and 'ruler' (1.5). God acts in three ways: he 'loves' us, 'frees' us, and 'makes' us priests (1.6).

John uses letters, as well as numbers, as a way of revealing patterns in the fabric of the world. He calls the Lord God 'Alpha and Omega' (1.8). These are the first and last letters of the Greek alphabet, equivalent to our 'A to Z'. My family has to put up with me shouting at the telly whenever an advert comes on for 'omeega' 3 supplements, or when James Bond succumbs to a bit of shameless product placement: 'Rolex?' 'Omeega' (*Casino Royale* 2006). Greek has two kinds of letter 'o'. One is (literally) little-o, 'o-micron'. The other is big-o, 'o-mÐga'. For me 'o-meega' jars as badly as saying 'A to Zee'.

Is this pedantry (bad) or accuracy (good)? They are two sides of the same coin. Bible scholars may aim for the latter, but still end up sliding into the former. When it comes to John of Patmos, being scrupulous about patterns of numbers and letters is never pedantry. But it is not mystery either. Or magic. His patterns of numbers and letters are like the patterns of human life (birth, growth, decay, death) or times (spring, summer, autumn, winter): they are signs of the divine hand at work in creation. They show that God has turned the cosmic abyss of random chaos into something meaningful – we may almost say, 'readable'. This is what lies behind another John's famous Gospel prologue: for the Greek word for a rational principle is *Logos*. It can also be translated 'Word' (the capital letter is ours, not John's).

And so to Doubting Thomas. It is not fair to criticize him for doubting, despite his famous nickname. Quite apart from anything else, doubt is not a sin. What this Gospel passages shows is not that Thomas requires certainty when he should have had faith, though that is what preachers – myself formerly included – sometimes argue. What Thomas is demanding is evidence. And his making that demand is not presumptuous or suspicious; it is rational. We are created by a rational God, in his likeness, and we are called to conform to the image of his Son, who is Rationality itself. It is not unreasonable for Christians to want to be reasonable.

Another thread of connection running through the readings is witness. Peter declares that he and his companions are witnesses of all that has happened. In a world when stories were mostly transmitted from one generation to the next verbally, and where there was no modern technology for recording events, the evidence of witnesses is of supreme significance. If trustworthy people tell stories, that is moderately convincing. If trustworthy people (remember how Peter was to insist that they were not drunkards, but sober truth-tellers, Acts 2.14–15) tell extraordinary stories about someone rising from the dead, that requires a greater step of trust. The witnesses may be judged by how far they live in accordance with the claims they make.

Peter and the others will go on, outside the New Testament record, to die for their faith: the ultimate proof of their commitment to the Resurrection. But we should not forget little, ordinary proofs that are also evidence for their commitment to the Truth. Years before, they all left their own lives behind to follow the man who, they later said, had risen from death. Yes, they let him down when it mattered most. But even that was not enough in the end to deter them, for they turned back, and became witnesses once more. Now there is a pattern for us to recognize, take to heart and imitate.

The Third Sunday of Easter

[Zephaniah 3.14–end]; Acts 9.1–6 [7–20]†; Psalm 30;
Revelation 5.11–end; John 21.1–19

†The reading from Acts must be used as either the first or second reading.

With this Gospel, Peter's discipleship comes full circle. Years before, he was called from his work catching fish to become a fisher of people. Matthew records that call with a command from Jesus: 'Follow me!' Once more, in today's long Gospel, Jesus commands Peter to follow, but this time that call means something more.

At his first call, Peter had no idea what following Jesus would mean. Characteristically impulsive, he reacted to an invitation from a charismatic stranger. Perhaps he used to dream, as he fished, of a life that was working to live, instead of living to work. Our life choices begin like that too. We make those choices (what subject to study, what job to do, where to live) in faith, rather than in certainty.

After his friend died, Peter went back to his old life as a fisherman (John 21.3). Maybe he took comfort in his grief from its familiarity, re-awakening old skills on which he had once depended. This time Jesus' command, 'Follow me!', is almost the last word in a long conversation between a mortal man and his friend, over whom death had no more dominion. In fact, the conversation goes on a little longer (outside this appointed lection), but it still ends with Jesus repeating the command, 'Follow me!'

In between the first call and this last conversation, Peter has learned, grown and changed. He had formerly made promises, but had not delivered on them. He had told lies about himself (Matt. 27.74). He had failed repeatedly and had to pick himself up and go on, knowing that he had failed. But despite the failures, he still went to the tomb of the man he followed. He still gathered with the other disciples, to take comfort from speaking of the one they had loved and lost, as friends do.

Peter knew what he had left undone (acknowledging discipleship, Matt. 27.75) and what he ought not to have done (Matt. 26.56; John 18.10, 27). But how should he go on trying to follow Jesus now that the purity of his commitment to 'the Messiah, the Son of the living God' (Matt. 16.16) was spoiled?

The way Peter responded to his failures is precisely what made him worthy to be Jesus' rock, the foundation of the church (Matt. 16.18).

The Lord knew this was who Peter truly was. He knew him better than Peter knew himself.

It would be easy to stop here and conclude that Peter was a great man and that we must honour him, perhaps even entrust him with our prayers. Such reverence is a good instinct, but there is more to be embraced in his story. It is precious because we observe its beginning and we also hear of its end (John 21.18–19). When we contemplate the lives of holy men and women, we can choose to look at them for what they are in themselves (in Jesus' case, as a 'sacrifice for sin', according to the BCP Collect for Easter 2). But we need to balance our veneration of what they are with how they teach us by what they do ('an ensample of godly life').

Peter is a prototype for our life's vocations. As once we chose our studies, career, home, without knowing how our lives would unfold as a result, so we have also chosen our vocations: to Christian discipleship (baptism, confirmation), to a relationship with 'mutual society, help and comfort' (matrimony), perhaps to service (in ministry, including ordination). With each vocation, we commit ourselves to vows and promises without any knowledge of what life might throw at us or how we will respond when we are tempted to let go the love we had at first (Rev. 2.4). We trust that we will somehow make good on our commitments, 'the Lord being our helper' (BCP Ordinal).

It is possible to live a life that takes no such bold steps into the unknown. By shrinking the world to what is within our easy reach, we can pull up the drawbridge of our minds and contract our view to what feels safe. Paul tried that. But the love of Christ broke through and claimed him just the same. Three times Jesus asks Peter, 'Do you love me?', reminding him of those three dreadful denials (John 18.17, 25, 27). But Luke supplies the exegesis (15.6–7): strive for repentance, not perfection.

The Fourth Sunday of Easter

[Genesis 7.1–5, 11–18; 8.6–18; 9.8–13]; Acts 9.36–end†;
Psalm 23; Revelation 7.9–end; John 10.22–30

† The reading from Acts must be used as either the first or second reading.

Dorcas the needlewoman reminds us how unusual Luke the evangelist is in paying so many women the compliment of a personal existence by naming them. I have been a needlewoman, knitting and dressmaking, since childhood. I still knit, but no longer tailor my own clothes; it is time-consuming, and I am now more cash rich (relatively), but time poor. Long before I realized Dorcas was a needlewoman from the Bible, I had a tin of pins from the brand, 'Dorcas'. It promised ultrafine pins that would not mark cloth or turn rusty.

When Dorcas dies, it sounds a straightforward, natural death: 'she became ill and died' (Acts 9.37). People must have liked her: their first thought was to send for Peter, and when he came, he was surrounded by widows 'weeping and showing tunics and other clothing that Dorcas had made', (9.39). This homely detail is touching. Dorcas the needlewoman will not be remembered for mighty acts of power, but for the clothes she made. When people wear them, they will think of her.

I know how this feels when I wear my ordination stole for weddings and baptisms. My aunt embroidered it, my mother made the lace cross at the nape, and it was made up by a friend who also made my wedding dress. All three of them, now gathered to glory, are remembered every time I wear it. All kinds of clothing can carry memories for us, and contain meaning.

It is not soppy to be touched by the memories that simple objects can evoke. Look how the cockerel has become a symbol for Ukraine, 'bloody but unbowed'. A lingering scent on a scarf, a handwritten memo fallen out of a book, the savour of familiar food: all these can, for a moment, bring the dead to life, albeit only in our minds.

It is not naive or wrong to hope for miracles, either. But we should listen carefully to what Luke tells us. He does not say that they summoned Peter expecting him to revive Dorcas, or that Peter prayed for her to be restored to life. In fact, Luke goes out of his way to emphasize that she was dead. Peter turned not to a person but a 'body' (9.40: *soma*) to speak his command, 'Tabitha, get up!' It reminds me of Jesus' words, *talitha koum* (Mark 5.41), and perhaps it was intended to.

Dorcas was one of Jesus' sheep. So, presumably, was Simon the tanner, whose job description still survives in English as a personal name. So, certainly, was Peter. When Jesus makes his self-disclosing statement in John 10 – 'the Father and I are one' – he is only part-way to the fullness of revelation that emerges by the end of the Gospel. The seven great 'I am' sayings show that Jesus was not completely avoiding disclosure of his identity, but rather sowing the seeds of it where they will thrive (the first, the Bread of Life is in Chapter 6, the last, the true Vine, is in Chapter 15). None of those is a political title like 'king' or 'anointed'. Without context and instruction, they remain enigmatic, even the simplest one, which is also the one most closely associated (in the Hebrew Bible) with kingship: 'I am the good Shepherd' (10.11).

That final sentence of this Gospel lection, 'the Father and I are one' (John 10.30) is dramatic. We can think of it as provocative in its effect, a piece of evidence providing ammunition for the Jewish authorities to work up their picture of Jesus as a blasphemer. The very next sentence says that they gathered stones to stone him for his supposed blasphemy against the oneness of God.

From John 17, we know that Jesus prays later on for the unity or 'one-ness' that is between himself and the Father to exist also among his followers. This might seem to belong to a later strand of New Testament thought, when Christians were deciding how to ground and grow the Church. But it lies behind a polemic in Corinthians, 'anyone who glues themselves to the Lord is one Spirit' (1 Cor. 6.17: NRSV and NIV translators supply 'with him'). It is front and centre in the sublime language of Ephesians 4.5–6). A noble ideal is also, for Christians, a statement of fact, a done deal: 'you have died, and your life is hid with Christ in God' (Col. 3.3).

The Fifth Sunday of Easter

[Baruch 3.9–15, 32—4.4 *or* Genesis 22.1–18]; Acts 11.1–18†;
Psalm 148 [*or* 148.1–6]; Revelation 21.1–6; John 13.31–35

† The reading from Acts must be used as either the first or second reading.

One key factor in the survival and spread of Christian faith is also the source of a potential flaw. Peter and the Jerusalem Christians, Paul and the diaspora Christians, John of Patmos and his churches, all survived the dangers of being a new faith, and conflicts with their neighbours, and opposition to some of the authorities of the Roman empire. They did so by being courageous and constant, by knowing what they stood for and believed in.

That cohesiveness grew from a sense of common purpose – an exalted purpose too, nothing less than cooperation with the salvific plan of God. But the first Christians had a problem. Were they a new form of an old faith or a genuinely new faith? Luke meets the problem head on, with Peter as the hero who cuts the Gordian knot.

Peter's vision is so important that Luke tells the story twice. He did not have to do so. In the Scriptures, we come across stories in which a conversation takes place, and then takes place all over again, in full, when it is reported to someone (Genesis 13.32–4 is a good example). The lectionary tends to disguise this by leaving out the repetitions. But there is another way: summarize the contents of a reported conversation. Matthew finally resorts to this at the end of the parable of the sheep and the goats (25.44).

Luke's repetition of the story has two aims. First, he simply wants to reinforce the teaching it contains. Second, he wants to send the reader a message: by the time Peter tells his vision in direct speech, Luke the narrator has already reported it as a historical fact (Acts 10.9–16).

The Jerusalem Christians had initially been shocked at Peter's mingling with gentiles. With this careful groundwork, though, they accept without further questioning, and even with celebration (11.18), the inclusion of those gentiles within the new covenant of God's grace. There are still plenty of details to be worked out, as the Jerusalem Council in Acts 15 makes clear. But the principle has been established. God's grace is no longer to be confined within racial or social boundaries.

And now we come to the potential flaw. Thanks to Luke's narrative skill, we never doubt that Peter will succeed in his argument. But we are also aware, from our contemporary experience of church life, how easily disputes rooted in differences of religious behaviour can intensify and divide.

If the faithful in Jerusalem had behaved then as some Christians do today, Christianity would have shrivelled into oblivion. It makes good sense for churches now to put thought and effort into mission at the door, to make people feel welcome, valued and affirmed. But still the dark side of our strong identity is constantly challenging that outward-looking Easter faith. Pull up the drawbridge! Circle the waggons! Bar the outsiders who want to downplay our hallowed traditions!

In the Gospel, John's Jesus does not straightforwardly support Peter's vision in Acts. In Chapter 13, Jesus' teaching takes on an urgent quality, because the moment of his arrest is at hand. Time is short. God is going to 'glorify' him 'at once'. At this moment of high tension, when outward appearance (a conversation among friends) is at odds with inner reality (isolation, fear, incomprehension), Jesus gives the disciples an extraordinary gift. Not an object, but a principle. It is a principle that we take for granted ('of course we ought to love one another'), and so fail to notice the shocking description: 'A NEW commandment? How can this be?'

There have been no new commandments for centuries. There have been interpretations and clarifications of the 613 commandments in the Mosaic law. There has been Jesus' own summary of the law (Mark 12.28–31). But this is different. It is specific to those within the community of faith, for they are to model their love for one another on the love Jesus has shown to them. If people want to know who is a Christian, this love is what they will be looking for.

The people who followed Jesus have been revealed as a new faith. The new faith has a new commandment. And it has a new holy city too, 'the new Jerusalem' (Rev. 21.2) given by the Lord. For he is not the guardian of what is antique, but the one who makes all things new (Rev. 21.5).

The Sixth Sunday of Easter

[Ezekiel 37.1–14]; Acts 16.9–15†; Psalm 67;
Revelation 21.10, 22—22.5; John 14.23–29 *or* John 5.1–9

†The reading from Acts must be used as either the first or second reading.

It is a relief to discover that the heavenly Jerusalem contains a river and tree. Without such delights of nature, it seems an uncomfortable place, covered in metal and jewels, and cube-shaped. Not a comfy armchair in sight. The thought of there being no darkness is particularly unappealing. A city that is all blazing light is a recipe for migraine.

But I am being too literal. That is not how John of Patmos means it. If it were a literal picture, how could the single tree of life stand 'on either side of the river'? He is evoking Ezekiel 47.12, but his own symbolism demands both a single tree and also symmetry (an aspect of beauty) in the heavenly city. There is no temple in the city, and therefore no sacrifice. But this is not a deprivation. In the presence of God, sacrifice becomes redundant. Our access to the divine will go beyond anything we could hope for on earth. And yes, John declares that there will be no night there, because the city will have God's glory and the Lamb to light it. As for the gates, they will not be shut because the city has no need of protection or defence.

John's language evokes other prophetic visions (Isa. 60.19; Zech. 14.7) to underline that his prophecy is authentic, a confirmation of what was foretold long ago. But the power of his vision is more rapturous than logical. He moves us with words of love and wonder, giving hope that death is not the end.

Paul's vision is different. It is a message for right now, in the form of travel directions. He must forget going to Asia, and head for Greece (Macedonia is in the mountainous north of that land). So, the text goes on, 'we' came to Philippi (the same place where Caesar's supporters overcame the assassins Brutus and Cassius in 42 BC). Blink, and you will miss it. But open your Bible commentary and you could lose yourself in the sheer mass of scholarship on what is, after all, a mere change of verb form from the third person ('Paul', 'they') to the first person ('we').

What this untidy text reveals is the sticking together of two sources. Luke the historian has so far been telling a story about what Peter, then Paul did. But suddenly, and without explanation, it is as if he opens his notebooks and continues the tale by transcribing notes from his diary.

True, it is a clumsy use of sources, perhaps an unfinished draft. But the benefit is that it allows us a glimpse of the author at work. We are suddenly hearing eyewitness testimony from someone who travelled with Paul, who was there to watch Lydia and her household being baptized.

There are two possible Gospels for this Sunday. One, John 14.23–29, looks forward explicitly to the giving of the Holy Spirit. The choice of the other, John 5.1–9, for the run-up to Ascension and Pentecost, needs a bit of explanation. It begins by mentioning an unspecified festival of the Jews. One early tradition identifies this as Pentecost, the festival of 'weeks'. Here is the implicit reference to Christian Pentecost. Unfortunately, the text is confused at this point: just look at the wodge of footnoted 'other authorities' in NRSV. Did an angel stir up the waters, giving them healing properties? Was the place called Bethesda ('house of mercies' or 'house of flowing') or Bethsaida (confusing it with a place in Galilee)? Despite this clutter of variants, it is clear that the pool (which has been excavated, complete with its 'five porticoes') was partly filled by springs. So the invalid man is referring to water bubbling up from below (5.7): the seeming miracle of the water's movement gave rise to hopes of healing. Being first into the waters meant catching the curative capacity at its strongest.

The sick man had gone there for 36 years without success. He had put his faith in the magic of angelically kinetic water. Jesus repeatedly warned people not to demand signs and miracle. Now he ignores the magical pool and simply tells the man to get up and walk. So was the man's disability all in the mind? No. He is really healed – by the words of the Word, which are more powerful in their effect on us – body, mind and spirit – than any holy hot tub.

The Seventh Sunday of Easter (Sunday after Ascension Day)

[Ezekiel 36.24–28]; Acts 16.16–34†; Psalm 97;
Revelation 22.12–14, 16, 17, 20–end; John 17.20–end

† The reading from Acts must be used as either the first or second reading.

A slave girl makes money for her owners by her 'spirit of divination'. Joseph Fitzmyer's superb commentary on Acts (in the Anchor Bible series) translates this as a 'spirit of clairvoyance': her value lies in her ability to see into the future. He also gives a literal rendering of the Greek: a 'python spirit'. Not because it was a snake, or a comedy classic, but alluding to the mythical creature Python which guarded the oracle at Delphi.

If the girl or her owners are faking clairvoyance, then Paul's word of command to the python spirit will have no effect. But she must really have had the power to tell the future, because Paul's words rob her of it. Her trade, and with it her value, evaporated. I wonder what became of her.

The unknown future is a thread running through today's readings. When Paul and Silas are miraculously freed from their bonds in prison, their gaoler is so terrified for his own future that he contemplates suicide. Perhaps here is early evidence for the Christian ethical perspective on suicide, running counter to Roman belief that it could be a noble act.

With Paul's reassurance, the gaoler realizes that the future may be unknown in its details, but that its direction is up to him: 'Sirs, what must I do to be saved?' The answer comes in a slightly odd form, but it is not a typo: 'on' (*epi* in Greek) instead of 'in'. He must believe 'on' the Lord Jesus. This was the AV rendering. The RSV changed it to 'in'. The NRSV changed it back again to 'on'. This hints that believing 'on' is unlikely to mean exactly the same as believing 'in' (Fitzmyer opts, alas, for 'in').

Not being an expert in ultrafine nuances of New Testament Greek, I feel free to think of believing 'on' Christ as a state in which we can place ourselves, rather than a theological formula we can sign up to. Christ is our corner-stone, our 'sure foundation': to believe 'on Christ' is to stand on a place of blessed assurance.

In the Gospel, Jesus too is looking to a future the short-term details of which are unclear. We should not conclude that as he prays, he already knows it all. For what, then, would be the meaning of praying at all? The verb helps us. It is subjunctive: the form in which we express what is potential or conditional. He prays 'that they may be one'. This is not a statement; it is a prayer. It may happen. But it may not.

As in our intercessions, so in our Lord's, there is a commitment of trust to an unknown future by having faith in the God we know. Our prayers are real prayers. We pray that God 'may' do something, because we accept that he is sovereign and that we are mortal, and our vision is restricted, while his gaze is infinite.

Jesus' prayer reminds us, by its use of the subjunctive, that God will not force us to be one. We have a choice, and (so far in the history of Christianity) we have chosen not to be one. Verbal subterfuges like redefining the faith to exclude those we disagree with are mere sophistry.

In the words of the prayer, Jesus has already given his disciples the glory that his Father has given to him (John 17.22). But when? It is hard to see the bestowing of this glory in anything that has preceded this point in the Gospel. The disciples have certainly beheld glory, but they have not yet received it. If we look back to John 17.1, it confirms that the glory is in the future, whereas in this passage it has already been given. It is as if the prayer is collapsing time into eternity – in which 'past', 'present' and 'future' are terms whose meaning is redundant.

It may seem trivial to be talking about details of grammar in Jesus' great prayer. But only when we do can one supreme, sublime moment come into focus (17.24). As well as praying to his Father for things that 'may' come to be, he switches to a definite statement: 'I want', rather than 'I would like.' 'I want my disciples to be where I am, to see my glory.' Truly we can answer with John of Patmos, 'Amen. Come Lord Jesus'.

Pentecost (Whit Sunday) C

Acts 2.1–21† *or* Genesis 11.1–9; Psalm 104.26–36, 37b
[*or* 104.26–end];¹ Romans 8.14–17 *or* Acts 2.1–21†;
John 14.8–17 [25–27]

† The reading from Acts must be used as either the first or second reading.

Grammar makes a difference to the theology of these readings. In Romans 8, why does the NRSV repeat the noun 'Spirit' (not in the Greek) in 'the Spirit intercedes' (8.27)? Surely it is to avoid having to choose between the Spirit's grammatical gender ('it': neuter), Western theological gender ('he': masculine), and, sometimes, Eastern theological gender ('she': feminine). Calling the Spirit 'the Advocate' makes him masculine. Calling the Spirit 'Holy Wisdom' makes her feminine. Calling the Spirit 'Spirit' makes it neuter, because 'spirit' in everyday English is a stuff, not a person. What clearer proof do we need, in gender-sensitive times, that language matters to how we understand things? And that language makes no difference at all to the essential nature of the thing itself?

According to Peter, the prophet Joel had foreseen this day of Pentecost, which was to be different from all previous fiftieth-days-since-Passover. It would be a time of prophetic speech no longer confined to the trade union of prophets, but instead lavished upon on men and women, old and young alike. Later, the Church came to regulate the Spirit (if that isn't an oxymoron) through a clerical trade union instead. The contest of priestly and prophetic voices and attitudes continues to govern how Christians access the God we all believe in.

Our celebration of (as it were) freedom of speech contains a difficulty for many readers: the list of nationalities in Acts 2. Most are straightforward to pronounce, but some are not. The real impact of the reading is in the maths of the list. Fifteen nationalities, but only 12 apostles. It cannot be that the apostles have learned a language each. The message is transformation, not translation.

Why are the tongues of flame divided? The image of a forked tongue first of all suggests deceit. This may be because of the snake in Genesis 3.4–5, or because of vague memories of dialogue in old-fashioned cowboy films: 'white man speak with forked tongue.' Lancelot Andrewes' first Pentecost sermon muses on this puzzle, observing that the tongue

---

1 Psalm 104.26–36, 37b in Common Worship equates to 104.24–34, 35b in BCP and NRSV.

can be the best (Ps. 108.1 in the BCP version) or worst (James 3.6) of our members. True, the first divided tongue was a sign of the first deceit; but Acts 2 turns the symbol inside out (the theological word for this is 'recapitulation'). This time, division is a blessing, not a curse. This time, 'the message has gone out to the ends of the world' (Ps. 19.4): the 'division of tongues', says Andrewes, is a 'reversing of the curse of Babel' (Gen. 11).

The divided tongues of fire tell us that God's Spirit is calling to all the peoples of the earth, but his/her/its work does not end there. There is an ongoing work of education to be done, an enlightenment to dawn upon us so that, now God has spoken directly to us, we can learn to talk to him. In Romans, Paul states (8.26) that we do not know what we ought to pray for (so NIV: not 'how we ought to pray', NRSV). But the Spirit does the work of prayer for us, with groans that cannot be put into words. Here is a firm encouragement, if we strive to follow that example, to make use of silence in private prayer and corporate worship. If even the Holy Spirit lets go of words in communicating with God the Father, we must be incapable of finding adequate speech. The best conclusion we can draw from this is that God gives us what Augustine calls 'the inferior cacophony of words' because we are not yet ready for pure communication that does not need articulate speech.

This is not a case of us developing our fluency through instruction in prayer. The Spirit is our Advocate, standing between us and God, saying for us what we cannot put into words for ourselves. This is how we should intercede for others too. Using many words is not necessarily a virtue in prayer (Matt. 6.7) or a gift of the Spirit. In court, advocates have a specialist skill in persuasion. In faith, the Advocate has two roles: the first is to plead on our behalf, as counsel for the defence; the other is to be the prosecuting counsel who exposes the failings of the world.

Trinity Sunday

Proverbs 8.1–4, 22–31; Psalm 8; Romans 5.1–5; John 16.12–15

John's Gospel for this Trinity Sunday so dazzles with its depth of meaning, that in worship it risks crowding out all else from our minds – readings, prayers and hymns. So the challenge is to use it as a torch, to cast its bright light into obscure corners of the mystery of faith.

Even as I began to read John 16.12, I immediately had to pause. What does Jesus mean when he says, 'you cannot bear them now'? I had always thought of it as 'bear' in the sense of 'endure'. Thus Jesus would be pointing forward in time, with predictions of his own imminent passion and prophecies of their consequent persecution. His soon-to-be (in the Gospel narrative) or recently inaugurated (according to the Church's calendar) apostles are as yet ill-equipped to cope with either.

Looking more carefully, I think that this may be wrong, or at least only part of the truth. For the verb does mean 'bear', but in the primary sense of 'carry off', 'carry away'. That shifts our point of view. Jesus is telling the disciples that now is not the moment for them to be proclaiming abroad all that he has taught them. For a little while longer, the good news is still good news only for the chosen few.

There is, then, much still to be said; but it has to wait until after his death and Resurrection. What we have here is nothing less than a plan for the future of the Church. Not a diagram of contents and dimensions, though, but something more flexible. Something much too precious to be entrusted to stone (like the ten commandments) or paper (like the law, prophets, and writings) or even to memory, like the powerful, variable memories of the individuals we know as Matthew, Mark, Luke and John himself.

This plan is the Holy Spirit. John's readers would have been waiting, as last week we too were waiting, for the moment when the Scripture revealed how the Spirit was being poured out. On Trinity Sunday, we move on to the interwoven being of the Holy Three. Proverbs reminds us that the divine Wisdom is a way of understanding the Spirit. Romans reveals the true nature of the relationship between the Father and (on the one hand) the Son who justifies us, and (on the other) the Spirit who communicates God's love to us.

The teaching that our God is three Persons in one Being (or Essence) was teased out of texts like these, in which the Holy Three is not set out as a sum or diagram, but narrated, as the story of a relationship, in terms of its actions and effects.

In John, Jesus has a clear vision of his relationship with human beings as having a direction and a destination. Theologians call this 'eschatology'. In Greek, the closeness of Son and Spirit is even clearer than in the English, because embedded in the Greek verb for 'guide' (*hodegesei*) is that earliest name for the new faith; the verb can be more fully translated as, 'he will guide (someone) on *the way* (my emphasis)'.

In a rush of future-tense verbs, Jesus revealed that the new faith would look to the future, as a journey to a destination. In Romans, Paul speaks to us from an early moment in that future (well within living memory of the first Pentecost). He too is looking forward: 'hope ... hope ... hope.'

Paul sees the Holy Spirit as the channel through which God's love is communicated to his people, both Jew and gentile. The Spirit has not been dabbed, dripped or drizzled, but poured out, in an act of stunning generosity. That has been lived Christian experience for a little over two decades when Paul writes to these Christians whom he did not evangelize. His summary of faith is dazzling too: it ties together God's love, Christ's justifying sacrifice, and the Holy Spirit's communication between divine and human.

On Trinity Sunday, we learn that 'Truth' is our companion and destination, with the word (the Bible) as our guidebook on the journey. The Holy Spirit is our sacred sat-nav: we input our intended goal, and it gives us directions. Even though sometimes we ignore it, thinking we know better, it exists only to get us home. Last week the Church, this week the Trinity: together they form the triumphant fulfilment of the Incarnation.

Proper 3
Sunday between 24 and 28 May inclusive
If this follows Trinity Sunday, Proper 3 is used (see page 288).

Proper 4
Sunday between 29 May and 4 June inclusive
(if after Trinity Sunday)

Continuous: 1 Kings 18.20, 21 [22–29] 30–39; Psalm 96;
Galatians 1.1–12; Luke 7.1–10
Related: 1 Kings 8.22–23, 41–43; Psalm 96.1–9; Galatians 1.1–12;
Luke 7.1–10

In one respect this story speaks to both my academic interests: theology and Classics. When I began postgraduate study, working on the portrayal of soldiers in Latin literature, I quickly realized the importance of centurions.

My interest in the portrayal of soldiers was one reason why the first translation I published was not of some early Christian writings, but the *Gallic War* of Julius Caesar. Working on that devious text gave me insight into the pivotal part played by centurions not only in real-life battles, but in the imagination and mythology of Rome herself (and doubtless of inhabitants of the empire both Roman and foreign).

Centurions occupy a unique place of intersection between officers and men (the closest modern British equivalent is the regimental sergeant-major). When leaders are cowardly or incompetent, or when soldiers act rashly or from greed and bloodlust, a centurion comes to the fore to embody the proper mode of action to both groups. It is impossible to tell how much of what we read in Roman histories reflects reality, but in any case the process is not all one-way. Iconic leadership on the page can inspire its like on the field, as well as vice versa.

'Centurion' is a job description, deriving from the hundred soldiers (a 'century') such men typically commanded. The structure of the Roman army was unlike that of the modern British army. In the latter, there are few gradations of rank among ordinary soldiers, but more among officers. The Romans, though, had fewer ranks at the top; but a precise 'pecking order' within every century.

So when the centurion tells Jesus, 'I also am a man set under authority, with soldiers under me' (Luke 7.8), he is speaking with precision. He wins the reader as he won first Jesus, then Luke, by having the insight to recognize someone with authority, who wields true power. Yet he and Jesus never meet.

We know that the centurion is a good man (7.4–5). Local Jewish elders go to Jesus to plead on his behalf. This is how winning favours worked then, and still does. Being too direct or too demanding risks causing offence. Using an intermediary allows both parties to save face if a request is refused. It is worth noting that, for once, the Jewish leaders are given a creditable part to play, for they start their plea with a favourable character sketch of this good centurion (for so we should surely call him).

This centurion's place is precisely encapsulated by verse 8, spoken – we must keep reminding ourselves – via a representative. We have already discovered that he trusts the Jewish leaders to speak on his behalf. And that he is right to do so, because they plead his case sincerely (and successfully). We should be asking ourselves, how can this man be so certain that Jesus, whom he never meets, is even capable of healing his slave?

Undoubtedly, the reputation of being a powerful healer would have gone before Jesus, and Luke often draws our attention to the ways in which the good news about him was spread abroad. But the good centurion has been posted in or near Capernaum for quite a while. Long enough to get a synagogue built, at any rate. He must have seen plenty of healers and wonder-workers – some deluded, some deceiving, some even successful – come and go.

One of the key virtues of a good centurion is judgement. He has to be able to weigh a man's motivation, character, ability, at a glance, to know who will stand firm in the vanguard, and who will run away if placed in the rearguard. So keenly honed is this ability that, even before he heard of Jesus, he has seen past barriers of 'the customs of the ancestors' (*mores maiorum*: so fundamental to Roman morality), and of language, geography, history, to discern what is worthwhile in the life of the people where he is posted.

Now this good centurion's judgement sees past routine cynicism at yet another charlatan or snake-oil salesman, to discern a man of God who can grant his prayer and save his slave. So Jesus does him equal justice in return, as one busy man of faith to another, and heals the slave. It is no accident that the last words upon our lips before we take holy communion are often those of the good centurion.

Proper 5
Sunday between 5 and 11 June inclusive
(if after Trinity Sunday)

Continuous: 1 Kings 17.8–16 [17–end]; Psalm 146;
Galatians 1.11–24; Luke 7.11–17
Related: 1 Kings 17.17–end; Psalm 30; Galatians 1.11–end;
Luke 7.11–17

Luke arranges this episode within his Gospel to mark a progression in Jesus' ministry, from healing the sick to raising the dead. Not that this supernatural feat is unique, even within the Gospel, for in the next chapter, Jesus will go on to raise Jairus' daughter too.

On that occasion (in contrast with the raising of Lazarus in John's Gospel, 11.1–44), there will be doubt as to whether the girl is dead or not. Luke draws attention to that doubt, saying that some scoff at Jesus' assertion that she is not dead but 'sleeping' (8.52). We might think of her being unconscious, perhaps, or in a coma.

Here, though, there is no mention of sleeping. The man, only son of his widowed mother, is definitely dead. By taking action to help her, Jesus, consciously or unconsciously, imitates a miracle of the prophet Elijah in 1 Kings 17.

In modern times, when we are sensitized to the importance of safeguarding, no Christian priest or healer should dream of separating a child from its parent, taking it to an upper room, and laying their own body three times across that of the child. Elijah the Tishbite, though, exercised a ministry directed by God's personal command. We must rely upon his effectiveness as a prophet, and God's affirmation of him, to reassure us that – judged by the standards of their time – his actions are not improper.

We are still entitled, though, to ask why he took the boy to an upper room, and why he 'stretched himself' upon the child. Answering the first may be straightforward, even if it seems primitive to our sophisticated ears. I think that Elijah took the boy upstairs because upstairs is closer to heaven than downstairs. If the 'upper room' was in fact a kind of outdoor space on the roof of the widow's home in Zarephath, this becomes plainer still.

We Christians tend to think that it does not matter where we go to pray, never mind in what direction we orientate ourselves. But in early times, some Christians turned to Jerusalem as Muslims still turn to

Mecca. One early Christian writer advises opening the window when praying, to remove every possible obstruction to clear communication. In such a critical situation, getting as close to God as possible makes sense.

Something similar may be at play in Elijah's covering of the boy's body with his own. He asks God to let the boy's 'soul' (*nephesh*) return to him. This physical contact may be a means by which the divine word, flowing through him, enlivens the dead boy. Similarly, physical touch (the laying-on of hands) is even today essential for confirmation, unction or ordination.

Jesus is greater than Elijah, as John the Baptist (the true second Elijah) was aware. So we need not be surprised that on this occasion he chooses not to use physical contact at all (at other times he does use touch to heal). Instead, he heals by words alone. Between Elijah and the widow of Zarephath there had been a pre-existing obligation: she had fed him, so he was in her debt. Not so with Jesus and the widow here. Elijah had shown his distress at the turn of events by referring to their bond of obligation, 'O LORD my God, have you brought calamity even upon the widow with whom I am staying, by killing her son?' (1 Kings 17.20).

'The LORD listened to the voice of Elijah', says the anonymous author of 1 Kings (17.23). Thus, the raising of the boy happened as an 'ordinary' miracle, a prayer uttered and answered with a 'yes'. Not so in this Gospel. Jesus does not ask God to bring a dead body back to life. He addresses the boy directly, as one who is still a person and not a corpse: 'Young man, I say to you, rise!'

Luke makes it impossible for us to doubt the miraculous quality of the sign by resorting to explanations about states of coma or unconsciousness. He simply states, 'The dead man (the Greek word, *nekros*, can be a noun, 'corpse', or adjective, 'dead') sat up and began to speak' (7.15). The next words, 'he gave him to his mother', are exactly the same as in the Greek version of 1 Kings 17.23. Jesus' act in giving back a life looks ahead to what he will one day do for each of us.

Proper 6
Sunday between 12 and 18 June inclusive
(if after Trinity Sunday)

Continuous: 1 Kings 21.1–10 [11–14] 15–21a; Psalm 5.1–8;
Galatians 2.15–end; Luke 7.36—8.3
Related: 2 Samuel 11.26—12.10, 13–15; Psalm 32;
Galatians 2.15–end; Luke 7.36—8.3

If we catalogued social crimes, 'causing a scene' would probably be on the list somewhere. This woman is definitely guilty of it. How she gatecrashed dinner at the house of Simon the Pharisee we do not know. But her weeping, anointing and kissing made for an embarrassing scene for Simon's guests.

With a degree of reserve that is practically British in its reticence about another social crime, 'making a fuss', Simon says nothing. But he is thinking, and Luke tells us what he is thinking: it is nothing to do with the woman. It is about his guest, Jesus.

How come this so-called prophet, he thinks, does not see this woman for the sinner she is? Either his countenance was unusually expressive, or, more likely, Jesus' divine insight perceives the direction of Simon's thought. But now it is time for Jesus to commit a social crime in his turn. He starts complaining (or so it seems) about the service. Bad enough in a restaurant, but in someone's home?

We once had friends to lunch with their children, and when the (to us) perfectly acceptable plate of food was put in front of one of the children, he glanced at it, then declared, 'Yuck, I'm not eating *that*!' We too said nothing. But we did not forget. The incident, as such incidents will, became established as a family legend.

Jesus was a guest in Simon's house. We can only guess at the reason why he had been invited. Perhaps Simon wanted to confirm his suspicions about the new teacher, or perhaps he was both genuinely curious and genuinely hospitable. It is possible to be both friendly and censorious, for we are not a logical species.

We can only guess, too, at the true significance of these marks of welcome – water, a kiss, oil (Luke 7.44–46) – which Jesus has not received. If we apply the lesson of the parable Jesus goes on to tell, the meaning must be that Simon and the woman are both sinners in need of forgiveness. I find it hard to imagine the Lord Jesus as a discontented customer in a restaurant, grumbling about poor service. The point, surely, is not that Simon has been a neglectful host, only that he does not recognize the goodness in what the woman is doing.

Luke's is not the only Gospel to record a woman anointing Jesus with precious perfume. In Matthew (26), Mark (14) and John (12) there are many differences in detail, but the meaning of the woman's act is similar: the anointing is done in preparation for burial.

Here, the meaning is quite different, but completely in keeping with Luke's understanding of Jesus. This Gospel episode is a presentation of forgiveness in dramatic form. Jesus is more than simply a healer and teacher; he is the bringer of God's forgiveness, and the one whose calling, whose whole being, is to communicate the nature of that forgiveness.

So we come to the heart of this drama of forgiveness. For us, it is not the moment when he tells the woman, 'Your sins are forgiven'. That matters most to her, of course, but for us who read her story, the lesson is in what precedes that forgiveness. It is a lesson about the meaning of forgiveness itself.

I struggle with the translation of the Greek here, for so much depends on it. In the various versions I have underlined the tricky word, a mere three letters in Greek (*oti*): NRSV: 'her sins, which were many, have been forgiven; hence she has shown great love.' That is a legitimate translation. The NIV fudges it so badly that I cannot find a word to underline: 'as her great love has shown.' I used to think the AV gave the best as well as most straightforward translation, 'for she loved much'. NJB agrees with that: 'because she has shown such great love.'

Here is the curse of the translator: that a choice has to be made, between a cause ('for', 'because') and a consequence ('hence'). If the word *oti* signifies a cause, the woman is forgiven because she showed love. Put another way, love determines her deserving of forgiveness. If it means a result, then her loving behaviour arises from her experiencing of forgiveness. The message in the original text teaches something more complete. Love evokes forgiveness AND forgiveness evokes love.

Proper 7
Sunday between 19 and 25 June inclusive
(if after Trinity Sunday)

Continuous: 1 Kings 19.1–4 [5–7] 8–15a; Psalms 42, 43 [*or* 42 *or* 43];
Galatians 3.23–end; Luke 8.26–39
Related: Isaiah 65.1–9; Psalm 22.19–28; Galatians 3.23–end;
Luke 8.26–39

I have mentioned before my admiration of Bible commentator Joseph Fitzmyer. In this episode of the demoniac and the pigs, his comment on the puzzle of geography (Gadarene? Gerasene? Gergasene?) made me laugh out loud, which is rare when reading Bible commentaries: 'a stampede of the pigs from Gerasa to Lake Gennesaret would have made them the most energetic herd in history!' (p.736).

We do not know where this exorcism happened. But we do know that for Luke it demonstrates Jesus' compassion for gentiles. The mere existence of a herd of pigs indicates that we are not in Judea. Mark says there were two thousand pigs, which sounds like a lot even for a modern livestock farmer. But it may be intended simply as indicating a large number.

The episode stands out among Jesus' miracles as grotesque, perhaps because we quickly jump to visualizing flying pigs. Galloping horses might have been majestic, but pigs not so much. This element of the grotesque should not distract us. A deep darkness is at work, and the threat it poses to human wellbeing is real. Jesus asks the name of the demon, and in a chilling glimpse of horror there comes a multiple voice from the possessed individual (the exact response varies between Luke and his source Mark): 'My name is Legion: for we are many.'

Here is an uncomfortable window into the dark side of fractured humanity. Films and dramas sometimes make use of this chilling effect, by having one creature speak with the voice of another. This instance is yet more fearsome, for one being is inhabited by two voices at the same time, and speaks in both singular and plural.

To have no secure identity, no selfhood, is indeed a nightmare for any human individual. We are all patchwork personalities, stitched together from scraps of others' opinions and expectations, interwoven with our own memories and character. To have two names is bad enough – when the demons speak they give their name, Legion, not the name of the man whose being they have invaded. But to have no true individuality, wavering instead between singular and plural, is frightening. As an image of mental illness or a suffering soul, it is powerful.

So is the response of the people who witness the death of the pigs and the destruction of Legion. They want Jesus to go away (8.37) for his power frightens them more than the demon-possessed man did. Their fear of what they cannot understand inhibits their ability to respond to Jesus. Whereas 'perfect love casts out fear' (1 John 4.18), here fear is a barrier preventing them from falling in love.

Paul's Galatian Christians have fallen out of love already (Gal. 1.6), but he has to remind them of what they should be doing about it. Christian life ultimately transcends the earthly – Paul echoes Jesus' teaching on male and female (3.28; Mark 12.25). But they also have to live in the present, as they wait 'in joyful hope'.

Until the time of Jesus, they had the law to guide them. The NRSV makes the law a 'disciplinarian', which sounds rather negative. The AV is closer and kinder, 'the law was our schoolmaster'. The Greek word, 'pedagogue', is one we know in English, where it can also be neutral, or have a negative tinge.

Our own experience of teachers colours our response to this. I have learned much from my teachers, though from a few the only lesson was not to teach as they did: through fear, caprice or sarcasm. In an unequal power dynamic (Matt. 8.9) like that of teacher and pupil, I try to remember Jesus' high expectations (Luke 12.48).

I now believe that no teacher really teaches anything. You cannot put facts into brains. All you can do is stir up the fire. That is what the law could do, and did, for those who followed it, like Paul himself. It was a teacher: it gave him parameters and enthused him with possibilities. But it could not put the blessed assurance of justification into his brain.

Isaiah had long before held out that hope, setting aside the teacher's syllabus and confirming what every person called to faith knows: that God is there to be found even by those who do not seek him. He calls to us, just as we call to him, 'Here I am!' (Isa. 65.1; 1 Sam. 3.5).

Proper 8
Sunday between 26 June and 2 July inclusive

Continuous: 2 Kings 2.1–2, 6–14; Psalm 77.1–2, 11–end
[*or* 77.11–end]; Galatians 5.1, 13–25; Luke 9.51–end
Related: 1 Kings 19.15–16, 19–end; Psalm 16; Galatians 5.1, 13–25; Luke 9.51–end

Galatians 5 encourages us to tackle a question that has energized Christian thinkers for centuries. We can frame it in Pauline terms, as a war between flesh and spirit, or draw from the embedded Pauline teaching a more abstract formulation of the problem of good and evil.

This was a lifelong preoccupation of Augustine. He was just as limited as we are by the circumstances of his intellectual formation. Did his dualistic belief in eternal powers of good and evil draw him into Manichaeism? Or was it Manichaeism which taught him to see good and evil as opposite and equal powers locked in eternal conflict?

We still use the term 'Manichee' or 'Manichaean' to refer to someone with a dualistic world view of a cosmic struggle between light and darkness. This is rather a simplistic take on that ancient religion: religious history is written by the winners, so we would not expect Manichaeism to get a fair press. Yet it cannot have been entirely without merit, for it captured the imagination of Augustine for nine years.

In the end, it was not the theology or ideas of Manichaeism that ceased to feed Augustine's spiritual hunger. It was meeting one of that religion's great teachers and discovering that he was a bombastic poseur. In the same way, Christians today may have high ideals about following the teachings of their faith, but a dull or incompetent minister can be enough to drive them away from one church community and into another. In religious teaching, the medium is (to some extent) the message.

Paul's list of evils to be avoided is markedly longer than his list of fruits of the Spirit (15 negative items against nine positives). If balance were the only thing that mattered, 'the works of the flesh' would easily trump those of the Spirit. Good and evil, though, are not a matter of arithmetic or ratios.

There is a more excellent way, and it was accepted and taught by Augustine, principally because he realized the inadequacy of dualistic systems. That alternative is the theology that evil is an absence of good. It is a less unsatisfactory solution than dualism, but it is still not without difficulties. What do we make of God creating evil (Isa. 45.5)? Or the scriptural evidence of the existence of Satan and demons? This question is in no danger of being fully answered any time soon. But it will not hurt us to admit there is a difficulty here, and to be ready to explore it with those searching for an intellectually credible faith.

The other readings also work against simplistic dualism. When following the related readings track, it is often tempting to take the old covenant reading as identifying a problem that is 'solved' under the terms of the new covenant. Elijah allows Elisha to hold one final holy barbecue before he leaves behind his plough and follows the man of God. Jesus, on the other hand, takes a more extreme line: he will not even permit a son to bury his dead father.

Many commentators have struggled to avoid the stern, plain sense of Luke's Gospel. Surely Jesus cannot have meant what he said to be taken literally? It must be one of his 'hard sayings', a tough message in uncompromising language, that nothing is more urgent than the kingdom. Even filial duty must make way for it.

For us, though, a decision to follow Jesus is not literal or immediate. We do not feel the pressure of impending judgement; for us, the act of 'following' means study, imitation, commitment, prayer, fellowship, not a literal stepping where the Lord's feet have passed only seconds before.

There is a crumb of comfort in this command to leave the dead to bury their dead (which, to be honest, I would not even have tried to obey, if the person concerned were one of my parents). It is hidden by the shift from Greek to English: the word the NRSV translates as 'looks back' could be rendered more precisely as 'keeps looking back'.

If our hearts keep backsliding to past loves and former loyalties, we will be unable to give ourselves wholly to following Jesus. That leaves a tiny bit of latitude for those of us who would rather be called to follow the model of Elisha and Elijah, by not ignoring family obligations altogether.

Proper 9
Sunday between 3 and 9 July inclusive

Related: 2 Kings 5.1–14; Psalm 30; Galatians 6.[1–6] 7–16;
Luke 10.1–11, 16–20
Related: Isaiah 66.10–14; Psalm 66.1–8; Galatians 6.[1–6] 7–16;
Luke 10.1–11, 16–20

This Gospel comes in two parts, setting aside the declaration of woe (Luke 10.12–15) that is omitted. The first part is Jesus' instructions to the 70 (or 72, depending on the Greek text used) when he sends them out to proclaim the kingdom message and to show the effects of the kingdom by healing the sick.

He gives them unexpectedly precise instructions, 'unexpectedly' because he could have focused on the message, 'say this ... explain that ...' In fact most of his attention goes on how the 70 are to be equipped, and how they must behave.

At the beginning of these instructions, Jesus makes an admission: he is deliberately making their task harder. He did not have to make them hit the road preaching without baggage or equipment, but that is what he has chosen to do. The admission itself takes the form of a simile. Everyone in those days would understand it, as we still do: 'I am sending you out like lambs into the midst of wolves.'

The 70 will be defenceless, at the mercy of anonymous forces like weather, or their own cold and hunger, but also vulnerable to the animosity of anyone who is suspicious of strangers, especially strangers disturbing a peaceful status quo. What is the point of insisting on this weakness, when common sense dictates ensuring their security as the best way to get the message out?

The answer lies in who the message is for. At this relatively early point in Jesus' ministry, 'the kingdom of God' is a message of a straightforward kind. No redemption has yet been effected by Jesus' salvific sacrifice on the Cross. Any faithful Jew could respond positively to the preaching of the 70 while still remaining a faithful Jew.

At least one purpose in Jesus' lambs-among-wolves programme, perhaps the most important, is its effect on the 70 themselves. They must learn to accept being vulnerable, meeting with hostility, enduring hardship, isolation, deprivation. They must learn to adapt themselves to the needs of any who show themselves receptive to the message. They must accept that they are utterly reliant on God for the necessities of life, and trust him to provide for them.

After a time (the duration is not specified), the 70 return, and their return is joyful (10.17). They sound more than joyful; they sound excited, perhaps amazed by the power they have found within themselves: 'even the demons submit to us!' In the previous chapter (9.40), they had failed to exorcize such spirits of evil, but now, even when Jesus himself is not present, his very name is enough to cast them out.

Now for the second part of the Gospel. Jesus' reaction to this enthusiastic return is mysterious, making a link between mission and exorcism, and so setting a pattern for the Christian future: 'I watched Satan fall from heaven like a flash of lightning' (10.18). The verb form points to this observation being continuous: we could translate 'I watched over and over'. Christians came to associate this verse with Isaiah 14.12: 'How you are fallen from heaven, O Day Star, son of Dawn!', so merges Satan and Lucifer into one. But generations continue to puzzle at how Lucifer (the name means 'Bringer of light') could be a fitting name for the Adversary.

Much in this passage remains unclear (at least it does to me), but there is surely an important message for the 70 in the fact that, at the moment when Satan falls from heaven in a flash of light, their names are being recorded in heaven. His place is lost at the same moment, and as part of the same shift, as theirs is secured. Jesus' observation of the actions of the 70 also *real*-izes the fall of Satan. Their mission becomes, in that moment, salvific – not yet for all, true, but undoubtedly for them.

What Jesus is really doing is turning the attention of the 70 away from their own wonder-working successes and on to the real point of the exercise. What have they learned, once he concludes his explanation of what has taken place? They have learned that their faithful obedience, their overcoming of fear and hardship, their recognition of Jesus' authority, have earned them the place in heaven for which they long. There is cause and effect in being lambs and being written in the Lamb's book of Life (Rev. 21.27).

Proper 10
Sunday between 10 and 16 July inclusive

Continuous: Amos 7.7–end; Psalm 82; Colossians 1.1–14; Luke 10.25–37
Related: Deuteronomy 30.9–14; Psalm 25.1–10; Colossians 1.1–14; Luke 10.25–37

Obeying God is supposed to be easy. Deuteronomy says, 'surely this commandment is not too hard for you' (Deut. 30.11). Jesus corroborates it: 'my yoke is easy' (Matt. 11.30). So once we hear today's Gospel, it ought to be simple for us to turn its message into moral action.

The parable of the good Samaritan does not exist, strictly speaking. For it is never described as a parable. The good Samaritan is not likened to anyone; the message is drawn from the entire story, not from the points of contact or comparison. Too good not to share is Fitzmyer's observation that the priest, the Levite and the Samaritan are the equivalent of our 'Englishman, Irishman and Scotsman'.

The Gospel makes two characters, not one, the baddies: the priest and Levite who pass by on the other side. I feel rather sorry for them, as I hear sermon after sermon filling out their back story so as to conclude that they stand for religious intransigence or hardheartedness.

I would like to know how common it might be at that time for people to encounter the unburied dead in their environment. Roadsides are a place for the poor and desperate to wait, either to rob, like those who attacked the traveller, or to beg. It is not unlikely that some who begged might die if they were not helped. Also, the traveller did look half-dead. They may have assumed that he was already beyond their aid.

The reason we suppose that the priest and Levite deliberately avoided helping is that they passed by 'on the other side'. But we are not told that they changed sides to avoid encountering the half-dead traveller. All that we can say for certain is that they did not react to him. Perhaps they deliberately avoided taking notice of him, as we might a *Big Issue* seller we walk past every day. Equally likely is the possibility that he simply escaped their notice because the sight of the unburied destitute was nothing out of the ordinary.

It is in the nature of a Bible story like his that we get only the information we strictly need to evaluate the message. Why the others passed by is not the point. They simply stand for 'what most people would do'. Our gaze must remain on the Samaritan. He was 'moved with pity'. That is less earthy than the Greek original, which says *esplanchnisthe*: 'his guts were churned.' It is not in our brain or heart that we feel compassion, according to the Bible, but in our guts (Col. 3.12). Imagine the sort of reaction we have to news of casualties in war, or victims of famine: the impact is 'gut-wrenching'.

So our guts are where we feel compassion for the suffering of others. The name of the feeling this gives rise to is 'mercy'. We could explore the relationship between mercy and pity. But the story is perfectly accessible without fine distinctions and arguments about moral abstracts. Much more important than finessing definitions of these qualities is the form in which the lesson is delivered.

Jesus does not preach at the man who stood up to 'test' him. We must not criticize the lawyer for doing so. He is sensible to check that this new teacher is not peddling fake truth. He shows wisdom in trying to 'make himself righteous' (put himself in a right relationship with God) by asking how to identify his 'neighbour'. The beauty of Jesus' teaching method is that he makes the lawyer answer his own question.

I think that Jesus knew the lawyer would give the right answer because he had asked the right question in the first place. Perhaps it was something his own conscience had been struggling with for years. Sometimes the point at which people pluck up the courage to ask a question is years apart from the moment it first began to trouble their conscience or spirit.

It is a pity that the NRSV and other translations do not deliver exactly what the Greek says for the answer, although it is understandable, for we do not have a natural English equivalent phrase. The answer in 10.37 to the question 'Which one was the neighbour?' is, literally, 'The one who did mercy upon him'. This is not the first time that the Gospel has told us that merciful feelings are no substitute for merciful actions.

Proper 11
Sunday between 17 and 23 July inclusive

Continuous: Amos 8.1–12; Psalm 52; Colossians 1.15–28; Luke 10.38–end
Related: Genesis 18.1–10a; Psalm 15; Colossians 1.15–28; Luke 10.38–end

The meeting by the oaks of Mamre is called a 'theophany', which means the appearing of a divinity. The text begins by affirming that Abraham does meet God there ('the Lord appeared'). But when it comes to identifying the three beings who come to Abraham, the ground is less certain.

From early times, Christians detected a pre-Christian glimpse of the Trinity in this encounter. By the fourth century, when the Trinity was coming to its full theological expression, debate on whether to keep the Old Testament/Hebrew Bible as part of Christian revelation had been settled, but many of the christological readings that have become standard in later centuries were still being worked out. Mamre is one such.

The historical-critical method has long been established as standard practice in biblical scholarship. So we could explain inconsistencies in the Mamre encounter by means of the documentary hypothesis (the theory that Genesis is constructed from four sources, J, E, D and P). But the mystery of Mamre resists a pedestrian approach. It is better to accept the text as it stands and accept that the author (or editor, or redactor, or compiler) has reasons for telling the story like this.

The three figures do not draw near to Abraham; they simply materialize in front of him. The author of Genesis struggles to make pronouns fit realities, though not in quite the way that we do nowadays. Are they one, or three? 'The Lord' appeared (singular). They were 'three men' (plural). Abraham spoke to 'them' using the term, 'My Lord' (singular). He spoke to them as more than one (plural). All very odd.

Telling a theophany in story form makes it easier to grasp (we have all entertained unexpected guests at times). In Colossians, Paul takes a different path, expressing God's reality by making statements in abstract terms. This passage is inspiring and daunting at the same time. I do not think that I have yet fully appreciated the meaning of 'in him all the fullness of God was pleased to dwell' (1.19; or 'Christ in you, the hope of glory', 1.27), though I sense a link to Johannine Incarnation-theology.

Some scholars see Colossians 1.12–20 as a christological hymn reflecting a baptismal liturgy; others as a pre-Pauline body of teaching that

Paul has incorporated into his letter, as he does elsewhere (Phil. 2, 1 Cor. 11). Either way, Paul has received teaching about Christ in a highly concentrated form, which incorporates past and future, as well as the present, into the 'fullness' of Christ's identity. We need help from thinkers, storytellers, artists and musicians, to dilute it into a palatable form that can be imbibed and absorbed over time.

Line after line of this Christ hymn reveals the divine nature and reality as complete within itself, yet gathering to itself what is fractured and alienated, to heal it and reconcile it. Tackling the content of Colossians 1.15–28 can feel like walking in to a rich banquet convinced that you only have time to grab a sandwich and slurp a Starbucks. It's all too beautiful, too much. The cumulative force of truth after truth about God and Christ is overwhelming: once we start to hear those words speak to us of the God we pray to and worship, we can find ourselves with nothing left to cry but our unreadiness and unworthiness, 'Who will rescue me from this body of death?' (Rom. 7.24).

It is easier to hear divine truth in story form, when people, not principles, are the vehicle by which God enables seeds of faith to take root and grow. This Gospel passage from Luke 10 is (frankly) annoying in its lack of appreciation for those behind-the-scenes heroes without whose selflessness church life could not flourish. It is tough to be told off for being too considerate and helpful. But annoying or not, it makes the point that the proper way for a Christian is neither asking for praise as their reward nor finding other means of winning approval, but solely fixing one's attention on Christ. Charles Wesley got this just right, so I hope his words will be widely sung this Sunday:[1]

> For ever would I take my seat
> With Mary at the Master's feet:
> Be this my happy choice;
> My only care, delight, and bliss,
> My joy, my heaven on earth, be this,
> To hear the Bridegroom's voice!

---

1 Charles Wesley, 'O Love divine, how sweet Thou art!', hymn, 1749.

Proper 12
Sunday between 17 and 23 July inclusive

Related: Hosea 1.2–10; Psalm 85 [*or* 85.1–7];
Colossians 2.6–15 [16–19]; Luke 11.1–13
Related: Genesis 18.20–32; Psalm 138; Colossians 2.6–15 [16–19];
Luke 11.1–13

I had to smile when I read Luke 11.8. Here is Gospel truth that even a dog can grasp. Daniel the spaniel sleeps shut in our kitchen, but every morning at daybreak he goes out through the dog flap to the garden gate and howls as loudly as possible. This is not because he wants to get into the garden but because he wants to come upstairs and sleep on our bed with us. By annoying the neighbours, he forces us to open the kitchen door and let him up. Perhaps we should think of being 'cunning as *spaniels* and gentle as doves' (Matt. 10.16).

There is more to this Gospel than canine wisdom. But first, another theology-dense passage from Colossians. Verse 2.8 contains two exciting references. The first calls to mind a fifth-century church historian called Socrates. Socrates is our main historical source for all the fighting over theology that went on in the fourth century. This left him with a distaste for doctrinal finessing and elaborate arguments about putting God into words. He alludes to Paul's criticism of 'philosophy and empty deceit' in justification for his view. And I want to cheer him on.

The other is the use of the term, 'the elemental spirits of the universe'. The Greek term *stoicheia* means 'components' or 'elements' of a whole. In speech, *stoicheia* are syllables of sound. In writing, they are letters of the alphabet. One influential Greek philosopher taught that all matter is composed of four *stoicheia* – earth, air, fire and water.

Paul uses the term to connect Greek ideas about matter with his conception of forces of the universe, the *kosmos*, that 'war against the soul' (1 Peter 2.11). In Galatians 4.9, he makes a parallel point about these 'weak and worthless elements'. If they are in fact 'elemental *spirits*', as some versions translate, that hints at individual personhood rather than impersonal forces. The ontology of evil spirits is too ambitious a subject to tackle here, but this passage is an important source for such an inquiry.

One thing we know for certain: Christian life will not be untested bliss. Alongside the message of justification by faith for the individual, Paul sets a cosmic dimension to the Christian message, which he explores in

Colossians and elsewhere. Christ challenges earthly powers (2.15), and those 'elemental spirits' alike. Both enemies are real.

Our individual existences are constantly being shaped by our environment. Like a pattern of river erosion, experience and circumstance carve trackways upon us where we are yielding (like limestone) and divert around us where we are tough (like granite). Some parts of us are worn down (conscience, confidence and trust are prone to such erosion), while others are built up (wisdom at one extreme, vanity at the other). But when we are incorporated into a structure, that structure gives us a strength beyond what we can have as individuals.

So when I read Luke's version of the Lord's prayer, I am struck by the phrasing, 'forgive us our sins, for we ourselves forgive everyone indebted to us'. We know Matthew's version better: not 'for we forgive' but 'as we forgive'. Luke's Jesus implies that our forgiving of others is a necessary precursor to God's forgiving of us. Matthew's Jesus suggests a balance in which the measure of forgiveness we give will also be the measure we get. Both are daunting.

What both versions of our great prayer show is that pure individualism is not the Christian way. The ability to forgive is a fundamental ethical principle of our faith, as these doubled injunctions make clear. Every Christian needs to be both forgiven and forgiving. Not surprisingly the former is less painful than the latter, probably because our contrition is rarely as complete as it should be, so making us ill-equipped to value full forgiveness at its true price.

The passage from Genesis draws our eye back from New Testament revelation into the world of the patriarchs. Here is a chance for God to show us that he is both reasonable and righteous. This dialogue between God and Abraham establishes the principle that a collective punishment for individual wrongdoing is an injustice unworthy of God. The Lucan Lord's prayer takes this a stage further. Unless Christians are a living temple, a Church, united as the 'body of Christ', there is no 'us' to be forgiven.

Proper 13
Sunday between 31 July and 6 August inclusive

Continuous: Hosea 11.1–11; Psalm 107.1–9, 43 [*or* 107.1–9];
Colossians 3.1–11; Luke 12.13–21
Related: Ecclesiastes 1.2, 12–14; 2.18–23; Psalm 49.1–12;
Colossians 3.1–11; Luke 12.13–21

The lections for this Sunday evoke Robert Frost's vision of the road 'less traveled by'. First we have the more worn path: a theological problem arises in one reading (usually from the Old Testament) and is 'solved' in another (usually the Gospel).

In this case we have the Preacher, or Teacher, in Ecclesiastes, in the person of King Solomon, lamenting the pointlessness of human striving for excellence, success or wealth, when mortals are doomed to go 'the way of all flesh' (1 Kings 2.2 in the Douai-Reims Bible version). Then comes Paul, encouraging his readers to forget earthly things and set their hearts on things that are above. Last, when we hear the readings in liturgical order, the Gospel upholds Solomon's view that self-enrichment is vanity, but gives a different vision of God's priorities, drawing upon that.

If this is the well-worn path, it is so for a good reason. In worship, a preacher often has to explain that what the congregation take as evidence of divine approval may be nothing more than human vanity. A significant proportion of the Christian message runs counter to what most people think of as 'good'. The Gospel imperative outweighs family obligations and sometimes seems downright unreasonable in the demands it makes. Turn the other cheek! Go the extra mile! Pray for persecutors! Leave the dead unburied!

What about the 'less traveled' approach? It too has valuable insight to offer, though that insight may come somewhat treacled with long words and sticky theology. When we choose the grassier path, our take on the Colossians passage will have implications for how the other two lections are read as well. I am thinking of the question it raises of realized versus future eschatology.

Colossians has already revealed itself as a challenging letter to understand theologically, though rich in spiritual material. But at some point, each reader must make up their mind whether they wish to include it among letters like Romans, Corinthians and Galatians, which are indisputably written by Paul himself; or to consign them to a category of 'deutero-Pauline' writings (with Ephesians in particular).

What drives this division of material (among other things) is a perception that one key characteristic of the undisputed letters is what is known as 'future eschatology'. This portrays the fulfilment of God's purposes as belonging in future time. We might think that future eschatology is a virtual tautology, for if eschatology means things to do with the end-time, that must by definition be in the future.

But no. There is an alternative vision, in which the fulfilment expected in the end-time is perceived as having taken place and as already being lived by the Christians to whom Paul (or A. N. Other) is writing. The label for this is 'realized eschatology'. Opinion ebbs and flows between extremes of radicalism and conservatism, but many readers would agree that Colossians speaks of the end-time (*eschaton*) as having happened. As often, proof comes in the form of the verb: 'you *have* died' (3.3).

The question that demands an answer, then, is this: if the 'end' has already happened, and if we are living the Resurrection life in Christ right now, why does that Resurrection life look so much like the life before Christian truth dawned upon us – as we go on failing to live up to gospel ideals?

I do not find it difficult to accept that Paul wrote Colossians (or Ephesians for that matter). Like the preacher and orator he was, he tailored his message to the needs of the recipients. And it would be very surprising, given the depth of his wisdom and reflection in and on Christ, if his understanding had not developed and matured in the years between his conversion and his martyrdom. But fitting the two visions together is problematic.

When we turn to the Gospel, help comes in an unexpected form: we do not need to tease it out of the text, for God speaks directly, showing the rich man the error of his ways and corroborating Solomon's sense of irony about working for wealth that others will enjoy. The Gospel has a different take on that irony, though: the rich man was a fool because he planned to be happy tomorrow. Better to leave the future to take care of itself and take the road 'less traveled', by investing our valuables with God and being happy today.

Proper 14
Sunday between 7 and 13 August inclusive

Continuous: Isaiah 1.1, 10–20; Psalm 50.1–8, 23–end [*or* 50.1–7]; Hebrews 11.1–3, 8–16; Luke 12.32–40
Related: Genesis 15.1–6; Psalm 33.12–end [*or* 33.12–21]; Hebrews 11.1–3, 8–16; Luke 12.32–40

Many of us glaze over when preachers utter that dreaded phrase, 'as it says in the original Greek …' Imagine the think-bubbles: 'Who cares?' 'This isn't helping!' I have probably been the cause of such dread myself, for I find the urge to dive into language questions irresistible.

Still, you do not need ancient languages, only your own mother tongue, to see how verbs teach a message. Look at the form, as well as the meanings, of each 'doing' word. In this Gospel, much of what Jesus teaches is cast in the form of a command called an 'imperative'. In this Gospel there are eight: 'Do not be afraid … sell … make … be dressed … have … be … know … be ready.'

Imperatives, or commands, are the most basic form of teaching. When you teach a toddler, or a dog (Daniel the spaniel strikes again), you keep it simple: 'Stop!' 'Down!' 'Leave it!' Once children mature into reasoning, self-aware beings, commands alone are insufficient. Unlike a dog, a child can ask (and do so repeatedly, driving parents distracted): 'Why?'

There are different ways of managing this teaching transition. Some parents never progress beyond the imperative form. They give all their teaching in the form of orders. Perhaps they enjoy power and control. Or they may lack confidence in the reasons underlying the command, so try to cover up their insecurity or inconsistency ('Do as I say, not as I do!').

By being taught well, people learn to progress beyond imperatives to more subtle forms of teaching – narratives and stories like this one about Abraham in Genesis 15. Bible readings about Abraham speak loud and clear to modern blended families which, like his, are touched by sibling rivalry, or long for posterity through children, or fight over inheritances. If we are looking for something to learn, we will not only find it spelled out for us in simple commands. We have to respond to the imperatives ('do not be afraid … look … count'), learn the story and contemplate the meaning, all at the same time.

Contemporary with the compiling of the book of Genesis was the Greek storyteller Aesop. He gave us tales with simple moral messages, like the tortoise and the hare, or the frog and the scorpion. In this Gospel,

Jesus blends commands and stories together: he takes teaching-by-story to a higher level through a special form called parables, with many layers, and messages that look simple but are quite the reverse.

The best parable stories connect with our own experience and help us to see through the eyes of other people: the good Samaritan, the sower – and here, the servants and their master. Two non-scriptural parables which I would love to preach on but cannot (because both make me cry) are the Selfish Giant, and Mary Jones and her Bible. As with Gospel parables, we may identify with the rescuer or the rescued, the seeker or the giver.

There is a third form of teaching in Scripture, of which Hebrews is a prime example. In Chapter 11, the writer lists lives lived in faith before the time of Christ, then gives an interpretation (11.13–15). This leads on to Abraham, who left all that he knew to follow a command ('do not be afraid', Gen. 15.1), trusting in a story as yet untold (15.3–4). The logical conclusion ('therefore') is that 'God is not ashamed to be called their God' (Heb. 11.16). Hebrews will not be most Christians' favourite book, but it is in the New Testament because it is full of reasoned teaching that we need to know, even if it lacks the purity of commands or the appeal of stories.

All Scripture is 'god-breathed' (or 'inspired by God': 2 Tim. 3.16), and every verse contains meaning. But not every verse contains the same meaning for everyone, or at all times and in all places. Some parts speak to us at particular stages of life, or in particular moments of need.

The clearest teachings will always be commands, from the moment of creation ('Let there be light', Gen. 1.3) to the end of Revelation ('Come, Lord Jesus!', 22.20). The most moving will be stories, in which we find ourselves, and our families, friends, foes and fellow worshippers.

But there must still be room for theology, as the glue binding verse to verse and Christian to Christian, across centuries, continents and testaments. For theology shows us how to defend, and proclaim, the authority of our texts of transformation.

Proper 15
Sunday between 14 and 20 August inclusive

Continuous: Isaiah 5.1–7; Psalm 80.1–2, 9–end [*or* 80.9–end]; Hebrews 11.29—12.2; Luke 12.49–56
Related: Jeremiah 23.23–29; Psalm 82; Hebrews 11.29—12.2; Luke 12.49–56

At this stage of the summer, university students have (mostly) passed exams, and graduated (we hope); while families await the publication of school pupils' exam results. So I wish the lectioneers had included verse 30 in the Jeremiah reading: 'I am against the prophets, says the LORD, who steal my words from one another.' Plagiarism and other exam cheating, we are told, is on the increase at present. Yet even back in the sixth century BC, would-be prophets were pinching one another's prophecies and passing them off as their own.

Why not put equivalent effort into listening to God? I recently watched a documentary about Jim Jones, the cult leader and mass murderer. His talent for communicating was extraordinary. His reputation was untainted by expensive tastes for bling or supercars. Did that mark him as a true prophet? The programme wondered whether, if he had died before the mass murder that cemented his evil reputation, he would have been celebrated as a visionary supporter of racial integration.

Nobody expects to mix Mass with mass murder. But this is where my imagination led me, prodded by Jeremiah's warning about false prophets. Falsehood can consist in claiming to be what you are not, like the prophets who were not really prophets at all. Or it can call to mind students who put effort into deceiving that they could have expended on study. Latin has two forms of the same word to express deceit. *Simulatio* is pretending to be what you are not. *Dissimulatio* is pretending not to be what you are. The false prophets were both kinds of liar; like Jim Jones, who was more excited by the power than by the truth of Christianity.

In Hebrews, we glimpse another side to religious experience: the courageous faithful, who did not count the cost of their discipleship, or who reckoned it a price worth paying. The writer piles hero upon hero, one extraordinary example after another. Then he astonishes us with his conclusion: despite it all, they had to wait for us – *us!* – in order to obtain that perfection ('fulfilment' is a better translation) bestowed on us in Christ. We all win the prize together. This is the way of the gospel, not the way of the world. I point out to those who mock my football allegiance that every season, 19 out of 20 [= 95%? I am terrible at maths] Premier League teams 'fail'.

The Gospel is every bit as demanding as the terrific (in both senses) texts that precede it. We have seen false prophets 'weighed in the balance and found wanting' (see Dan. 5.27). We have seen the heroes of the Judaeo-Christian story having to wait until a time when we are ready. When we turn to the Gospel, there is not a comfortable word in sight, for Jesus issues a message that is frankly frightening.

He speaks of fire, and we recall the Lord saying that his word is like fire (Jer. 23.29). He speaks of his own death as a form of rebirth (Luke 12.49–50): and we, the baptized, are obliged to confront the question of what our baptism might cost us. Could it mean that our spiritual rebirth will lead to our physical death, as it did with the Jesus? And the martyrs?

Jesus is equally fierce when it comes to prophecy. For him, foretelling the future seems as easy as predicting the weather. Prophesying is not astonishing people with the unimaginable, but perceiving what is plain to the eye of faith. This perception comes at a price: 'what pressure I am under!' The weight of providence is crushing him.

Many an examination candidate could say that they feel the same. The only relief from such pressure comes from facing it, and facing it down. But not by lying or cheating. When the author of Hebrews reminds us that we are surrounded by a great cloud of witnesses, he means to inspire us with the thought that the heroes of our faith are all about us, seen and unseen. But those famous words have a solemnity about them at least as powerful as the oath that witnesses swear (or affirm) in court, to tell 'the truth, the whole truth, and nothing but the truth'. Our words and actions do not pass unscrutinized, and we should live our lives as if that cloud of witnesses is testifying to everything we do and are.

Proper 16
Sunday between 21 and 27 August inclusive

Continuous: Jeremiah 1.4–10; Psalm 71.1–6; Hebrews 12.18–end; Luke 13.10–17
Related: Isaiah 58.9b–end; Psalm 103.1–8; Hebrews 12.18–end; Luke 13.10–17

Does human society need peace and security if it is to flourish? In a recent (2022) world ranking of safest countries, Britain came in at 34 out of 163. A school report might say, 'Should do better'. But it could be worse. By the same index, the four least peaceful countries in 2022 were Russia, Syria, Yemen and Afghanistan.

General prosperity contributes to making countries peaceful and secure for inhabitants. Money can buy comforts, of course, but genuine wellbeing depends on people feeling noticed and nurtured. Sometimes this is framed in negative terms: freedom from evils such as pain, fear, exploitation or oppression. Or it could be expressed positively: wellbeing through access to a functioning legal system, an honest judiciary, governance that protects democracy and free speech, accessible health care, and a military that is content to keep a low profile.

Isaiah surveys times of construction and destruction in his nation's history, calling to mind Ecclesiastes 3.3, 'a time to break down, and a time to build up' (3.3). Which is more important to maintaining peace and security? Isaiah chooses the intuitive option: destruction is negative, and construction is positive. The time of ruin is over: now is the time to build and strengthen, putting an end to instability, one of the factors that diminish any nation's global peace rating.

The New Testament also looks at the past and future of a nation, and favours stability and security, despite the tension in Hebrews between realized eschatology ('you have come', 12.18, 22) and future eschatology ('here we have no lasting city', see 13.14). The author takes us through a cluster of images for our destination to inspire us with the vision of a nation possessing security through its location, resources, fortification, and finally its people and those who govern them (a mountain, a city, a gathering, an assembly, God and his Christ).

We are promised an 'unshakeable kingdom'. But can we even imagine such a thing? The word for what cannot be shaken (*asaleutos*) is rare, if only because, in human living, unshakeableness is rare. The visionary kingdom of Hebrews is the only unshakeable one in Scripture. All the others have either been flawed from their inception, or have flourished at the beginning yet gone on to crumble away.

Hebrews calls us to remember the book of the Exodus, and how the children of Israel had a chance to behold the awe-full presence of God. When we experience theophany, says Hebrews, it will not be something that can be touched. At least, so the NRVS and NIV have it. We need to go carefully. The text is not stating that the non-physical is superior to what is physical. No gnostic heresy here. An uncommon word for 'touch' is used (12.18), one that suggests touching something to find out about it, like when blind Jacob touches his son to make sure he is blessing Esau (Gen. 27.21 in the Septuagint, the old Greek translation of the Hebrew Bible). 'Grope/feel for' gets close, suggesting understanding things by means of our physical senses.

Hebrews is saying that what awaits us is something we cannot interpret by means of ordinary human powers. Thus there is no conflict with the healing story in Luke's Gospel, in which physical touch has an unambiguously positive value. Luke makes his points about Jesus mostly through narrative, not theological argument. This means that he does not need to provide a 'how' or 'why', only a 'what'. I expect he had many stories to draw on in which Jesus healed someone. This example tells of a woman no longer young. Perhaps post-menopausal osteoporosis was exacerbating her kyphosis. At best, she might inspire pity; at worst, disgust.

Luke helps us to see her through Jesus' eyes. She is not an insignificant 'old woman'. Rather, she is an honoured 'daughter of Abraham'. As with many Gospel healings, it was her wellbeing, not her life, that needed to be restored. By affirming that she has a place of dignity within her nation, Jesus highlights both her value as an individual, and the rightness of striving for collective health and happiness.

He ended her disability through touching her, and immediately she stood upright and praised God. In this simple movement, touch and healing are tied together for ever in Christian history: so celebrating a precious contribution to the peace and wellbeing of us all.

Proper 17
Sunday between 28 August and 3 September inclusive

Continuous: Jeremiah 2.4–13; Psalm 81.1, 10–end [*or* 81.1–11]; Hebrews 13.1–8, 15, 16; Luke 14.1, 7–14
Related: Ecclesiasticus 10.12–18 *or* Proverbs 25.6–7; Psalm 112; Hebrews 13.1–8, 15, 16; Luke 14.1, 7–14

For this Sunday, we have a choice between Proverbs and Ecclesiasticus (which the NRSV calls Sirach). The former is a paltry couple of verses corroborating the theme of the Gospel. Sirach offers more food for thought, with its opening message: 'The beginning of human pride is to forsake the Lord' (10.12).

Sirach is one of the scriptural books that the Church of England ranks as 'Championship' rather than 'Premier League'. Article 6 of the 39 Articles says it is to be read for 'example of life and instruction of manners'. This reading proves its value by stating an important principle in Christian ethics: 'all sin is pride' derives from its statement (10.13) that 'sin is the beginning of pride'.

But is forsaking the Lord a sin? Apostasy has always been a difficult thing for the Church to make sense of: how can people ever abandon faith if it is self-evidently the truth, the whole truth and nothing but the truth? If faith itself cannot be imperfect or inadequate, the responsibility must lie with individuals. Thus, we end up with people who lose their faith being not only outside the Church but also responsible for their own predicament – even, in less tolerant times, for their own damnation.

Hebrews offers a partial solution. It tells Christians to look to their leaders: 'consider the outcome of their way of life, and imitate their faith' (13.7). Virtually all of us who profess and call ourselves Christians can think of at least one person who has had such a positive effect on us. They may have inspired our faith, nurtured it, challenged it or simply lived it alongside us.

Yet that is not to deny that bad leadership can have the opposite effect. It can repel people, causing them to doubt a God in whose name wrongdoers exercise their authority. In recent years, all the churches have faced scandals rooted in inadequate or non-existent safeguarding. This has been mixed into a toxic brew by some blind-eye-turning, peaceful-life-preferring, institution-protecting, justice-and-restitution neglecting leaders. The advice given by Hebrews, though, insists that leaders set an ethical example and follow it themselves. It is not enough to appear good; they, like us, need to *be* good as well.

This principle that all good leadership is by example goes some way to explain the crisis in UK political leadership that led to a series of five prime ministers in eight years (between 2016 and 2024). Very few of us expect our leaders to be perfect. We have feet of clay, and so do they. Indeed, we respect them for being honest about the fact. But normalizing a tangential relationship with the truth corrodes the invisible ties that bind government and society together.

And so we come to the bit where Jesus is the answer to all these problems. That makes for yawn-worthy predictability in sermons. But in reality, Jesus is always our answer: our rock, unchanging, through past, present and future (Heb. 13.8). He is the reason we stay faithful despite every scandal, every leader ruined by sin exposed or hypocrisy laid bare.

Unlike the apocryphal books, Luke's Gospel has the highest degree of authority of any book of the Bible (shared with Matthew, Mark and John). It can be used to establish doctrine (the virginal conception, for example). But it is a vital source of examples of life and instructions of manners too.

To be judged presumptuous for taking the place of honour produces a human reaction that is more a matter of instinct than conscious thought. The NRSV says 'disgrace', but this is not quite right. Disgrace is something imposed on us from the outside. Other versions reveal that the reaction comes from deep within: the AV says 'with shame', and the RSV follows it; the NIV nails it with 'humiliated'. Following Jesus' encouragement not to be presumptuous can save us from humiliation.

But when we are confronted with the failures of Christian leaders, and the trail of broken lives and disillusioned souls that they leave in their wake, we must not just stay silent, 'knowing our place'. If society and Christian fellowship are to thrive, we must resist pecking-order humility. We should challenge wrongdoing wherever we confront it, however great the authority of those we call out. As the epigraph over the Old Bailey commands, we must 'Defend the children of the poor and punish the wrongdoer' (Ps. 72.4, Coverdale's translation).

Proper 18
Sunday between 4 and 10 September inclusive

Continuous: Jeremiah 18.1–11; Psalm 139.1–5, 12–18 [*or* 139.1–7]; Philemon 1–21; Luke 14.25–33
Related: Deuteronomy 30.15–end; Psalm 1; Philemon 1–21; Luke 14.25–33

In this Gospel, Jesus tells the crowds about a builder and a king who have to calculate the cost of what they plan to do. Both of them begin by 'sitting down'. The verb 'sit down' looks redundant – after all, it makes no difference what posture is adopted for the business of reckoning costings.

In reality, though, people often need to 'sit down' as a first step in dealing with something serious. It may be different in practice, but on telly, police officers always ask people to sit down before they deliver bad news. Here, the act of sitting down highlights the seriousness of the builder's calculations, and the king's. Getting it wrong could be ruinously expensive, or just plain ruinous.

This triggered a trawl through the Oxford English Dictionary for another idiomatic verb. I was looking for a use of the verb 'turn' which seems to be devoid of meaning, yet marks the seriousness of a conversation, especially in colloquial English. 'She turned round and said to me ... I turned round and said to her.' 'Turned round' sounds redundant, but it turns static into kinetic, and conversation into drama.

In the Gospel, the building of a tower and planning of a war are already dramatic. Sitting down equates to calming down, resisting impulsive action, or being carried away by enthusiasm and emotion. Jesus urges his followers not to act on impulse but to think cautiously and act rationally. What is being demanded of them is extreme. If we all took Luke 14.33 wholly at face value, the churches would all be empty while monasteries and convents would be full to bursting.

This seriousness is further highlighted when we take on board the full force of 14.27. Christians naturally think of hardships in terms of taking up their cross. But at the time when Jesus delivers this teaching, the Cross as a historical event lies in the future. Either he is exercising divine foresight, or Luke is muddling up who said what, to whom, and when.

If it is the latter, I can sympathize. I am constantly forgetting who said what and when. Sometimes whole sentences slide through my brain without registering at all. 'What time will you be home tonight?' 'I just told you that.' Words can be slippery. And I am not alone in this experience.

When we come to Paul's letter, words are certainly being slippery. But this time intentionally so. He plays on the name Onesimus ('useful', Philemon 10–12: a male equivalent of function-based slave names like 'Glycera', meaning 'sweetie'). And he also uses a rhetorical device called 'praeteritio' – this means mentioning something in the process of mentioning how you are not going to mention it.

Paul writes, 'I am bold enough ... to command you to do your duty, yet I would rather appeal to you on the basis of love' (Philemon 8–9). His message is a command, but framed as loving counsel – a not uncommon stratagem now in church circles, as well as long ago. Philemon surely heard the real message, that it was his duty to treat Onesimus as a brother, rather than punishing him as a slave. Hence the shift between verse 15 and verse 20. The subtext is that Philemon, if he wants to be counted as Paul's brother, must himself count Onesimus as a brother.

Paul needs to tread cautiously here, because he is interfering between a man and (according to laws of the time) his property. Subtlety, he hopes, will get the right response from Philemon without alienating him. It is the opposite of the style of persuasion found in the reading from Deuteronomy: no subtlety, no careful persuasion there. Instead the command is stark. On the one hand stand life, and prosperity, and blessings. On the other, death, and adversity, and curses.

The distinction is pure, absolute, which is what gives such impact to the challenge it issues. It made me think of two old-fashioned hymns which are rarely sung now. One is 'Who is on the Lord's side?' (to a marvellous marching tune, *Rachie*). The other was perhaps a Sunday-school hymn, 'Trust and Obey', with its tune of the same name, and its rousing chorus: 'Trust and obey, for there's no other way | To be happy in Jesus, but to trust and obey.' Being happy in Jesus may be a New Testament ideal, but the command to trust and obey is pure Deuteronomy.

Proper 19
Sunday between 11 and 17 September inclusive

Continuous: Jeremiah 4.11–12, 22–28; Psalm 14; 1 Timothy 1.12–17; Luke 15.1–10
Related: Exodus 32.7–14; Psalm 51.1–11; 1 Timothy 1.12–17; Luke 15.1–10

Christianity lays great weight upon repentance (in Greek, *metanoia*, 'change of mind'). It is a tricky term. Its meaning is almost exclusively religious. So it is not a word many people are exposed to in the course of their everyday life.

This is not because Britain is no longer a Christian country. It is because Christian wrong, and Christian sorrow for wrong, are a different kind of thing, a particular stage in our growth towards moral maturity. Christian sin is not a matter of offending social rules and conventions, but rather a straying from the path of righteousness. Christian repentance is not a matter of wishing you had not done something, but rather of being sorry for having done something because you recognize that it was wrong.

In ordinary life, we talk about things we do wrong; and about being sorry for them. In church, we talk about sin and repentance. The gap between those two attitudes is infinite, because what fills the gap, between one kind of sorry and another, is God.

The parable of the lost sheep makes this point perfectly. The sheep was not wicked because it strayed from the flock. Nor is the flock morally superior because it stayed where it was. Even more than the sheep, the coin, being inanimate (so taking Jesus' point about repentance a stage further), could not have an intention of any sort.

This puts all the focus back on the ones who do the searching, the shepherd and the housewife. Luke 15 is principally a lesson about God and his mercy, a challenge to our besetting fear that, by doing wrong, we may put ourselves beyond forgiveness.

Like the parable that follows them, these two parables are unique to Luke. What spurred Jesus into delivering them was the attitude towards wrongdoing shown by the scribes and Pharisees. Again uniquely, their misguided attitude is so harmful that it requires three parables, one after another, to vanquish it completely. If we gauge the importance Jesus placed on any precept by the amount of time he devoted to teaching it, then what he is telling us in Luke 15 is his most important teaching of all.

Jesus is doing more here than calling out the scribes and Pharisees for their judgementalism. They were, we are told, 'grumbling' – an insidious form of joy-killing human behaviour. Luke highlights this by using a very distinctive verb, *diagonguzein*. This is what, in the AV, is called the 'murmuring' of the Israelites (in Exodus, Numbers and Deuteronomy) and Luke seems to have pinched it from there to characterize the baddies in his Gospel.

Because the word is so unusual (it is used in exactly the same way for the story of Zacchaeus in Luke 19.7), it sticks out of the text, demanding to be noticed. In Luke, then, Jesus is making a strongly critical statement: to grumble at him for consorting with 'sinners' is akin to grumbling at God and resisting his will for his people, standing between them and the promised land. No wonder the scribes and Pharisees were ready to hand him over to the Romans on whatever charge they could think of to get rid of him.

This is where I must stray a little from the clearly marked path of the lectionary, and hope that readers are in a forgiving frame of mind. For the parables of the lost sheep and the lost coin do not stand alone; they need to be read together with the third and greatest parable of the three, perhaps the greatest parable of all, and surely the longest: the prodigal son.

We can try to re-label it, for it really is, as a thoughtful preacher sometimes reminds us, the parable of a father and his sons. But it will always be best known by its traditional name. Although we never hear all three parables together in a Sunday Eucharist, whenever the Gospel is Luke 15.1–10, we should always be prepared to listen for the voices of the prodigal, and his forgiving father, and his jealous brother. By the time that Jesus turns from lost sheep and coins, and takes human beings as his example, this comforting lesson should have been taken firmly to heart: we are not judged on how strenuously we strive to be good, but on how honestly we repent of our wrongdoing.

Proper 20
Sunday between 18 and 24 September inclusive

Continuous: Jeremiah 8.18—9.1; Psalm 79.1–9; 1 Timothy 2.1–7; Luke 16.1–13
Related: Amos 8.4–7; Psalm 113; 1 Timothy 2.1–7; Luke 16.1–13

Amos makes uncomfortable reading. He pronounces 'woe' on indifference to suffering; neglect of religion; dishonesty; and exploitation. Do we feel as if we are selfish, exploitative? Perhaps only a few of us have grossly exploited our position, like a dishonest police officer with a vulnerable victim, or an immoral teacher with a naive pupil. I have never bought the needy for a pair of shoes. But I have sometimes bought shoes, when I could have spent the money on something more worthwhile.

If we have not the self-discipline to be generous with this world's goods; or if our faith is insufficient to make us observe the tenets of our religion ungrudgingly; or if we resort to spiritual contortions to shunt the sufferings of others out of sight and mind, at least we can have the decency to accept that we need to hear God's 'woe' upon us. We can acknowledge failing, even if it does not bring about the fullest repentance of a grace-filled heart.

Stern Old Testament 'woe' may send us off in search of New Testament comfort instead. But the reassurance in 1 Timothy comes with a calling. It is a prayer for peace: not the ultimate spiritual vision, that 'peace which passes all understanding' (Phil. 4.6) but rather 'peace-and-quiet', an absence of violence (at one end of the disturbance-spectrum) and hassle (at the other end).

Living (mostly) peaceably in our habitations (Ecclus. 44.6) has been a privilege of British life for decades now. But we do not value it as we should. In Bible days, life was precarious, war was normal, and there was no welfare state. In those circumstances, which most of us can barely imagine (while the few who remember them are getting fewer year by year), how could we not pray for kings and rulers?

What may strike us as obsequious or quietist must at the time have been a cry from the heart, a yearning response to the Spirit's 'groans too deep for words', of which Paul writes elsewhere (Rom. 8.26). To know where you will spend the night, to have confidence that there will be food enough for those you love to eat their fill, to trust that what you call your own will not be taken from you unjustly, to close your eyes at night without fearing the morrow – these are not unreasonable aspirations, and it is proper for Christians to pray for them for themselves as well as others.

In the days when the BCP was our only prayer book, prayers for the sovereign were a daily duty. They do not speak challenging truth to power, or express any higher calling for her Majesty's subjects than to 'serve, honour, and humbly obey'. What virtue they do still embody is a common desire for peace and wise exercise of authority.

Amos and 1 Timothy share a vision that combines straightforward morality with devotion. Not so the Gospel, with its strange parable, its paradoxical commendation of dishonesty. In the ancient world, paradoxes were a way of teaching philosophy (the art of reasoning). My favourite is the Cretan liar paradox: 'All Cretans are liars', says the Cretan. But if he is telling the truth he is lying; and if he is lying, he must be telling the truth.

In the parables, a 'master' (of slaves; in most older versions the translation, 'servants' is preferred) usually stands for God. This might mean that God approves of dishonest means, provided that the end is a good one. But we cannot call even the steward's motivation 'good'. It is nothing more noble than self-preservation and pride. One scholar found it so embarrassing for the master to praise the steward that he argued the word 'praise', must really mean 'condemn'! If there are no easy answers to the moral meaning of that praise, we can at least be sure that such puzzles help us not to over-simplify Jesus' message.

There are two things that I take away from this parable that shine with perfect clarity amid the dark enigma of the paradox. One is that the only person who has been wronged by the steward's behaviour is the master. The other is that the master chooses to remit the debt in an act of undeserved generosity and forgiveness. This confirms that he stands for God, because that is the very definition of divine grace.

Proper 21
Sunday between 25 September and 1 October inclusive

Continuous: Jeremiah 32.1–3a, 6–15; Psalm 91.1–6, 14–end
[*or* 91.11–end]; 1 Timothy 6.6–19; Luke 16.19–end
Related: Amos 6.1a, 4–7; Psalm 146; 1 Timothy 6.6–19;
Luke 16.19–end

Some Bible readings, like *Hamlet*, are 'full of quotes'. People who never go to church know that, 'money is the root of all evil'; or 'fight the good fight'; or call an uncrossable division a 'great gulf fixed'.

In the BCP, the 'great gulf' Gospel is set for Trinity 1, the first Sunday in green time. Good, because the story of Dives and Lazarus (Dives is the Latin word for 'rich man'; we never learn his name) expresses two principles of the life of grace that we can grow into during this period.

The first principle is general: use wealth aright. There are penalties for selfishly misusing it. This links to Amos and to 1 Timothy. And it never hurts to be reminded that it is not money that is evil, but the love of it (1 Tim. 6.10).

The second principle is targeted, at the Pharisees, and at the future. The distress of Dives when he is 'tormented in this flame' is painful to read. It highlights a problem for Christians that has always troubled the thoughtful and charitable: how can a loving God consign people to eternal torment from which there is no hope of reprieve?

A Christian understanding of punishment allows for an element of retribution. If wrongdoing carries no penalty, the considerate, cooperative majority cannot be confident that their acts of trust are safe, and that harms done will require amends. That way lies social chaos. But there can be no Christian understanding of punishment where the penalty outweighs the offence (eternal torture by burning for neglecting a beggar?) or that makes no room for repentance.

Whatever we personally think about the reality of hell as a place of punishment in the next life, it is helpful to separate out the belief that actions (and inactions) can and should have consequences, from the conviction that hell is a torture from which no repentance can ever deliver us. There is greater scriptural support for the former than for the latter.

The rich man is tormented: but not only by his own physical sufferings. The object of his distress, in other words, is more than just himself. He has learned a truth about the demands of divine justice. But although he is unable to benefit from this himself, he tries to get the message to his brothers, so that they can learn from his mistakes.

He is not permitted to do so. It is a plain confirmation of the words of the psalmist, 'No man may deliver his brother: nor make agreement unto God for him' (49.7, Coverdale translation). We can help, guide, support. But every servant of God must find the Way for themselves.

The parable of Dives and Lazarus is the only one that names a character. Calling it 'Dives and Lazarus', as I have done thus far, obscures this intriguing fact. Luke alone records the story. It belongs to a category of material unique to Luke, which must have come from a hypothesized source we no longer possess. Bible scholars call it 'L'.

Lazarus' name is stated, but the rich man's is not. Women are used to this kind of depersonalizing in Scripture. It makes them, instead of unique individuals, either representative types, or tools. Mrs Noah, Mrs Potiphar, Lot's daughters, Pharaoh's daughter, Jephthah's daughter, the witch of Endor, the Queen of Sheba: grand and humble alike, they are only a means to some narrative end.

If this is true of the rich man, as we must now refer to him, it does not mean that he does not matter. By being named, Lazarus can matter to us as a unique person. But by being unnamed, the rich man could be any one of us who have done as he did. He becomes a silent reproach, a mirror to hold up.

More than anyone else, the rich man reminds me of 'doubting' Thomas, for he must once have ignored the evidence of others (Moses and the prophets), as his brothers are still doing. Even a resurrection from the dead will not convince them. Thomas had thought he needed to see for himself before believing in the Resurrection. Others did well to believe without seeing. This spectrum of reactions shows us that although some 'need no repentance' (Luke 15.7), most of us are on a journey between ignorance and understanding. There is still so much to learn.

Proper 22
Sunday between 2 and 8 October inclusive

Continuous: Lamentations 1.1–6; *Canticle:* Lamentations 3.19–26 or Psalm 137 [*or* 137.1–6]; 2 Timothy 1.1–14; Luke 17.5–10
Related: Habakkuk 1.1–4; 2.1–4; Psalm 37.1–9; 2 Timothy 1.1–14; Luke 17.5–10

The final verse of a Principal Service lection sometimes has a 'ker-ching', 'back-of-the-net' feel about it, because we find it to be a key to unlock the rest of the passage. This Habakkuk reading is like this. For many preachers, that famous last verse (famous because Paul made it so, in Romans 1.17) will be at the heart of what they aim to share with their congregation.

Without the right training to give us 'eyes to see' and 'ears to hear', Habakkuk 2.4 looks like just another statement about a godly life. It takes a further step into Christian belief before we learn that what it fully means is not just, 'righteous people live in a faithful way', but, 'a person's righteousness consists in having faith in God, not in correct behaviour or in belonging to a particular people'. We could even argue for expanding it to mean, 'through their innate instinct for a true relationship with God, some people are accounted righteous, and they will live (for ever)'.

Equally resonant in this present time are verses 2.2–3, which touch the worsening sore of our discontents and fears for the future, but which also have the capacity to heal it. The Lord's command is brief: 'Write the vision!' Like Habakkuk long ago, that is the call to which I here respond. God's vision is for the 'appointed time', but we are not to know the moment (Matt. 24.36), so cannot risk delaying our righteousness. Now is the time, the day (2 Cor. 6.2).

The Gospel likewise has its particular challenge to us. But it is not easy to define. Once more, it would look simple if we knew our Bibles less thoroughly. We could take Luke 17.7, for example, at face value, as a reminder that we are the Lord's servants: 'Who among you would say to your slave … "Come here at once and take your place at the table"?' But what, says the Bible-believing Christian, about the foot-washing in John 13? That is exactly what Jesus our Lord does for the disciples and, by extension, for us!

By reminding us of the way of the world, today's Gospel helps us to see how outrageous is the service rendered by the servant king. But if we want to understand it in its own right, rather than by reading it in combination with John 13, it looks as if Jesus is reproaching them. Their expectations, of what a life in the Lord's service is going to be, look unrealistic and idealized.

That may be the idea behind the first part of the Gospel too. I have never met a Christian who has successfully told a mulberry tree to go and plant itself in the sea (readers who know better can write in, of course). I hope this does not mean that I and all my Christian brothers and sisters are total failures.

Reading closely, carefully, sheds some light. The 'apostles' as Luke calls them (thinking forward to after the Resurrection) ask Jesus for something that they probably think will please him. Perhaps they are even trying to impress him. At least it is better than when they wheedled for the grandest seats at the banquet. 'Lord, increase my faith' is a prayer most of us have prayed more than once. Many of us have sung it (in the setting by Loosemore). Its great virtue is that it voices our awareness that our faith needs help.

So we get as far as seeing that our faith needs help, and that friendship with Jesus is not about 'mates' rates' or shortcuts to sanctity. The slaves in his parable do not expect a reward, for they have only done their duty. Their perception of themselves, depending on which translation you use, is that they are 'worthless' (NRSV), 'unworthy' (RSV, NIV) or 'useless' (NJB, following the Latin Vulgate, *inutiles*). All these translations are accurate, but also unpalatable.

Thank goodness for the reading from 2 Timothy. Paul does not explain how this all goes together. Instead, he embodies it: self-discipline, suffering, a holy calling. Grace and trust, and the indwelling Spirit.

If the disciples thought that Jesus would magically transform them, they must have been disappointed. It was not magic that made them into mighty men of valour (Judg. 6.12) like Paul; it was love, and shame, and suffering. The same may be true for us.

Proper 23
Sunday between 9 and 15 October inclusive

Continuous: Jeremiah 29.1, 4–7; Psalm 66.1–11; 2 Timothy 2.8–15; Luke 17.11–19
Related: 2 Kings 5.1–3, 7–15c; Psalm 111; 2 Timothy 2.8–15; Luke 17.11–19

The *Jewish Encyclopedia* (1903) says that Naaman was the archer who 'drew his bow at a venture' (1 Kings 22.34, AV). The NRSV says only that the archer shot 'unknowingly'. Either way, that bowshot hit a significant target: wicked king Ahab.

This identification comes from the rabbis of old. They further suggested that Naaman's leprosy was inflicted either for arrogance, or for enslaving the Jewish maiden (2 Kings 5.2). In both cases, his physical sickness was a punishment.

In the mind of generations of readers, and perhaps in the mind of the author too, sin and sickness went together. But we should re-evaluate that causal link in the light of the Gospel drama that the lectionary provides to follow it, in which only one out of ten lepers cleansed by Jesus returns to give thanks. That cleansed leper is, like Naaman, a foreigner (in this case a Samaritan).

One reason why this is an interesting option for the 'related lections' track is that Luke's Gospel has mentioned Naaman by name in an earlier chapter (4.27). There the evangelist refers to him as a Syrian: 'There were also many lepers in Israel in the time of the prophet Elisha, and none of them was cleansed except Naaman the Syrian.'

Who can fathom the ways of lectionary compilers? But if I had to choose between the Luke 4 and Luke 17 to go with 2 Kings 5, I too would have chosen the latter. In Luke 4, Naaman was an example of faith outside Israel. That example fits with Luke's emphasis on the inclusion of the gentiles. But there are many similar examples of blessing for gentiles in this Gospel. If we choose Luke 17 instead, we still gain insight, but not into one historical exemplar; rather, we learn of the inclusivity and gratitude that are fundamental to the message of Jesus.

Luke 17, then, is more than a nominal link between the Old Testament/Hebrew Bible and the Gospel. It is a glimpse into the priorities of the divine mind. 2 Kings 5 is not the only time the Old Testament/Hebrew Bible pits the religion of Israel, based on covenant and steadfast love, mutual loyalty and trust, against the religions that it made to look ridiculous with their incantations and elaborate enchantments, promises of foretelling the future, and realities of failure. Elijah's contest with the prophets of Baal is surely the supreme example here (1 Kings 18.20–40). But it is a powerful theme in Daniel too (Chapters 2, 4, and 5).

So religion that stashes secret ritual expertise in the hands of a powerful few is set against the Judaeo-Christian divine–human relationship based on mutual blessing. It ought to be intriguing to us Christians that so many of our hymns and songs tell of God's blessings upon us, while others flip the coin and celebrate our blessings upon God. Blessing is a reciprocal relationship. The pre-Pauline fragment ('the saying is sure') in 2 Timothy 2.11–13, probably an early hymn, exemplifies this reciprocity:

> If we have died with him, we will also live with him;
> if we endure, we will also reign with him;
> if we deny him, he will also deny us;
> if we are faithless, he remains faithful.

Naaman did not want the cure he was offered. Two things were stumbling blocks in his path. One was national pride: 'Is not the river Thames at least as grand and historical as the Seine or the Rhine or the Tiber?', we might ask. The other was that it was too easy. Where was the '*hocus pocus*', the '*abracadabra*', the '*expelliarmus*'? Where was the difficulty, the cost, the physical effort? But no words are needed from Naaman or Elisha. No 'steep and rugged pathway' had to be climbed.

What healed Naaman was also twofold. First, he stopped expecting fancy words and opted for actions (the seven dips in the Jordan). Then, most important of all, he submitted to a divine decree without fully understanding it, and he did so not out of blind faith, but out of hopeful obedience ('at a venture' we might say, in the sense of being prepared to take a risk).

There was a time when Augustine thought that Christianity's lack of refinement (literary, cultural, social) was beneath a man of his brilliance. Eventually he embraced the loveliness of lowliness. But Naaman the foreign leper got there first.

Proper 24
Sunday between 16 and 22 October inclusive

Continuous: Jeremiah 31.27–34; Psalm 119.97–104;
2 Timothy 3.14—4.5; Luke 18.1–8
Related: Genesis 32.22–31; Psalm 121; 2 Timothy 3.14—4.5;
Luke 18.1–8

2 Timothy says that all Scripture is inspired by God, and is useful for 'training in righteousness'. And so it is. But the training, we know, does not always come in the form of simple instructions. In this Gospel, it take the form of an example drawn from daily life. When Paul (or his disciple) said this of Scripture, he was certainly thinking of the Old Testament/Hebrew Bible, for the New Testament was still being written.

The message in Luke 18 echoes what Jesus was revealing in Luke 11.5–13. We need to be persistent in prayer. His parable uses a weaker case to prove a stronger one. If even an unrighteous person, asked repeatedly for something by someone who is 'unimportant', does the right thing at last, how much more will our God of righteousness hasten to help us when we pray to him?

I could not help thinking of Augustine and his mother Monnica in this context. She was desperate for him to become a Christian. She wept and prayed about it unceasingly. She even got hold of a bishop and badgered him to intervene. The bishop put up with her pestering for as long as he could before eventually losing patience: 'Let me be! It is impossible that the son of your tears should perish!'

History records that the bishop was right. Monnica's son did become a Christian. And he was a loving son who, like many children, forgave his parent even things which could be called, colloquially, 'unforgiveable'. So history does not record how exceptionally annoying he too must have found her refusal to let the matter drop. Sometimes thinking of Monnica reminds me to button my lip.

That bishop was not like the selfish friend or the unjust judge in Jesus' parables. He did not give her what she wanted. He was a wise pastor, and knew that the heart must be open to receive the truth, and that being 'puffed up' (in self-reliance) and 'hardened' (by hostility) would not be remedied by any words, even episcopal ones. Augustine's hard heart needed to become receptive to that mysterious mingling that Christians experience in the confluence between our yearning for God, and God's for us.

This parable is helpful to anyone who is struggling in prayer. Luke himself explains to us that its purpose is to remind us to pray always and not lose heart (18.1). He is addressing worries about the *Parousia* (18.7–8), that coming of the Son of Man that Christians in his day had been looking forward to for some decades. But I detect another kind of worry, the same one as underlay Monnica's bishop-badgering: worry because answers to prayer are not forthcoming. And the fears that stalk beside it: is my faith too weak? Is God rejecting me? Is he even there?

If we take 2 Timothy 3.16 as our guide, we are to look to the holy writings for training in righteousness, which is what the Gospel provides. But if we are to achieve this, we first need reassurance about God himself. The parable does not mean that God is unjust. It means that if even an unrighteous person sometimes does the right thing, God will hear and grant justice to those who pray. That needs asserting because the evidence, and our experience, are not always clear.

I suspect that one reason why the story makes the judge unjust is that Jesus needs us to stop focusing solely on the reactions (or lack of them) of the being we are praying to. Prayer could achieve something valuable, in other words, even if it evoked no change of heart in the unjust person. This is because, as Augustine has said, 'we do not pray in order to inform God, but to fortify ourselves'. In his case, Monnica's tears did not 'persuade' God to make her son a Christian, so giving her what she prayed for. They were a part of her relationship with God, not her son's.

Just one closing thought drawn from the Genesis reading: seeing God face to face left Jacob bruised and in pain. Unlike the widow, he got a response without praying for one. If the stories of Jacob and of the widow lead us to conclude that how prayer works is an unpredictable mystery, it is a conclusion that will not surprise anyone who has ever prayed.

Proper 25
Sunday between 23 and 29 October inclusive

Continuous: Joel 2.23–end; Psalm 65 [*or* 65.1–7];
2 Timothy 4.6–8, 16–18; Luke 18.9–14
Related: Ecclesiasticus 35.12–17 *or* Jeremiah 14.7–10, 19–end;
Psalm 84.1–7; 2 Timothy 4.6–8, 16–18; Luke 18.9–14

The Old Testament/Hebrew Bible reading reminds me of a fun word that is overdue a revival: 'jeremiad'. It means a long series of dreary complaints. Not that we are short of words for whinging. In the course of a lifetime, we get many a dollop of the prophet Jeremiah, but does the word 'jeremiad' fit them?

This is our faith as many perceive it: longwinded and depressing. But when I hear the cry of God's people, '… you, O LORD, are in the midst of us, and we are called by your name; do not forsake us!', I believe that such a prayer will be answered, because it comes from a place of truth. For today, at least, Jeremiah does not utter a jeremiad, but rather affirms his hope for a future lived in God.

It is tempting to linger over the arresting image of God as a weary traveller (perhaps feeling as we might when crawling along a traffic-laden motorway); and as a stupefied weakling, and this despite the fact the land through which God travels is in fact his own. And that the fullness of his might may at any moment descend upon the enemies of God's people. The tired traveller and the weedy weakling were such shocking images for God that some early commentators applied them to Israel instead.

When we turn to Paul in 2 Timothy, we are surprised again. The predominant image is that of a mighty hero, reinforced by artistic rhetorical phrasing: 'I have fought the good fight, I have finished the race, I have kept the faith.' This is no trick of the translator. It is there in the Greek too, a series of verbs each at the end of its clause for emphasis, and each one in the perfect tense. That is the tense of fulfilment: the clue is in the name 'perfect' which in Latin means something brought to completion. It is the same tense Jesus used on the cross for his dying words, 'It is accomplished' (John 19.30).

Heroic language demands heroic action. In ancient Greece, heroes were powerful men of action: physically commanding, courageous, dedicated to protecting and increasing their glory and honour. But Paul maps the language of heroism onto a courage that co-exists with weakness, to show how God overturns human preconceptions. It is a proof text for Paul's wisdom that 'whenever I am weak, then I am strong' (a fine biblical paradox: 2 Cor. 12.10).

Paul is describing his impending death. In a second striking image, he calls himself a 'libation'. This refers to a type of offering made to God or a god/s in which wine, or grain, or perfume, is poured out. Unlike the ritual sacrifice of an animal, it needed no special expertise, so it was a way for ordinary people in their domestic sphere to connect with the divine. By likening himself to something inanimate, he underlines that he is not resisting. Rather, he refers to himself in the passive, the grammatical voice of suffering, in which we let things be done to us instead of doing them ourselves like heroes would.

Paul is surely thinking of a wine offering, for this would model his death on the sacrificial death of Jesus (as Stephen also did, Acts 7.59). Paul is a willing victim, as his Lord was before him; but he is also more than a victim. The *victima* or sacrificial animal goes to its death in ignorance of its impending fate. But the Christian, Paul's example shows us, goes to death willingly, cooperating faithfully, trustingly, in the mysterious purposes of God.

By the time we get to the Gospel reading, Scripture has already stretched our minds to embrace ways of thinking about God and humankind that do not necessarily come naturally. This is not one of those Sundays when the Gospel resolves a theological problem raised by the preceding lections; instead, all three subvert our expectations. Luke prepares us for this with a remark that shows what he thought Jesus' message was: 'He also told this parable to some who trusted in themselves that they were righteous and regarded others with contempt' (Luke 18.9).

In the Gospel parable, the person we expect to be righteous, the Pharisee, turns out to be anything but, while the self-knowledge and humility of the tax-collector are reckoned to him as righteousness. First impressions are not always right.

The Last Sunday after Trinity
(*if observed as* **Bible Sunday**)

Isaiah 45.22–end; Psalm 119.129–136; Romans 15.1–6;
Luke 4.16–24

I have often quoted Romans 15.1–2 in the context of disputes between groups of Christians or, more often, between Christian individuals. Understood in a spirit of charity, this text expresses beautifully the nature of Christian forbearance.

But what about when we are not feeling charitable? Then, describing one side as 'strong' and the other as 'weak' could seem patronizing (at best) or downright dismissive (at worst). Who, our opponent might ask, do you think you are, to call us weak because we uphold different standards of, for example, food purity or morality?

On Bible Sunday, the charitable approach yields a message about equality of respect between those who apply the authoritative writings of their faith to the letter and those who approach them in a more free-spirited way. The distinction is Paul's own, for he remarks in 2 Corinthians 3.5–6 that 'God ... has made us competent to be ministers of a new covenant, not of letter but of spirit; for the letter kills, but the Spirit gives life.'

This makes me think of a similar situation in which committed, well-informed people hold very different views and practise different approaches: Bible translation. Translators may talk in terms of 'dynamic equivalence', when getting the gist across in terms meaningful to readers of that time is the main priority; and 'formal equivalence', when preserving the shape and ideas of the original is to the fore.

The AV is decidedly 'formal equivalence': it tracks the structure of Paul's convoluted Greek, sometimes at the expense of yielding comprehensible English. The Today's English (Good News) Bible and Contemporary English Version both adopt 'dynamic equivalence'. They are focused on getting across the message in modern terms, without readers needing to grasp a lot of historical concepts.

Neither method yields perfect results. I often grumble when I am not happy with the way a translation has been done, but I do not doubt that there is an honourable rationale underlying it, even if the translators have not disclosed the fact in a footnote.

That is a good principle in Christian living more generally. We should contemplate that, where disagreement happens, it is just as likely to be a mistake, or oversight, or an ambiguity imposed by a word limit or ban on footnotes, as it is to be a deliberate deceit inflicted on Christ's flock.

When it comes to applying rules and customs for daily living laid down in Scripture (which, for Paul, has to mean the Old Testament/Hebrew Bible), we might understand the 'strong' as those who are robust enough to cope with the demands of freedom in interpretation, rather than sticking to narrow definitions in (as it might appear to an outsider) a fruitless quest for certainty.

But if we took this approach, we would have to admit that doing so presupposes first a moral high ground, and then that we, and those like us, are in possession of that high ground. That does not seem to leave much room for listening to other points of view or being prepared to adapt our own – which is exactly what we criticize our opponents for. And by this point in the exchange, no one doubts that beneath the smiles and outward friendliness, there is a real battle going on.

Perhaps it makes a difference that Paul is writing to a church he did not found. The advice he gives here may be adapted from arguments he used when trying to reconcile recalcitrant Corinthian factions. If so, his advice about the strong and the weak may not be countering present discord, but trying to stop it before it begins. That would explain why there is disagreement about who the 'weak' and 'strong' are.

Paul did not write Romans 15.1 to teach us how to read the Bible. But he was taking arguments developed in one context and applying them to another. So we too can adapt Romans 15.1 to a specifically scriptural question: what is the proper way to interpret Scripture?

Both sides in this debate tend to despise and distrust the other. 'They ignore the Bible whenever it doesn't suit them.' 'They quote selectively, and discount what doesn't uphold their pre-formed opinion.' Paul does not get into fancy hermeneutics. He quotes a psalm (69.9) – 'The insults of those who insult you have fallen on me' – and applies the actions of Christ as foretold in the Old Testament to the behaviour to be expected of Christians in the New. We can do likewise.

All Saints' Day
or **Sunday between 30 October and 5 November** *if this is kept as* **All Saints' Day**

Daniel 7.1–3, 15–18; Psalm 149; Ephesians 1.11–end; Luke 6.20–31

The teaching of Jesus in the last part of this Gospel is so well-known that I have never, I realize now, given it the attention it deserves. But 'familiarity breeds contempt' is not a truism that we should ever be happy applying to the Bible!

In the past, I have made the lazy assumption that each command in Luke 6.27–31 was making the same sort of demand on us. The fact that they are all counter-intuitive encourages this. The life of a Christian is a topsy-turvy thing, in which curses (poverty, rejection, injustice) turn out to be blessings; and blessings such as wealth and status become curses that cut us off from God.

So we begin at the beginning. 'Love your enemies.' How is this possible? It does not, after all, say 'behave lovingly', which most of us could probably manage at a push. It just says 'love'. I sometimes find myself listening to young adults who are unhappy because they feel attracted to someone who does not reciprocate. They may rack their brains to think of ways to change themselves so as to win the other person's affection. I try to help them see that feelings of attachment cannot simply be created like this. They either happen or they don't.

When love does not awaken naturally in us, it is just not possible to conjure it out of thin air. That makes this Gospel command difficult to understand and apply to our lives. It makes me think of Dickensian heroines who try to mould themselves into whatever some other person requires them to be. They shoulder the burden of emotional fakery to conform to a purpose they have been conditioned to regard as higher than their own happiness.

One way to solve the puzzle is to blame the speaker, Jesus. Perhaps his teaching is unreasonable. But that is not an answer Christians can accept. Another unacceptable way to solve it is to say that the fault lies with God the Father for putting such extreme words into the mouth of his Son. That will not do either. We could take the time-honoured course of blaming ourselves (it saves so much time!), but this would be wrong too.

In the end we get what must be the right answer because it is the only answer left, like Sherlock Holmes after a three-pipe problem. The difficulty can only lie in the words themselves: to be specific, with the word, 'love'.

We are used to hearing that there are different kinds of love in the Bible. In English we need workaround words to distinguish love for God from love for our life-partner or children, our work, our favourite book or music. The love word used here refers to specifically Christian love (*agape*). But even when we know this, we cannot 'solve' the problem; for we still do not know how it is possible for us to evoke true Christian love within ourselves.

The answer is right in front of us, in the passage itself, though when we read it as a simple list of 'aims and objectives for Christian people', that answer is hard to spot. So think of 'love your enemies' as the course objective for the Christian learner: then what follows is the course materials you need to work through to win your coveted qualification.

We cannot make ourselves love people even when they are nice or kind or generous. Making ourselves love our enemies is impossible unless we act upon the other instructions. Doing good to those who hate us is a practical step. It does not depend on an emotion but on human resolve and commitment. Blessing those who curse, and praying for abusers, is practical too. It can liberate us from cycles of wrong and retaliation, and from other people's agendas. Perhaps their enmity and abuse comes from a place of pain. But it is their problem, it does not have to be ours too – though we must also consider the possibility that some fault lies in us.

Turning the other cheek, and giving more of our stuff to people who take from us, are also ways of loving others. Instead of doing emotional gymnastics, we must live the values that we aspire to, until they catch light in us. The flame may not be especially bright or hot. But imperfect love is still better than no love at all.

The Fourth Sunday before Advent
(for use if **All Saints' Day** is celebrated on 1 November)

Isaiah 1.10–18; Psalm 32.1–8; 2 Thessalonians 1; Luke 19.1–10

It is no fun being short. Time and again, you are at some performance or event, but seated behind someone blocking your view. There are no handy sycamore trees in a theatre. In a football stadium, when people in front of you stand up to get a better view, you stand up too, passing the misery backwards.

Zacchaeus is short. But he wants to see the same spectacle as everyone else, so he climbs a tree. The fact that it is a sycamore is a factual detail like the mention of Jericho as the setting for this episode, and the unique personal name. This kind of detail makes us trust the narrator of the story, because it proves that he has mastery of specifics.

Zacchaeus is short. He is a tax-collector. He is wealthy. His name suggests that he is Jewish. There is an obvious parallel with Levi, another tax-collector, in Luke 5. That episode likewise included a meal and a warning about judging Jesus adversely for his readiness to mix with 'sinners'.

What makes Zacchaeus unique is the description of his appearance. Four centuries later, when Jerome the Bible translator described the heretic Pelagius as walking 'like a tortoise', and 'fat on Scottish porridge', it marked history's first physical description of a British person. Such descriptions are unusual: no one thought to record for posterity the appearance of Jesus, or Paul, or Augustine, in their own day.

Luke is not directing his readers to make judgements about Zacchaeus based on his lack of height. Not in the way that Jerome does when he spits his venom at Pelagius. His stature is purely functional. The climbing of the tree happens for one reason – to enable him to see Jesus. By Gospel irony, it has the reverse effect – enabling Jesus to see Zacchaeus.

Perhaps this is the first time that anyone has looked properly at Zacchaeus, or has really seen him for who he is. People have seen the role, the work, the tax-collector. They have seen, and have turned away in disgust, in much the same way as we might, if simultaneously revolted and fascinated by some gruesome sight on television.

This does not faze Zacchaeus. He is surely well accustomed to being an object of other people's hostility and disgust. His attention is all on the excitement of Jesus' having noticed him in a way he is never usually noticed. This may explain why he is so happy at the thought of Jesus' coming not just to eat with him but to stay with him too. He is certainly happier than I might have been if some stranger, even a celebrity stranger, were to invite himself into my home.

His happiness at having been 'seen' – for once in his life affirmed instead of spurned – brings us to the heart of the story. Two options are before us: treating people as outcasts, rejecting them, sends them a message that they will only be welcome within society's fold when they have changed, repented, reformed their lives in conformity to social norms and expectations. That is Zacchaeus' situation in Luke 19.2.

Then there is the second option: the example of Jesus. He notices a sinner. He talks to a sinner. He asks the sinner to invite him in. And when people turn their hostility and judgement upon Jesus instead, he shakes it off, and declares to Zacchaeus that 'today salvation has come to this house' (19.9).

Zacchaeus' eagerness to see Jesus (19.3) suggests that his transformation began long before it became visible. It then unfolded in stages, in a dialogue between saviour and saved. Naturally this attracted the hostility of those who believed in repentance first and forgiveness afterwards.

It is central to Luke's message that Jesus is the seeker-out of the lost, and Zacchaeus proves it by taking immediate action. He offers restitution, and compensation too, as concrete signs of what the Lord's welcome means to him. His transformation began with his eagerness to see Jesus. It blossoms because the Lord treats him with courtesy and warmth.

Zacchaeus reminds us first of Levi, but he makes an even better pairing with the prodigal son. Both are unique to Luke. Both have made themselves social outcasts by their own behaviour and choices. Both encounter divine love, which they never expected and knew that they did not deserve. Both, in other words, are us.

The Third Sunday before Advent

Job 19.23–27a; Psalm 17.1–9 [*or* 17.1–8]; 2 Thessalonians 2.1–5, 13–end; Luke 20.27–38

The first thing I thought of saying about this Gospel might prove awkward to incorporate into a sermon if I were preaching on this Sunday. Luke 20.32 states that, after having seven husbands and trying to make babies with all seven of them, 'the woman also died'. Well, frankly, I'm not surprised.

The Sadducees were trying to test Jesus on the institution of marriage. This version of it later became known as 'levirate' marriage: if a man died without issue, a brother could marry the widow to raise up children for his brother. The word 'levirate' does not indicate a role for members of the tribe of Levi: it comes from a Latin word, *levir*, meaning a husband's brother.

They weaponized that poor (and, I hope, imaginary) woman with her seven husbands. A modern equivalent might be atheists or secularists trying to trip up a Christian on the problem of evil or on anthropomorphic depictions of God. The Sadducees knew, in other words, that this conundrum would prove awkward for their religious opponents, the Pharisees. The jury seems still to be out on whether Jesus was himself a Pharisee; but Paul certainly was (Acts 23.6).

This clash of religious beliefs leads us to expect an answer focused on the Resurrection. But Jesus holds part of his response back. First we have something to learn about the institution of marriage.

It would have been uncontroversial once to say that marriage is primarily for the procreation of children. Now we have moved so far from a one-size-fits-all theology of marriage that many people would find such a statement surprising, even shocking.

Selling a romantic vision in which marriage is the fulfilment of every dream takes many forms. Even the simplest marriage token is not immune. A wedding ring may acquire many meanings in the course of a marriage. But one thing it cannot signify is the eternity of that marriage. Christian marriage is not an eternal state. It is dissolved by death. The rationale behind this is that marriage secures legitimate issue, which matters to human society in historical time. When the world ends, though, and the time for further procreation likewise ends, marriage itself is done with. So it is divinely instituted, but bound to human time. Whatever else that gold band signifies, it cannot be the eternity of the bond between husband and wife.

The unbroken circle of the ring can still signify God's perpetual love for both parties. One of my favourite moments in the Common Worship Marriage Service comes when the minister prays to God, 'you enable us to share in your work of creation: bless this couple in the gift and care of children'. That can be a reminder that everything we do to build up our common life, as a couple or a society, a nation, even the whole human family, binds us more closely to God, in whom is our first beginning and our final end.

Beyond the bickering between religious parties, Jesus is establishing a more significant fact of faith: that the way we make our commitments in this life has consequences for the life of the world to come. He does not rebuke the Sadducees for treating the woman as a pawn in their theological game. He does not need to, because he makes it clear that he does not see her as they do. She is not a baby factory, or a means of massaging the fragile egos of the seven brothers who are fixated on having legitimate offspring. In the life of the world to come, human sexual dimorphism will have run its course.

We could let this Gospel story lead us into a debate about the resurrection of the body versus the immortality of the soul. That is relevant and important, but I doubt we would get closer to the truth than have our forebears in the faith. Paul says what he can about it in 2 Thessalonians, then moves on; while Job's cry of faith is notoriously difficult to pin down precisely in the mind of the writer.

Eventually we may decide that it is enough, for now, to resolve to support marriage as an inclusive institution, embracing commitment, creativity and community; and not merely a means of self-expression or self-improvement. That is already quite a lot for 'the children of the Resurrection' to be getting on with.

The Second Sunday before Advent

Malachi 4.1–2a; Psalm 98; 2 Thessalonians 3.6–13; Luke 21.5–19

Two of the Remembrance Sunday lections are straightforward. Malachi promises healing after a time of conflict. In Luke, Jesus prophesies war and oppression at the beginning of the end-time. Sitting oddly in between is 2 Thessalonians, which, instead of mentioning special military operations, reads like an endorsement of the so-called 'Protestant work ethic'.

I use those inverted commas because that idea is not biblical. It comes from a German sociologist, Max Weber, who linked Protestantism with capitalism, arguing that the latter emerged from a mindset inculcated by the former. If this is right, the New Testament reading could be showing us that capitalism is the root of war and oppression, a breeding ground for inequality and conflict.

Whatever our take on politics and theology, there is no doubt that Paul has shaped his language with precision. The word he uses for 'idleness' is *ataktos*. In it you can see the same word-root that has given us 'tactics' and 'tactical', and that is unsurprising, because it is a military word, mainly used in Greek to refer to disorderly, unsoldierly behaviour. Go back to the first word of the reading and you find that it too is military ('command', NRSV; NJB tries to demilitarize the Greek by translating it as 'urge').

Here is a useful reminder that the language of war was not as repellent and morally negative for those first Christians as it has later become for many of us. This example of military language does not work up an elaborate comparison between the life of a Christian and that of a soldier. It is more like another passing resonance, 2 Timothy 4.7 ('I have fought the good fight') from a lection of three weeks back. The marvellous elaboration of Ephesians 6.13–17 ('put on the whole armour of God') is on a different scale.

Decades ago now, I wrote my doctoral thesis on battle narratives in the Roman historians Caesar and Livy. I was interested then, and still am, in how historians compose their accounts to prompt, drag or inveigle their readers into sharing their own interpretation of an action. When I find military language in the New Testament, I ask myself why it is especially desirable for the writer to use it right there. Often the answer is that military language is another aspect of topsy-turvy Christian values. Paul 'fights the good fight' right at the moment when he has surrendered without a fight to his soon-to-be executioners. He uses it in Ephesians in a nuanced way; for having already urged upon them the values of peace (4.1–3), he then has to stir them to a form of warfare. Though it is not physical, it is still dangerous, relentless, and requiring the utmost cooperation and concord for success.

Words are slippery things. It can be risky to take them at face value. One person's morally neutral description of a colour may be another person's racist insult. Or a word may change its meaning completely: Latin *egregius* meant positively outstanding, while English 'egregious' means 'outrageous'. 'Literally' now means 'metaphorically' {Oxford English Dictionary 1c}.

The Greek historian Thucydides famously anticipated George Orwell by describing how words change their meanings when societies and circumstances come into conflict. In his case, war was the catalyst: 'The usual meaning of words was changed to suit; irrational recklessness became loyalty and courage … the cause of all this was ravenous hunger for power.'

War opened the door to revolutionary change as Athens went to war with Sparta. Change in society brought change in meaning and in values, as experience shifted people's perceptions. After decades of relative peace in Europe, 2022 saw a similar shift because of the war between Russia and Ukraine. We have become so used to the equation 'war + conflict = evil', that we now need to change our thinking as well as our language: this is not a storybook contest between 'goodies' and 'baddies'. It is real.

Soldiering can be a noble vocation. That applies both to metaphorical soldiering (like Paul or Jesus or us) and also literal soldiering. Ukrainian forces fighting to free their homeland from foreign invasion and tyranny have won our admiration for their courageous sacrifices. Russian conscripts attract our pity. Perhaps it is time to sing 'Onward Christian soldiers' and 'Stand up, stand up for Jesus' once more, with gusto and a clear conscience.

Christ the King: The Sunday next before Advent

Jeremiah 23.1–6; Psalm 46; Colossians 1.11–20; Luke 23.33–43

In 2022, for the first time in 70 years, the celebration of Christ's kingship took place with a king sitting on the throne of this United Kingdom. It is now over 100 years since the feast of Christ the King was instituted, by Pope Pius XI.

The readings for the end of the Church year, Christ the King, have powerful emotional effects on me, from goose bumps to the pricking of tears. Colossians triggers the former when we are assured of a share 'in the inheritance of the saints in light'. And when we are promised rescue and redemption. Then the gaze shifts onto Christ as we only glimpse him here: the head, the beginning, the firstborn, the maker of peace.

This vision is not just for us; any more than Christ is only Christ insofar as he relates to us. When we are children, we see adults chiefly in terms of their relationship to us. It is one of the many pains of adulthood that we begin to see adults, our parents most of all, as they are in themselves. Strong and patient, sometimes, but often also needing rescue.

And yet God's majesty endures. Christ is king, we might say (borrowing from psalm 99), 'be the people never so unpatient: he sitteth between the cherubims, be the earth never so unquiet'. Or we could borrow from Habakkuk (2.3), 'the vision is yet for an appointed time, but at the end it shall speak, and not lie'. We live, and travel, in hope. As the world descends into darkness, and light fades, this vision keeps us on the road, travelling in the right direction.

The vision of Christ the King speaks to us on the eve of Advent in the same way as the vision of Christ transfigured prepares us, year after year, on the threshold of Lent. Even as the darkness deepens, and 'change and decay in all around [we] see', we receive the assurance of that share in the inheritance of the saints which we have been promised.

With it comes the reminder of the foundation on which that vision has been built: 'righteousness'. It is not always easy to value at its true worth. It can mislead people who confuse it with self-righteousness. We need to be reassured that it is a good which consists of 'solid joys and lasting treasure', not prim piety.

I think of this verse as I find it in the AV, written in capitals: 'THE LORD OUR RIGHTEOUSNESS'. My old Welsh Bible does the same, 'YR ARGLWYDD EIN CYFIAWNDER'. The capital letters emphasize what might otherwise escape our notice: that something private and precious is being disclosed to us, a name of God (also at Ex. 3.15). There is nothing, however, so noble, so inspiring, that a soupçon of scholarship cannot bring it down to earth. I find that there is debate between those who translate closely, as our NRSV and AV do, and those who prefer a narrower take on Jeremiah 23.6, restricting the reference to a prophecy of Christ, rather than a disclosure about God ('the Lord our righteous *Saviour*', NIV).

There is no time, no space, to ponder now the meaning of that sacred name. Or the meaning of righteousness. For the Gospel must be heard too. I doubt that I am alone in finding myself moved to the point of tears by that exchange between Jesus and the penitent thief. At the moment when the atonement is being effected ('making peace through the blood of his cross', Col. 1.20), we see in miniature the playing out of a drama of redemption that has been going on ever since that (literally) crucial moment. The undeserved suffering of Jesus (somehow, mysteriously, inexplicably) turns the heart of a wrongdoer and inspires repentance and real contrition.

So great is the faith of the penitent thief that he receives from the Lord that blessed assurance we all hope for at our dying: 'this day you will be with me in paradise.' Here, then, is the Christian hope in a pure form. That the Lord is our righteousness, we have been told. That our admissions of wrongdoing, however flawed, bear fruit, we have discovered, when first we confessed the faith. That the Lord effects our redemption, we do believe, helped by the readings for Christ the King. Even our failures, sins and times of unbelief cannot undo that. So thank you, Pope Pius.

www.ingramcontent.com/pod-product-compliance
Lightning Source LLC
Chambersburg PA
CBHW060546080526
44585CB00013B/467